Lost to the Collective

Lost to the Collective

Suicide and the Promise of Soviet Socialism, 1921–1929

Kenneth M. Pinnow

Cornell University Press
Ithaca and London

First published 2010 by Cornell University Press

Printed in the United States of America

Library of Congress Cataloging-in-Publication Data

Pinnow, Kenneth Martin.
  Lost to the collective : suicide and the promise of Soviet socialism, 1921–1929 / Kenneth M. Pinnow.
      p. cm.
  Includes bibliographical references and index.
  ISBN 978-0-8014-4766-2 (cloth : alk. paper)
  1. Suicide—Soviet Union—History.   2. Suicide—Political aspects—Soviet Union.   3. Soviet Union—Social conditions—1917–1945.   I. Title.

  HV6548.S65P55   2010
  362.280947'09042—dc22   2009024186

For my parents

Contents

Acknowledgments

This book has been a long time in the making and could not have been completed without the generosity, support, and intellectual sustenance provided by a number of individuals and collectives.

I am deeply indebted to those who have educated and mentored me during my lifetime. Martin A. Miller, the late Warren Lerner, Edna Andrews, Stefan Pugh, and William H. Chafe were instrumental in cultivating my interest in history and all things Russian when I was an undergraduate at Duke University. At Columbia University, I had the good fortune of studying during a period of incredible historical change and intellectual ferment. I learned the art of the historian's craft from Leopold Haimson and Richard Wortman, who pushed me to engage history at a deeper intellectual as well as emotional level. Silvana Patriarca helped me to see that the seemingly dry history of statistics can be a fascinating avenue of exploration, while Nancy Stepan guided me through the rich landscape of medical history, a world that I now have the privilege of sharing with my students. During his year at Columbia, Stephen Kotkin was instrumental in pushing me see the Soviet past in a new light. I am especially grateful to Mark von Hagen, my dissertation adviser and now friend, who nurtured my original ideas for this project and provided encouragement as well as thoughtful counsel along the way to its completion.

One of Mark's earliest pieces of advice—to select a graduate school according to the caliber of its students—could not have been more prescient. Much of my learning has come from the rich conversations and intellectual exchanges with members of my cohort at Columbia, sometimes in such less rarified spaces as Cannon's Pub or the Blue Marlin (both of which are now sadly part of New York City history). In particular, Peter Holquist was and continues to be extremely generous with his time and ideas. My fellow travelers Igal Halfin, Jochen Hellbeck, Chuck Steinwedel, and Amir Weiner will no doubt see their influence in this work as well. Much of my thinking about Soviet medicine and deviance has been shaped during numerous exchanges with my good friend and colleague Fran Bernstein. Fred Corney keeps me current with his knowledge of new historical trends and laughing with his good-natured cynicism about our endeavors as academic historians. Above all, I have immense gratitude and respect for Yanni Kotsonis, whose dear friendship has sustained me personally and whose keen mind has pushed me intellectually.

Numerous people contributed to this book at various stages of its completion. I would like to thank the organizers and participants of several workshops where I tested ideas and received constructive feedback. In particular, I have in mind Michael David-Fox, Angela Brintlinger, Ilya Vinitsky, Fran Bernstein, Christopher Burton, Dan Healey, and David Wright. Eliot Borenstein deserves special mention for helping me to untangle some particularly complex problems of translation. My colleagues at Allegheny College merit thanks for providing a supportive environment in which to live, work, and write. I am also deeply indebted to those who read and commented on all or portions of the book, most notably Fred Corney, David Hoffmann, Yanni Kotsonis, John Lavelle, and the external reviewers. This book has benefited immensely from their insightful criticisms and suggestions, and any shortcomings are entirely of my own doing. Among the staff at Cornell University Press I would like to thank John Ackerman for his fine editorial comments and unstinting support for the project, Ange Romeo-Hall for her smooth shepherding of the book's production, and Jamie Fuller for her excellent revisions of the manuscript.

I could not have written this book without sustained periods of work in the archives and libraries of the Russian Federation. My research was funded at various junctures by the International Research and Exchanges Board, the American Council of Teachers of Russian, the Academic Support Committee of Allegheny College, the Jonathan Helmreich Fund, and the Bruce Harrison '45 History Fund. In Russia, I benefited from the professionalism and assistance of the staffs at the Russian State Library and numerous archives, most notably the Russian State Military Archive, the State Archive of the Russian Federation, and the State Archive of Iaroslavl' Oblast. Mark Borisovich Mirskii helped me to get my work off the ground in Moscow, while Lena Morozova and her family opened up their home to me on too many occasions to count. Most of all, I wish to thank Mikhail Poddubnyi, naturalist and historian of medicine, who uncovered vital sources for the project and was my constant intellectual companion during my investigations. His humor and friendship were perhaps my most valuable discoveries in Russia.

Sections of this book have been modified from previously published materials. Chapter 2 contains elements from "Violence against the Collective Self and the Problem of Social Integration in Early Bolshevik Russia," *Kritika* (Summer 2003), and Chapter 5 builds on work that appeared in "Lives out of Balance: The 'Possible World' of Soviet Suicide during the 1920s," in *Madness and Madmen in Russian Culture,* ed. Angela Brintlinger and Ilya Vinitsky (University of Toronto Press). I thank the publishers for allowing me to use them here.

Most special thanks are in order for my wife and accomplice, Barbara Riess, who expertly read countless drafts and can probably recite the book by heart. She pushed me when I needed a push and found me whenever I became lost in the book. I owe her more than words can express and look forward to our intellectual journeys in the years ahead.

I dedicate this book to my parents. They are the ones who encouraged my exploration of the world and who instilled a joy of life that allows me to see the flicker of humanity in even the darkest sides of existence.

Introduction

In late December 1925, Sergei Esenin, the enfant terrible of early Soviet poetry, used his own blood to pen his final words: "In this life there is nothing new about dying. But then again there is nothing new about living." He then proceeded to hang himself from the heating pipes of his room in the Leningrad Hotel Angleter. Esenin's theatrical last act quickly became the topic of much discussion, rumor, and speculation, some of which continue to this day.[1] It set off debates in the Soviet press and within political circles about the role of art and the artist in the revolution, the meaning of suicide under Soviet socialism, and the state of Russia's youth. This latter concern stemmed in part from the immense outpouring of public grief among young people and from disturbing reports that students and adolescents were killing themselves while in the thrall of Esenin's words and ideas. In fact, suicide during the late 1920s and well into the 1930s became closely associated with the novel Soviet condition known as "Eseninism" (*eseninshchina*), a diagnosis that conveyed cultural

1. There is, for example, continued speculation among Russian nationalists that Esenin was murdered by the Bolsheviks, who then made his death appear to be self-inflicted. They read Esenin's death as yet another case of "foreign" Soviet power destroying native Russian culture. These speculations about Esenin's murder are addressed in A. V. Maslov, *Petlia i pulia. Issledovanie obstoiatel'stv gibeli Sergeia Esenina i Vladimira Maiakovskogo* (St. Petersburg, 2004).

decadence (*upadochnichestvo*), individualism, and a general loss of faith in the Bolshevik Revolution.[2]

The possibility of a "suicide epidemic" (*epidemiia samoubiistv*) among Soviet youth deepened more general anxieties about the course of the revolution at the height of the New Economic Policy (NEP). Adopted in 1921 by the Bolshevik leadership as a series of ad hoc responses to the devastation and social unrest wrought by years of war and upheaval in Russia, the New Economic Policy allowed for the partial restoration of a market economy and an easing of ideological restrictions in the cultural sphere. Despite official professions of faith in the future, the NEP suggested that achievement of the socialist dream would be postponed indefinitely. This evolutionary course split the Bolshevik Party and called into question the very survival of the revolution. Some observers worried that Soviet Russia was adrift, threatened by a host of enemies both internal and external.[3] An upsurge of suicides among youth was particularly troublesome to the regime given the importance of young people as the generation that bore the seeds of a new socialist world that was coming into existence. Suicide, together with such related problems as alcoholism, sexual hedonism, and venereal disease, signaled the political as well as moral "degeneration" of this key social group and implied the dogged presence of old mentalities and lifestyles that the Soviets strove to eradicate.[4]

The shadow of an earlier suicide epidemic only added to the scare power of self-destruction during the 1920s. In the years following the 1905 revolution, Russia was wrenched by an apparent outbreak of despair that both horrified and fascinated the public. Writers, journalists, and physicians made the rise of suicides synonymous with the reactionary politics, immorality, and social dislocation of the late tsarist period. Doctors, in particular, sought to frame suicide as an illness that simultaneously reflected and contributed to the degeneration of Russian society. Homing in on the many suicides among young people, they condemned the autocracy's failure to cultivate a healthy population in a biological, psychological, and moral sense. Moreover, they strongly criticized its resistance to the open

---

2. Gregory Carleton contends that the response to Esenin's suicide must be understood as part of the wider debate over sexuality and culture during the 1920s. See his *Sexual Revolution in Bolshevik Russia* (Pittsburgh, 2005), 107–12.

3. Eric Naiman sees anxiety as a distinguishing feature of Soviet culture and politics during the NEP years. See his *Sex in Public: The Incarnation of Early Soviet Ideology* (Princeton, 1997), 5–12.

4. On the significance and challenge of youth to the Soviets, see Anne E. Gorsuch, *Youth in Revolutionary Russia: Enthusiasts, Bohemians, Deliquents* (Bloomington, 2000); and Igal Halfin, *Terror in My Soul: Communist Autobiographies on Trial* (Cambridge, MA, 2003).

collection of statistics and the adoption of progressive policies aimed at reducing suicides through positive rather than negative measures. The post-1905 suicide epidemic, therefore, seemingly reaffirmed the need for a more thoroughgoing revolution in Russia, one that would transform society and usher in a new, more modern system of governance.

The Bolshevik takeover of October 1917 allowed for the fulfillment of these revolutionary imperatives. Its leaders not only promised to eliminate the various "ills" of industrial capitalism and autocratic rule but also opened up expanded possibilities for social exploration and intervention. Over the course of the 1920s, suicide—as both an individualized drama and a broader social phenomenon—became the object of integrated study within a number of institutional and political settings that formed the party-state system created by the Bolsheviks.[5] Forensic-medical experts began the process in 1920 when they organized the collection of data through a specially formulated questionnaire (*anketa*) designed to elicit information about the social and physiological dimensions of self-destruction. Moral statisticians quickly joined the effort when they established a national registration program that reflected the Soviet regime's deep desire for knowledge about the population. Joining these professionals was a set of investigators who emerged from the country's new political configuration. Activists in the Bolshevik Party and the Workers' and Peasants' Red Army (RKKA) displayed an intense interest in suicide as part of their broader responsibility for monitoring the political and moral well-being of two key constituencies that were responsible for spreading and defending the word of the revolution. Taken together, these various explorations into suicide reflected a common belief in the power of the expert to unravel the mystery of self-destruction and a common desire for order and rationality through the application of science to the body politic.

This book explores the Soviet regime's growing claim on suicide during the formative decade of the 1920s. It argues that responses to suicide reflected the way that the individual and society—and the connection between them—were imagined and constructed through a mixture of rhetorical strategies and concrete politico-scientific practices. In particular, the handling of self-destruction provides us with a valuable window into

---

5. Regarding terminology, the Russian personal noun *samoubiitsa* signifies one who commits suicide and is thus rendered as "the suicide." In terms of describing the act itself, Soviet investigators routinely used the word *samoubiistvo*, which translates into "suicide," and to a lesser extent *samounichtozhenie*, which translates into "self-destruction." I employ both terms interchangeably except when quoting, in which case I follow the wording of the original text. For the sake of linguistic variety I also occasionally use the term "self-killing." This latter formulation is consistent with the Russian "to kill oneself" (*pokonchit' s soboi*).

how the Soviets understood the sources of the personality, conceptualized human relationships, defined norms and responsibilities, and sought to transform the quality of subjective experience. Such an approach emphasizes the historically and culturally contingent nature of suicide's significance. As Michael MacDonald and Terence Murphy note, every era and every society have possessed their own "hermeneutics of suicide, a set of institutions, procedures, and beliefs that identified suicidal deaths and assigned them meanings."[6] In the case of early Soviet Russia, the recording and interpretation of suicides were integrated within a governmental apparatus that combined modern precepts of population management with the transformative ethos of revolution. The person who committed suicide during the 1920s fell under the jurisdiction of new institutions that aimed not simply to describe the objective state of affairs in the country but also to reveal and shape the subjective state of affairs inside the individual.

Suicide is therefore treated here as a problem of modern government rather than an existential drama. By themselves, the abundant source materials on suicides in the archives and libraries are evidence of the fact that self-destruction was understood as a distinct problem demanding attention by the Soviet state, the Bolshevik Party, and a host of experts. Moreover, their content and form are suggestive of a new style of politics that emerged during the 1920s and shaped not only the meaning of self-destruction but the entire texture of everyday life. Compared with its autocratic predecessor and European contemporaries, the Soviet regime was infused with a more insistent desire to access and restructure both the subjective and the social realms.[7] This aspiration found partial expression in the numerous experiments designed to create new living patterns and to forge the New Soviet Man and Woman who would populate the future socialist world. It also sanctioned a wide-ranging set of efforts to study the population at virtually every level of existence, including sexual relations, human psychology, physical health, and political attitudes. Many of the tools used to make self-destruction legible and open to investigation—medical examinations, standardized questionnaires, statistics, and a variety of surveillance techniques—were also applied to the rest of the population. Suicide, then, provides a fitting object for examining the overlapping

6. Michael MacDonald and Terence R. Murphy, *Sleepless Souls: Suicide in Early Modern England* (Oxford, 1990), 221.

7. On the search for subjectivity as a distinct element of Soviet modernity see Peter Holquist, "What's So Revolutionary about the Russian Revolution? State Practices and the New-Style Politics, 1914–21," in *Russian Modernity: Politics, Knowledge, Practices*, ed. David L. Hoffmann and Yanni Kotsonis (London, 2000), 87–111.

spheres of governmental action toward both individuals and society during the 1920s.

Focusing on a single object of analysis, this book broadens our picture of the early Soviet regime and deepens our understanding of the possibilities as well as the limits of social investigation after the Bolshevik Revolution. It sets out the key technologies of government, reveals the techniques of individuation and group formation, and illuminates the production of the knowledge that animated the regime and now serves as the basis for much of our historical understanding of the Soviet order. In the hands of the Soviets, suicide became a medium for debating the course of the revolution, for understanding the relationship between society and the individual, for rationalizing the intervention of various "experts" into the social realm, and for implementing a shared political ethos organized around the assumption that society was a discrete entity that could be sculpted according to scientific principles. Ultimately, the meaning of Soviet suicide was shaped by a combination of organized rituals, statistical-medical studies, and government interventions into the life of both the individual and the collective. An exploration into these practices shows how their creation and implementation helped to forge the Soviet population as an aggregate whole that could be (re)organized through a blend of scientific and political measures. Such interventions in turn influenced human subjectivity, promoted certain forms of human relations, and defined what it meant to be an individual in the socialist world.

This book therefore seeks to understand how governmental officials and social scientists conceptualized, studied, and gave meaning to suicide. For this reason its narrative is heavily weighted toward the voices, actions, and aspirations of those who created the information we now have available regarding self-destruction in the USSR during the 1920s. The story of suicide's transposition into statistics, autopsy reports, secret political summaries, and other forms of social knowledge sheds light on institutional and everyday sites of social investigation that have been either overlooked or used differently by other historians. It also reveals the formation of novel practices in the Bolshevik Party and the Red Army, which gave a clear political edge to the meaning of Soviet suicide and helped to establish a distinct form of medicopolitics that embraced the totality of the individual. Because these various governmental interventions promoted certain ways of thinking and acting on the part of the observer as well as the observed, suicide functioned as a stimulant for the creation of new understandings and the formation of governmental practices that together substantiated the Soviet experiment.

SUICIDE AS A HISTORICAL PROBLEM

Total mastery of the problem proved quixotic for those Soviets who investigated self-destruction during the 1920s. Nevertheless, the tangible result of their endeavors is an impressive array of information, both published and "top secret," that today allows the historian access to the world of Soviet suicide. Statistical data and medical opinion, for example, are available in the publications of the Central Statistical Administration (TsSU) and the People's Commissariat of Public Health (Narkomzdrav), the Moscow-based homes of moral statistics and forensic medicine, respectively. In the local and central archives of Russia one finds autopsy reports, completed and half-completed statistical forms, investigatory protocols, and a plethora of documents outlining the organizational efforts that went into the creation of these very materials. There is also documentation that captures personal and public reactions to suicides, including those of the country's leaders and political elites; of families, friends, and neighbors; and of the investigators who sought to make sense of the seemingly incomprehensible. Finally, we have a degree of access to the suicides themselves. Their final notes, words, and gestures were often dutifully transcribed, and thus preserved, as part of the official record.

Historians of suicide face an interpretative challenge when dealing with such source materials. Indeed, they experience most acutely what all historians must confront—namely, the matter of how to reconstruct the subjective world of the past. Even today data on suicides are inherently problematic given the tendency of families to conceal acts of self-destruction, the vagaries of certain forms of suicide, and the variations of definition and categorization intrinsic to the process of recordkeeping across national borders and cultures. Of still greater significance for historical interpretation is the nature of suicide itself. Because the subject and the object of suicide are one and the same person, a completed act ends in the annihilation of its author and, according to one scholar, creates a "black hole" of meaning that begs to be filled in by others.[8] Consequently, we are not always sure whose voice is contained in the records, which are shaped by the demands and constraints of the individuals, institutions, and culture that brought them into being.[9]

Despite these interpretative dilemmas, scholars have produced a rich and growing body of literature that affirms the great potential for

---

8. Irina Paperno, *Suicide as a Cultural Institution in Dostoevsky's Russia* (Ithaca, 1997), 2.

9. See, for example, the trenchant critique of suicide statistics in Jack Douglas, *The Social Meanings of Suicide* (Princeton, 1967), 163–231.

examining suicide historically. A small number have adopted an empirical approach, reconstructing rates of suicide as best they can in order to identify patterns among different social groups and according to such broader processes as industrialization and urbanization. In so doing, they have both replicated and challenged the sociological theories of Émile Durkheim, who in the late nineteenth century made suicide the key barometer of social integration and thus the basis of his argument for sociology as a distinct discipline. Looking beyond the statistics, historians interested in the lives of ordinary men and women have sought to recover popular beliefs and personal experiences. Suicide, in their hands, is revealing of attitudes toward religion and death, assumptions about the limits of human endurance, and the trials and tribulations faced by people in their everyday lives. Scholars have also explored the contested meanings of self-destruction as put forth by religious and cultural figures, governmental authorities, and a diverse group of professionals concerned with suicide's metaphysical and social implications. Taken as a whole, the richly textured literature highlights the shifting experience of self-destruction across time and space, thus establishing suicide as an ideal object for studying social, political, and cultural change.[10]

Suicide has proven particularly fertile ground for exploring the structures and forms of European modernity, a somewhat "natural" endeavor given the fact that self-destruction was reified as a marker of "civilization" and the concomitant breakdown of "traditional" values and lifestyles during the nineteenth century. Most notably, Michael MacDonald and Terence Murphy shaped the field with their highly influential model of suicide's "secularization" in early modern England. They suggest that a combination of political, economic, and intellectual changes led to greater leniency and sympathy for the suicide, which in turn promoted a shift away from religious understandings and toward our more familiar medical and psychological explanations of self-destruction.[11] Different aspects of this model have since been modified by scholars working on the history of suicide in earlier periods and among different parts of Europe.[12] Most notably, Susan Morrissey's ambitious study of suicide in Imperial Russia has called into question the overly linear quality of most historical narratives.

10. On the general trends in recent historiography see the excellent review by Róisín Healy, "Suicide in Early Modern and Modern Europe," *Historical Review* 49, no. 3 (2006): 903–19.

11. Michael MacDonald, "The Secularization of Suicide in England 1660–1800," *Past and Present*, no. 111 (May 1986): 50–100; and MacDonald and Murphy, *Sleepless Souls*.

12. For a critique of MacDonald's conclusions see Donna T. Andrew, "Debate: The Secularization of Suicide in England 1660–1800," *Past and Present*, no. 119 (May 1988): 158–65.

Where MacDonald and others see modern ideas and beliefs displacing traditional ones in a sequential pattern, Morrissey instead sees a more complicated process of "conversion and translation." Extended to the present work, such scholarship reinforces the fact that attitudes toward suicide, including those of the Soviets, are fundamentally a "hybrid" of the old and the new.[13]

Historians of Europe have also noted the modern state's growing interest in suicide. Indeed, the move to secularize and decriminalize self-destruction in the nineteenth and twentieth centuries resulted in greater rather than less state involvement. Consistent with their monopoly on violence, modern governments have demonstrated an abiding interest in stopping acts of aggression both between citizens and directed against one's own self. Toward this goal, they have adopted a variety of measures to prevent suicide and lessen its demographic and moral effects on the population, including laws against the incitement of suicide by others and strategies to encourage citizens to work actively against suicides.[14] In addition, the rise of modern population politics, which emphasize the rational regulation of the social order and the promotion of individual potential, facilitated the expansion of different disciplines into the study and management of self-destructive behavior.[15] Physicians, psychiatrists, and sociologists, among others, have all staked a claim to expertise on suicide as both a general and an individual phenomenon. In the process, suicides went from being considered criminals to being seen as sick or troubled people who required treatment and whose actions stirred the therapeutic as well as coercive powers of the state.

The history of suicide in the nineteenth and twentieth centuries is therefore closely linked with the rise of "the social" in Europe.[16] Suicide

13. Susan K. Morrissey, *Suicide and the Body Politic in Imperial Russia* (Cambridge, 2007), 3–8, 346–53. Irina Paperno has also identified the presence of transfigured religious tropes within the sociological and medical discourse of the nineteenth century. See her *Suicide as a Cultural Institution*, 26–44.

14. Healy, "Suicide in Early Modern and Modern Europe," 916–17. In the case of Nazi Germany, we see a slightly different dynamic at work. While the regime encouraged healthy citizens to preserve their own lives, it welcomed suicides among the sick and injured as a way for them to relieve the nation of their burdensome existence.

15. One could argue that this process actually flowed in the reverse direction. The study of suicide in the nineteenth century was key to the rise of many modern state concerns and practices, including population surveillance, the medicalization of human behavior, and the development of sociology as a distinct discipline. See Ian Hacking, *The Taming of Chance* (Cambridge, 1990); and Hacking, "How Numerical Sociology Began by Counting Suicides: From Medical Pathology to Social Pathology," in *The Natural Sciences and the Social Sciences: Some Critical and Historical Perspectives*, ed. I. Bernard Cohen (Dordrecht, Neth., 1994), 101–33.

16. The rise of the social as a field of knowledge and administrative practices is elaborated in David G. Horn, *Social Bodies: Science, Reproduction, and Italian Modernity* (Princeton,

was among the facts of everyday life that were used to create new disciplines (social science, social hygiene, social work, etc.) that attended to the population as an aggregate whole with its own distinct properties and interests. The statistics of self-destruction were in fact critical to the formulation of social "laws" that called into question notions of free will and suggested that however undesirable, deviant acts like suicide were a predictable and hence natural part of society. Thinking in terms of populations, moreover, provided an additional rationale for what Michel Foucault termed "governmentality," or the organized practices through which subjects are governed both individually and as part of the collective body (what Foucault respectively called "anatomo-politics" and "bio-politics"). As Bruce Curtis observes, the idea of the population, a largely statistical abstraction that posited the interdependence of its individual members, gave rise to "new orders of knowledge, new objects of intervention, [and] new forms of subjectivity."[17]

The link between the art of governance and subjectivity suggests that suicide also broaches the problem of the self and human agency. In his discussion of what he calls "making up people," the philosopher Ian Hacking has argued that suicide is emblematic of the multidirectional process of identity formation. Citing Foucault's two poles of governmentality—the individual and the species body—he suggests that the nineteenth-century construction of statistical categories for suicide, including its motives and means, provided new ways for people to understand and articulate their actions.[18] Scholars have since fleshed out the hermeneutic circle of suicide. In particular, Irina Paperno's fine examination of suicide's dialogic quality raises important questions about the autonomous self and the nature of social facts. Her work on late Imperial Russia demonstrates the inability of suicides to escape the broader discourse of self-destruction; when articulating their motivations through the language of writers, journalists, and medical doctors, suicides seemingly confirm the power of such social observers to make sense of, and potentially control, the self-destructive personality.[19] Of course, notions of the suicidal personality are themselves historically contingent and dependent on more general understandings of the individual. To take one example, definitions of the suicide as a

1994); and Bruce Curtis, "Surveying the Social: Techniques, Practices, Power," *Histoire sociale/ Social History* 35 (2002): 83–108.

17. Bruce Curtis, "Foucault on Governmentality and Population: The Impossible Discovery," *Canadian Journal of Sociology* 27, no. 4 (Fall 2002): 507.

18. Ian Hacking, "Making Up People," in *Reconstructing Individualism: Autonomy, Individuality, and the Self in Western Thought,* ed. Morton Sosna, Thomas C. Heller, and David E. Wellbery (Stanford, 1986), 234–35.

19. Paperno, *Suicide as a Cultural Institution,* 204–5.

"sick" person accompanied the rise in the early nineteenth century of "social man," a quantifiable and partitive being who was deemed reflective of society and thus open to various governmental interventions.[20] Despite the arguably progressive nature of such outlooks, however, modern understandings of suicide elide human agency no less than belief systems that ascribed suicide to a sinful nature or devilish incitement. Attributions of the self-destructive impulse to social, psychological, or even biological forces both confirmed the power of the scientific disciplines over the individual and offered a degree of consolation by proffering the idea that no right-thinking member of society would choose to end his or her life voluntarily.[21] In terms of human agency, suicide, an act at once intensely personal and socially meaningful, simply cannot escape the culture in which it is embedded.

THE SOVIET SOCIAL SCIENCE STATE

The historically contingent problems of modernity and government also frame this book. Soviet investigators were drawn to suicide as part of their broader concern for the population. In their own ways they all understood society as an artifact and aspired to refashion it—and its individual members—through rational, scientific practices. In many respects, then, Soviet responses to suicide drew upon and transformed the pan-European debates about the management of urbanization, industrialization, mass politics, and other manifestations of modern life.[22] As a consequence, the facts of Soviet suicide—including many of the analytical and statistical categories—look quite familiar and do not differ fundamentally from the work of other Europeans during the early twentieth century. Nevertheless, the Soviets acted according to a different set of assumptions about the individual and the role of the state and expert in people's everyday lives. Their sense of the possible, as well as the scope of their interventions, was greatly emboldened by a revolutionary politics that aimed to unleash the power of science and the state toward the creation of a socialist order. This radical expansion of the social in Soviet Russia had profound implications for researchers and their objects alike. Both found themselves participat-

---

20. Horn, *Social Bodies*.

21. Lisa Lieberman, *Leaving You: The Cultural Meaning of Suicide* (Chicago, 2003).

22. Michael Halberstam, "Totalitarianism as a Problem for the Modern Conception of Politics," *Political Theory* 26, no. 4 (August 1998): 459–88; and David L. Hoffmann, *Stalinist Values: The Cultural Norms of Soviet Modernity, 1917–1941* (Ithaca, 2002).

ing in the all-embracing governmental project that was at the heart of the emerging "social science state."[23]

By positing the Soviet regime as a social science state, I argue for regarding the modern social sciences as a style of culture and politics— indeed, as a way of making sense of the world. Despite the closure of academic sociology in the early 1920s, a fact that has led scholars to see the Bolshevik Revolution as spelling the death of the discipline in Russia, the social sciences flourished during the early Soviet period under different names and in a variety of locations outside the university setting.[24] Statistics, questionnaires, and other types of social investigation were not only compatible with Bolshevik dictatorship but also an essential feature of the revolutionary project. They were the primary means by which the regime came to know the population and conditions within its borders and by which it mapped out its transformational ambitions.[25] Thinking of the social sciences as a technology of government helps to explain why the scientism of Bolshevism merged so well with the sociological inclinations of professionals for whom the theories of Durkheim were as relevant as those of Karl Marx. It was not just ideology but the assumptions and conceptual tools that signify the social realm that shaped the interventions and activities of the state and its investigators. Visions of Russian society—past, present, as well as future—were structured around numbers, organismic metaphors of the body politic, and a combination of biological and medical theories that applied equally to the political and social spheres.[26]

The notion of the social science state also situates the Soviet experiment within the stream of modernity and continues the argument against Soviet exceptionalism. A growing number of historians have identified various affinities between the Soviet Union and its European counterparts,

23. In this respect, Soviet citizens were increasingly modern. See Jane Caplan and John Torpey, eds., *Documenting Individual Identity: The Development of State Practices in the Modern World* (Princeton, 2001), 1–12.

24. Alex Simirenko has described the 1920s as a "period of decline" for sociological research, with much work being carried out in "covert form." See "An Outline History of Soviet Sociology with a Focus on Recent Developments," in *Soviet Sociology: Historical Antecedents and Current Appraisals,* ed. Alex Simirenko (Chicago, 1966), 19. On the fate of academic sociology after 1917 see Elizabeth A. Weinberg, *Sociology in the Soviet Union and Beyond: Social Enquiry and Social Change* (Hants, UK, 2004), 2–7.

25. Francine Hirsch emphatically makes this point in her study of Soviet ethnography. See *Empire of Nations: Ethnographic Knowledge and the Making of the Soviet Union* (Ithaca, 2005).

26. On the continuation and radicalization of liberal notions of human behavior, most notably the theory of degeneration, under the Bolsheviks see Daniel Beer, *Renovating Russia: The Human Sciences and the Fate of Liberal Modernity, 1880–1930* (Ithaca, 2008).

noting such important commonalities as the welfare state, the deployment of mass politics, and broad governmental interventions into the realms of the family, education, and health. In this way, David Hoffmann and other scholars have broadened our understanding of the Soviet regime by demonstrating that the assumptions and aspirations of modernity shaped the Soviet experience as much as Bolshevik ideology did.[27] Nevertheless, recognition of shared origins and features does not mean overlooking the distinctive qualities of Soviet population policies. Key in this regard are the radicalized quality of many Soviet practices, the stronger emphasis placed on ideology and politics, and the greater insistence on revealing and shaping the subjective affairs of the individual.[28] Daniel Beer, for example, frames Soviet responses to crime and other social threats as a particularly radical adaptation of what he calls "liberal modernity." If, according to Beer, late tsarist Russia was a "laboratory of modernity," then Soviet Russia was a vast testing ground where many of the potentialities of modern thought were realized, expanded, and redefined amid the drive toward a particular end point—the harmonious socialist society.[29]

Soviet modernity was as much a rhetorical move as it was a distinct set of practices and outlooks. In many respects, Soviet investigators were drawn to the problem of suicide precisely because of its linkage in scientific and political discourse to the changing landscape and existential pressures of modern life. Across Europe suicide was seen as a "natural," if undesirable, fact of the modern world, representing both sign and source of social breakdown and pathology. It therefore provided an invaluable window into the workings of society and pressing questions about human nature and its potential for transformation. Within the context of the Soviet experiment, the study of suicide also enabled investigators to conceptualize the distinctive features of postrevolutionary life and to define themselves against both the autocratic regime and their contemporaries in other countries. Seeking to develop and expand the technologies of modern government—such as statistics and surveillance—they saw themselves at the forefront of building a socialist Russia that would overcome its past as well as the alienation and dislocation associated with other industrialized

---

27. Hoffmann, *Stalinist Values*, 7–10; Hoffmann, "European Modernity and Soviet Socialism," in *Russian Modernity*, 249–60; and Stephen Kotkin, *Magnetic Mountain: Stalinism as Civilization* (Berkeley, 1997), 18–21.

28. Peter Holquist, "What's So Revolutionary about the Russian Revolution?" 87–111.

29. Daniel Beer, "Blueprints for Change: The Human Sciences and the Coercive Transformation of Deviants in Russia, 1890–1930," *Osiris* 22 (2007): 47; and Beer, "'Microbes of the Mind': Moral Contagion in Late Imperial Russia," *Journal of Modern History* 79, no. 3 (2007): 531–71.

and urbanized nations. No less than their object of study, the social experts regarded themselves as hallmarks of the modern world.

The experts who populated the Soviet social science state were a varied bunch ideologically and frequently served as both social workers and social investigators. Doctors and psychiatrists in particular embraced the revolution as an opportunity to get closer to the people. They attempted to do so through enlightenment campaigns, the dispensary system of health care, and a plethora of social surveys into such matters as living conditions, reading habits, sexual practices, and the sources and patterns of self-destruction.[30] Statisticians, many of whom were carryovers from the tsarist administration, were also busily engaged in gathering economic and demographic information about the population as part of their self-professed mission to provide empirical material for the Soviet state.[31] Working with and alongside the scientific community was a new set of experts primarily concerned with the individual as a political being. Bolshevik Party officials and Red Army political instructors routinely gathered information about the everyday lives and subjective beliefs of communists and soldiers. In addition to fulfilling their many tasks, they were exhorted to give proper attention to the individual, which meant studying people from all sides and carrying out a personalized dialogue with each one about matters great and small. These interventions provided the Soviet regime with abundant information about the lifestyles, "moods" (*nastroeniia*), and ideological "health" of these key participants in the revolutionary project. They also formed the basis for a distinctive form of medicopolitics that aimed to make surveillance an everyday operation. This surveillance would function in a vertical top-down fashion but also in a horizontal fashion, a process of mutual observation among the citizens.

A different type of social history is therefore told in these pages. Instead of treating society as a preexisting given, the book explores the formation and radical expansion of the social as a site of governmental action during the 1920s. In particular, I contend that the advent of the Soviet social science state marked a key moment in Russia's development. For the first time the state fully embraced the statistical conception of the population and, accordingly, the potential of modern governmental

---

30. See, for example, Frances Lee Bernstein, *The Dictatorship of Sex: Lifestyle Advice for the Soviet Masses* (DeKalb, IL, 2007); and Dan Healey, *Homosexual Desire in Revolutionary Russia: The Regulation of Sexual and Gender Dissent* (Chicago, 2001).

31. Alain Blum and Martine Mespoulet, *L'anarchie bureaucratique: Pouvoir et statistique sous Staline* (Paris, 2003).

practices to achieve a legible and integrated social order. To be sure, this understanding of the population and government did not emerge overnight and was hardly restricted to the Bolsheviks.[32] The key historical question is when and why it finally achieved the backing of state power and in what forms. Recent scholarship by Peter Holquist and Joshua Sanborn has focused on the revolution of 1905 and the outbreak of war in 1914 as important catalysts in Russia's move toward a more modern, activist state consciously engaged in shaping the population.[33] Oleg Kharkhordin has also related Bolshevik techniques of group formation to religious practices, while Irina Paperno's and Susan Morrissey's studies of suicide in Imperial Russia suggest that the modern social sciences recast a variety of traditional attitudes toward individuals and their relationship to the world.[34] While recognizing these developments and antecedents, this book emphasizes the qualitatively and quantitatively distinctive character of social exploration after 1917. Under the leadership of the Bolsheviks, who insisted that everything and everyone was open to scrutiny, social investigators found unprecedented possibilities for intervention within a regime that broke down the conceptual as well as physical barriers to a unitary understanding of the population and to its all-encompassing study. By contrast, social investigators in tsarist Russia decried the absence of reliable statistics and other governmental technologies needed to intervene in the general population. Their primary obstacle was a regime and populace that could not see self-destruction as an injury to the society at large, since individuals were defined by their relationship to their estate (*soslovie*), the sovereign, or God and not necessarily by their equivalent relationship to society as a whole.[35] The redefinition of these relationships under Soviet power resulted in a changed political, social, and cultural

---

32. Since the late nineteenth century, for example, populists and other members of the intelligentsia had been dreaming of an integrated social order and looking to sociology as a utilitarian tool of social transformation. See, for example, Alexander Vucinich, *Social Thought in Tsarist Russia: The Quest for a General Science of Society, 1861–1917* (Chicago, 1976).

33. See Joshua A. Sanborn, *Drafting the Russian Nation: Military Conscription, Total War, and Mass Politics, 1905–1925* (DeKalb, IL, 2003); and Peter Holquist, *Making War, Forging Revolution: Russia's Continuum of Crisis, 1914–1921* (Cambridge, MA, 2002).

34. Oleg Kharkhordin, *The Collective and the Individual in Russia: A Study of Practices* (Berkeley, 1999).

35. Yanni Kotsonis examines the corporatist social structure as an impediment to holistic conceptions and governmental policies in his recent work on taxation. See Yanni Kotsonis, "'No Place to Go': Taxation and State Transformation in Late Imperial and Early Soviet Russia," *Journal of Modern History* 76 (September 2004): 531–77; and Kotsonis, "'Face to Face': The State, the Individual, and the Citizen in Russian Taxation, 1863–1917," *Slavic Review* 63 (Summer 2004): 221–46. More broadly, Bruce Curtis contends that the shift toward seeing a "population" as opposed to a concern with "populousness" necessarily involved a

terrain that made the study and shaping of the collective a defining characteristic of the new regime.

GRAPPLING WITH THE INDIVIDUAL

This book emphasizes the centrality of the individual to the Soviet project. While the ruling ideology certainly narrowed the field of possibilities in its rejection of the private realm as a legitimate space and of liberal understandings of autonomy as central to personal rights and identities, it simultaneously opened up new and often unprecedented avenues for thinking about and acting upon the person.[36] Thus, rather than mattering less, the individual mattered differently within the context of a regime that encouraged its members to think about themselves primarily as collective or social beings. In particular, the aspiration to break apart, analyze, and shape the personality (*lichnost'*) not only provided a catalyst for the broad study of suicide but gave an added political dimension to its meaning in light of the regime's ultimate transformational goals. Faced with the continued presence of suicides during the 1920s, the Soviets cast them as vestiges or residues of the old bourgeois order that had yet to be expunged from everyday life. In particular, their understanding was tied to the indeterminacy of the New Economic Policy. The ephemeral and murky character of this transitional epoch meant that some people—notably the young, the politically immature, the physically exhausted, and the dispossessed prerevolutionary elites—would lose their sense of place and fall into despair. Only when the new forms of everyday life and new forms of people were made a reality would the dangers of suicide and other bourgeois illnesses disappear. In the meantime, the regime set about obsessively studying the body politic and looking for elements of disease within, lest the remnants of the old world pollute the new one.[37]

Suicide, perhaps more than any other form of human behavior, forced the Soviets to confront the individual. It was a form of individuation that raised thorny questions about autonomy, agency, and responsibility and the right to live and die as one chose. In many respects, Soviet responses

---

shift from relations to practical equivalences. See Curtis, "Foucault on Governmentality and Population," 505–33.

36. In this respect, the present book continues the observations of Stephen Kotkin, who emphasizes the productive or creative aspects of power and not just its potential to limit or restrain. See *Magnetic Mountain*, 21–23.

37. The discourses of the transition period are explored in Naiman, *Sex in Public*, and Gorsuch, *Youth in Revolutionary Russia*, 18–27.

were a continuation of modern theories that stripped agency from the individual. However, particularly in Bolshevik Party discourse, acts of suicide provoked debate as well as consternation about individual will and autonomy. Being Marxists, the Bolsheviks accepted historical and social laws as fact; however, being part of the political vanguard, they also professed a deep belief in their ability to shape history, and often cast suicide as a willful act committed out of spite or despair.[38] These unresolved tensions over the relative importance of impersonal forces and personal volition eventually spilled out beyond the party itself to affect other spheres of social investigation. In the case of Soviet statistics, for example, party activists in the late 1920s began to criticize the law of large numbers, which assigned regularities to different forms of human behavior, for suggesting the impotence of political or state activity. Simply capturing reality through numbers became increasingly inappropriate for a regime that sought to change reality, an ideological shift that helped to bring down Soviet moral statistics.[39]

Recognition of the individual also coexisted uneasily with the idea of the collective. Suicide went against a key tenet of Soviet belief—the idea that human potential and freedom could be realized only after the false dichotomy between the public and private self was destroyed along with the bourgeois ideology that had produced this unnatural split. Most strikingly, Soviet social experts during the 1920s framed isolation as unhealthy, unnatural, and dangerous for both the self and the rest of society. To be alone and outside the collective risked a loss of purpose and meaning. It opened one up to unhealthy thoughts and dangerous ideological influences. It provided the grounds for a metaphorical, if not always literal, death. Bolshevik Party officials, in particular, gave a twist to the broader association between suicide and alienation, interpreting acts of self-destruction as the product of an egoistic love for the self that privileged the "I" over the "we."[40] Thus they worked simultaneously to promote and contain the individual through the collective, with the goal being the creation of social individuals who would recognize themselves through the group. The rituals surrounding suicides in the party and Red Army were as much about diagnosing and reaffirming the collective's health

---

38. On the issue of will and consciousness see Halfin, *Terror in My Soul,* 14–15.

39. Blum and Mespoulet, *L'anarchie bureaucratique,* 201–6.

40. This way of seeing the suicide went slightly against the grain of modern theories of violence, which posited suicide as an act of aggression turned inward and murders as acts of aggression turned outward against other human beings. A fine summary and critique of these attitudes and their origins can be found in N. Prabha Unnithan et al., *The Currents of Lethal Violence: An Integrated Model of Suicide and Homicide* (Albany, 1994), especially 7–34.

as they were about promoting a particular reading of the act. In this way, the self-destructive behavior of the individual served as a catalyst for individual as well as group formation.

Soviet professionals also grappled with the challenge of understanding the individual (the part) and his or her relationship to society (the whole). Their intense interest in studying and caring for the personality—a "unitary complex" composed of hereditary, biological, sociological, psychological, moral, and ideological elements—suggested multiple points of intervention and solidified the centrality of the individual (as well as the expert) to the search for an integrated social order.[41] This was the thinking behind the many investigations into the "criminal personality" during the 1920s and the rationale behind the search for the sources of the "suicidal personality" (*lichnost' samoubiitsa*). The challenge was to determine the elements that made up a "healthy," or conversely "pathological," type of person and then to promote or limit them accordingly. Some forensic doctors took a rather literal approach to the problem when they emphasized the importance of autopsy, which meant breaking down the body in order to identify the physiological signs and causal agents of the self-destructive personality. Still others opted for performing a metaphorical autopsy on the social body, using questionnaires and clinical methods to gather the particulars that would together make up an aggregate picture of suicide. In this manner, they sought to reveal statistical regularities and to visualize the social organism. The part and the whole came together most clearly, however, in the strongly interdisciplinary approaches that characterized much of the Soviets' work on criminals, suicides, and other deviants. Doctors and psychiatric specialists, for example, argued for a biosocial theory of the suicidal personality that posited self-destruction as the end product of the uninterrupted interplay between external surroundings and the internal self. Through this framework the suicide was cast as an unbalanced individual who reacted pathologically to events that healthy people could manage normally. Researchers could therefore acknowledge the particularities of each case without jeopardizing their abiding interest in society as a whole.

Such variations of thought and emphasis in regard to the suicidal personality reinforce the fact that we should not confuse a commonality of interests with a uniformity of outlooks and aspirations. While embracing

---

41. On the significance of "personality" as a concept and site of intervention see Kharkhordin, *Collective and the Individual,* 175–212; Halfin, *Terror in My Soul,* 189–91; and Derek Offord, "*Lichnost'*: Notions of Individual Identity," in *Constructing Russian Culture in the Age of Revolution: 1881–1940,* ed. Catriona Kelly and David Shepherd (Oxford, 1998), 13–23.

the opportunities of the new social terrain, Soviet investigators varied in their understanding of the limits and possibilities of their cognitive reach. Moral statisticians in the Central Statistical Administration were rather circumspect about the usefulness of numbers for revealing subjectivity, limiting them to the role of objectively capturing the national picture of suicide. Unable to penetrate the inner thoughts and motivations of the individual, the statisticians opted instead to count the number of people who had died by their own hands and to measure how this deed was related to such measurable factors as education, marital relations, occupation, and the revolution's effects on the position of the sexes in society. Facing a similar dilemma, forensic-medical experts disagreed over whether the truth about suicide ultimately lay in aggregate information or in the individualized details that one gathered from the concrete study of the body. Proponents of the latter approach stressed the importance of direct observation, although one detects a hint of utopianism that belied the emphasis on concrete materiality. Their inability to see the physiological signs of suicide did not cause them to question their existence; rather, they explained this failure as the product of a faulty or limited cognition that would be rectified through repeated observations or through new technologies developed in the future. Reflecting their Marxist-based ideology, investigators in the Bolshevik Party and Red Army combined both scientism and faith in their approach to studying the social realm. Because total and direct knowledge of the individual was deemed central to the proper operation of the collectivist society, the presence of suicides and other asocial phenomena suggested the opposite—the still incomplete state of surveillance and information gathering. In their different ways, then, the responses to suicide suggest a common technocratic impulse inherent in the modern social sciences, notably the belief that social progress and control were determined in large measure by the state's ability to see its population.[42]

Although this book does not focus on the act of suicide itself, it nevertheless offers evidence of individual participation in the formation and functioning of the Soviet social science state. The handling of the suicide was not a unidirectional process with the state and its representatives simply transposing their categories and assumptions onto a powerless population. While a successful suicide certainly opened up the individual's life story to reshaping in the hands of others, Soviet responses did not negate, and in some cases promoted, the inherently dialogic quality of self-destruction.

42. For a critical examination of this imperative see James C. Scott, *Seeing like a State: How Certain Schemes to Improve the Human Condition Have Failed* (New Haven, 1998).

For one thing, individual suicides had the power to shape the reading of the case through their selection of methods, staging of the act, and choice of words used to describe feelings and motivations, which in some instances contradicted and in others reinforced the dominant interpretative paradigm. Friends, family, and witnesses also participated by providing investigators with their understanding of the event. Even the suicide's body, a seemingly fixed entity that could be assigned a particular significance, provoked a variety of different responses in the hands of different kinds of experts. More broadly, the creation of a "collective opinion" and the shaping of political attitudes in the Bolshevik Party and the Red Army encouraged the group to engage the suicide, whose words and actions were exposed to scrutiny in an effort to inscribe them within a communal narrative. In the hands of the Soviets, the act of suicide remained an interpretative struggle as well as an incitement to making meaning.

Many of the projects examined here are thus permeated by the nagging sense of a *lack* of control over the population. They offer additional confirmation that anxiety, as much as utopianism, was the leitmotif of the early Soviet period. Socially and economically, the products of dislocation— notably unemployment, homelessness, infectious disease, prostitution, family discord, and abortion—undermined the state's ability to fulfill its ambitious welfare agenda. Politically, Bolshevik visions of the future were animated by fears of ideological corruption among the faithful. Reflecting the utopian's predicament, their revolutionary dreams were beset by the contradiction of having to create something completely new out of the preexisting human and social material. Looking more broadly, however, the Soviets' pervasive unease reflects the universal condition of modernity. Surveillance of the population, which promises to provide ever greater amounts of information about the social world, rarely provides certainty or greater control. This elusiveness, argues Anthony Giddens, is the direct consequence of the deeply "sociological" and "reflexive" character of modern life, whereby the objects of investigation continually alter their behavior in response to the ideas and interventions of the investigators. The resulting hermeneutic circle can affirm not just one's assumptions but also one's fears.[43]

Ultimately, then, suicides challenged the aspirations of Soviet investigators and the social science state. Their actions raised questions about

---

43. Giddens writes, "The discourse of sociology and the concepts, theories, and findings of the other social sciences continually 'circulate in and out' of what it is they are about. In doing so they reflexively restructure their subject matter, which itself has learned to think sociologically." See his *The Consequences of Modernity* (Stanford, 1990), 36–45.

human perfectibility, signaled social breakdown as well as individual despair, and brought into sharp focus the limits of human knowledge and control. Indeed, the act of self-destruction frustrated Soviet investigators since it suggested the continued presence of beings whose isolation had escaped detection or whose internal selves remained opaque. It also raised questions about the overall health and well-being of Soviet society during the difficult transition to socialism, making the study of suicide a deeply self-reflexive enterprise. This troubling fact only intensified the desire to access the personality in the hopes of reforming it and had the potential to feed into more pessimistic calls for isolating and/or destroying irredeemable social elements.[44] By intruding violently into the dreams of Soviet social investigators, suicide acted as a vehicle for the creation of a scientific-political apparatus that was designed for the comprehensive care of the population. The following chapters tell the story of the unfolding and the workings of this apparatus.

THE STRUCTURE OF THE BOOK

The book explores the practices and meanings surrounding Soviet suicide at a number of mutually reinforcing levels. Chapter 1 looks at suicide under the old and new regimes in order to provide a general background and to examine the rise of the population as an object of government. Using the "suicide epidemic" of 1906–14 as a starting point, it outlines the discourse of suicide as a social problem and demonstrates that studies of self-destruction in Russia were dependent on certain understandings of the individual and society. Suicide, in particular, was understood as a sign of social breakdown and alienation and was associated with the challenges of modern life. An examination of responses to these challenges before and after 1917 suggests that the position of social investigators vis-à-vis the state was dependent on the way that the autocratic and then Soviet regime conceived of the population as an object of administration. The affinity between Bolshevism and other modes of modern social science is evident

---

44. Daniel Beer contends that a redefinition of heredity and social danger in terms of social class led the Soviet regime to increasingly pursue more pessimistic measures toward threatening individuals. See his *Renovating Russia*. Bolshevik attitudes toward the permanence of human nature are also explored in Amir Weiner, "Nature, Nurture, and Memory in the Socialist Utopia: Delineating the Soviet Socio-Ethnic Body in the Age of Socialism," *American Historical Review* 104, no. 4 (October 1999): 1114–55; and Eric D. Weitz, "Racial Politics without the Concept of Race: Reevaluating Soviet Ethnic and National Purges," *Slavic Review* 61, no. 1 (Spring 2002): 1–29.

in the new centers of social investigation that arose during the 1920s and made suicide an object of governmental concern.

Chapter 2 examines the politics of suicide and the Soviet individual. The Bolshevik Party largely condemned suicide and responded to acts among its ranks by organizing special gatherings to discuss the meaning of such incidents. These meetings of the faithful produced a "collective opinion" that criticized suicide as a form of desertion from the socialist cause and an act of individualism not becoming a true Bolshevik. They also promoted the practice of "mutual surveillance" among individuals as central to maintaining the health of the *kollektiv*. In this way, Bolshevik responses to suicide were embedded in the larger project of creating social individuals who recognized themselves through the group. Although the meaning of self-destruction was contested in the party, the individual member could not be understood outside the framework of the collective.

Chapter 3 investigates professional power and expert knowledge. It focuses on the Department of Forensic-Medical Expertise, a new state institution that undertook the first national survey of suicide in Russian history, and a group of university-based doctors who autopsied suicides in the search for the physiological origins of the suicidal personality. I investigate the competing explanations of suicide as the product of either bodily degeneration or environmental forces and demonstrate that the focus on the particulars of the human body was in tension with the desire of some forensic doctors to represent their discipline as a branch of Soviet social medicine. The work of the forensic doctors not only reinforces the fact that biological understandings of the individual were compatible with the Soviet regime but shows that the real line of debate among forensic doctors was over the relative importance of particular facts and aggregate information. The story of Soviet forensic medicine therefore suggests that debates about suicide were also debates about professional identity and the sources of social knowledge and scientific truth.

Chapter 4 continues the theme of professional knowledge by examining the relationship between statistics and Soviet modernity. Attention here is given to the Department of Moral Statistics inside the Central Statistical Administration. I explore how the Soviet Union became statistical and describe the efforts of moral statisticians to standardize the collection of materials relating to social problems like suicide, crime, and abortion. In particular, the chapter reveals that moral statisticians interpreted their activities within a gendered discourse of "civilization" that made the numbers—both the patterns read from them and the manner in which they were gathered—symbolic of progress and Soviet distinctiveness. In so doing, I demonstrate that Soviet modernity was in part a rhetorical endeavor. Numbers served as a means for the moral statisticians to inscribe suicides and themselves into the larger story of Russia and its historical development. Ultimately, however, the moral statisticians found themselves written out of the Soviet project in the late 1920s and early 1930s. Their definition of the scope and purpose of moral statistics placed them at odds with increasingly politicized and instrumentalist conceptions of social knowledge.

The closing narrative in chapter 5 probes the formation of social and political bodies within the Red Army, one of the primary sites for building socialism during the 1920s. It looks at the efforts of the Political Administration (PUR) to study suicides as part of its larger responsibility for maintaining the "political-moral condition" of the troops. I argue that the Political Administration operated in a radically expanded social terrain and that its activities came closest to expressing the ideals of the Soviet social science state. Seeking total knowledge and transparency, PUR was dependent on the study of individuals and the statistical mapping of the aggregate in order to comprehend the suicidal state of mind and to see patterns of self-destruction within the military population. Information set in motion a comprehensive effort to transform individual subjectivity and regulate the larger organism of the military. The result was a distinctive form of politico-medical therapeutics.

The book concludes with a brief look beyond the 1920s to the 1930s, when suicide and other social pathologies disappeared from public discourse under Stalin. A survey of the sources suggests that investigations into suicide continued in secret during the 1930s, while the act was recast as a social anomaly unrepresentative of the newly constructed socialist order. Most notably, responsibility now shifted to the individual amid the final construction of socialism in Russia. The renewed emphasis on human agency was not simply a move to absolve Soviet society of responsibility. It can also be interpreted as a particular response to the vagaries and uncertainties modern life. For the very rise of the social science state was stimulated by the desire to end the conditions that produced the isolation and despair of suicide.

1

Suicide and Social (Dis)Integration in Revolutionary Russia

Russia experienced a demographic nightmare between 1914 and 1923. All told, some 30 million people are estimated to have perished from a combination of military strife, socioeconomic upheaval, famine, and disease. Countless more were displaced. During the civil war period 1918–21, in particular, Russia's cities were depopulated as its urban denizens migrated to the countryside in search of food and fuel, a fact that caused deep consternation for the Bolsheviks since it depleted the proletarian social base in whose name the October Revolution of 1917 had been made.[1] Beyond the physical shifts and losses, however, there also lurked the less visible danger of widespread mental alienation and emotional damage among the survivors. This potential threat to the country's future presented physicians and psychiatrists with enormous challenges as healers and with extraordinary opportunities as researchers of the human condition. Faced with the specter of mass social breakdown and individual anomie, many plunged headlong into the study of the population.[2]

1. William G. Rosenberg, "Problems of Welfare and Everyday Life," in *Critical Companion to the Russian Revolution 1914–1921,* ed. Edward Acton et al. (Bloomington, 1997), 633–44; and Catherine Merridale, *Nights of Stone: Death and Memory in Twentieth-Century Russia* (New York, 2000), 101–6.

2. See, for example, V. P. Osipov, "O dushevnoi zabolevaemosti i dushevnykh boleznikakh v perezhivaemuiu epokhu i ee posledstviiakh dlia dushevnogo zdorov'ia naseleniia v

One of the first medical efforts took place under the auspices of the newly formed Narkomzdrav, which aimed to centralize and equalize the delivery of health care throughout the country. In 1920 its Neuro-Psychiatric Subsection conducted a broad investigation into the "nervous system and psyche of the Republic's population." A rather bleak report resulted. It concluded that both the military and civilian populations had suffered severe psychological trauma and raised questions about the significance of the damage for future generations. Amid all the bad news, however, the report's authors did identify one positive trend—suicides and suicide attempts in Russia had fallen sharply since the outbreak of war in 1914. Most notably, suicides among school-aged children had all but stopped, while the broader "suicide epidemic of the reactionary period 1906–1914" had come to an end. The report's authors confessed that these conclusions were based more on impressions than on "precise statistical data," but they were hopeful that a newly formed "commission for the study of suicides in Russia" would sort out the "reasons for these [positive] influences" on suicide.[3] In fact, the commission's creation within Narkomzdrav's Subdepartment of State Expertise foreshadowed a much more extensive set of efforts to understand and control self-destruction throughout the decade of the 1920s.

The timing of this interest in voluntary death might seem a bit perplexing, given the scarcity of resources and the fact that the number of suicides and attempted suicides, even if they were known in 1920, paled beside deaths from disease, warfare, and other forms of violence. However, from a broader perspective it is fully consonant with suicide's historical and cultural significance in Russia and the rest of Europe. The primary author of the Health Commissariat's 1920 report, the psychiatrist Leonid Alekseevich Prozorov, had himself been an influential figure in the fight against suicide before the Bolshevik Revolution, indicating the continuity both of personnel and of their concerns across the chronological divide of 1917.[4] In addition, the report's reference to the "suicide epidemic of the reactionary period 1906–1914," which suggested that even suicide could not escape politicization, underscored the fact that concern over suicides had a deep history in prerevolutionary

---

budushchem," *Priroda*, nos. 10–12 (1921): 2–21; and A. M. Tereshkovich, *Vliianie voiny i revoliutsii na psikhicheskuiu zabolevaemost'* (Moscow, 1924).

3. Report of the Neuro-Psychiatric Subsection of Narkomzdrav dated June 28, 1920, GARF, f. 482, op. 3, d. 9, ll. 77–78ob. The report speculated that the prohibition of alcohol since the war's beginning was one factor behind the lower incidence of suicide.

4. The commission being organized to study the problem of Soviet suicide also included several members of a prerevolutionary committee that struggled against self-destruction.

Russia. The Russian public, generally speaking, had grown accustomed to thinking about rates of self-destruction (as well as mental health) in terms of what they said about the prevailing political and social order.[5] At various times they signified the anomie of modern life, the state of education and the country's youth, the moral tenor of society, the injustices of the market economy, and the dangers as well as promises of mass politics. Within the Russian scientific community, moreover, the decision of the individual to commit suicide represented more than just the loss of a person; it also raised a whole set of questions about human nature and the quality of relationships among human beings. Studying suicide therefore allowed Soviet researchers to look intensively at individuals and to dissect group life, making the voluntary end of a relatively few people too important to be completely ignored, even amid the cacophony of anguish and death swirling around Russia in the early 1920s.

A survey of responses to suicide after the revolutions of 1905 and 1917 provides a foundation for the chapters that follow and allows us to identify the distinctive as well as more universal qualities of Soviet approaches to self-destruction. Soviet investigators, despite their desire to distinguish themselves and the new social order from the tsarist era, could not fully escape the prerevolutionary past. In addition to reading their actions and findings against the so-called suicide epidemic of 1906–14, they used many of the same categories, explanatory frameworks, and technologies to make sense of suicide, a fact that reflected both the continuity of certain actors and the sway of the broader pan-European discourse about self-destruction in the modern world. In particular, commentators during the two postrevolutionary periods shared an understanding of suicide as a social phenomenon that functioned as a barometer of social health and integration, or the degree to which the individual was bound to the larger community. The result was a series of efforts to study suicide scientifically in the hopes of creating a rational social order through a mix of individualized interventions and broad surveys of the population.

Well before 1917, then, the discourse on suicide in Russia blurred the boundaries between the individual (the part) and society (the whole), making the one legible through the other. However, the move to treat the individual as a social body found more fertile ground within the collectivist framework of Soviet socialism. Indeed, the responses to suicide during the early Soviet period embraced a politico-statistical conception of the population that depended on both the creation of an administrative

---

5. On mental illness as a social indicator, see Irina Sirotkina, *Diagnosing Literary Genius: A Cultural History of Psychiatry in Russia, 1880–1930* (Baltimore, 2002), esp. chap. 4.

infrastructure and the implementation of a more modern style of governance. Unlike the tsarist regime, which had seen the people primarily as legally defined subjects and thus had difficulty creating equivalences among them, the Soviet state was organized around the management, shaping, and transformation of the population as a conceptual whole.[6] The governmental ethos that animated this approach made "social diagnostics," or the application of medical language and statistical practices to the population, an essential part of the Soviet landscape after 1917. It accounts for the rise of new state institutions concerned with gathering information about the citizenry. It also helps to explain why many doctors and other social investigators found greater opportunities under Soviet power to study suicide and to participate more generally in the campaign to "renovate" Russia.[7] Thus the story refracted through the prism of Soviet suicide is the story of the rise of specific governmental attitudes and practices in Russia, which made possible the radical expansion of the social and with it the expansion of various forms of expertise designed to manage this field of knowledge and policy.[8]

MEDICAL DIAGNOSTICS AND THE SUICIDE EPIDEMIC OF 1906–14

Suicide in the nineteenth century signified disintegration. Commentators throughout Europe connected it to the dissolution of the self and the breakdown of social bonds, and to the alienation, nervousness, and pressures associated with modern life. The axiomatic link they established between suicide rates and civilization offered a powerful explanation for the apparent rise of self-destruction across the continent as the century moved forward. It also led to a host of associated truths: that levels of suicide were greater among more advanced nations as compared with "backward" peoples, among city dwellers as compared with rural inhabitants, among men as compared with women, and among the upper classes as compared with the masses. Suicide thus became emblematic of the dark side of progress, a visible marker of the difficult transition from the intimate personal

6. On this distinction see Peter Holquist, "'Information is the Alpha and Omega of Our Work': Bolshevik Surveillance in its Pan-European Context," *Journal of Modern History* 69, no. 3 (September 1997): esp. 419–21.

7. I borrow the term "renovate" from Daniel Beer's *Renovating Russia: The Human Sciences and the Fate of Liberal Modernity, 1880–1930* (Ithaca, 2008).

8. For a valuable discussion of "the social," including its definition as a field of knowledge and administration, see Bruce Curtis, "Surveying the Social: Techniques, Practices, Power," *Histoire sociale/Social History* 35 (2002): 83–108.

relations of traditional life to the quickening pace and more atomistic world of cities, industry, mass communications, and mental labor.[9]

The meaning of suicide was also closely linked to those disciplines that defined the individual as a social body whose condition was representative of the larger social organism. Statistics, for example, helped to make individual actions significant for the rest of society and thus the business of investigators who professed a desire to monitor and maintain its wellbeing. What seemed to be deeply voluntary or individualistic acts, determined solely by the actor's personal whims, were increasingly seen in the nineteenth century as the product of "social laws" or forces outside the individual. In fact, suicide statistics played a critical role in the construction of society as an entity that could be studied—and ultimately regulated—by the state and various experts. It is no coincidence that Émile Durkheim chose suicide as the vehicle through which he sought to establish the "new science" of sociology as a distinct field with its own object of inquiry.[10]

Although its overall rate of suicide placed the Russian Empire in the "less civilized" category of nations, there, too, suicide was interpreted in terms of modernity. In the press and specialized journals, educated Russians portrayed suicide as a barometer of "change, insecurity, and flux," and they regarded the rise of suicides in major cities like Moscow and St. Petersburg as tangible proof that higher rates of suicide were an inevitable, indeed almost natural, byproduct of urbanization, industrialization, and capitalist economies.[11] Explanations of suicide in late-Imperial Russia, for example, frequently employed the trope of the unsuccessful journey or transition from the tradition-bound countryside to the inhospitable world of the modern city. In these stories, the urban newcomer encountered corruption, immorality, and economic injustice instead of human warmth and support. Isolated and despairing, the displaced person committed suicide and became yet one more victim of Russia's move into the modern world.[12]

---

9. Irina Paperno, *Suicide as a Cultural Institution in Dostoevsky's Russia* (Ithaca, 1997); and Lisa Lieberman, *Leaving You: The Cultural Meaning of Suicide* (Chicago, 2003). Lieberman emphasizes the fact that the concern over suicide and social dislocation was shared by Europeans of all political stripes.

10. Ian Hacking, *The Taming of Chance* (Cambridge, 1990), chap. 20; and Theodore M. Porter, *The Rise of Statistical Thinking 1820–1900* (Princeton, 1986), chap. 2.

11. Susan K. Morrissey, "Suicide and Civilization in Late Imperial Russia," *Jahrbücher für Geschichte Osteuropas* 43, no. 2 (1995): 207. On the link between capitalism and suicide, see P. Gaikovich, "Samoubiistvo v voiskakh russkoi armii za 15 let," *Russkii vrach*, March 10, 1907, 344.

12. Morrissey, "Suicide and Civilization," 212–14.

Suicide in Imperial Russia was also closely linked to specific moments of profound political and social change. The notion of the suicide epidemic first entered public consciousness well before 1905, during the Great Reform era of the 1860s–1870s that saw the emancipation of the serfs, the easing of censorship, and the establishment of new institutions in the spheres of law and local self-government. In the hands of journalists and writers such as Fyodor Dostoevsky, this early suicide epidemic came to symbolize a variety of conditions and anxieties, including the disintegration of Russian society, the limits of human comprehension, and the loss of traditional morality caused by the rise of atheism and radical political philosophies. Russia's medical community also entered into the fray at this time, offering a view of the epidemic that challenged Christian notions of free will and called into question the autocratic regime's paternalistic claims over the welfare of its subjects. Many of these same issues and interpretations, albeit with some variation, would resurface in the debates after the 1905 revolution.[13]

Between 1906 and 1914, the so-called suicide epidemic became a ubiquitous presence in the popular press and medical-scientific literature. Newspapers in particular stoked both public horror and fascination with daily announcements of suicide and sensationalized accounts of young people killing themselves in the most theatrical fashion, an indication of the fact that suicides were aware of their audience and helping to shape the discourse surrounding the epidemic.[14] Many observers argued that the suicide epidemic was an expression of the deep malaise affecting most Russians after the revolution, which had resulted in only partial victories and the splintering of the opposition after Tsar Nicholas II promised basic political reforms in October 1905. In addition to rising levels of suicide, they also pointed with alarm at a host of other social maladies, including an increase in hooliganism, mental illness, physical violence, and various forms of sexual hedonism, especially among young people. Each of these phenomena, like suicide, suggested a coarsening of life that engendered pessimism, introspection, and lack of concern for others. Their very existence raised questions about the viability of the social organism as then constituted.[15]

13. Paperno, *Suicide as a Cultural Institution*, 94–104. Paperno identifies several differences. Most notably, the post-1905 debate placed greater emphasis on sexuality and the pernicious influence of decadent literature.

14. On the role of the commercial press in shaping the debates about suicide, see Susan K. Morrissey, *Suicide and the Body Politic in Imperial Russia* (Cambridge, 2007), 325–28.

15. On the social and cultural atmosphere, see Laura Engelstein, *The Keys to Happiness: Sex and the Search for Modernity in Fin-de-Siècle Russia* (Ithaca, 1992); Joan Neuberger,

One of the most noteworthy features of the post-1905 response to epidemic suicide was the heightened visibility of the scientific community, which increasingly set the terms for public debate and opinion in Russia.[16] Consistent with the widespread use of bodily metaphors to conceptualize both society and its problems, physicians took the lead in describing the epidemic and prescribing preventative and curative measures. They organized special investigative commissions, held special sessions on suicide during meetings of their professional associations, and published numerous articles and books on the subject.[17] Most significantly, medical investigators were responsible for establishing the very fact of the suicide epidemic, particularly in the major capital cities of Moscow and St. Petersburg. Through statistics and case studies they not only set out the general parameters of the problem but also established that certain population groups were more susceptible to the epidemic than others. Doctors discovered alarmingly high rates of suicide among the country's unemployed as well as inside Russia's prisons, military, and educational system, all spaces where suicides were most visible and surveillance most common.[18]

Russian physicians, like their counterparts in the rest of Europe, argued that suicide was a matter of public health and social policy, rather than simply a moral problem, whose roots were above all in the environment.[19] Most vocal in this regard was Dmitrii Nikolaevich Zhbankov, chief administrator of the Pirogov Society of Russian Physicians, the main professional organization of the Russian medical community. A tireless social commentator and devout populist, Zhbankov expressed deep anxiety about the rampant violence and general devaluation of life that he observed in Russian society after 1905. He shared his apprehension at regular intervals in articles written about suicide and what he termed the

Hooliganism: Crime, Culture, and Power in St. Petersburg, 1900–1914 (Berkeley, 1993); and Julie V. Brown, "Revolution and Psychosis: The Mixing of Science and Politics in Russian Psychiatric Medicine," *Russian Review* 46 (1987): 282–302.

16. Daniel Beer, "'Microbes of the Mind': Moral Contagion in Late Imperial Russia," *Journal of Modern History* 79 (September 2007): 537.

17. Good bibliographies of the literature can be found in M. F. Teodorovich, *Samoubiistvo. Ukazatel' literatury na russkom iazike* (Moscow, 1928); M. N. Gernet, *Ukazatel' russkoi i inostrannoi literatury po statistike prestuplenii, nakazanii i samoubiistv* (Moscow, 1924); and the list compiled by the physician Grigorii Gordon in E. Diurkgeim, *Samoubiistvo. Sotsiologicheskii etiud* (St. Petersburg, 1912), xxv–xxxii.

18. L. Prozorov, *Samoubiistva voennykh* (Moscow, 1914); N. A. Bekker, *Samoubiistva v Russkoi Armii. Statisticheskii ocherk* (Kiev, 1914); and Gaikovich, "Samoubiistva," 344–45.

19. This move was the result of larger and more complex factors, including the shift toward understanding moral issues in medical terms. See Daniel Beer, "The Medicalization of Religious Deviance in the Russian Orthodox Church," *Kritika* 5, no. 3 (Summer 2004): 451–82.

"epidemic of trauma" (*travmaticheskaia epidemiia*). Applying the methods of epidemiology and the language of bacteriology to the collective psychology of the population, Zhbankov plotted the "course" (*khod*) of the epidemic of trauma according to several key indicators of violence—pogroms, acts of terrorism, the death penalty, and suicides.[20] In his explanatory comments, he likened the cause of this broader epidemic to an "infectious pathological matter" and traced its origins back to April 1903, when the "microbes of misanthropy" were planted in the body politic during a series of coordinated pogroms against Jews living in Kishinev. From here the disease spread slowly to different parts of Russia, only to explode in the revolution of 1905 and its bloody aftermath.[21]

Within medical discourse, suicide symbolized the literal, as well as metaphorical, decomposition of the Russian social organism. In particular, Russian physicians relied heavily on the concept of "degeneration," a highly flexible theory of physical and moral decline, to account for the threat that individual suicides posed to the rest of society. First articulated by the French physician Bénédict-Augustin Morel in 1857, degeneration theory combined biology with social and historical factors to suggest that the environment could imprint itself on the human body and thus influence later generations.[22] Russian doctors, criminologists, and other professionals interested in the human psyche were particularly concerned at the fin de siècle about the susceptibility of the least developed and most unstable members of society to various moral and psychological "contagions." This understanding of deviance had clear applicability to the suicide epidemic, given the latter's apparently infectious quality and its connection to post-1905 collapse. More important, degeneration theory reinforced the belief that individual suicides were both sign and source of social breakdown, which then could be remedied through a mixture of sociopolitical reforms and medical treatments aimed at the individual and the broader population.[23]

20. Zhbankov also focused periodic attention on rapes and other acts of sexual violence, criticizing pornography and decadent literature for unleashing the repressed impulses of the individual. Engelstein, *Keys to Happiness*, 266–68.

21. D. N. Zhbankov, "Travmaticheskaia epidemiia v Rossii (aprel'–mai 1905 g.)," *Prakticheskii vrach*, August 13, 1905, 635–36. Zhbankov here was referring to the infamous pogrom of Easter 1903 that followed rumors of the ritual murder of a young boy committed by Jews. See Merridale, *Nights of Stone*, 70–71. Merridale, like Zhbankov, places the pogrom within the framework of a broader "culture of death" in Russia around the time of the 1905 revolution.

22. Richard A. Soloway, *Demography and Degeneration: Eugenics and the Declining Birthrate in Twentieth-Century Britain* (Chapel Hill, NC, 1990), 38–39; and Daniel Pick, *Faces of Degeneration: A European Disorder, c. 1848–c. 1918* (Cambridge, 1989).

23. Daniel Beer argues that initial optimism gradually gave way to more pessimistic and coercive approaches toward the deviant population. See his *Renovating Russia*.

The rhetoric of pathology was also essential to Russian physicians' efforts to position themselves as experts on suicide and the broader social realm. As Irina Paperno has suggested in her study of suicide in the nineteenth century, language was essential to solving the issues of individuality within the debates about the nature of self-destruction. In particular, the popular metaphor of the social organism, which easily lent itself to the application of medical terms and ideas, played a critical role in conceptualizing individuals and their relationship to the rest of the population. The corporeal language facilitated the construction of the "social man," who embodied society and whose actions were shaped by social laws similar to those found in nature.[24] Such an understanding allowed investigators to move freely back and forth between the part and the whole and thus to comment on the health of society through the observation of the individual.

Diagnosis and prophylaxis therefore went hand in hand. Dmitrii Zhbankov, for his part, called suicide the most "dangerous symptom" of "the internal disintegration [*razlozhenie*] of society." When conditions in society were favorable, he claimed, people valued their lives and turned to suicide only under the most unbearable circumstances. Conversely, when conditions were intolerable, as they were after 1905, the value of life—one's own as well as that of others—was cheapened. Not only did people take their own lives more easily, but the continuous stream of suicides desensitized society as a whole and made it increasingly indifferent to the plight of those in despair, thereby continuing the cycle of social dissolution.[25] Dr. Grigorii Izrailevich Gordon, an independent activist who spearheaded the medical community's response in St. Petersburg, echoed Zhbankov's concerns and language. He agreed that suicides were becoming an "everyday event" (*obydennoe iavlenie*) in Russia. Over the course of numerous articles and presentations, Gordon anxiously warned his readers about the larger danger of suicides, particularly among students and children, to society as a whole. "If suicides in general are, as some people think, a grave and ominous symptom of the degeneration [*vyrozhdenie*] of society," he wrote, "then the suicides of children are the saddest expression of this degeneration."[26]

---

24. Paperno, *Suicide as a Cultural Institution*, 30, 38–43.

25. "Itogi travmaticheskoi epidemii v Rossii s 1 iiuliia 1907 g. do 1 iiuliia 1908 g.," RGALI, f. 199, op. 1, d. 19, ll. 32–33; D. N. Zhbankov, "Travmaticheskaia epidemiia v Rossii (fevral' 1905 g.–iiun' 1907 g.)," *Prakticheskii vrach*, September 22, 1907, 683; and "Vnutrenniaia letopis'," *Prakticheskii vrach*, December 13, 1909, 883.

26. G. Gordon, "Samoubiistva molodezhi i ee nervna-psikhicheskaia neustoichivosti," *Novyi zhurnal dlia vsekh*, no. 9 (September 1912): 105.

Russian physicians also regarded suicide as an "indicator" (*pokazatel'*) of morbid spaces within the body politic. To take one major example, Gordon focused heavily on the classroom environment to explain an alarming rise of suicides among school-aged youth. According to his analysis, student suicides in Russia were "victims" (*zhertvy*) of an atmosphere that was poisoned in both a literal and figurative sense. The harsh school regime—which placed too much emphasis on grades and formal examinations and too little on hygiene, personal freedom, humane interactions, and physical exercise—created fertile ground for suicides by producing young people who were nervous, unstable, and prone to overreaction. All that was needed was a spark to set things in motion, which came in the form of poor grades, a harsh reprimand, the threat of punishment, or the mocking of other young people.[27]

The emphasis on the environmental origins of self-destruction was apparent even when physicians recognized suicide's subjective qualities. During an address to the First Congress of Psychiatrists and Neuropathologists in September 1911, the noted St. Petersburg professor of psychiatry Vladimir Mikhailovich Bekhterev raised the question of individual motivation and character for understanding suicide. Bekhterev acknowledged the importance of statistics for highlighting general trends and establishing the correlation between broad indicators; however, he also stressed the need for studying suicides as individuals in order to discover why only certain people killed themselves. In particular, Bekhterev called for clinical investigations into heredity, physiology, and mental-nervous makeup. Yet when it came to wrapping up his talk and offering suggestions on how to fight suicides, the famed psychiatrist devoted most of his discussion to broader social and political measures. He linked the rise and fall of suicides to the political situation in the country and preached the importance of economic redress, expanded charity, mutual-aid societies, and fundamental school reforms.[28]

In addition to blaming the autocratic regime for creating the general conditions that had produced the suicide epidemic, physicians were also critical of its response to the problem of self-destruction. The suicide in Imperial Russia potentially fell into the domains of law, religion, and medicine. According to the 1845 criminal code that functioned up to 1917, successful suicides were to have their last will and testament voided and

27. G. Gordon, "Samoubiistva uchashcheisia molodezhi," *Novoe slovo*, no. 9 (September 1911): 33.

28. V. M. Bekhterev, *O prichinakh samoubiistva i o vozmozhnoi bor'be s nim* (St. Petersburg, 1912), 4–5, 20–22.

their bodies denied Christian burial, unless it could be proven that they were insane or acting in a state of momentary delirium caused by illness. Attempted suicides were to be handed over to Church authorities for penance, presumably in the hope of saving their souls. Considered as policy, such laws demonstrated the autocratic state's strong interest in promoting Christian values within the secular legal system as well as its tendency to see the threat of punishment as a deterrent against future cases of suicide (this was the reasoning offered by the authors of the 1845 criminal code). The primary concern, in both respects, was with maintaining order and obedience, thereby leaving the matter of the individual's soul to the Church.[29] Although implementation of these laws varied in practice, the late nineteenth-century debates about the juridical position of the suicide in Russia suggest that representatives of the legal and ecclesiastical realms were struggling to define their relationship to the suicide, whose body and mind were at various times the responsibility of police, doctors, and clergymen.[30]

Russian physicians, not surprisingly, were eager to claim the body and mind/soul (*dusha*) of the suicide as their own. They were highly suspicious of the belief that suicide could be treated like a crime and reduced through a mixture of legal or punitive measures. In a lengthy essay published in 1912, Grigorii Gordon questioned proposals to strengthen the law by also depriving attempted suicides of any familial rights. Gordon argued that such regulations were easily skirted, and most important, they ended up making life worse for the survivor and relatives alike. Similarly, he believed that religious sanctions against suicide, exemplified by a 1909 circular of the Holy Synod reminding Orthodox priests of their obligation to refuse burial rites for suicides whose mental incapacity had not been proven, also hit hardest against the survivors. Finally, Gordon raised doubts about proposals to construct special halfway houses that would shelter attempted suicides until they had calmed down. The suicidal mindset, he argued, was the result of a long process that could not be undone so

29. The above account of suicide within the Russian legal system is taken from Paperno, *Suicide as a Cultural Institution*, 58–66. It should be mentioned that the 1845 criminal code also included a provision against instigating or participating in a suicide. This clause survived the revolutionary changes of 1917 and linked the performance of suicide in Russia to issues of paternalistic power and social order. See Susan Morrissey, "Patriarchy on Trial: Suicide, Discipline, and Governance in Imperial Russia," *Journal of Modern History* 75 (March 2003): 23–58.

30. According to Susan Morrissey, rates of prosecutions against suicides, as well as guilty verdicts against them, began to decrease around the mid-1800s. See her *Suicide and the Body Politic*, 99–104.

easily and quickly. Indeed, in Gordon's view, the weakness of these various measures was the underlying failure to understand suicide as a "complex social phenomenon." The fight against suicide needed to be about making life more, rather than less, appealing. Toward this goal, Gordon called for fighting against alcoholism, improving the school environment, and limiting the sensationalized reporting of suicides in the popular press, all of which would promote healthier minds and bodies, especially among young people.[31]

When physicians surveyed the state's policy toward suicide, they detected a tendency to focus on the means rather than the deeper causes of self-destruction. Among the most visible examples was the proposal of the St. Petersburg *gradonachal'nik* (city governor) to restrict the sale of vinegar essence, a readily available cleaning product that doubled as a popular instrument of self-poisoning (especially among women). Physicians serving on the medical council (*meditsinskii sovet*) of the Ministry of Internal Affairs, who met to discuss the proposal in 1909, agreed to support the sale of more diluted forms of the offensive liquid, but they rejected its outright ban as being detrimental to the poor and ultimately ineffective against the determined suicide.[32] Doctors working outside the government, however, loudly criticized the proposed restrictions on vinegar essence as yet another example of shortsighted, bureaucratic thinking. In an article devoted to suicides among women, Dr. Sofiia Bogatina condemned the "general conditions of Russian reality" for causing the recent rise in suicides and noted that the government's response ignored this essential fact. "The struggle against the...current suicide epidemic," she declared, "should be directed not against liquid ammonia and the essence of vinegar, as some of our administrators think, but against the conditions that nourish poverty, unemployment, and that unlimited oppression and arbitrariness so characteristic of our post-October constitutional fatherland."[33] To crit-

---

31. G. I. Gordon, "Sovremennye samoubiistva," *Russkaia mysl'*, no. 5 (1912): 89–92.

32. Assumptions about the fundamentally social nature of suicide predominated even in these official circles. Dr. L. N. Malinovskii, the chief medical inspector, was almost fatalistic in his assessment of the issue, stating that suicides always rose during periods of "political excitement" and thus the *gradonachal'nik*'s proposal would have little effect on the number of Russians taking their own lives. In other words, broader conditions had created the grounds for the increase in suicidal urges, and these impulses would find an outlet one way or the other. "Vnutrenniaia letopis'," *Prakticheskii vrach*, October 11, 1909, 721.

33. Sofiia Bogatina, "Samoubiistva sredi zhenshchin," *Zhenskii vestnik*, no. 11 (November 1910): 222. Bogatina here was referring to the political order that resulted from Tsar Nicholas II's so-called October Manifesto. Issued at the height of the 1905 revolution, the manifesto promised basic civil liberties and a series of reforms that, at least on paper, made Russia a constitutional monarchy.

ics such as Bogatina, attacks against the means rather than the root causes only reinforced the image of an autocratic regime that was either unable or unwilling to recognize its own complicity in the suicide epidemic.

Debates about the suicide epidemic were therefore intertwined with broader debates about the care and governance of the population. Having long prided themselves on their activism and social conscience, Russian physicians regarded the fight against suicide as a logical extension of their self-professed role as social workers among the people.[34] This meant taking the lead role in educating and mobilizing the larger community around the problem of suicide. It also meant adopting a critical stance that linked the prevention of suicide to broader reforms in the realm of society, economy, and politics. Dmitrii Zhbankov, for example, argued that the government's tepid response to suicide failed to take the problem seriously and overlooked the need for change. He called for "fundamental prophylactic measures" and the genuine "renovation" (*ozdorovlenie*) of Russian society, by which he had in mind the expansion of civil liberties, the cessation of government repression, and the end to unemployment and other conditions that devalued life.[35]

Medical doctors were especially critical of the government's failure to collect reliable information about suicides, which they deemed a major hindrance to the fight against suicide and one more sign of Russia's overall backwardness as a nation. According to an anonymous commentator in the journal *The Russian Physician,* the systematic analysis and annual publication of figures on student suicides was common practice among "the civilized [*kul'turnye*] countries of Western Europe." Russia, in sharp contrast, was just now making an effort to know the extent of the problem among its students.[36] The lack of statistics, in other words, was not just a sign of government indifference but also evidence of a deeper problem: the Russian state's halting adoption of a more modern, progressive approach to the population.[37]

---

34. On the self-identity of the Russian medical profession, see Nancy Mandelker Frieden, *Russian Physicians in an Era of Reform and Revolution, 1856–1905* (Princeton, 1981).

35. D. N. Zhbankov, "Travmaticheskaia epidemiia v Rossii (aprel'–mai 1905 g.)," *Prakticheskii vrach,* August 27, 1905, 686; Zhbankov, "Travmaticheskaia epidemiia v Rossii (fevral' 1905 g.-iiun' 1907 g.)," *Prakticheskii vrach,* September 22, 1907, 683; and "Vnutrenniaia letopis'," *Prakticheskii vrach,* January 24, 1910, 79. Zhbankov also lamented the fact that the "renovation" of the country had been turned over to bureaucrats. See "Travmaticheskaia epidemiia v Rossii (aprel'–mai 1905 g.)," *Prakticheskii vrach,* August 13, 1905, 635.

36. "Khronika i mel'kie izvestiia," *Russkii vrach,* September 22, 1907, 1327. Grigorii Gordon, for his part, held up the Prussians as the example to be followed in Russia. Gordon, "Samoubiistva detei," in *Trudy XI Pirogovskogo S"ezda,* ed. P. N. Bulatev (St. Petersburg, 1911), 2:56–57.

37. On the link between statistics and modernity, see Hacking, *Taming of Chance.*

To be fair, the government of Tsar Nicholas II did not completely over-look suicides, and there were indeed signs of Russia's move toward becoming statistical. Acts of suicide within the military were counted, broken down, and published as part of the general accounting of sanitary and health conditions among the troops.[38] Local statistical committees, such as those belonging to the Moscow and St. Petersburg city governments, also gathered information about cases of self-inflicted deaths within their respective regions.[39] Most notably, the Ministry of Education's Medical-Sanitary Division attempted to systematize the study of suicides and accidents throughout the Russian Empire's school system, a process that had begun rather haltingly in the 1880s. Starting in November 1905, the heads of all educational institutions were to submit a detailed report every time one of their students committed suicide, together with a number of supporting materials—autopsy reports, physicians' conclusions, and suicide notes. They were also requested to complete a brief questionnaire (*oprosnaia kartochka*) in order to standardize the information being passed along to the center. Although there is evidence that these requests met with resistance, notably in the judicial branch, Dr. Grigorii Vital'evich Khlopin, the director of the Medical-Sanitary Division, collected sufficient information to produce in 1906 an elaborate study of suicides committed within the school system. This work was followed by the annual publication of volumes filled with detailed statistical information, suggesting the extensiveness of the education ministry's efforts.[40]

There were limitations to these official statistics. Most notably, they applied only to discrete groups, which made it difficult to speak in terms of national patterns or the population as a whole. Grigorii Gordon in particular expressed frustration over the lack of a nationwide counting in a 1909 essay that discussed suicide rates in different countries. He could only speculate about the true number of Russian suicides and long for the day when he and other social investigators would have a national statistical network at their disposal: "It will only be possible to answer this ques-

---

38. These were the *Otchety o sanitarnom sostoianii russkoi armii*, published by the Main Military-Medical Administration as a supplement to the *Voenno-Meditsinskii zhurnal*. The *otchety* listed suicides among "sudden deaths" without comment or analysis.

39. See, for example, I. Serkov, "Samoubiistva v Moskve v 1908 i 1909 gg.," *Izvestiia moskovskoi gorodskoi dumy* 34, no. 5 (May 1910): 1–12. The Moscow data came primarily from the Provincial Statistical Committee, which counted suicides among general deaths, and from police reports.

40. G. V. Khlopin, *Samoubiistva, pokusheniia na samoubiistva i neschastnye sluchai sredi uchashchikhsia russkikh uchebnykh zavedenii. Sanitarno-statisticheskoe issledovanie* (St. Petersburg, 1906). For a more complete analysis of the ministry's efforts, see Morrissey, *Suicide and the Body Politic*, 320–22.

tion [of suicide rates] with any sort of precision when in our country, as abroad, there function state or public statistical bureaus that would note and register all cases of suicide. However,...we [currently] have nothing like this here." Significantly, he emphasized that having the instruments of government would do more than simply overcome Russia's statistical backwardness. It would also bring about a fundamental change in popular psychology regarding the meaning of individual acts like suicide for the nation as a whole. Gordon lamented, "The vast majority of them [suicides], especially within the villages and small cities, completely escape attention and that is why in our country we do not yet see suicides as important social phenomena demanding the most serious attention."[41]

Many within the medical community also looked with suspicion on the official figures, arguing that they were incomplete, unsystematic, and downright tendentious. In one article Gordon went so far as to argue that contrary to the official data, St. Petersburg probably occupied first place in the world according to the number of annual suicides, and he cast doubt as to whether Russia really was at the bottom of the table according to national rates of self-inflicted deaths.[42] Khlopin of the Education Ministry's Medical-Sanitary Division also came under criticism for failing to treat his source materials with sufficient skepticism. While the public hygienist Dr. Natan Vigdorchik lauded Khlopin for his "scientific conscientiousness" and "thoroughness," he argued that the official information had to be approached with extreme caution since school officials had a vested interest in shaping the way a suicide was represented and interpreted. Specifically, they might overlook certain causes or emphasize others in order to escape accountability for the young person's suicide. In the opinion of Vigdorchik, this basic fact skewed Khlopin's conclusions about the main causes of suicide in the schools, shifting responsibility away from the school regime itself and onto Russian society as a whole.[43]

Some physicians sought to overcome the lack of accurate information by gathering their own statistical data from sources outside the purview of the state. For his part, Dmitrii Zhbankov methodically clipped the daily

---

41. G. I. Gordon, "Samoubiistva v Rossii," *Bodroe slovo*, no. 15 (August 1909): 72. One could also read Gordon's comments as indicative of the medical profession's sense of isolation from the masses, who like the state viewed physicians and their larger ambitions with suspicion. On the position of the professions, see Harley Balzer, "The Problem of Professions in Imperial Russia," in *Between Tsar and People: Educated Society and the Quest for Public Identity in Late Imperial Russia*, ed. Edith W. Clowes, Samuel D. Kassow, and James L. West (Princeton, 1991), 183–98.

42. Gordon, "Sovremennye samoubiistva," 75.

43. "Vrachebnye otkliki," *Prakticheskii vrach*, no. 38 (1906): 643–45.

announcements from various newspapers, which he would then combine to create an aggregate picture of the suicide epidemic.[44] Although not without their flaws, such materials were deemed sufficient to establish the main character of the epidemic and to make general statements about its causes, course, and dimensions. Writing about the traumatic epidemic in 1907, Zhbankov stated, "The collected data are important for their *relative* significance; they more or less reliably indicate how both the entire epidemic in general and its individual expressions *have developed over time.*"[45] In a similar vein, Grigorii Gordon acknowledged the incompleteness of his statistics regarding school-aged suicides. Nevertheless, he argued, even these imperfect numbers were disturbingly high and greater than those provided by Khlopin and the Ministry of Education.[46]

The desire for empirical knowledge was an important factor behind the establishment of two independent bodies to investigate suicide—the Commission on the Fight against School Suicides, founded by the St. Petersburg-based Russian Society for the Preservation of the People's Health in October 1910, and the Commission for the Study of Suicides, which was formed under the auspices of the Pirogov Society in December 1912. In its first appeal to the public, the Pirogov commission cited the absence of precise data as the "primary difficulty" before it and turned to "all of Russian society" with a request that it provide printed works, letters, and other materials relating to suicide.[47] Similarly, the Commission on the Fight against School Suicides claimed that the first step in its struggle was to reveal the "true scale and causes" of youth suicide. It therefore called on "all people who hold dear the interests of the adolescent generation and the future of the motherland [*rodina*]" to provide the commission with detailed information about the causes and circumstances of every student suicide. In addition, the commission composed its own question-naire (*anketa*) to be completed by school physicians, parents' commit-tees, teachers, and others on the occasion of each suicide in the school system.[48] This questionnaire, which was developed with reference to the

44. Many of these clippings are among Zhbankov's personal papers and materials. "Lichnyi fond Dmitrogo Nikolaevicha Zhbankova," RGALI, f. 199.

45. Zhbankov, "Travmaticheskaia epidemiia v Rossii," *Prakticheskii vrach*, September 1, 1907, 624 (emphasis in the original).

46. Gordon, "Samoubiistva uchashcheisia molodezhi," 30; and Gordon, "Sovremennye samoubiistva," 83–84. Khlopin in turn claimed that there were inaccuracies in one of Gor-don's articles. Spravka of June 1, 1917, RGIA, f. 733, op. 199, d. 105, l. 317.

47. "Doklad Komissii po izuchenii samoubiistv v Rossii," in *Doklady pravleniia i komissii XII-mu Pirogovskomu s"ezdu vrachei (S.-Peterburg, 29 maia–6 iiunia 1913 g.)* (Moscow, 1913), 40–41.

48. "Zhurnaly zasedanii otdelenii i komissii Russkogo Obshchestva okhraneniia narodnogo zdraviia," *Zhurnal Russkogo Obshchestva okhraneniia narodnogo zdraviia*, no. 3

official form used by the Ministry of Education, contained additional questions about religion, sexuality, alcohol usage, family history, and other factors deemed essential for a more complete and objective picture of the problem.[49]

It is tempting to read these debates over information and the autocracy's response solely as a struggle between a reform-minded public on the one hand and a reactionary government on the other. The dispute over the quality and availability of information, however, also reflected an ongoing struggle between differing conceptions of the population and its management. Despite the growing importance of statistical knowledge to the machinery of state, Russian officialdom in the Old Regime continued to look upon the tsar's subjects as a countable group that was organized hierarchically according to irreducible legal estates or social orders (*sosloviia*). This way of seeing people certainly recognized interrelationships and did not preclude the adoption of organized measures to promote productivity and general well-being; nevertheless, defining them by their differences hindered the establishment of statistical equivalences between individuals and groups that would allow them to be compared and rearranged almost at will.[50] By contrast, Russian physicians who studied suicide professed a more expansive and flexible understanding of Russian "society" (*obshchestvo*), which traditionally denoted only the educated members of the public as opposed to the masses, or the "people" (*narod*). Theirs was fundamentally a politico-statistical conception that regarded each individual as a social body whose thoughts and actions were part and parcel of the larger whole.[51] "Society," explained the psychiatrist Vladimir Ivanovich Iakovenko in 1907,

> is an organized aggregate of individuals. Everything that we observe in the psyche of the separate person becomes a component part in the psyche of the entire society; conversely, the ideas, feelings, and volitional urges prevailing in the social organism inevitably find reflection in some way on the

---

(March 1911): 45. Grigorii Gordon and Vladimir Bekhterev were among the members of this commission.

49. See the discussion of the questionnaire in *Zhurnal Russkogo Obshchestva okhraneniia narodnogo zdraviia*, no. 3 (March 1911): 49–52, 55–57.

50. One scholar distinguishes this Old Regime outlook for its concern with "populousness" rather than "population." See Bruce Curtis, "Foucault on Governmentality and Population: The Impossible Discovery," *Canadian Journal of Sociology* 27, no. 4 (Autumn 2002): 507–11.

51. The concept of the "social body" is developed in David G. Horn, *Social Bodies: Science, Reproduction, and Italian Modernity* (Princeton, 1994).

individual person [*lichnost'*] and his mental life, since under the current conditions there is no, and can be no, individual life in absolute isolation.[52]

Conceived in such a manner, individual actions like suicide and crime could not be viewed outside the framework of society and thus held meaning for everyone, especially the investigator concerned with the condition of the social organism. To read the individual was thus to read the social world in which he or she moved.

This latter conception of the population rationalized a range of therapeutic approaches that combined broad social reforms with measures directed at the individual. Russian physicians imagined a vicious circle of disease, concluding that a sick society could produce sick individuals, who in turn threatened the health of the entire social order. This was especially evident in the medical debates about suicide and the educational system, which, together with the family and the Church, were responsible for cultivating future generations of Russians. As noted above, physicians and psychiatrists worried that the school regime itself was responsible for alarmingly high rates of suicide among students, particularly those enrolled in the middle schools. Vladimir Bekhterev, for example, faulted the school system for its failure to produce young people who were idealistic and cognizant of their larger importance to society. He lamented that Russian schools focused primarily on education (*obrazovanie*) in the narrow sense of book learning and the imparting of knowledge and skills. Instead, they needed to devote greater attention to the "self-perfection of the person" (*lichnoe sovershenstvovanie cheloveka*), by which Bekhterev meant a more individualized approach that stressed physical education and the ethical and moral "upbringing" (*vospitanie*) of the student. Ultimately, argued Bekhterev, an amelioration of wider social conditions would not be sufficient to combat suicides if the individuals who inhabited this world

52. Vladimir Iakovenko, "Zdorovye i boleznennye proiavleniia v psikhike sovremennogo russkogo obshchestva," *Zhurnal Obshchestva Russkikh vrachei v pamiat' N. I. Pirogova* 13, no. 4 (May 1907): 269. Iakovenko claimed that the revolutionary moment in Russia provided an extraordinary opportunity to examine the "psyche of Russian society," since it brought into greater relief the laws that operated on society and its members. For example, he interpreted the changed calculus of suicides and other pathologies as indicating the disruption in the normal operation of social laws: "If the usual monotonous social life promotes a continually fixed number of suicides, criminals, and mentally ill individuals, then, under the condition of general agitation, this contingent must be supplemented by still other unbalanced individuals who were standing on the border of mental health and who were unable to maintain their mental equilibrium under unusual conditions of social life" (280). A similar case for revolution as a moment of revelation was made in N. A. Vigdorchik, "Politicheskie psikhozy i politicheskie samoubiistva," *Obrazovanie*, no. 12 (December 1907): 51.

were not healthy enough—in both a physical and a mental sense—to overcome the difficult moments that would inevitably occur during their lifetimes.[53]

Physicians and psychiatrists like Bekhterev were essentially arguing for the cultivation of healthy citizens who were conscious of themselves as social beings with responsibilities toward the larger population. Moreover, they considered the medical profession uniquely positioned to study and treat both poles of the equation for social health—the part and the whole. With their special knowledge of the human body and increasingly of the human mind, physicians claimed a certain power over the individual, whose thoughts and actions could be better understood through clinical research, autopsy, and expert analysis. At the same time, the popular usage of bodily metaphors to represent the population, as well as the redefinition of moral issues as fundamentally medical problems, extended the applicability of this specialized knowledge to society as whole. Medical diagnostics increasingly became a form of social diagnostics with numerous implications for the types of roles that physicians would play in the community and the government. These could range from a general influence, such as providing parents with educational material on how to raise their children, to more direct interventions in the lives of people, including the examination of bodies and the counseling of individuals.[54]

In post-1905 Russia, therefore, concern over suicide and suicide statistics also reflected doubts about the nature of the autocratic regime. When physicians spoke about the need to have an exhaustive and centralized accounting of the population, they were not simply stating their faith in the revelatory powers of positivist science; rather, they were also speaking as outsiders who desired a regime that would recognize and promote the exercise of medical power for the benefit of the general welfare.[55] As historians have noted, Russian physicians and other liberal professionals were

---

53. Bekhterev, *O prichinakh samoubiistva*, 22–24.

54. On the concern of the school physician with the hygiene of the "soul" (*dusha*) and "mood" (*dushevnoe nastroenie*) as well as the body of the student, see the discussion of Gordon's presentation to the Pirogov Society, *Trudy XI Pirogovskogo S"ezda*, 71. The Ministry of Education's instructions of June 4, 1905, for school physicians included the constant observation of students and their environment, participation in pedagogical councils, and the registration of all deaths and sicknesses. "Instruktsii dlia vrachei srednykh uchebnykh zavedenii Ministerstva Narodnogo Prosveshcheniia," TsIAM, f. 459, op. 3, d. 4542, ll. 20–21ob.

55. Nancy Frieden, for example, argues that Russian physicians had a Janus-faced relationship with the autocratic state. While the state was a key instrument in modernizing the country and uplifting the population, it also thwarted the development of an autonomous profession because of its suspicion of independent activity outside its control. *Russian Physicians*, 14.

not necessarily opposed to greater state power despite their difficult relationship with the tsarist government, which looked with deep suspicion on independent initiatives. In fact, after 1905 many increasingly looked to the state as the only instrument capable of achieving genuine reform and lifting the Russian people from their benighted condition. The fundamental issue for them was not centralized state power per se but the ideas or ethos that animated this power.[56]

Russian social investigators possessed an activist vision of themselves and the state but found it incompatible with the tsarist regime's vision of order, proximity, and subordination. Indeed, autocracy, which vested legitimacy in the single person of the tsar, was at odds with the idea of the participatory and self-conscious citizen implied by the medical community's ideal image of itself and the people.[57] Achievement of this vision was dependent on a dual revolution in Russia. Not only would the regime need to recognize the importance of the social expert, but people also had to alter the way that they understood society and the place of the individual within it. Such changes in subjectivity and the ethos of the state would together facilitate the production of information and promote its rational application for the benefit of the population. However, the revolutionary transformations required for the complete realization of this modern governmental project would have to await the Bolsheviks' seizure of power in October 1917.

SUICIDE AND SOCIAL DIAGNOSTICS IN THE 1920s

The regime that emerged out of the revolutionary struggles of 1917 profoundly altered the political and institutional landscape in Russia. It gave rise to an all-encompassing social science state that was driven in part by a new guiding ideology—Marxism, which remained, at least until Joseph Stalin's consolidation of power, an intellectual tool for trying to understand the world in order to change it.[58] Refusing to recognize a private realm, the ruling Bolsheviks sought to bring the entire population into the sphere of the centralized state, whether as citizens under its care, workers

56. Yanni Kotsonis, *Making Peasants Backward: Agricultural Cooperatives and the Agrarian Question in Russia, 1861–1914* (London, 1999), chap. 4; and John F. Hutchinson, *Politics and Health in Revolutionary Russia, 1890–1918* (Baltimore, 1990).

57. Yanni Kotsonis, "'Face-to-Face': The State, the Individual, and the Citizen in Russian Taxation, 1863–1917," *Slavic Review* 63, no. 2 (Summer 2004): 222.

58. Martin Malia, *The Soviet Tragedy: A History of Socialism in Russia, 1917–1991* (New York, 1994), 172.

in its employ, or pariahs under its watchful gaze and supervision. State and society were in this sense no longer separate entities. New institutions like the People's Commissariat of Public Health, which often functioned like professional networks that supported a range of outlooks and agendas, were created to manage all facets of economic and social life in accordance with the ideal of the scientific state.[59] Thus, the October Revolution brought about a radical change in the position of physicians, statisticians, and other intellectuals interested in the social realm. No longer speaking to the state, they now found themselves speaking within it.

Thanks to the continuity of personnel as well as the power of the broader discourse of society, the analytical and cultural framework established before 1917 continued to shape responses to suicide during the 1920s. We see similar categories, concepts, and terms being used across the revolutionary divide, although with different emphases, meaning, and logic that reflected the changed political culture of the early Soviet period. Most significantly, the practice of social diagnostics was expanded and institutionalized as part of the Bolsheviks' utopian goal of reshaping human nature. Viewing the population as a "collectivity of citizens," the new regime regarded surveillance, enlightenment campaigns, and political education as essential tools for knowing and molding individual belief.[60] This cognitive shift, coupled with the new regime's revolutionary ideology, validated the politico-statistical conception of the population and greatly expanded the social domain beyond that of the prerevolutionary era. This in turn made the social sciences and its practitioners essential instruments of the Soviet state, which now became the sole patron of explorations into "everyday life" (*byt*).[61]

The debate over epidemic suicide in Russia reemerged after the end of the civil war and the introduction of the New Economic Policy in early 1921. Depicted variously as a tactical retreat before the final assault on the fortress of communism or as a betrayal of the revolution, the NEP allowed for the restoration of a limited market economy in the hopes of stabilizing

---

59. Mark B. Adams, "Eugenics as Social Medicine in Revolutionary Russia: Prophets, Patrons, and the Dialectics of Discipline-Building," in *Health and Society in Revolutionary Russia*, ed. Susan Gross Solomon and John F. Hutchinson (Bloomington, 1990), 200–201.

60. Holquist, "'Information is the Alpha and Omega of Our Work,'" 417–21.

61. To recognize the state's dominance, however, is not to suggest the uniformity of its actions and outlooks. Indeed, scholars have demonstrated the competing interests and visions within the Soviet state; moreover, the fates of various research and reform projects rose and fell along with their individual patrons. See, for example, Susan Gross Solomon, "David and Goliath in Soviet Public Health: The Rivalry of Social Hygienists and Psychiatrists over the *Bytovoi* Alcoholic," *Soviet Studies* 41, no. 2 (April 1989): 254–75.

the country after years of war, famine and disease, and economic collapse. In terms of Soviet culture and everyday life, the period 1921–29 is noteworthy for its lack of clarity and consistency both within and outside the Bolshevik Party. If such conditions allowed for relative experimentation and freedom, they also produced an atmosphere of angst over the future of the revolution and the meaning of individual thought and action.

Within the Bolshevik Party, the introduction of the New Economic Policy led to suicides and resignations among its most disenchanted members, fostering from that time forward a strong link between suicide and "desertion" in Bolshevik discourse.[62] By the mid-1920s, in fact, the number of suicides in the party had become significant enough that the leadership was openly addressing the problem within the context of discussions about so-called party ethics, which were themselves emblematic of the confusion over what was permissible in the new revolutionary society.[63] Less publicly, party officials fretted among themselves over the growing frequency of suicides, especially in the League of Communist Youth (Komsomol) and the Workers' and Peasants' Red Army (RKKA). Several secret reports spoke of a suicide epidemic in the military, while others noted the outbreak of suicides in certain units or party cells.[64] This trend toward higher rates of self-inflicted deaths raised troubling questions about the health of the party membership.

Bolshevik responses to suicide were ambivalent despite references to a single party line toward the matter of self-inflicted death. Some leaders suggested a sympathetic approach to their comrade-suicides, blaming the increase in suicides and other mental-health problems on the fact that

62. On resignations (and suicides) after 1921, see Leonard Shapiro, *The Communist Party of the Soviet Union,* 2nd ed. (New York, 1971), 313–14; Robert Service, *The Bolshevik Party in Revolution: A Study in Organisational Change 1917–1923* (New York, 1979), 163–66; and Merle Fainsod, *How Russia Is Ruled* (Cambridge, MA, 1962), 244.

63. According to figures for the first quarter of 1925, roughly 14 percent of all party members and 12 percent of all candidate members who died during this period were suicides. "Ubyl v sostave RKP(b)," *Izvestiia TsK RKP(b),* September 7, 1925, 5. By comparison, the percentage of deaths from suicide in Leningrad was much lower. For the same quarter (January–April 1925), suicides made up slightly fewer than 3 percent of all deaths in the former capital city. For the entire year 1924, this figure was roughly 2 percent. See *Biulleten' Leningradskogo gubstatotdela,* no. 16 (October 1926–July 1927): 273; and *Biulleten' Leningradskogo gubstatotdela,* no. 12 (January–March 1925): 155.

64. See, for example, "Ob uchastivshikhsia sluchaiakh samoubiistv sredi chlenov partii and RLKSM," GARF, f. 374, op. 27, d. 21, ll. 128–37ob; and "O samoubiistvakh, sovershaemykh chlenami partii," GARF, f. 374, op. 27, d. 21, ll. 62–73. References to a suicide epidemic (linked to poor material conditions in the army) are found in the July 27, 1924, report of Andrei Sergeevich Bubnov to the Council of People's Commissars, RGVA, f. 9, op. 26, d. 111, l. 141; and "Material'noe polozhenie i nastroeniia komvzvodov RKKA. 23 iiunia 1923 g.," RGVA, f. 9, op. 3, d. 195, l. 106ob.

a portion of the membership was simply too "nervous" or "exhausted" from the hardships of underground life and revolutionary struggle to overcome the challenges facing them.[65] Aron Aleksandrovich Sol'ts, a key figure in the Bolshevik Party's Central Control Commission (TsKK), acknowledged before a gathering of the faithful at Sverdlov Communist University in 1924 that indeed a "rather large number" of suicides had taken place in the preceding few years. However, he appealed for calm and argued against any sort of panic, since these suicides were "natural and understandable" at the present time. "We are living through such an epoch," proclaimed Sol'ts, "when the nerves of a large number of people have been so tested and tried that they no longer have the strength to do what the party demands of them." Nevertheless, despite the suggestion that suicides were the legacy of past sacrifices on behalf of the party, Sol'ts cast the act of suicide in personal terms and invoked the notion of individual responsibility. He argued that by committing suicide, these individuals had not only demonstrated a kind of internal "rottenness" (*chervotichina*), but had also revealed themselves to be "poor party member[s]." True Bolsheviks, argued Sol'ts, held firm no matter what the circumstances and fought to overcome the obstacles placed before them.[66]

Other leading Bolsheviks were more direct in their denunciation of suicide as a sign of weakness and ideological wavering. Emel'ian Mikhailovich Iaroslavskii, the secretary of the Central Control Commission who directed a special probe into party suicides in the mid-1920s, argued that suicides must be "sharply condemned." Speaking on party ethics in 1924, Iaroslavskii digressed from his prepared remarks to address the question of self-destruction. "We cannot in any way," he proclaimed, "justify the fact of suicides among comrades, not to any degree. Furthermore, we cannot think that for them this was the only way out [of their situation]."[67] In this, he echoed Sol'ts, who also criticized suicides for concluding that there was "no way out" (*vykhoda net*) from their predicament besides killing themselves. Those who threatened to commit suicide if they were expelled from the party, for example, missed the point entirely. If they truly

---

65. Concerns about nervous exhaustion (neurasthenia) among the party *aktiv* were ubiquitous throughout the 1920s. A May 1925 report, for example, stated that 76.4 percent of party members examined by a medical committee in the Altai Province had some form of neurasthenia. "V remontnuiu komissiiu pri altgubkome RKP(b)," RGASPI, f. 17, op. 68, d. 138, ll. 52–53ob.

66. A. A. Sol'ts, "O partetike. Doklad, chitannyi v Kommunisticheskom universitete im. Ia. M. Sverdlova," in *Partiinaia etika: Dokumenty i materialy diskussii 20-kh godov* (Moscow, 1989), 279–81.

67. E. Iaroslavskii, "Nuzhno surovo osudit' samoubiistva," *Pravda*, October 9, 1924, 4.

were good Bolsheviks, they would work hard to prove that a mistake had been made rather than commit suicide (and essentially confirm the judgment of the party).[68]

Linked to the idea of desertion, an association whose origins are traceable to the Platonic tradition, suicide within Bolshevik discourse came to represent a loss of faith in the revolution as well as the triumph of individualism.[69] By choosing suicide, these party members had placed their personal lives over the interests of the collective (*kollektiv*). They had degenerated from the ideal type of Bolshevik, demonstrating through their actions a loss of consciousness about themselves and the historical conditions at work during the 1920s. Indeed, Bolshevik discourse of the 1920s is filled with anxious speculation about the possibility that the NEP would lead to moral and political degeneration because it asked members to put off their dreams of an immediate communist utopia and seemingly granted a new life to the capitalist foe in the country. The loss of revolutionary ardor as well as the ideological corruption from contact with the remaining bourgeois elements threatened to undermine the weakest members of the party, causing them to lapse politically and to succumb to thoughts of self-destruction.[70]

Fears of an emotional, psychological, and moral letdown extended to Soviet society as a whole. As we shall see in later chapters, the Soviet debate over suicide was driven in part by signs of a steady rise in the number of suicides throughout the 1920s and the question of what this increase said about the new socialist order. Most commentators rejected the idea that Russia was once again in the throes of a suicide epidemic. Emel'ian Iaroslavskii conceded that there had been a momentary spike in party suicides following the introduction of the New Economic Policy in 1921, but he flatly rejected any speculation about "mass suicides" (*massovye samoubiistva*) in the country. Perception, he argued, was being mistaken for reality. The return to peacetime simply made "these deaths stick out."[71] Five years later, however, the debate over epidemic suicide was still alive. A team of authors writing in the journal *Revolution and Culture* sharply criticized

68. Sol'ts, "O partetike," 280–81.
69. On the ancient Greek assertion that suicide was the equivalent of a soldier's desertion from his post, see Alexander Murray, *Suicide in the Middle Ages*, vol. 2, *The Curse on Self-Murder* (Oxford, 2000), 125.
70. Bolshevik notions of degeneration are explored in Igal Halfin, *Terror in My Soul: Communist Autobiographies on Trial* (Cambridge, MA, 2003), esp. 99–108.
71. Iaroslavskii insisted, "As a whole the number of suicides in the USSR is lower than in any bourgeois country." "Nuzhno surovo osudit'," 4.

the analogy drawn by some between suicides among party and Komsomol members during the 1920s and the "period of reaction 1907–9." Using an ingenious logic to justify the public discussion of suicide, they claimed that suicides had not been sufficiently addressed in the Soviet press precisely because their numbers were not very large and thus did not seem to be a pressing matter.[72]

Investigators outside the Bolshevik Party also took on the question of the Soviet suicide rate as part of their explorations into the mental and physical health of the population. Although medical personnel noted a worrisome upsurge in mental disorders related to the traumatic experiences of war and social upheaval, most argued that the revolution had had a salutary effect by reducing the number of people who were taking their own lives. A team of physicians studying the impact of famine in Russia made such a contention in 1922:

> Generally speaking, it seems (since we know that precise statistics do not exist) that our revolutionary epoch is notable for its extremely small percentage of suicides. If after the first Russian revolution the gloomy years 1907–10 were a time of reaction and a true suicide epidemic along with the ebb of social energy, general fatigue, and confusion, then the situation is now reversed: a revolution triumphant, an abundance of the most diverse creative affairs, and a general lifting of moods have in recent years made suicides a very rare phenomenon in our country.[73]

Nevertheless, there were fears that as the euphoria of making revolution wore off and the realization of the arduous task of rebuilding the country set in, the number of people killing themselves was starting to rise. To some it appeared as though Russia was again experiencing a period of drift amid the "humdrum days of revolution."[74]

Comparisons to the post-1905 period seemed especially relevant given the growing alarm over Soviet youth, who, like their tsarist-era predecessors, demonstrated a particular propensity for suicide. Correspondents reporting for exiled opposition groups described an atmosphere of gloom inside the universities and spoke frequently of a suicide epidemic

72. M. Dubrovskii and A. Lipkin, "O samoubiistvakh," *Revoliutsiia i kul'tura*, March 15, 1929, 33.

73. L. A. Vasilevskaia and L. M. Vasilevskii, *Golodanie. Populiarnyi i mediko-sanitarnyi ocherk* (Ufa, 1922), 16. Suicide and famine are also discussed in L. A. Mirel'zon, "K voprosu o samoubiistve u golodaiushchikh," *Sovremennaia meditsina*, nos. 4–6 (May–July 1924): 61–70.

74. "O samoubiistve. Nasha anketa," *Vecherniaia moskva*, January 9, 1926, 2.

plaguing the student body.[75] The international communist Victor Serge also claimed that suicide in Soviet Russia had a particularly youthful complexion. "Leningrad," he wrote, "lives at a cost of ten to fifteen suicides a day, mainly among the under-thirties."[76] Such impressions were confirmed and promoted by the available data. Soviet statisticians contended that one of the distinguishing features of their national suicide rate was its distribution according to age. Whereas in other countries the likelihood of suicide increased as a person got older, in Russia the inclination to suicide was greatest among people living in the prime of their lives, i.e. individuals in their early to midtwenties.[77]

With the suicide of the poet Sergei Esenin in late 1925, the association between suicide and Soviet youth became even more firmly entrenched in popular and official discourse. The press, which usually contained laconic announcements of suicides under the section heading "Incidents," now published reports of ritualized suicides by young people as well as the revival of so-called suicide clubs, all of which recalled the decadent and deflated atmosphere of the post-1905 era.[78] Internal party documents also expressed concern over the growing number of suicides in the Komsomol that were linked to Esenin's death and writings.[79] Consequently, the act of suicide was included among a range of practices and attitudes that constituted Eseninism, a wastebasket diagnosis used by Soviet officials and cultural critics to delineate what they deemed pathological in society. Transmitted through decadent literature or by human carriers, Eseninism was thought capable of literally "infecting" (*zarazhat'*) individuals and destroying their connection to the revolution, the party, and society as a

75. "Epidemiia samoubiistv," *Sotsialisticheskii vestnik,* July 24, 1924, 13–14; and "Samoubiistva sredi molodezhi," *Sotsialisticheskii vestnik,* June 20, 1924, 16–17.

76. Victor Serge, *Memoirs of a Revolutionary, 1901–1941,* trans. and ed. Peter Sedgwick (London, 1963), 193–96, 199. Serge's claim about the daily number of suicides was based on his work as a newspaper editor in Leningrad.

77. S. Novosel'skii, "Samoubiistva, ubiistva i smertel'nye neschastnye sluchai v Leningrade," *Biulleten' Leningradskogo gubstatotdela,* no. 14 (July–September 1925): 121–22. This distinctive age-related trend was also noted before the revolution.

78. "Proisshestviia," *Izvestiia TsIK,* December 22, 1926, 6. A number of suicides at the Higher Artistic Theatrical Schools (Vkhutemas) in Moscow were reported in the wake of Esenin's death. Similarly, from a school in Eisk came the account of a schoolgirl who was strangled per her request by a male companion. Both apparently belonged to a suicide club. G. Pokrovskii, *Esenin—Eseninshchina—religiia* (Moscow, 1929), 53; Constantin V. Ponomareff, *Sergey Esenin* (Boston, 1978), 155–56; and S. Ingulov, "Protiv khuliganstva v pechati," *Zhurnalist,* no. 10 (October 1926): 3. On the prerevolutionary suicide clubs, see Morrissey, *Suicide and the Body Politic,* 341–44.

79. "Boleznennye iavleniia v organizatsii (informatsionnyi obzor)," RGASPI, f. 17, op. 85, d. 66, ll. 68, 70.

whole by placing the "I" (rather than the "we") at the center of their world-view. The resulting isolation spelled the moral and political disintegration of the person, leading to suicide and other antisocial forms of behavior.[80]

The official responses to Esenin's death emphasized the importance of integration as a means of reducing suicide and argued that Soviet Russia, thanks to its collectivist underpinnings, was in a favorable position to promote a sense of belonging among its people. A few days after the poet killed himself, for example, the daily newspaper *Evening Moscow* published a series of articles titled "On Suicide: Our Questionnaire," which asked leading medical, legal, and political authorities to share their thoughts on suicide.[81] These experts provided a varied list of causal factors, including mental illness, nervous exhaustion, loss of interest in life, and a host of psychological and physiological conditions. However, they were unanimous in their understanding of suicide as a socially conditioned and socially meaningful act. Each regarded suicide as the product of a rupture between the individual and the larger social body.

In his contribution to *Evening Moscow,* Leonid Prozorov, the Moscow psychiatrist who had authored the 1920 report on the nation's mental health, stressed the benefits of the individual's integration into society. He wrote, "One must emphasize and note the life-preserving force of the collective. Human beings are 'social animals' for whom solitude is fatal." Russia's chief medical examiner, Iakov L'vovich Leibovich, agreed, arguing that the prevention of suicides depended on the degree to which the "'tone' of sociability [*obshchestvennost'*] and the force of collectivism" could be maintained in Soviet society. Improved socioeconomic and living conditions, mental hygiene, and physical labor were not sufficient by themselves to lower rates of suicide; rather, Leibovich believed in the need to "strengthen the collective feelings produced by the revolution." Representatives from outside the medical field arrived at similar conclusions. Iakov Aleksandrovich Berman, a member of the Supreme Court of the Russian Soviet Federated Socialist Republic (RSFSR), argued against a legislative approach to suicide prevention, instead contending that the only

---

80. The equation of Eseninism with individualism is forcefully made in Pokrovskii, *Esenin*, 51–52. For a flavor of Eseninism's diverse meanings and usages see also *Upadochnoe nastroenie sredi molodezhi: Eseninshchina* (Moscow-Leningrad, 1927); I. Bobryshev, *Melkoburzhuaznye vliianiia sredi molodezhi* (Moscow-Leningrad, 1928), 98; and M. O., "Esenin i eseninshchina (Disput v teatre Meierkhol'da)," *Izvestiia TsIK,* December 22, 1926, 3.

81. In addition to those mentioned here, the respondents included Nikolai Semashko, head of the People's Commissariat of Public Health; Nikolai Pavlovich Brukhanskii, a psychopathologist who had conducted a detailed study of suicides in Moscow; and Vasilii Alekseevich Giliarovskii, a noted professor of psychiatry at Moscow State University.

way to fight against suicide was to "pull young people more forcefully into social life" and to raise their genuine interest in the "great tasks of socialist construction." Finally, Emel'ian Iaroslavskii linked suicide to pessimistic attitudes that developed as a consequence of the individual's alienation from society. He claimed that the study of some two hundred suicides confirmed "that in the vast majority of such cases the suicide results from the person's isolation from the collective and a sense of social belonging [*obshchestvennost'*]."[82]

Nikolai Aleksandrovich Semashko, the country's chief physician as head of Narkomzdrav, also emphasized the importance of social integration in a lengthy newspaper article that directly addressed speculation about a possible suicide epidemic after Esenin's death. His article "Are We Threatened by an Epidemic of Suicide?" began by acknowledging that suicide could assume an epidemic character, and he called for caution when speaking openly about suicides lest the public debate itself provoke additional acts of self-destruction. However, Semashko emphatically rejected the idea that Soviet Russia was in danger of an epidemic like the one that occurred during the "reactionary epoch 1906–8." He argued that the October Revolution was by contrast a fundamentally healthy event for the population. As proof he cited statistics provided by Narkomzdrav's Department of Forensic-Medical Expertise, which found that the number of suicides in Russia (per million in population) had declined approximately 25 percent since the pre-1914 period. According to Semashko, this decrease was the result of the heightened "mood" and great "feeling of public-mindedness [*chuvstvo obshchestvennosti*]" fostered by the conditions of war and revolution. October, he contended, had produced unprecedented levels of "social enthusiasm" among the population, which translated into lower levels of suicide as people thought less about their personal life and more about the greater good.[83]

Semashko forcefully rejected theories about a racial inclination to suicide and instead maintained that individual factors such as heredity, changes in the nervous system, and everyday "upheavals" mattered only because of the broader environment. Here too he found support in the statistical information provided by the Department of Forensic-Medical Expertise, whose data suggested that motivations of a so-called social

82. "O samoubiistve. Nasha anketa," *Vecherniaia moskva*, January 7, 1926, 2; "O samoubiistve. Nasha anketa," *Vecherniaia moskva*, January 9, 1926, 2; and "O samoubiistve. Nasha anketa," *Vecherniaia moskva*, January 11, 1926, 2.
83. N. A. Semashko, "Ugrozhaet li nam epidemiia samoubiistv?" *Izvestiia TsIK Sovetov*, January 22, 1926, 5.

nature—material need, shame and fear of punishment, misfortunes, etc.—predominated over all others. Semashko could therefore argue that thanks to the Bolshevik Revolution, the conditions no longer existed for a repeat of the post-1905 suicide epidemic. True, Soviet Russia continued to experience some suicides, but these "antisocial acts" would not "grow thickly on revolutionary soil." In fact, Semashko boasted that Soviet Russia possessed a "reliable inoculation [*nedezhnaia privivka*]" against epidemic suicide. Referring to the heightened collectivism of the revolution and the growth of dispensary care for mental health, he proclaimed, "The foundations for the struggle against suicides in our country are unlike anywhere else in the world."[84]

The explanations provided in Semashko's article were fully consistent with the dominant understandings of prerevolutionary physicians and point to a key source of intellectual affinity between liberal professionals and the new Marxist rulers of Russia. Most notably, Semashko and his fellow doctors emphasized the role of the environment in shaping the suicidal individual, although one should be careful not to interpret such inclinations as a rejection of the biological factor. This Lamarckian orientation was extremely popular among the prerevolutionary intelligentsia, given their critical reading of Russian history and the state of Russian society. In particular, Lamarckianism allowed them to blame the autocracy for the downtrodden condition of the masses and to speculate that one could improve the physical and moral state of the people by fundamentally changing the circumstances in which they lived and worked. Such thinking fit rather well with Marxism's emphasis on environmental factors and social transformation. It provided a strong impetus for non-Bolshevik physicians, statisticians, and other professionals to find common cause with the radical reconstruction of everyday life that was at the heart of the Soviet project.

Of course, the revolutionary politics and class ideology of the Soviet regime lent a distinct flavor to the discourse of suicide and social integration during the 1920s. Commentators like Semashko and the contributors to *Evening Moscow* all emphasized that Soviet Russia was uniquely positioned to reduce suicides among its population. They pointed to the fact that the revolution provided people with a cause greater than themselves, suggesting that individuals could realize their true selves in the task of building socialism. They also highlighted the innately collectivist nature of the ruling proletariat, whose members were said to be less prone

84. Ibid., 5.

to suicide and fostered an environment where individuals could identify their personal interests with those of the group. At their most utopian moments, a few Soviet commentators even envisaged a future world where suicide disappeared altogether from everyday life along with any distinctions between the I and the we.[85]

Such optimism was tempered by the realization that at least in the foreseeable future suicides would continue to exist as the country made the difficult and sometimes painful transition to socialism via the New Economic Policy. In fact, throughout the decade of the 1920s the concept of the transition period (*perekhodnyi period*) was a powerful means for explaining the persistence of suicide and other social illnesses after the revolution. Like the human body going through puberty, the Soviet social organism was thought to lack the stability that characterized a mature society. Old morals, habits, and human relationships, especially those between men and women, were being destroyed, but new forms had yet to fully take shape (hence, the importance of the debates about communist ethics). One result of the numerous contradictions in Soviet life was a variety of social pathologies that reflected the absence of clear boundaries and clear identities. According to Soviet commentators, the descent into personal and moral dissolution would be most pronounced among the former ruling classes that now found themselves on the losing side of history and without a place in the new social order. The disintegration of these "former people," much like a diseased and decaying body, posed a major threat to the well-being of the rest of the population and to the revolution in general.[86]

Within the conceptual framework of the transition period, suicides could be understood as the temporary product of the general contradictions of Soviet society. Commentators like Nikolai Semashko stressed the fact that the complexities and "abnormalities" in everyday life, particularly

85. The psychoneurologist and Bolshevik Party member Aron Borisovich Zalkind, for example, is said to have claimed that in the future society, when people "live according to knowledge rather than faith, and according to science rather than mysticism," there would be no more suicides. L. A. Prozorov, "Profilaktika i terapiia samoubiistva," in *Nevrologiia, nevropatologiia, psikhologiia, psikhiatriia. Sbornik posviashchennyi 40-letiiu nauchnoi vrachebnoi i pedagogicheskoi deiatel'nosti Prof. G. I. Rossolimo 1884–1924* (Moscow, 1925), 55.

86. The idea of suicide as the product of the general confusion in Soviet life found powerful expression in *The Right to Life, or the Problem of Being Nonparty,* a short story written by Panteleimon Romanov in 1926 and published in 1927. Hounded by internal doubts and insecurities about his place in Soviet society, the protagonist Leonid Sergeevich Ostankin concludes that he cannot live a normal life and opts for suicide as a way to end his predicament. Romanov, "Pravo na zhizn', ili Problema bespartiinosti," in *Izbrannye proizvedeniia* (Moscow, 1988), 252–91.

in the spheres of marital and sexual relations, "wore out the nervous system" and provided grounds for the "disturbances" that led to suicide.[87] Others pointed to the difficult economic conditions prevailing throughout the country, which led to massive unemployment and dampened the future prospects of already impoverished students and young people demobilized from the Red Army. Moreover, there always remained the deep concern that the most active Bolsheviks were exhausting themselves prematurely and ruining their nerves as a result of their heroic efforts to build socialism.[88]

Leading Bolsheviks and social commentators also explained suicides in terms of the broader "struggle for a new everyday life" (*bor'ba za novyi byt*) during the 1920s, a campaign that aimed to remake society at the smallest level of physical and mental existence. Assuming that suicide would not exist in the ideal world of the future, they represented self-inflicted death as a "vestige" or "residue" (*perezhitok*) from prerevolutionary culture that had yet to be expunged from Soviet life. It was one more bourgeois illness that contradicted the new proletarian values championed by the regime. The literary critic P. Ionov, for example, called suicides and other social pathologies "grimaces of the old departing world," an image that chillingly evoked the belief that bourgeois society was in its final death throes.[89] Conceived in this manner, suicides were never really representative of the imagined socialist order, only the byproducts of the struggle to re-create society on a new basis. Yet their continued presence during the transition period was a cause of concern. Whether isolated events or in clusters, they signaled the existence of unhealthy attitudes, environments, and ways of living, all of which threatened to pollute the future world that was being constructed.

The anxieties provoked by this unsettled state of affairs explain the Soviet regime's rather obsessive efforts to map, contain, and eliminate illness within the body politic. Indeed, I argue that this underlying sense of uncertainty was a critical factor behind the Bolsheviks' heavy reliance on the practice of social diagnostics. Leading the way in this regard was the party's Central Control Commission. Created at the Ninth Party Congress (October 3–10, 1920) to oversee discipline and ideological purity among the faithful, the Central Control Commission from the outset depicted its

---

87. "O samoubiistve," *Vecherniaia Moskva,* January 7, 1926, 2.

88. On the fears of rampant nervous exhaustion and premature aging among the party *aktiv* and young people more generally, see David Joravsky, *Russian Psychology: A Critical History* (Oxford, 1989), 337–38; and Frances Lee Bernstein, *The Dictatorship of Sex: Medical Advice for the Masses* (DeKalb, IL, 2007), 82–89.

89. P. Ionov, "Bez cheremukhi," *Pravda,* December 4, 1926, 5.

mission through the language and imagery of health. Matvei Konstanti-novich Muranov, then secretary of the Central Control Commission, ar-gued that the creation of the commission, whose branches were instructed to "promote the good health [*sodeistvovat' ozdorovlenie*] of our party and the revelation of its collective opinion [*obshchestvennoe mnenie*]," reflected the need to monitor internal illness in order to fulfill the Bolsheviks' larger historical mission of building international socialism. At the time, illnesses (*bolezni*) primarily referred to bureaucratic attitudes and abuses of author-ity that threatened the revolutionary spirit of the party after its assumption of power. Originally applying to the threat posed by the hidden presence of careerists and nonproletarian elements among the membership, the concept of illness gradually expanded over the course of the 1920s and came to signify a wide variety of moral and political transgressions, includ-ing the commission of suicide.[90]

Noteworthy in the early descriptions of the Central Control Commis-sion is the emphasis placed on both collective and personal self-diagnostics. "As the party of the proletariat," Muranov proudly declared in 1920, "our party had the courage on its own to pose the question of its illnesses."[91] It was a theme that continued during the debate at the Second Party Ple-num of the TsKK in 1924. There, a draft resolution on the question of party ethics proclaimed, "We have nothing to fear from openly discuss-ing these [party] illnesses. In fact, only by drawing the active attention of all candidates and members to these questions and only by creating a definite party opinion on these matters, will we protect the party from arbitrary decisions regarding them and allow ourselves to deal with these illnesses."[92] Such declarations about the willingness of the Bolshevik Party to recognize and tackle its illnesses head on were in sharp contrast with representations of the tsarist regime as willfully ignorant and largely silent about the ills of society after 1905. They reflected the party's preoccupa-tion with monitoring and shaping the beliefs of its members, who merited special care as the active agents of socialism and the transmitters of the new socialist culture to the rest of the population.

The Central Control Commission therefore represents the incarnation of the therapeutic logic that shaped Bolshevik ideology and governance. An instrument of prophylaxis, the TsKK had to watch over the cadres,

---

90. "Ot kontrol'noi komissii vsem chlenam RKP" and "Iz polozheniia o kontrol'nykh komissiiakh vsem partiinym organizatsiiam RKP," in *Partiinaia etika*, 125–28. On the link be-tween illnesses and foreign elements inside the party see "O partetike. Proekt predlozhenii prezidiuma TsKK II plenumu TsKK RKP(b)," in *Partiinaia etika*, 155–57.

91. "Ot kontrol'noi komissii," 125.

92. "O partetike," 157.

prevent their degeneration, and eliminate pathologies before they threatened the healthy members. According to Matvei Muranov, the primary
defense against sickness followed two basic lines: (1) the removal of threatening individuals through the periodic "purging" or "cleansing" [*ochishche-
nie*] of the party membership and (2) the active creation of a "collective
opinion that establishes the limits of the permissible and keeps an eye on
the fulfillment of these norms."[93] Muranov and the Bolshevik Party were
basically applying the logic of preventative medicine to the realm of politics, including the removal of the offending matter from the body and the
development of the body's internal resistance against disease agents.

Beyond the Bolshevik Party, the practice of social diagnostics was extended to the rest of the population as part of the Soviet regime's conscious
efforts to create a citizenry that was healthy in a physical, mental, and political sense. This ambitious goal rationalized a comprehensive approach
by the state to the care of the individual and the larger population. For example, the Commissariat of Public Health, which coordinated the country's centralized health care system, sought to promote well-being through
a combination of therapeutics and education. Enlightenment campaigns
against infectious disease, alcoholism, and sexually transmitted diseases
emphasized that Soviet citizens had a responsibility to maintain their personal health and to monitor their own behavior. These campaigns, which
assumed the internalization of certain values and beliefs, sanctioned an
expanded and more active role for social investigators among the people.
For the achievement of health in Soviet Russia demanded the possession
of knowledge about individual subjectivity and behavior as much as it required information about the objective signs of disease.[94]

Images of the prophylactic power of the Soviet system rested heavily
on the activist state engaged more fully and directly in people's lives. As
head of Narkomzdrav, Nikolai Semashko claimed that the expanded delivery of psychiatric services to the masses would reduce the number of
suicides in Russia by promoting "the improvement [*ozdorovlenie*] of the
nervous-mental health of the population."[95] Other commentators talked
optimistically about the enhanced prospects for fighting suicide through
the positive, rather than negative, application of state power. Instead of
using the law to punish or threaten, as had been done in tsarist Russia,

---

93. "Ot kontrol'noi komissii," 126.
94. On enlightenment strategies in the fight for sexually healthy citizens, see Bernstein,
Dictatorship of Sex; and Tricia Starks, *The Body Soviet: Propaganda, Hygiene, and the Revolutionary
State* (Madison, WI, 2008).
95. Semashko, "Ugrozhaet," 5.

the legal mechanisms of the Soviet state would be directed toward the "elimination" and "standardization" (*normirovanie*) of those areas of everyday life linked to "the rise and cultivation of ideas about 'voluntary' death." According to the psychiatrist Leonid Prozorov, one could reduce suicides through laws that promoted "the improvement of the population, the fight against social diseases and alcoholism, and the proper organization of school affairs, etc." Quite similar to the program put forth by Grigorii Gordon in 1912, Prozorov's vision of suicide prevention depended on the state's involving itself more deeply in matters of personal health, behavior, and the upbringing of the individual. It was a prescription that dovetailed nicely with the regime's broader interest in creating the new Soviet man and woman.[96]

These ambitions led to a vigorous system of information gathering that produced a virtual flood of data about the population during the 1920s. Soviet institutions routinely conducted surveys, carried out time-budget studies, and quantified all forms of human activity with the aim of governing on a more rational and scientific basis.[97] Statisticians, for their part, welcomed the opportunity to exercise their particular expertise on behalf of the state and the people. In 1921, for example, the moral statistician Dmitrii Petrovich Rodin argued that the collection of information about suicide was part and parcel of any modern government. Responding to skeptics who doubted the ability to collect accurate data on self-destruction, he wrote, "I doubt that it's even necessary to prove the importance of organizing suicide statistics.... If the state must know its income and expenditures as well as its illnesses, then the state should also know the character and dimension of a social illness like suicide." Moreover, Rodin believed that this knowledge was particularly important "in a state with a socialized economy, a unified [system of] medicine, and in a state of general accounting." He clearly had in mind the centralizing and rationalizing tendencies of the Soviet government.[98]

Two central state organs formed in the early 1920s took the lead in gathering and publishing information about Soviet suicide—the Department of Moral Statistics in the Central Statistical Administration and the Department of Forensic-Medical Expertise in the People's Commissariat of Public Health. Led and staffed by individuals who had been active prior

---

96. Prozorov, "Profilaktika i terapiia samoubiistva," 51–53.

97. Richard Stites notes the utopian elements of such measuring in his *Revolutionary Dreams: Utopian Vision and Experimental Life in the Russian Revolution* (Oxford, 1989), 161–64.

98. D. Rodin, "O postanovke statistiki samoubiistv v Rossii," *Vestnik statistiki*, nos. 5–8 (May–August 1921): 94.

to 1917, both of these institutions played an important role in setting the parameters of the debate on suicide during the 1920s, as evidenced by Semashko's use of the forensic-medical data to buttress his case against a return of epidemic suicide.[99] As we shall see in subsequent chapters, they undertook ambitious programs that aimed to provide a national accounting of self-destruction based on specially formulated questionnaires completed by doctors, statisticians, and other members of the state apparatus. Within the context of the Soviet regime, they were able to expand and realize many of the agendas for social research that had first been broached in the tsarist era.

Sympathetic patrons inside the Soviet state also facilitated the growth of interdisciplinary efforts to study crime, suicide, and other forms of antisocial behavior. Most notable in this respect was the Moscow-based State Institute for the Study of Criminality and the Criminal (founded in October 1925 under the auspices of the People's Commissariat of Internal Affairs) and the network of similar "laboratories" (*kabinety*) that sprang up in cities across the USSR.[100] Bringing together representatives from a variety of specialties—among them medicine, moral statistics, psychiatry, and criminal anthropology—these institutes sought to develop a unified approach to deviant behavior, including suicide. According to Mikhail Nikolaevich Gernet, the head of the Department of Moral Statistics who also played a leading role in the creation of the Moscow institute, the very rise of "scientific" investigations into criminality reflected the "socialist character" of the new regime. They were an attempt, he claimed, to introduce a greater measure of planning and rationality into the efforts to combat and prevent crime. In particular, the participants sought to formulate an integrated program that recognized both environmental and organic factors in shaping human thought and behavior. Statistical studies of the population, for example, were coupled with clinical examinations of the human body and psychological evaluations of individuals in the hopes of revealing the entire personality of the criminal.[101]

99. The continuity of personnel in the early Soviet statistical agencies is a key theme in Alain Blum and Martine Mespoulet, *L'anarchie bureaucratique: Pouvoir et statistique sous Staline* (Paris, 2003).

100. In addition to the State Institute in Moscow, there were similar bodies operating in other cities and regions, including Leningrad, Odessa, and Irkutsk.

101. "Proekt rezolutsii po dokladu prof. M. N. Gerneta—'Izuchenie prestupnosti i prestupnika,'" Otdel rukopisei RGB, f. 603, k. 3, d. 17, l. 6. According to Gernet's original proposal, the scientific-research work of these laboratories was to follow two primary lines: the study of criminality as a social phenomenon and the study of the criminal personality as the product of "certain social (and biological) interactions."

This interdisciplinary model extended to suicide as well. In October 1923, a special commission was established to investigate all registered cases of suicide in the capital city of Moscow. The commission was chaired by the psychopathologist Nikolai Pavlovich Brukhanskii and adopted a profoundly biosocial approach to suicide. Brukhanskii was joined in the effort by representatives of various disciplines, among them Professor Viktor Bunak, a specialist in criminal anthropology, Vil'gelm Grombakh, director of the Moscow city health department's psychiatric section, and Mikhail Gernet. The commission also coordinated its activities with a number of government and city institutions in order to collect as much information as possible about every suicide that occurred within Moscow, a method that allowed the commission to examine 349 out of 359 registered cases of completed and attempted suicide occurring over the six-month period from December 1, 1923, to May 31, 1924. The commission relied heavily on the Laboratory for the Study of the Criminal Personality, the Institute of First Aid, and the various hospitals and psychiatric clinics throughout Moscow, each of which was instructed to gather information about acts of suicide that fell within its jurisdiction.[102] Moreover, Mikhail Gernet, who also served on the faculty of Moscow State University's Department of the Social Sciences (FON), involved students taking his course on criminal law in order to give them practical experience in both moral statistics and criminology. The students responded to calls from the police or ambulatory services and used a special questionnaire to collect detailed information about the sociological and psychological dimensions of suicide. As a result, Gernet claimed to have in his possession countless suicide notes and other materials that reflected the mindset of the self-destructive individual.[103]

In addition to its practical accomplishments, which included the publication in 1927 of Brukhanskii's ambitious study *Suicides,* the Moscow suicide commission was significant as an expression of the developing relationship between the state, the scientific expert, and the population under Soviet power. Specifically, it represented an attempt to lessen the distance between investigators and their primary object of study—society— and thus overcome the nagging sense of separation that had plagued many doctors and professionals during the tsarist era. The psychiatrist Petr Borisovich Gannushkin, for example, saw the published results of the

---

102. N. P. Brukhanskii, *Samoubiitsy* (Leningrad, 1927), 15; and Brukhanskii, "O samoubiistvakh i samoubiitsakh," *Klinicheskaia meditsina* 4, no. 3 (March 1926): 110.
103. M. N. Gernet, "Kratkie vospominaniia o moei universitetskoi rabote posle oktiabr'skoi revoliutsii," Otdel rukopisei RGB, f. 603, k. 1, d. 16, l. 2.

Moscow commission as an important sign that such a move was indeed taking place in Soviet Russia. Gannushkin claimed that where previously the "voice" of the psychiatrist had been muffled by the "high walls" of the clinic, the "specialist" now enjoyed "full rights" to participate in "all fields of life," including the school, the factory, and the prison. This perhaps idealized move into the arena of everyday life not only enlarged the realm of scientific practice but also expanded the possibility for gathering detailed and exhaustive information about the population. Indeed, Gannushkin heaped praise on Brukhanskii's data as perhaps "the only material of its kind" in the world.[104] Mikhail Gernet likewise saw the Moscow project as yet one more example of the new possibilities for studying suicide and the social order under Soviet power. "Of course," he emphasized in a short autobiographical sketch, "such work was impossible under tsarism."[105]

BOLSHEVISM AND SOCIAL SCIENCE

Gernet's comments raise the important question of why the practice of social diagnostics expanded so dramatically in Russia during the 1920s. The image of the Soviet state connecting to the masses through the intervention of its experts certainly contrasts with representations of an unmotivated autocratic regime that resisted the push to develop the nation on the basis of scientific or specialized knowledge. It would also seem to blur the image of the Bolsheviks as instinctively wary of professionals who, like the Bolsheviks themselves, claimed a certain power over the social world and its inhabitants.

The broad answer lies in the redefinition of politics in Russia during and after 1917. Russia's revolutionary moment resulted in a "political ecosystem" that not only facilitated the application of modern political practices (mass parties, ideologies, mobilization, etc.) but also promoted the use of modern state practices (statistics, surveillance, etc.) in order to transform both individuals and their social environment.[106] As a result, when the Bolsheviks took power and began to reconstruct Russian society

---

104. P. Gannushkin, "Vstupitel'naia stat'ia," in Brukhanskii, *Samoubiitsy,* 7–8.

105. Gernet, "Kratkie vospominaniia," l. 2. Elsewhere, Gernet distinguished the Soviet-era work on criminality as a matter of proximity, claiming that before 1917 "scientists had no access to criminals." "Istoriia izucheniia v Rossii prestupnosti i prestupnika," Otdel rukopisei RGB, f. 603, k. 2, d. 2, l. 42.

106. Peter Holquist, "What's So Revolutionary about the Russian Revolution? State Practices and the New-Style Politics, 1914–21," in *Russian Modernity: Politics, Knowledge, Practices,* ed. David L. Hoffmann and Yanni Kotsonis (London, 2000), 88.

on Marxist-Leninist principles, they were able to attract individuals of varying backgrounds and political inclinations to their revolutionary project. While the Bolsheviks found themselves in need of the experience and knowledge offered by so-called bourgeois specialists, these physicians, statisticians, and other professionals found in the Bolsheviks a champion of the broad values of science, reason, enlightenment, and the application of state power toward the comprehensive care of the population. Even if these different actors could not always communicate through the language of Marxism-Leninism, they frequently found common ground in the language of health, numbers, and social science, sharing many of the same words if not the exact meanings. Thus, we have doctors and Bolsheviks alike speaking about illness, degeneration, and making life healthier (*ozdorovlenie*) as part of their search for a rational social order. The party in any case lacked the power and internal cohesion to impose a single understanding of these concepts and principles during the 1920s. This opening created the possibility for many experts to read their own hopes and visions onto the emergent Soviet state, and perhaps even to believe that they would be able to create the kind of state that they had long desired.[107]

To be sure, a shared search for a rational social order did not necessarily mean an absence of conflict and unlimited freedom. The Soviet regime's hostility toward religion, for example, made it difficult to study the connection between suicide and faith, which was an important element of investigations in Europe. Moreover, not everyone chose to participate in the Soviet experiment, and those who did professed a variety of motivations ranging from the most practical to the most idealistic. Dmitrii Zhbankov, for his part, administered the remnants of the Pirogov Society until its dissolution in February 1925, but he rejected the establishment of a centralized medical system as the antithesis of his populist vision of community-based medicine. Still, he continued to collect information about suicides as part of a study on mortality among physicians during the 1920s, and in April 1918 he gave an update on the epidemic of trauma, where he speculated that the "picture of self-destruction" would no doubt be "dismal" if statistics were made available.[108] Much less

107. Alain Blum and Martine Mespoulet, for example, emphasize the growing conflicts over the course of the 1920s between the professional ideals of early Soviet statisticians and the increasingly political demands of the ruling Bolsheviks. See their *L'anarchie bureaucratique*.

108. "Travmaticheskaia epidemiia (nekotorye itogi smertnykh kaznei v 1918–19 gg.," RGALI, f. 199, op. 1, d. 19, l. 115; and "Itogi smertnosti vrachei za 1914–1925 gg.," RGALI, f. 199, op. 1, d. 21, l. 4ob. Zhbankov did, however, work "for Soviet power" by cataloging the

is known about the fate of Grigorii Gordon, the leading medical expert on suicides among children and school-aged youth before the revolution. A brief glimpse is provided by a letter he wrote in January 1925 to Mikhail Gernet. In it, Gordon requested raw statistical material for Russia and/or the USSR so that he might work once again on the question of suicide in general and among young people in particular. He explained that he was most interested in studying the "awful rise in the number of suicides" that seemed to go against the patterns set out by Durkheim in his influential tome *Suicide*.[109]

Gordon's reference to Durkheim, whose theories were central to the work of the Departments of Forensic-Medical Expertise and Moral Statistics, is an additional confirmation of the fact that Soviet social diagnostics were shaped by more than just Marxist notions of class and society. Indeed, to assume that the Soviets operated solely by class logic is to overlook the tensions and different registers within Soviet discourse. While the regime was driven by a particularistic vision of class conflict and communist comradeship, its representatives also spoke in terms of a unified Soviet citizenry and of the population as the sum of its parts. Social diagnostics in the early Soviet era were therefore constructed upon elastic understandings of the individual as a social being and of society as a distinct entity that could be studied, managed, and rearranged along scientific lines. In contrast to the prerevolutionary period, when the autocratic state had defined and ordered people in terms of their relationship to the tsar, Soviet individuals were now defined in terms of their relationship to the larger kollektiv, a cognitive shift that made their thoughts and actions legitimate objects of study and intervention. This way of thinking about the individual and the population lent the Soviets' investigations into suicide a decidedly modern cast and helps us to distinguish their efforts from those of their tsarist predecessors. For although there are noteworthy elements of continuity over the chronological divide of 1917, the postrevolutionary landscape of the 1920s stands out for the rise of a social science state whose primary object was the population and its care.[110]

---

society's library, which was eventually moved to the Central Medical Library. "Pirogovskoe Obshchestvo: Deiatel'nost' D. N. Zhbankova v etom obshchestve," RGALI, f. 199, op. 1, d. 24, l. 172.

109. Letter of January 12, 1925, Otdel rukopisei RGB, f. 603, k. 9, d. 69, ll. 1–2. There is no evidence among Gernet's papers regarding whether or how he replied to Gordon's request.

110. On the centrality of the population as the hallmark of modern governance, see Curtis, "Foucault on Governmentality and Population."

2

Suicide and the Collective Individual in the Bolshevik Party

In March 1925 a group of young communists in Leningrad wrote to Emel'ian Iaroslavskii, secretary of the Bolshevik Party's Central Control Commission, for some advice on party ethics. Could he tell them, they asked, whether or not they had acted correctly in expelling the Komsomol member Fedorov for desertion from the party? Fedorov had committed suicide, and their posthumous action against him had been lampooned in the newspaper of the Leningrad Komsomol organization. Now these young people sought clarification, and perhaps some justification, from one of the party's leading voices on suicide and communist ethics.

Iaroslavskii replied by letter. He began by stating that suicides among healthy, young people deserved condemnation. In particular, the suicide had erred in taking a life that belonged to the collective. Nevertheless, it would be incorrect to expel an individual from the party after the fact and solely for the reason of suicide. "After all," he wrote, "he [the suicide] can no longer offer any words in his defense." According to Iaroslavskii, the Central Control Commission never expelled members without first hearing their side of the story. Therefore, the suicide Fedorov had to be treated like someone who could not be present at the inquiry into his case.[1]

---

1. GARF, f. 374, op. 27, d. 21, ll. 263–263ob, 266–67.

I suggest that the deceased Fedorov was indeed present at his inquiry, just not in the way Iaroslavskii had in mind. Instead of an active interlocutor, he was a more passive presence in the form of the words, actions, and gestures captured in official records, remembrances, and testimonies, as well as in any notes he left behind and in the manner of the death that he scripted. This body of knowledge now belonged fully to others, who gave it new meaning in terms of the fixed end point—the act of suicide—and in terms of the larger cultural understanding of suicide and self-destructive behavior. In Soviet Russia, as in any country, the completed suicide resulted in nothing less than the retrospective renarration of the individual's life and death.

This process of renarration achieved a particular form within the collectivist framework of the Bolshevik Party, which sought to redefine the boundaries between the part and the whole. Acts of suicide among party members violated idealized conceptions of the collective as a space where the individual would achieve genuine self-realization as a member of the group. Party investigators and theoreticians, like Iaroslavskii, argued that suicide was an illegitimate response to life's travails because the individual belonged to the collective, which suffered harm from the act. In response, both the civilian and military wings of the Bolshevik Party used the language and methods of social investigation, gathering statistics and other types of information about suicide in the belief that these data were indicators of social integration and organizational well-being. Moreover, suicides were a catalyst for constructing new practices appropriate to the regime's transformative goals. Each one potentially set in motion a whole range of efforts to shape the texture and experience of individual and group life.

This chapter examines the responses to suicide in the Bolshevik Party and reveals how the Bolsheviks sought to make the ideal of social integration a reality. It argues that the party's internal debates about suicide must be interpreted within the context of the regime's efforts to build a collectivist social order composed of new types of men and women. Bolshevik discourse stressed the inherently social nature of the individual, based on the belief that human potential and freedom could be realized only after the false dichotomy between the public and private self was destroyed. The emphasis on the collective did not negate the development of the individual, if by this we have in mind distinct persons rather than the liberal notion of autonomous agents. Indeed, the Bolshevik regime actively fostered self-awareness and self-discovery as part of its revolutionary project. Public confession, autobiography, and diary writing were all tools by which men and women would truly become conscious of themselves and their relationship to society and the revolution.[2]

Suicides among Bolshevik Party members provoked a distinct set of practices that were aimed at forging the kollektiv within the challenging environment of the New Economic Policy. Central to these practices were the joint articulation of a "collective opinion" (*obshchestvennoe mnenie*)[3] and the promotion of mutual surveillance as a means of fostering communal relations, strengthening both group and individual accountability, and preventing future acts of self-destruction. Such efforts conveyed a certain vision of civic responsibility and social solidarity based on understandings of the individual as an integral, but potentially threatening, element within the collective. Moreover, they were a manifestation of the broader system of Soviet government, which aimed to develop persons who were appropriate to the particular needs and possibilities of the socialist society.[4] The historical exploration of suicide, in other words, provides insights into two critical questions facing the new rulers of Russia: how was the Soviet individual to become social and how was unity to be defined under Soviet power?

SUICIDE AND THE CREATION OF A COLLECTIVE OPINION

To commit suicide is to hand over one's self and story to others. Although suicides often try to shape how people will read their life and death by leaving behind a note or choosing a particular method of self-destruction,

2. Igal Halfin, *From Darkness to Light: Class, Consciousness, and Salvation in Revolutionary Russia* (Pittsburgh, 2000), 287–88; Jochen Hellbeck, "Self-Realization in the Stalinist System: Two Diaries of the 1930s," in *Russian Modernity: Politics, Knowledge, Practices*, ed. David L. Hoffmann and Yanni Kotsonis (London, 2000), 299; and Oleg Kharkhordin, *The Collective and the Individual in Russia: A Study of Practices* (Berkeley, 1999), 199–201.

3. I have chosen here to translate *obshchestvennoe mnenie* as "collective opinion" rather than use the more literal and common translation "public opinion." "Collective opinion" better conveys the distinguishing aspects of *obshchestvennoe mnenie* under the Soviets. In particular, it captures the idea of widely held views and beliefs that have been actively shaped and then consciously internalized by the members. This contrasts with the prerevolutionary notion of public opinion as a commonality of viewpoints that developed naturally among members of educated society (*obshchestvo*) through the free and rational exchange of ideas. On the distinctive characteristics of Soviet collective opinion see Kharkhordin, *Collective and the Individual*, 114–15.

4. On modern government and the socialization of individuals, see John W. Meyer, "Myths of Socialization and of Personality," in *Reconstructing Individualism: Autonomy, Individuality, and the Self in Western Thought*, ed. Thomas C. Heller, Morton Sosna, and David E. Wellbery (Stanford, 1986), 208–21.

death effectively robs them of control over their body and their biography. This inherent loss of control was sensed by the prerevolutionary physician Grigorii Gordon. Calling suicide notes a "mirror" of the individual, he observed that they "cease to be private property and become public property [*obshchestvennoe dostoianie*] from the moment when those who wrote them cease to exist."[5] Death, it seems, provides a new life for the suicide, whose end becomes the object of others' fascination, imagination, and need for explanation. The body, history, and memory of the suicide are taken over and reinterpreted by the broader culture.[6]

The making of suicide into public property achieved its ultimate expression in the hands of the Soviets. During the 1920s suicide became everyone's business within a revolutionary regime that deemed the collective as possessing interests that superseded, but ideally harmonized with, those of its individual members. In fact, suicide provoked much debate among Soviet commentators precisely because it contradicted the ideal of total unity between the part and the whole. Not surprisingly, this debate raged most intensely in the Bolshevik Party, which was represented as a living organism giving birth to a new breed of people and to the conventions and relationships—the so-called new everyday life (*novyi byt*)—of the future socialist society.[7]

Suicide by party members sharply interrupted the Bolsheviks' eschatological narrative of self-development. By joining the party, these individuals had taken an essential step along the road to becoming the new Soviet men and women who would build and populate socialism. It suggested that they had achieved a higher level of consciousness and that they possessed the strength of character and purpose to carry out the Bolsheviks' historical mission. Deemed "living projects," party members were expected to work on themselves continuously through education and reflection, active participation in the organization, and by overcoming the various obstacles that came before them and the party. In addition, membership also suggested the transcendence of petty individual desires and a willingness to sacrifice for the cause of socialism, if need be through

5. G. Gordon, "Samoubiitsy i ikh pis'ma," *Novyi zhurnal dlia vsekh*, no. 28 (February 1911): 107.

6. This process of reinterpretation is explored in Anne Nesbet, "Suicide as Literary Fact in the 1920s," *Slavic Review* 50, no. 4 (Winter 1991): 827–35; and M. Higgonet, "Suicide: Representations of the Feminine in the Nineteenth Century," *Poetics Today* 6, nos. 1–2 (1985): 103–18.

7. On the significance of organismic metaphors within Bolshevik thought, see Eric Naiman, *Sex in Public: The Incarnation of Early Soviet Ideology* (Princeton, 1997); and Eric van Ree, "Stalin's Organic Theory of the Party," *Russian Review* 52, no. 1 (January 1993): 43–57.

the ultimate sacrifice—one's life. Bolsheviks faced with the prospect of a martyr's death found consolation in the belief that immortality would be achieved through the kollektiv, which would live on and always carry a part of them within.[8]

Becoming the new Soviet man or woman was itself a heroic task fraught with its own challenges and dangers, especially under the trying conditions of the New Economic Policy. In a speech delivered at the Sverdlov Communist University in 1924, the university's rector, Martyn Nikolaevich Liadov, argued that those who joined the party were part of an elect group that was learning how to freely accept limitations on their personal will (*volia*) for the sake of the party as a whole. "For us," Liadov proclaimed, "the interests of the party are becoming more important than our own....We envisage the future society to be a society in which every person will feel that his interests coincide with the interests of the entire collective."[9] However, in the same speech, Liadov warned that in the near term suicide and other forms of unbridled individualism could result from this difficult transition. Gone were the old restraints on personal behavior—notions of sin, fear of social reproach, and internalized codes of morality—while new ones had yet to take their place. Without such "restraining centers" there was nothing to hold back egoistic impulses and desires, including those which led the individual toward self-annihilation.[10]

Liadov's portrayal of the developing relationship between the individual and the kollektiv reflected broader currents of revolutionary thought and tradition while at the same time expressing the special concerns regarding party youth as the bearers of the new culture. On the one hand, Liadov was preaching a form of revolutionary asceticism that celebrated the selfless radical who forsook all personal life, creature comforts, and earthly pleasures for the sake of the larger cause. On the other, he echoed Marxist conceptions of the proletariat as the source of universalistic, rather

---

8. I borrow the term "living project" from Igal Halfin, *Terror in My Soul: Communist Autobiographies on Trial* (Cambridge, MA, 2003), 21. The narrative and practices of personal development are also examined in Jochen Hellbeck, *Revolution on My Mind: Writing a Diary under Stalin* (Cambridge, MA, 2006). Bolshevik attitudes toward death and immortality are discussed in Catherine Merridale, *Nights of Stone: Death and Memory in Twentieth-Century Russia* (New York, 2000), 93–100; and Katerina Clark, *The Soviet Novel: History as Ritual*, 3rd ed. (Bloomington, 2000), 181–82.

9. Martyn Nikolaevich Liadov, *Voprosy byta (Doklad na sobranii iacheiki sverdlovskogo kommun. Un-ta)* (Moscow, 1925), 21–22.

10. Ibid., 32. The context of Liadov's comments was the marked increase in suicides among party members discussed in chapter 1. See also Viktoriia Stanislavovna Tiazhel'nikova, "Samoubiistva kommunistov v 1920-e gody," *Otechestvenaia istoriia*, no. 6 (1998): 158–73.

than particularistic, values. His discussion of the new human being emphasized that the workplace—the large-scale factory or enterprise—was another site where the collective psychology was being cultivated in Soviet Russia. There the workers labored together and learned to place the we over the I.[11] For this reason the Bolsheviks emphasized the importance of factory work experience and grew increasingly anxious during the 1920s about the large number of party members—such as students—who either lacked factory experience or no longer had living ties to the industrial workplace. Isolation from the factory was seen as a key ingredient in the growth of individualism and in the ideological and moral disintegration of the collective's constituent elements.[12]

Such emergent orthodoxies in Bolshevik thought about the individual helped to shape understandings of suicide. For many Bolsheviks, suicide could have no place in party culture because they viewed it as an individualistic act that put personal concerns over group interests. By this definition, suicide was committed by someone who lacked true self-knowledge as a social being with responsibilities that extended beyond one's immediate realm of existence. For example, P. Tsel'min, a leading figure in the Red Army's Political Administration (PUR), which was the military wing of the Bolshevik Party, contended, "He who is a conscious communist or a conscious worker cannot become a suicide because he does not belong to himself and is not his private property. Rather, he belongs to his party and to his class."[13] In a similar vein, party declarations frequently characterized the act of suicide as a violation of collective norms and responsibilities; killing oneself was a form of desertion that showed weakness, pessimism, and egoism in the face of personal difficulties or frustrations about the delayed advent of socialism. Responding to the 1924 suicide of the Red Commander Sukhanov, the collective of the Seventh Communications Regiment adopted a resolution condemning Sukhanov's behavior as unbecoming a true proletarian. It emphasized the duty of every individual to participate in the messianic cause of the revolution and proclaimed, "Our

---

11. Liadov, *Voprosy byta*, 20. More broadly, Marxist discourse emphasized the belief that the proletariat was the only social class untainted by the ownership of private property and thus the individualism that it promoted. See Halfin, *From Darkness to Light*, 96–104.

12. For example, a study of suicides in the Komsomol cited the "absence of a continuous link of the student with the factory and workers" as a critical component in the formation of "ideologically dangerous moods" that resulted in a loss of revolutionary perspective, a passion for Esenin, and suicide. "Boleznennye iavleniia v VLKSM," GARF, f. 374, op. 27, d. 1055, l. 67.

13. P. Tsel'min, "O samoubiistvakh," *Sputnik politrabotnika*, March 31, 1926, 22.

lives do not belong to us, but to the working class and all the oppressed of the world."[14]

This line of reasoning rendered suicide a deeply personal act that raised troubling questions about individual autonomy within the Soviet regime. In a notable departure from modern theories of self-destruction (which tended to downplay human agency by representing the suicide as a victim of mental illness or external social forces), Bolshevik thought ascribed a considerable degree of agency to the suicide. Such thinking was consistent with a mythology that emphasized the Bolsheviks' special ability to bend history and shape reality according to their Marxist principles.[15] Suicides, however, had displayed autonomy outside the movement by taking the fundamental question of life and death into their hands, thereby violating the belief that the personal and public self could not be distinguished.[16] Death in the cause of communism was possible, even welcomed by some as form of heroic martyrdom and immortality, but, as P. Tsel'min concluded in his article on party suicides, "Life and death cannot be decided on one's own."[17] None other than Vladimir Il'ich Lenin fell prey to this ethos after his death in early 1924. During the intraparty discussions about whether to embalm Lenin's corpse, several prominent Bolsheviks argued that the body should be preserved because Lenin belonged to the people and to the larger cause of the revolution and not to himself or his family. After all, they maintained, during his lifetime Lenin had renounced any personal or private life in order to devote his complete self to the revolutionary struggle.[18]

Taken to their extreme, such understandings implied that suicide in the Bolshevik Party was not self-murder in the literal sense of the word,

---

14. "Vypiska iz protokola obshchego sobraniia chlenov i kandidatov kollektiva RKP(b) 7-go polka sviazi ot 5/11-1924 g.," RGVA, f. 9, op. 28, d. 781, l. 31. In this respect, the suicide was the opposite of the new regime's championed values of inner strength, willpower, and unflagging optimism. For a discussion of these traits and their encapsulation in party discourse see Clark, *Soviet Novel*, 46–89.

15. This was in many respects a romantic view of personal development, which emphasized the ability of individuals to remake the world around them rather than be passively determined by it. See Halfin, *Terror in My Soul*, 53–54.

16. At least one 1924 gathering of the party emphasized the fact that the Bolsheviks differed from other socialists because they made no distinction between private (*lichnyi*) and public (*obshchestvennyi*) life. "O partetike. Proekt predlozhenii prezidiuma TsKK II plenumu TsKK RKP(b)," in *Partiinaia etika. Dokumenty i materialy diskusii 20-kh godov* (Moscow, 1989), 152–53.

17. Tsel'min, "O samoubiistvakh," 22.

18. Claudio Sergio Ingerflom and Tamara Kondratieva, "Pourquoi la Russie s'agite-t-elle autour du corps de Lénine?" in *La Mort du Roi. Autour de François Mitterand. Essai d'ethnographic politique comparée*, ed. Jacques Julliard (Paris, 1999), 264–65.

since it involved an act of violence perpetrated by one actor (the individual) against another (the self that belonged to the collective). In some respects, Bolshevik attitudes paralleled early Christian theology, which branded suicide a sin committed against God the Creator, and secular Petrine law, which defined suicide as a crime against the monarch. However, a slightly different calculus was at work in Soviet Russia, where the individual was thought to achieve greatest meaning through the collective and where the government actively sought to sculpt the population. There, suicides transgressed Soviet society or the Bolshevik Party, which endowed the individual with consciousness and purpose, instead of God or the sovereign. They also violated one of the principal tenets of socialism—the rejection of private property—by treating their lives and bodies as their own.

These lines of thought are clearly evident in one of the most unequivocal denunciations of suicide that I have uncovered from the early Soviet period. In 1930, the physician Vladimir Ivanovich Velichkin vigorously disputed the idea that individuals had complete control over their bodies and were therefore free to choose when they would die. "No one," he argued, "has a right to die according to his desire.... Reproduced by society, a person belongs to it, and only society, in the interests of the majority, can deprive him of life."[19] Velichkin's severe attitude toward suicide denied free will in the sense of the individual as a fully autonomous being separate from the rest. Instead, it gave society a claim on the individual, who committed a kind of sin against the creator by killing one of its progeny—himself or herself. The collective therefore had a right to punish or sanction these "murderers" for their misdeeds.

The conflation of the individual with the collective helps to explain one of the Bolsheviks' primary responses to suicide during the 1920s—the active formation of a collective opinion around the problem. As part of its concern with the party's moral health, the Bolshevik leadership early on emphasized the importance of expressing a clear and firm opinion on various ethical matters, which would help to guide members in their daily lives and keep them from succumbing to temptation.[20] It was an approach that also extended to self-destruction. Investigations into party suicides

---

19. Vladimir Ivanovich Velichkin, "Pravo na smert'," *Sovremennyi vrach*, nos. 17–18 (1930): 765–66. Velichkin was responding to Maksim Gorky's discussion of the poet Vladimir Mayakovsky's 1930 suicide, in which the great writer suggested that suicide might be justified or excused in some instances (such as a terminal illness that robbed the individual of his or her ability to be a productive member of society). For Gorky's comments see his "O solitare," *Nashi dostizheniia*, no. 6 (June 1930): 5–6.

20. "O partetike," 157.

routinely led to the recommendation that local organs work to organize collective opinion around every case of completed or attempted suicide.[21] In addition, the Red Army's Central Political Meeting sought to make this official policy in 1926 when it included the following call to action in its draft resolution on self-destruction: "We must create a negative collective opinion in the Red Army toward suicides as an unacceptable phenomenon..., incompatible with all the principles of the Red Army's construction and impossible to justify by any difficult conditions."[22] Similarly, the Central Committee of the Komsomol called for the publication of a brochure about suicides that would tell young people about the "disgracefulness" of the act and the "repugnance" with which they should regard suicides.[23] Such thinking about the need to shape young people's views was shared by local activists charged with investigating suicides in their area. The political instructor Gaitskhoki, who looked into a number of incidents within the Leningrad Komsomol organization, argued that the process of constructing a single, collective voice was essential to "eradicating" the problem of self-destruction. He called for "fostering around every case of suicide a collective opinion of the organization's members condemning this act, pronouncing it at a meeting of the party cells and collectives, and widely illuminating it in wall newspapers."[24] Still, despite such pleas for openness there were also concerns about giving too much attention to suicides, lest all the noise give the false impression that self-destruction was an endemic problem.[25]

Collective opinion was forged through a guided discussion of the suicide that allowed the party to shape the group narrative and remembrance. In the event of a self-inflicted death or suicide attempt, local party leaders were instructed to convene a special meeting of the affected cell or kollektiv. These gatherings of the faithful were part of the broader socialization process that emphasized the social nature of the individual in

21. Regional branches of the military's Political Administration listed the creation of a collective opinion among the basic measures for dealing with acts of suicide among the ranks. See, for example, the circular of May 12, 1924, to PUR from the Head of the Western Military District Political Administration, RGVA, f. 9, op. 17, d. 186, l. 133.

22. "Proekt rezoliutsii TsVPS o samoubiistvakh," RGVA, f. 9, op. 28, d. 1175, l. 42. The wording of such recommendations contradicts the findings of Oleg Kharkhordin, who contends that the Soviets constructed public opinion around individuals and not issues. See *Collective and the Individual*, 114–15.

23. "Boleznennye iavleniia v VLKSM," l. 68.

24. "V sekretariat leningradskogo gubkoma VLKSM," TsGAIPD (SPb), f. 601, op. 1, d. 735, l. 2.

25. "Samoubiistva v Krasnoi Armii i Flote za ianvar'–aprel' 1924 goda," RGVA, f. 9, op. 28, d. 738, l. 54.

Soviet Russia. On one level, they provided a venue where the group negotiated questions regarding how the individual should think, feel, and
behave under Soviet power. On another, they involved the diagnosis of the
entire collective. Since suicides had once helped to constitute the larger
whole and thus contained part of it within them, their separation from the
group could never be treated as a purely individual matter. Indeed, given
the logic of infection at work in Bolshevik discourse, the suicide suggested
not simply the degeneration of the individual but the possible existence
of unhealthy elements or environments that threatened the rest of the
kollektiv.

Suicide therefore highlighted the significance of the individual for the
well-being of the collective. It reinforced the fact that the party could treat
the kollektiv only through the study and care of its constituent members.
By killing themselves, suicides placed the question of the individual front
and center before the group and made their personal lives (as well as their
deaths) the object of contemplation.[26] Indeed, one of the striking aspects
of the party discussions was the emphasis given to the individual qualities
of the suicide. Emel'ian Iaroslavskii, who carried out a special investigation of party suicides in 1924, concluded that there existed no "general"
set of causes applicable to all party suicides; rather, he argued that each
case must be examined "on an individual basis" (*individual'no*).[27] More
broadly, the party's military wing was emphatic in its recommendation
that every instance of suicide undergo a thorough investigation. While
information gathered from such studies was eventually used to create an
aggregate picture of suicide and the party's health, the initial imperative
was to conduct a careful study that explored the history of the party member and the circumstances that had led to the suicide.[28]

Within the political meeting, the suicide functioned like a text that
could be interpreted and studied by the group in a controlled environment, often under the tutelage of a trained facilitator. Political instructors

26. In this respect, suicide was a form of individuation, according to Oleg Kharkhordin's
distinction between "individuality" and "individuation," with the latter signifying the process
of separating the individual from others in order to make him or her an object of study. See
Collective and the Individual, 164.

27. Iaroslavskii, "Nuzhno surovo osudit' samoubiistva," *Pravda,* October 9, 1924, 4. Iaroslavskii may have emphasized the individual character of suicide in order to establish a
boundary between the suicide and the rest of the organization, which he declared to be
healthy. Accordingly, he concluded that suicides had nothing to do with *partiinost'*—or the
state of the party organization.

28. For example, one report concluded, "In the future there must be deeper and more
attentive study of the causes and motives of every case of suicide." "O samoubiistvakh sredi
chlenov RKP(b) v partorganizatsii krasnoi armii i flota," RGVA, f. 9, op. 28, d. 736, l. 5.

helped the cadres dissect the life and death of the suicide in order to spread the "Soviet line" on suicide, including the kinds of people likely to kill themselves, the causes of self-destructive behavior, the warning signs of suicidal intent, and the implications of taking one's own life in a socialist society. The point of this exercise was to establish the significance of suicide in terms of the collective and its ultimate expression—the party. We must therefore regard such gatherings as part of the larger effort to get people to see themselves, and not just suicide, as inherently social.

The political meetings followed a general pattern. They began with a presentation of the evidence, moved on to an open discussion of the suicide, and concluded with the assembled members expressing a collective opinion in verbal and nonverbal form. Typically, the party cell or commission would adopt a resolution containing its diagnosis of both the individual and the collective. These resolutions were mostly negative in tone and content, as the group highlighted the particular mistakes or weaknesses of the deceased that had contributed to his or her disintegration. In addition, the collective also communicated its opinion through a number of symbolic gestures, including the posthumous expulsion of the suicide from the party or the refusal to accord the body any ceremonial honors, such as a funeral escort. By committing suicide, the deceased had placed his or her own interests above those of the collective; in response, the collective purified itself and formally recognized this separation by invoking the ultimate punishment for a social being—excommunication from the group.[29]

In this concern for maintaining—indeed, actively constructing—a collective opinion among the communist faithful, we see that social investigation was essential to individual and group formation in Soviet Russia. Speaking about suicide with a single voice reflected the idealized convergence of the part and the whole. It broke the silence around suicide and forced the group to confront the specter of illness within it. Moreover, the point of the exercise was not simply to find a common interpretative framework but to adhere to the "correct" (*pravil'nyi*) one.[30] Thus the creation of a collective opinion implied unity in thought, feeling, and cognition, as the party member spoke for the organization, which in turn spoke

29. Here, too, comparisons between such gestures and religious responses to suicide are unavoidable. As an act of ritual excommunication, for example, the refusal to escort the body or to provide it the usual honors echoed the practice of many churches—including the Orthodox Church—to forbid internment of the suicide in hallowed ground.

30. "Moskva. 10 iiunia 1927 goda. Svodka Politicheskogo Upravleniia Raboche-Krest'ianskoi Krasnoi Armii i Flota. No. 361," RGASPI, f. 17, op. 85, d. 126, l. 44.

for him or her. The part and the whole ideally came together in a single voice around the suicide.

The formation of the collective opinion had a dialogic quality even though the ultimate goal was to ascribe a particular meaning to an act that usually lent itself to multiple interpretations. In some instances, the struggle over meaning was carried out between the suicides and the kollektiv, which now functioned as the repository of their memory. This was the case with the Red Army commander Sukhanov, who shot himself in 1924 and left behind a note that blamed his death on severe material need. Sukhanov's claim was not out of the realm of possibility, since poor material conditions were a constant complaint in the Red Army and frequently cited in official documents to explain suicides. However, Sukhanov's comrades rejected his contentions and offered an alternative explanation based on their reading of his behavior prior to his death. According to the minutes of the party meeting, the kollektiv declared, "The causes given by Sukhanov in his letter as having motivated the suicide do not correspond to the true state of affairs. Because lately Sukhanov had become interested in women and spent all his time with them, not realizing the many possible consequences that can result from a captivation with petit bourgeois ideology."[31] Sukhanov, as diagnosed by the kollektiv, had degenerated both morally and politically as a Bolshevik, although he might not have been aware of his downfall. In this respect, the Bolsheviks were not unlike physicians and psychiatrists who claimed the ability to know the individual better than he knew himself. Sukhanov therefore went from being a victim of circumstance to being the perpetrator of a crime.

As a group practice, the ritualistic creation of a collective opinion also involved collective self-diagnostics and self-therapeutics. Acts of suicide were catalysts for introspective examinations of both the political health of the membership and the general conditions prevailing within the organization. This self-reflexive impulse was readily apparent in the stated goals of the meeting convened to discuss the death of Evgenii Funt, an assistant military commissar who shot himself in November 1924. The gathering set the following tasks for itself: "(1) to elucidate the general condition of the party organization in connection with the incident, and whether it is the result of amoral deviations among the members of our organization; (2) to outline a range of measures, having explained the essence of this suicide."[32] The idea here and at similar gatherings was to

---

31. "Vypiska iz protokola obshchego sobraniia chlenov," l. 31.
32. "Protokol No. 13: Ekstrennogo zakrytogo zasedaniia politsoveshchaniia 32-i str. divizii sostoiavshegosia 8 sentiabria 1924 g.," RGVA, f. 9, op. 28, d. 781, l. 50.

create a controlled environment where the question of suicide and other party illnesses could be discussed openly in an edifying manner that would strengthen relations within the membership and decrease the likelihood that others would commit similar offenses against the collective.[33]

Party cells of the Red Army routinely examined the social background, character, medical history, and service record of the suicides in order to identify those factors that might explain their degeneration. The political meeting held to discuss the suicide of Evgenii Funt began with a reading of various documents from his personnel file, which included a biographical questionnaire, as well as letters of reference and attestations. On this basis, several members in attendance concluded that Funt, a baker's son who "stood close to trade," had failed to develop into a "firmly seasoned communist" and therefore had never become a "committed member of the RKP." In other words, the suicide had never escaped his social background and lacked the political consciousness needed to correctly understand his personal problems within the larger context of the Soviet Union's difficult transition to socialism; instead, he "fell under the influence of difficult material circumstances and deserted in a disgraceful manner from the ranks of the RKP(b)." This diagnosis apparently made Funt's death more comprehensible to the rest of the group; comrade Burmakin, for example, stood before the gathering and stated, "One can expect such faint-heartedness and such acts from these [unseasoned] party members."[34]

Funt's questionable social background, in addition to his flaws as both an individual and a political figure, were deemed sufficient explanation for the organization to absolve itself of any direct culpability. The collective opinion organized around his suicide stated this explicitly:

> The political meeting, having thoroughly examined the question of comrade Funt's suicide on the basis of the available materials, establishes that this incident is in no way connected to the overall condition of the party organization as the consequence and result of its moral decomposition and instability. On the contrary, the divisional party organization is completely healthy, morally stable, and the line taken by the organization in relation to individual members is correct and requires no changes.... The political meeting calls on the organization to categorically denounce the phenomenon of suicide in the ranks of the party as one of the greatest crimes before the working class.

33. On the prophylactic character of these discussions see "Proekt rezoliutsii TsVPS o samoubiistvakh," RGVA, f. 9, op. 28, d. 1175, l. 42; and M. Dubrovskii and A. Lipkin, "O samoubiistvakh," *Revoliutsiia i kul'tura*, March 15, 1929, 33.

34. "Protokol No. 13: Ekstrennogo zakrytogo zasedaniia," ll. 50–52.

By declaring Funt a "temporary fellow traveler of the party," the collective suggested that his crime did not reflect fully on the condition of the "party organism." He could not stand for the larger group or collective because he was never truly part of it in the first place.[35] As the author of another investigation declared, the suicide of the Komsomol Schesnovich demonstrated that he "was a communist on paper but not in his worldview."[36]

This separation of the individual body from the collective was expressed literally in the case of Filatov, who killed himself in early 1924. After his suicide the party cell of the Lenin Command School in Tashkent determined that Filatov's suicide was the product of "romanticism," a state of mind that had no place within the ranks of the Bolshevik Party, and it labeled his death a "weak-willed" act of "cowardice" that "absolutely contradicts the principles of the Red Commander" and "communist ethics." Moreover, the party cell concluded that Filatov had revealed his true self by destroying it. His choice of death had exposed his petit bourgeois psychology, as well as his underlying devotion to "tsarist, Junker, and medieval traditions." The cell therefore sought to break with Filatov. After some debate, it posthumously expelled him from the organization, resolved to forgo any funeral escort of his body, and literally ceased referring to Filatov as "comrade" during its discussions. The message was clear: in death, as in life, the suicide never achieved full integration in the group.[37]

Even in this instance, however, the diagnostic performance of the party cell meeting was not restricted to the individual. Although the collective pronounced Filatov's deed completely inexcusable, it nevertheless drew a connection to general conditions prevailing inside the school and its political organs. When the cadet Petunin called on the command staff "to be more sociable" (*bolee obshchitel'nyi*), he intimated that the suicide was somehow related to the failure of school authorities to pay sufficient attention to the needs and concerns of individual students. For this reason, the group urged the leadership to conduct "intimate and concrete talks

35. Nevertheless, the political meeting made an effort to learn from Funt's suicide. It called for further investigation into the "difficult material conditions" of the command-political staff, suggested the organization of a campaign against suicide and other immoral actions, and resolved that further attention be paid to this case "as an example of insufficient party steadfastness and tempering existing among RKP(b) members." "Protokol No. 13: Ekstrennogo zakrytogo zasedaniia," l. 52.
36. "Zakliuchenie. Voenkom otdela artsnabzheniia R.K.K.A.," RGVA, f. 9, op. 28, d. 712, l. 103.
37. "Protokol No. 6: Obshchego zakrytogo partsobraniia 4-i Tashkentskogo Ob"edinennoi imeni tov. Lenina Komandnoi Shkoly," RGVA, f. 9, op. 17, d. 186, l. 25ob; and "Protokol No. 2: Obshchego partsobraniia iacheiki R.K.P. 2-i roty T.O.Sh.," RGVA, f. 9, op. 17, d. 186, l. 24.

with the cadets." Similarly, the collectively diagnosed cause of Filatov's action—"romanticism"—was also addressed within the context of everyday life at the command school. Members passed a resolution calling for a new direction in the party cell's "club work." Dances, parties, and other "romantic settings," which were said to foster romanticism and strengthen "bourgeois-philistine" ideology among the cadres, were no longer to be organized. The banning of such activities, it was argued, would help to "prevent acts that we find so offensive."[38]

The creation of a collective opinion always possessed this prophylactic intent. Party leaders conceived of the practice as a means of inoculating the collective and its members against ideological infection, an organic metaphor that stood for the active formation and internalization of norms and beliefs. In other words, collective opinion involved the promotion of the new individual "restraining centers" foreseen by Martyn Liadov in his discussion of everyday life. Through the story of the suicide, the party cadres would come to understand that killing oneself was an illegitimate response to personal difficulties or disappointments. They would develop a cognitive awareness of dangerous places, harmful literature, or even threatening social groups that should be avoided. Moreover, they would learn to recognize the signs of suicide that foreshadowed individual breakdown. Ideally, the group exercise in analysis would produce individuals who would be conscious of themselves and others as social bodies whose actions had meaning and consequences that extended beyond their immediate experience.

MUTUAL SURVEILLANCE AND INDIVIDUAL INTEGRATION

For the Bolshevik Party leadership, each suicide was a grim reminder of the embryonic state of the collective bonds being forged during the 1920s. It suggested that suicidal individuals—and the conditions that produced them—had gone undetected for days, weeks, or months until they finally made themselves known in the most horrific and irreversible manner. Only after the fact did the people who lived and worked alongside the suicides really get to know them. As suggested above, the very act of suicide forced others to ascribe certain significance to actions, words, or gestures that now, in retrospect, indicated emotional or mental, as well as political, instability on the part of the individual. This was certainly the case in

---

38. "Protokol No. 6: Obshchego zakrytogo partsobraniia," ll. 25ob–26.

the 1927 death of the regimental party bureau secretary whose noncommunist lifestyle had reportedly led him to commit suicide. The summary narrative of his death read:

> He [the suicide] approached his party duties formally and spread his demoralizing influence to individual members of his organization, dragging them into bouts of drinking and an alien [social] environment. Having embarked on a path foreign to the party he shot himself. Neither the party organization nor the political department could stop him, and the full extent of his disintegration [*razlozhenie*] only became clear *after* he committed suicide.

In many respects, what most disturbed the political leadership was not so much the suicide of a degenerate party member but the lack of comradely (*tovarishcheskii*) relations within the collective, which had allowed the individual to break away in the first place. The same report included an instance where timely intervention—a combination of material assistance, medical treatment, and "comradely moral support"—prevented the joint suicide of a party member and his wife.[39]

Bolshevik explanations of this collective breakdown were a variation on the narrative of alienation and failed transition that dominated modern discourse on suicide. In this version, the suicide resulted from the individual's failure to complete the journey to full political consciousness, as was the case with Evgenii Funt. On the surface, Funt's suicide was linked to the hard living conditions of the Red Army; in fact, Funt himself had sparked debate by calling on the party "to study everyday life" in his suicide note. Further investigation, however, suggested that the real problem was Funt's petit bourgeois wife, who had a taste for nice clothing and material goods. Her constant demands for a better lifestyle put pressure on Funt and created a tense atmosphere at home that gradually wore down his nerves and spirit. The Divisional Party Commission looking into the case concluded that the causes of Funt's suicide were both the abnormal relationship with his wife (whose negative qualities were strongly emphasized) and the fact that Funt was a young communist "who did not go through the crucible [*gornilo*] of the civil war and who had not been boiled thoroughly in the juice of the proletariat [*ne provarilsia v proletarskom soku*]." Funt, in other

---

39. "Obzor samoubiistv sredi chlenov i kandidatov partii v armeiskikh partorganizatsiiakh (po materialam OPK za 1925 g., 1926 g. i za 1-iu polovinu 1927 g.)," RGVA, f. 9, op. 28, d. 73, l. 2ob (my emphasis).

words, had never developed into the kind of person who could withstand the "pressure and pride" of his petit bourgeois wife.[40]

The Bolshevik version of the transition narrative also invoked a distinct notion of incomplete social integration. Suicide in Bolshevik discourse clearly signaled the fact that party members had failed to dissolve themselves within the collective and had instead developed a life and identity outside the group. Indeed, this theme of separation from the group ran throughout virtually all explanations of Bolshevik suicide. In his description of suicides in the party's military wing, P. Tsel'min used the metaphor of digestion, the process by which something is broken down and absorbed into the body, to account for instances of self-destruction. Suicides were in his opinion individuals who had never been fully digested (*ne perevarilis'*) by the organization.[41] Several years later, the authors of an investigation into suicides in the Moscow organization used a similar metaphor, arguing that suicides were often young people who had not been sufficiently "cooked in the cauldron of the party [*ne perevarennyie v partiinom kotle*]."[42] In both instances, the metaphors of digestion and cooking conveyed the idea of the party as an organic whole composed of individuals whose qualities had been blended together and transformed into something greater than themselves; consequently, isolation from the collective (*otryv ot kollektiva*) equaled social, political, and, in some instances, physical death.[43]

From such understandings arose the imperative to "envelop" or "encompass" (*okhvatit'*) the individual more fully within the collective. Political activists framed this goal as a matter of *vliianie*, or "influence," a concept that emphasized the environmental determination of human behavior and that figured prominently in Bolshevik notions of suicide and social integration. Both individuals and milieus were thought to exert an influence

40. "O sluchaiakh samoubiistva partiitsev i komsomol'tsev v chastiakh 32-i divizii (po ofitsial'nym politdoneseniiam Politotdela 32 politupravleniia PRIVO)," GARF, f. 374, op. 27, d. 21, ll. 34–34ob.

41. Tsel'min, "O samoubiistvakh," 20. The suicide's lack of complete digestion by the factory workplace is also cited in the study of the Leningrad Komsomol organization. "V sekretariat leningradskogo gubkoma VLKSM," l. 1.

42. Dubrovskii and Lipkin, "O samoubiistvakh," 34.

43. Iaroslavskii and other commentators cited isolation from the party and the working masses as a primary cause of suicides. Iaroslavskii, "Nuzhno surovo osudit'," 4; and Dubrovskii and Lipkin, "O samoubiistvakh," 35–36. The comrades of A. Karasev came to a similar conclusion about his suicide. As a result of Karasev's isolation from "social life," which meant that he did not partake in social or political work, he looked solely through the "prism" of his personal life and only saw the "negative side" of things. "Boleznennye iavleniia v organizatsii (informatsionnyi obzor)," RGASPI, f. 17, op. 85, d. 66, l. 67.

on the human mind and body, thereby shaping the self. Depending on the particular class nature of its source, as well as the condition of its object, an influence could have a positive or negative effect. A healthy milieu, such as a factory or a party collective, helped to foster political consciousness and a spirit of collectivism, while morbid influences emanating from social aliens (especially women like Funt's wife) or from a work of decadent literature (like that of Esenin) produced antisocial attitudes and degenerate morality. Amid the transition to socialism under the NEP, the Bolsheviks understood the individual's development as part of the larger struggle between the forces of revolution and counterrevolution or health and sickness. The weakest and least developed party members, especially those young people who had joined the party after the civil war or had never directly experienced the factory workplace, were considered the most vulnerable to unhealthy influences. They lacked the inner strength necessary to overcome obstacles and the willpower to resist corruption.[44]

A suicide therefore signaled the strength of unhealthy influences and, conversely, the weakness of the collective as well as the individual in resisting them. Addressing suicides and "decadent moods" among Komsomol members in schools of higher education, the Central Committee of the Komsomol concluded in 1926 that responsibility partly rested with the political organizations in these schools. It declared that the danger of "petit bourgeois moods" was "worsened by the fact that the party and union failed to repulse these moods with sufficient energy (in particular, there is almost no antidote [*protivoiadie*] to Eseninist moods, including the elaboration of a critical approach to his work and his deed)."[45] That same year, the political meeting of the Central Asian Military District drew a direct connection between the command staff's "susceptibility to its surrounding petit bourgeois milieu" and its isolation from the troops and the observed increase in suicides among the Red Army men under its authority. The political meeting contended that drinking and relaxing with "hostile elements" gradually distracted the officers from their custodial responsibilities. The resulting inattention increased the likelihood that soldiers gripped by "suicidal moods" would not be detected in time to prevent their deaths. In other words, there was no healthy "counterinfluence" on the part of the collective and its leadership.[46]

44. "V sekretariat leningradskogo gubkoma VLKSM," l. 1; Dubrovskii and Lipkin, "O samoubiistvakh," 33.

45. "Postanovlenie TsK VLKSM ob upadochnykh nastroeniiakh v vuzakh v sviazi so sluchaiami samoubiistv," GARF, f. 374, op. 27, d. 1055, l. 75.

46. "Informatsionnaia svodka Polit. Upravleniia RKKA. No. 336 ot iiunia mesiatsa 12 dnia 1926 goda," RGASPI, f. 17, op. 85, d. 127, ll. 192–93. On the need for the party to have

This understanding raised important questions about responsibility, a matter that was never far from the surface in Soviet responses to suicide. The political authorities recognized that in some instances the suicides were fully to blame; they had willfully masked or hidden their inner thoughts and feelings from those around them.[47] However, the reports summarizing instances of suicide in the Red Army were most frequently critical of commanders, political officers, and Red Army men for failing to recognize the tangible signs of suicide in time to prevent the tragedy from occurring. As early as 1924 the political administration of the Turkfront military district concluded, "Certain individuals, who are weak-willed, who lose heart under the influence of the environment and other attendant circumstances, who have hit bottom [*opuskaiushchiesia*], do not find timely support, influence, and assistance from their social [*obshchestvennyi*] and party milieu."[48] Several years later the political meeting of the Moscow Military District suggested that suicides came as a surprise only when commanders did not bother to understand the everyday lives of the soldiers in their units. It concluded,

> The insufficient knowledge of every Red Army man as an individual, the lack of interest in this knowledge on the part of the most immediate commander (the platoon commander) leads to the fact that suicide in the majority of instances takes the unit by surprise and seems completely unexpected. However, the inquiry [later] shows that the causes which provoked it were always in full view of the command staff and political instructor, but they ignored them, not having attached any significance to them. By not knowing the moods of the Red Army man it is impossible through educational work to strengthen those restraining impulses in him or to counteract these moods with the firm bases for eliminating them.[49]

A report on suicides in the military party apparatus also noted the lack of critical attention by some political organs to the behavior of individual soldiers in their units. It stated, "There are also instances when a party member disintegrates [*razlagaetsia*] before the eyes of the entire

its own counterinfluence (*kontr-vliianie*), see Redaktsiia, "Nashe zakliuchenie," *Voennyi vest-nik*, September 22, 1928, 53–56.

47. On soldiers concealing their personal experiences from others, see "Samoubiistva v chastiakh M.V.O. (Obzor za 1923 i 24 g.g. po dannym Prokuratory MVO)," RGVA, f. 9, op. 28, d. 739, ll. 49ob–50. See also the mention of suicides in S. Nevskii, "Litso, kotoroe skryto," *Voennyi vestnik*, May 21, 1927, 39–40.

48. "Obzor direktiva o samoubiistvakh v chastiakh Turkfronta za vremia avgust-dekabr' 1924 g.," RGVA, f. 9, op. 28, d. 781, l. 84.

49. "Samoubiistva v chastiakh M.V.O.," l. 49.

party organization, but the latter doesn't take any sort of preventative measures."[50] In essence, suicide signaled the need to promote the practices of mutual surveillance, which would bind the collective together more fully. The apparent inability or unwillingness of people to carefully observe others and then to respond properly if they detected something amiss meant that those servicemen who were in a state of personal crisis often remained unnoticed or alone until it was too late to help them.

The importance attached to these cognitive lapses surfaced in the very statistical categories used to arrange and compare suicides according to motives. Within the Red Army, failures on the part of commanders, political workers, and servicemen to realize when others were in trouble became formalized as a distinct group of causal factors linked to "service life." For the period 1927–29 the military's political organs classified 51 cases of suicide (out of 1,395 total cases) under the category "the inattention of superiors" and an additional 33 under the motive "inattention of and oppression by others." Both of these categories in turn fell under the broad heading that attributed suicides to the "fault of those around [the suicide]" (*vina okruzhaiushikh*). A common theme of incidents placed within this rubric was the failure of others to notice the individual's personal troubles and to take appropriate action. In each instance investigators concluded that the suicide had resulted from a dangerous combination: a callous officer or Red Army man plus an "extremely susceptible" (*ostro vospriimchivyi*) individual. For example, the higher authorities had ignored the deceased's entreaties for medical, material, or spiritual assistance, or they had taken disciplinary measures against the individual without being sensitive to how these actions might affect a mentally and emotionally vulnerable person.[51] This lack of mutual concern and attentiveness among the troops could be expressed statistically in a variety of formulations. Among the categories employed were "due to a bureaucratic and inattentive approach to individual comrades," "the inattentiveness of commanders to their underlings," and "abnormal relations among comrades."[52]

50. These were contrasted to suicides committed by individuals who displayed a disciplined and active public face before they unexpectedly took their own lives. See "Obzor samoubiistv sredi chlenov i kandidatov partii v armeiskikh partorganizatsiiakh," l. 3.

51. "Statisticheskii ezhegodnik za 1928/29 god. Politiko-moral'noe sostoianie RKKA," RGVA, f. 54, op. 4, d. 64, ll. 44ob, 45ob; and "Statisticheskii ezhegodnik. Politiko-moral'noe sostoianie RKKA (Sostoianie distsipliny, samoubiistva, chrezvychainye proisshestviia). 1929/30 god," RGVA, f. 54, op. 4, d. 69, ll. 32–33.

52. "Obzor samoubiistv sredi chlenov i kandidatov partii v armeiskikh partorganizatsiiakh," ll. 1, 3ob; "Samoubiistva v RKKA za 1926/27 god," RGVA, f. 9, op. 28, d. 73, l. 13ob; and "Samoubiistva M.V.O. za 1923 i 1924 goda," RGVA, f. 9, op. 28, d. 739, l. 4.

To promote the practice of mutual surveillance—the continuous observation by and of others—within the collective, the Red Army's political organization called for heightened sensitivity toward the needs and concerns of the individual. The report on the suicide of Evgenii Funt, for example, recommended that the party's organs in the Volga Military District take steps to know "the personal life and everyday living conditions of each party member...so that through the constant and daily observations of changes we have a full opportunity to prevent unethical and denigrating acts of the party member and, at the same time, avert accidents like this one."[53] Similarly, the special commission organized in the Western Military District concluded from its analysis of suicides, "There exists a need for an individual approach [*individual'nyi podkhod*] on the part of officers toward those under their command, the exposure by them of their subjective particularities (this is expected above all from junior officers), familiarity with the concerns of his family and service life, and an accounting of all these data when deciding any and all questions regarding the given individual."[54] According to K. Podsotskii, first secretary of the Political Administration, the rationale behind such calls for increased "attention to the life of the party member" was to prevent illnesses before they happened so that there would be less need for curative measures, such as the post-factum administration of disciplinary or exclusionary measures.[55]

As in the case of collective opinion, the therapeutic logic underlying these and other prescriptions was based on the conception of the individual as a social and political being. Such an understanding made the practice of mutual surveillance an essential goal of Soviet government and a key element of the Bolsheviks' strategy for preventing acts of suicide. Monitoring and promoting the well-being of the individual effectively became a necessary precondition for creating a healthy collective, which in turn exercised a positive influence on its constituent members. For example, the political activist Moseichuk hoped that the party cells would

53. Reprint of a letter of September 24, 1924, from Tret'iakov, head of the Thirty-second Division's political department, to the Military Commander and Executive Secretary of the RKP(b) cells of all units, RGVA, f. 9, op. 28, d. 781, l. 48.

54. "Samoubiistva v voiskakh Zapadnogo Voennogo Okruga," RGVA, f. 9, op. 28, d. 781, l. 68ob.

55. K. Podsotskii, "Vnimanie k zhizni partiitsa," *Voennyi vestnik*, April 9, 1927, 40–41. Podsotskii was a participant in the political leadership's debates about suicide inside the Red Army. He was present, for example, at the March 1926 gathering of the Central Political Meeting, which was devoted to the topic of suicide. See "Protokol No. 3: Zasedaniia tsentral'nogo politsoveshchaniia 24 marta 1926 g.," RGVA, f. 9, op. 28, d. 1175, l. 50.

take the following lesson from studying the 1929 suicide of comrade Ochk-ovskii: "It is necessary to decisively liquidate those cases when a party candidate remains for months isolated from the party environment and outside the party's influence."[56] More broadly, political reports on suicide in the party and the military routinely recommended that measures be taken to "create genuine party and comradely relations in the cells toward every party member." As part of this effort, the cells were to study "separately [*v otdel'nosti*] every commander, political worker, and Red Army man with the point of getting familiar with his life and his feelings [*perezhivaniia*] so that help might be given to any comrade when it is needed."[57]

Iaroslavskii, who strongly condemned suicides, also stressed the importance of devoting more attention to one's fellow comrades in his exchange with the young Leningrad Komsomolists cited at the beginning of this chapter. Claiming that there was another side to the matter of comrade Fedorov's suicide and expulsion, he emphasized

the need to devote more comradely attention to the *living*, especially those comrades who are sick, tired, and wavering, and who are experiencing any type of difficult circumstances. Then we will have fewer of these cases of desertion from the struggle by means of suicide. Then every member at the difficult moment will not just grasp at the straw of comradely sympathy [*sochuvstvie*]. Then the kollektiv will be the strong thread that keeps every individual in the kollektiv at the most difficult moment.[58]

Indeed, the message being sent from the party leadership to the rank and file was the importance of being proactive rather than reactive in the struggle against suicides and other party illnesses. As Vladimir Aleksandrovich

56. Moseichuk, "O nekotorykh momentakh prakticheskoi raboty v sviazi s chistkoi partii," *Voennyi vestnik*, May 21, 1929, 34–36. Specifically, Moseichuk criticized the local cell for "not taking an interest in how Ochkovskii worked and lived over the course of months, so that not a single measure was taken to protect him from the rot of his everyday life [*bytovoe zagnivanie*]."

57. "O samoubiistvakh sredi chlenov RKP(b) v partorganizatsii krasnoi armii i flota," l. 4ob; and "Obzor 'Samoubiistva v chastiakh UVO v period ianvar'-iiun' 1924 g.,'" RGVA, f. 9, op. 28, d. 738, l. 39ob. These measures were usually combined with calls to pull into social work those persons "who display a propensity toward individualism according to the particularities of their psyche or conditions of work." See, for example, "Samoubiistvakh v voiskakh Zapadnogo Voennogo Okruga. Doklad Komissii iz predstavitelei V/Prokuratury ZO, Voenno-Politicheskogo Upravleniia i Voenno-Sanitarnogo Upravleniia," RGVA, f. 9, op. 28, 781, ll. 68–68ob.

58. GARF, f. 374, op. 27, d. 21, l. 263ob. Emphasis in the original. Iaroslavskii made a similar argument about paying more attention to living comrades in his discussion of party suicides at the Second Plenum of the Central Control Commission in October 1924. "Nuzhno surovo osudit'," 4.

Antonov-Ovseenko, director of the Political Administration, made clear, it was fine to study suicides and to take lessons from them in order to identify the problems of everyday life that drove some comrades to kill themselves. But ideally the party should not have to wait to tackle these matters until after a suicide. "We do not need reminders," he declared, "in the form of the gunshots of despairing suicides."[59]

Suicides in the Bolshevik Party therefore provoked a set of participatory practices that aimed to recognize the individual as a distinct, but by no means autonomous, entity. Mutual surveillance, in particular, put into motion the reciprocal relationship between the part and the whole and differed from other forms of surveillance in that it functioned laterally as much as in a top-down manner. Thus, its correct operation depended on the active involvement of the people, who willingly took on this governmental responsibility and who became more thoroughly integrated into the collective as a result. In this way they moved closer to the ideal of becoming social beings while also promoting a distinctive form of Soviet unity where the individual achieved fulfillment through participation in the group.

The therapeutic logic behind Bolshevik social practices also suggested that greater integration would actually facilitate the development of mutual surveillance. Rather than conceal their sufferings from others out of fear of ridicule or an unsympathetic response, individuals would instead voluntarily come forward to share their personal concerns and problems. In other words, potential suicides would reveal themselves *before* they did so by taking their own lives. They would recognize their duty as members of the collective to seek treatment or help before they could infect others, who would in turn respond with comradely support.[60] In Soviet Russia socially integrated—and thus socially responsible—individuals were political beings who carried out mutual surveillance because they understood the need to see and be seen.[61]

THE STRUGGLE OVER MEANING

The discussion of Bolshevik practices is not meant to suggest the existence of a uniform and consistent set of attitudes toward suicide. Indeed, the conscious effort to create a collective opinion and to promote mutual

---

59. "Po povodu odnogo samoubiistva," *Voennyi vestnik,* March 8, 1924, 25.
60. On the desire for Red Army men to share their personal experiences with officers, see "Samoubiistva v chastiakh M.V.O.," l. 51.
61. On the Soviet imperative that every person must live a political life, see Hellbeck, *Revolution on My Mind,* 86–87.

surveillance was a dialogic process driven in part by the realization that multiple voices and interpretations continued to exist within the party, especially among the rank and file. Political officers and party activists therefore paid as much attention to the reaction among the membership as they did to the suicide, and their reports made note of incorrect or discordant interpretations. For example, even though the response of Evgenii Funt's party organization was deemed unified and healthy, investigators discovered some "independent opinions" (*otdel'nye mneniia*) that suggested a disconnect between the upper and lower echelons of the party. Several of Funt's comrades supported a proper funeral for him and wondered aloud why he was denied burial honors when such a distinction had been accorded to Lev Trotsky's secretary, Mikhail Glazman, who was also a suicide. Others raised questions of a more personal nature, telling each other, "If communists and commanders who are well provided for are going to shoot themselves, then what is there left for us to do?" In response, political workers held conversations with the Red Army men in order explain the matter "correctly," a move that reportedly kept these independent opinions from having a "dangerous influence" on other members.[62]

Ambivalence toward suicide was not restricted to the lower ranks of the Bolshevik Party. Even within the leadership, there were subtle yet significant differences. As noted in the previous chapter, some party commentators were more severe in their condemnation of suicides and less willing to see them as the sad byproducts of nervousness and overexhaustion. Moreover, the lack of unanimity surrounding suicide is evidenced by letters sent to Iaroslavskii in the mid-1920s as part of the larger debate about party ethics, itself a vexing collection of specific admonitions and vague proclamations about what constituted right and wrong in a socialist society. In addition to the letter of the Leningrad Komsomolists requesting clarification, the archives contain several pieces of correspondence questioning some of Iaroslavskii's assertions about self-inflicted death. One Bolshevik, for example, wrote that not all party suicides deserved to be condemned. To be sure, suicides who killed themselves on the grounds of "philistine misfortunes" certainly merited scorn as weak-willed, overly sentimental individuals "unsuitable for the new proletarian society of labor." However, the writer argued, they could not condemn comrades of "firm proletarian will" who knowingly committed suicide because their connection to the

---

62. "Vypiska iz vnesrochnogo doneseniia No. 5: Politupravleniia Privo ot 22/XI-1924 g.," RGVA, f. 9, op. 28, d. 781, l. 55; and "O sluchaiakh samoubiistva partiitsev i komsomol'tsev," l. 34.

party had been irreparably broken. He specifically had in mind Bolsheviks who had been "incorrectly expelled from the party." For these individuals, life outside the party was simply impossible, and the groundless expulsion was "a moral death that often leads to a physical death."[63]

The generally unsettled cultural and political atmosphere of the NEP further complicated the search for a uniformly articulated hermeneutics of suicide in the party. We see this clearly in the debate over the relationship between suicide and individual will (*volia*). The concept of will, which suggested human consciousness and freedom, was critical to Bolshevik self-identity and to Marxist-Leninist theories of human agency. Idealized visions of the true Bolshevik always presented a person who was steadfast and resilient in the face of all obstacles; in fact, Bolshevik notions of will stressed the importance of struggle for the attainment of genuine self-awareness. Moreover, as Igal Halfin has argued, within the framework of Marxism-Leninism, the notion of the will also had serious implications for understanding inner belief and the individual's commitment to socialism. The existence of human will implied the freedom to choose between right and wrong, between good and evil. True Bolsheviks consciously gave all of themselves over to the party and the cause of socialism.[64]

Although party members who committed suicide were routinely condemned as being faint of heart, Russian history provided examples of suicide as a heroic act of resistance against political or domestic despotism, which suggested that self-destruction could be an expression of self-sovereignty. Members of the revolutionary underground, for example, had killed themselves while in tsarist prisons or martyred themselves in selfless acts on behalf of the cause.[65] However, the idea that suicide could express strength of will or personal protest in the Soviet context was anathema to most Bolsheviks. In response to a question about self-destruction and individual will posed by the newspaper *Evening Moscow,* Nikolai Semashko emphasized the contingent meaning of suicide. A suicide committed by a Bolshevik in the face of torture by the Whites during the civil war could be considered an act of a strong will, but suicide in the face of personal difficulties during the 1920s represented weakness.[66]

---

63. Letter of October 21, 1924, GARF, f. 374, op. 27, d. 105, ll. 57–57ob.

64. Halfin, *Terror in My Soul,* 14–15. Oleg Kharkhordin has also noted the regime's conscious attempts to shape or train the individual will. See *Collective and the Individual,* 237–38.

65. On suicide as willful protest in Imperial Russia and its association with martyrdom, see Susan K. Morrissey, *Suicide and the Body Politic in Imperial Russia* (Cambridge, 2007), 33–38, 264–67.

66. "O samoubiistve. Nasha anketa," *Vecherniaia moskva,* January 7, 1926, 2. In the same issue, the psychiatrist Vasilii Alekseevich Giliarovskii cited the stoic Gaius Petronius as an

Similar logic applied to negative comparisons of suicides among revolutionary youth before and after the Bolshevik Revolution. According to a pair of authors, the meaning of suicide under Soviet power was different because the conditions that drove young revolutionaries to kill themselves after 1905—the frustrations and deprivations of the reactionary period following the heady and romanticized days of open struggle—did not apply to the current reality. "Social work and the application of one's energies toward the grandiose construction of socialism," wrote the authors, "are [now] accessible to every active proletarian, party member, and Komsomolist." These unprecedented opportunities explained why "among the party masses the will and struggle for life infinitely prevails over individual facts of pessimism and decadence."[67]

This reasoning also explains why the notion of suicide as protest was vehemently rejected by the Bolshevik leadership. The political act of killing oneself in the 1920s amounted to protesting against the dictatorship of the proletariat and the party itself. In other words, it smacked of counterrevolution and suggested capitulation, not heroism. In response to the argument that suicides among students amounted to a protest against their poor material conditions, bureaucratic attitudes, and the rudeness of other comrades, Vladimir Ermilov contended that such suicides actually represented the surrender of the individual. The influential editor of the Komsomol journal *The Young Guard,* Ermilov wrote, "In almost every suicide letter one hears the faint notes of self-disappointment [*razocharovanie v sebe*]."[68]

As indicated by the wave of suicides and resignations that followed the introduction of the New Economic Policy in 1921, suicide always had the taint of opposition in Bolshevik discourse. The fact that it was labeled a form of political illness also tied the act to a host of antiparty behaviors and attitudes. In the mid-1920s, the link between suicide and oppositionism became even clearer amid the power struggle between Lev Trotsky and the loose triumvirate of Joseph Stalin, Lev Kamenev, and Grigorii Zinoviev. Trotsky, whose "New Course" of 1923 called for greater openness in the party and warned of the party's overall degeneration, had attracted a substantial following among young communists, whom he regarded as critical

---

example of someone whose outlook made suicide an act of strong will, again suggesting that suicides could be interpreted differently depending on the context.

67. Dubrovskii and Lipkin, "O samoubiistvakh," 33.

68. V. I. Ermilov, *Protiv meshchanstva i upadochnichestva* (Moscow-Leningrad, 1927), 48; and Halfin, *Terror in My Soul,* 110. According to an internal Komsomol report, some students saw suicide as a protest against their impoverishment and poor living conditions. "Boleznennye iavleniia v organizatsii," ll. 70–70ob.

to retaining the party's revolutionary character. When the party's internal machinery was used to purge his supporters in the Komsomol and universities, a fresh wave of suicides—or at least threats of suicide—ensued.

The international communist Victor Serge, a supporter of Trotsky who was living in Leningrad, recalled in his memoirs that some young Bolsheviks expelled for supporting the New Course killed themselves over their plight. They reasoned that life outside the party was pointless and that the party had wrongly called into question their revolutionary commitment. Seeking to capture their voice, Serge wrote, "What use is it to live if our party refuses us the right to serve it? This newborn world is calling us, we belong to it and it alone—and look! In its name someone spits in our faces. 'You are disqualified....' Disqualified because we are the revolution's racked flesh, its outraged reason? It is better to die."[69] Such threats were hardly unique, nor were they restricted to members of the formal opposition; in fact, "expulsion from the party" was included among the list of motives used to categorize suicides throughout the 1920s.[70] Nevertheless, as the intraparty struggle intensified in the mid-1920s, the question of suicide as a response to one's political death only became more acute, since defeat deprived many Bolsheviks of the opportunity to play out their imagined role in the grand historical experiment of socialism.

In this context, the attempt to affix meaning to suicide was an element of the broader rhetorical struggle to define oneself or one's opponents in terms of the key conceptual dichotomies in Bolshevik discourse—loyalty/opposition, strength/weakness, optimism/pessimism, revolutionary/counterrevolutionary, collective/individual, and health/disease. We see signs of this battle after the 1925 suicide of the civil war hero and former "Left Communist" Evgeniia Bogdanovna Bosh, which provoked an intense debate within the party leadership about how to handle her burial. According to Victor Serge, the "more rigorous comrades" claimed that although suicide could sometimes be justified in the case of incurable illness (Bosh had been gravely ill since 1922), it nevertheless remained an "act of indiscipline." Bosh's suicide was to them "proof of Oppositional leanings." In a decision reminiscent of church sanctions against the body and memory of the suicide, party leaders denied Bosh an official funeral and refused to inter her ashes in the wall of the Kremlin: she had been

69. Victor Serge, *Memoirs of a Revolutionary, 1901–1941,* trans. and ed. Peter Sedgwick (London, 1963), 194.
70. See, for example, "Plan razrabotky materialov po samoubiistvam sredi chlenov RKP(b)," GARF, f. 374, op. 21, d. 27, l. 116.

banished from the sacred burial place of the revolution's heroes for the sin of standing against (and outside) the party.[71]

Oppositionists sought to reverse the discourse in their favor by portraying some suicides as the unfortunate result of a truly *revolutionary* outlook. In his obituary for the former Workers' Oppositionist Iurii Lutovinov, who shot himself in May 1924, Karl Radek cast Lutovinov's death as the product of too much rather than too little commitment to the revolution. He called Lutovinov the embodiment of "proletarian impatience" and argued that Lutovinov was never able to accept "the fact that it is impossible for the proletariat to jump instantly from capitalism to socialism, especially in such a petit bourgeois country as Russia." "He saw with his mind all the difficulties," continued Radek, "but everything in his nature rebelled against them. This conflict between the logic of mind and feeling left on him the tragic mark of internal breakdown [*razorvannost'*] and mental instability [*neuravnoveshennost'*]." Radek did not condone suicide, but he suggested that Lutovinov's act ought to be read as a sign of deeper problems within the party. In particular, he called for greater attention to those comrades who were experiencing a similar crisis over the fate of the revolution, a suggestion that echoed the more general calls to devote more attention to the party member as an individual. "Maybe," Radek concluded, "the death of Iurii Lutovinov will force us to speak more openly and more clearly about the difficulties of the revolution's development."[72]

The suicide of Trotsky's secretary, Mikhail Glazman, who had found himself caught in the vicious web of party ethics and denunciation, also reflects the discursive battle over the question of revolutionary purity and the collective health. On the surface, Glazman's death was the sad consequence of inner-party squabbling and overly zealous party officials. Several candidate-members in Glazman's housing cooperative accused him of a number of ethical violations—maintaining a personal relationship with his "father-speculator," using his position to help nonparty family members, employing a nanny in his household, and occupying more than his

---

71. Serge, *Memoirs*, 194.

72. Karl Radek, "Pamiati tov. Iuriia Lutovinova," *Pravda*, May 10, 1925, 5. Radek also sought to distinguish between the sign and source of internal party problems when discussing the issues facing communist youth, arguing that "suicide attempts should be seen as symptomatic of the fever engulfing our social organism." Cited in Halfin, *Terror in My Soul*, 110. Interestingly, Emel'ian Iaroslavskii would later speak positively of Radek's sober assessment of Lutovinov's suicide in comparison with the opposition's "hysterical" response to the suicide of Adol'f Abramovich Ioffe (see below). Em. Iaroslavskii, "Filosofiia upadochnichestva," *Bol'shevik*, December 31, 1927, 136–37.

fair share of living space. These accusations were forwarded to the party board (*partkollegiia*) of the Moscow Control Commission, whose working-class members investigated the charges and recommended that Glazman be expelled from the party. Notably, the charges were made public in a journal article that accused Glazman (without using his name) of personally engaging in the practice of speculation, a terrible sin for any Bolshevik. After his expulsion and public humiliation, Glazman killed himself in early September 1924.[73]

Soon after the suicide, a dispute arose between Trotsky and the Central Control Commission over Glazman's death. Though cast in terms of Glazman's honor and fate, Trotsky's response was also a push for greater openness inside the party as well as a broader attack on the growing bureaucratization of the organization. Trotsky was particularly angered by the results of the official investigation into the suicide. A special commission, which included his opponent Emel'ian Iaroslavskii, was appointed by the presidium of the Central Control Commission to look into the matter. It concluded that the accusations against Glazman were groundless, the result of misunderstandings and "petit bourgeois jealousy."[74] More important, the commission's members examined Glazman's record and reaffirmed his credentials as a revolutionary "who was prepared to give his life for the cause of communism." On the basis of these findings, they concluded that Glazman was not "an alien comrade of the party" and deemed his expulsion "absolutely incorrect." In an ironic twist, the special commission now argued for the removal as well as the prosecution of those who had libeled Glazman. It also accused the Moscow party board of failing to investigate the facts properly, although it discovered no malice behind this mistake and called for no action against its members.[75]

Trotsky agreed with the assessment of Glazman's character, but he rejected the official reading of the suicide. Whereas the Central Control Commission regarded the publication of the false accusations as the key motive behind Glazman's suicide, Trotsky blamed the party apparatus itself for driving Glazman to take his own life. The main culprits in his

73. The circumstances surrounding Glazman's suicide are reconstructed from documents of the Central Control Commission relating to the investigation into his death. These are contained among the papers of Vyacheslav Mikhailovich Molotov. RGASPI, f. 82, op. 2, d. 122, ll. 46–50.

74. For example, it established that Glazman and his wife occupied only a single room of no more than 50 arshin (approximately 117 square feet) and that the nanny was more like Glazman's "second mother," having raised him and his siblings since the early death of their mother.

75. RGASPI, f. 82, op. 2, d. 122, ll. 47–50.

mind were not the libelous accusers but the responsible workers of the party board who had voted to expel Glazman. In particular, they had failed in their duty to get to know Glazman's personality, a serious lapse given the gravity of their decisions for Glazman and other party members. This, according to Trotsky, explained why Glazman had committed suicide and why he had never made an effort to rehabilitate himself through the Central Control Commission. The superficiality of the party board's investigation had made him conscious of his "utter defenselessness" as a party member. The horror of this abandonment, Trotsky argued, was sufficient to "drive such a firm and honest comrade as Glazman to an act of despair."[76]

Trotsky's assessment was consistent with the general discourse linking suicide to the individual's isolation from the collective. However, his reading turned the standard narrative on its head. In Glazman's case it was the *party* that had deserted him and not the other way around. Glazman had found himself alone and abandoned by his comrades, outside the kollektiv that had given him meaning. His political life effectively ended by the callous actions of others, Glazman had opted for death rather than lead a purposeless existence. For this reason, Trotsky railed against the failure of the Central Control Commission to go after the people who had really driven Glazman to kill himself—the members of the party board "to whom is entrusted the political life and death of party members, who render the harshest sentence without having lifted even a finger to conduct a genuine check of the material."[77]

Trotsky's full attack came during his eulogy at Glazman's graveside. There he wove together a compelling narrative that juxtaposed the steadfastness and honesty of the deceased with the grave mistakes committed by the party apparatus. He used words like "firm," "courageous," and "true" to describe Glazman, who despite his secretarial duties was never a "bureaucrat" but a committed Bolshevik equally adept with Mauser pistol and stenographer's pad during the civil war. Trotsky also homed in on Glazman's attention to detail in order to highlight the tragedy of his death and the carelessness of others. "He hated mistakes," declared Trotsky, "but fate demanded that he himself fall victim to a 'mistake.'" Moreover, in a thinly veiled criticism of those who had first looked into the accusations against Glazman, Trotsky stressed that his secretary had always performed his duties with tact, displaying a keen ability to distinguish "what is important or unimportant, where lies truth and where lies falsehood." Indeed,

76. "Pis'mo t. Trotskogo (November 16, 1924)," RGASPI, f. 82, op. 2, d. 122, ll. 51–54.
77. "Pis'mo t. Trotskogo," l. 52.

the sad irony of Glazman's death lay in the fact that he was ultimately felled by members of his own party. Trotsky proclaimed, "He could anticipate death at the front from the enemy's bullet. He could await and did await the further development of [his] tuberculosis. But he could not abide and did not abide expulsion from the party. This blow he could not withstand."[78]

Trotsky's eulogy was an attempt to frame Glazman's suicide in terms of his campaign against the party's degeneration under the current leadership. What could be more telling of this degeneration than the fact that the party was now hounding its most honest and revolutionary members to their deaths? Glazman, not unlike other party suicides, was a victim of his comrades' failure to know him as an individual. More significantly, he was a victim of bureaucratic attitudes and heartless formalism, if not malicious intent. When Trotsky pressed to take this diagnosis public, the party leadership pushed back, arguing that the open discussion of the causes behind Glazman's suicide was simply too dangerous. The editors of *Pravda*, for example, claimed that mention of the causes in print "could provoke 'imitations.'" Trotsky took this reticence as one more sign of the party leadership's unwillingness to speak openly and truthfully about the condition of the party, an outsider's accusation not too unlike the prerevolutionary complaints against the obfuscation practiced by the autocratic regime. In his view, it was only by rehabilitating Glazman in the press and eliminating the possibility of similar expulsions that the party would actually prevent imitations.[79]

When Trotsky was himself expelled from the party in 1927, he chose not to imitate Glazman by committing suicide. However, his longtime friend and supporter Adol'f Abramovich Ioffe shot himself in the head, setting off an intense skirmish between oppositionists and party loyalists over the significance of the suicide. Supporters of Ioffe argued that his suicide was an act of selflessness and a "death in the name of life and struggle," a rhetorical move that went against the representation of suicide as the product of individualism and a lack of faith in the revolution. An underground leaflet proclaimed, "Ioffe's shooting is neither the manifestation of decadence nor a manifestation of social pessimism. Just the opposite. It is the manifestation of social optimism."[80] According to the secret transcripts of the funeral orations delivered at Ioffe's grave, Ioffe was depicted as a "fighter" who was not afraid to speak openly and honestly about the party

78. L. Trotskii, "Pamiati M. S. Glazmana," RGASPI, f. 82, op. 2, d. 122, ll. 55–58.
79. "Pis'mo t. Trotskogo," l. 53.
80. Iaroslavskii, "Filosofiia upadochnichestva," 135.

and his comrades, a not-so-subtle rebuke against the current leadership. Trotsky called for others to emulate Ioffe's life, not his death. However, he believed that Ioffe could not be reproached for ending his life "as if voluntarily." Having said and done everything that he could on behalf of the revolution, Ioffe had only his death to give.[81]

Ioffe offered himself as a martyr for the cause of the revolution. In his final letter, addressed to Trotsky, he sought to give his suicide a political cast and asked Trotsky to use his death to advance the opposition's struggle. The first part of the letter framed the decision to commit suicide within his larger philosophy about life and death. When an individual can no longer contribute to the greater good, Ioffe reasoned, he has a right to kill himself rather than go on living a life without meaning and purpose. This is why he had defended the right of Paul and Laura Lafargue to commit suicide many years before. Now it was his turn to act on his beliefs. The party leadership's attacks on the opposition meant that he could no longer hold a position of importance. Moreover, the leadership had taken measures that aggravated his worsening health, including a refusal to send him abroad for further medical treatment. "I know the party's negative attitude toward suicides," Ioffe wrote, "but I would contend that there's hardly a person who, having familiarized himself with my situation, would condemn me for [taking] this step." Finally, in the last section of his letter, Ioffe turned explicitly to politics and to the party's internal situation. Trotsky's expulsion, which he deemed a "disgrace" that signaled the start of the revolution's Thermidor, marked a critical moment in the fate of the opposition and the party as a whole. Unable to struggle in any other way, Ioffe called his death "the protest of a fighter" for whom, after twenty-seven years of standing at his post for the revolution, there was nothing left to do but "put a bullet in the temple."[82]

The counterattack against Ioffe and the opposition came from the pen of Emel'ian Iaroslavskii, who rebutted the claim that the party was degenerating by accusing Ioffe and his supporters of adhering to a "philosophy of decadence [*upadochnichestvo*]." Dissecting both Ioffe's letter and the words of the underground opposition, Iaroslavskii argued that the only people who saw Ioffe's suicide as an act of "social optimism" were "people who themselves have been soaked through with this putrid air of decomposition,

81. "Rech' tov. Kameneva," RGASPI, f. 82, op. 2, d. 189, l. 105; "Rech' tov. Rakovskogo," RGASPI, f. 82, op. 2, d. 189, ll. 106–7; and "Rechi, proiznesennye nad mogiloi tov. A. A. Ioffe v den' pokhoron 19 XI. 27 g.," RGASPI, f. 82, op. 2, d. 189, ll. 109–10.

82. Letter of A. A. Ioffe addressed to Lev Davidovich [Trotsky], November 16, 1927. RGASPI, f. 82, op. 2, d. 189, ll. 86–96.

decadence, and amoralism in relation to the Leninist party."[83] Under the distorting influence of the decadent philosophy, these "few thousand present and former party members" could only misread the state of the party, mistakenly view Ioffe as a victim of the leadership's retaliation against the opposition, and incorrectly see the expulsion of Trotsky (and Zinoviev) as signaling the loss of the party's revolutionary character. But the philosophy of decadence, Iaroslavskii asserted, would never penetrate deeply into the party because it was "healthier and stronger than ever.... Linked with the masses as never before, close to the proletariat, it *envelops* these proletarian masses as never before." In fact, Iaroslavskii boldly declared that the party was "so healthy" that it could reanimate the politically dead, a clear reference to the life force of the kollektiv. In contrast to the "decaying" opposition, it was "capable of infusing new living juices into every [member] who finds in himself the honesty to acknowledge and condemn his mistakes unconditionally, and of returning to these comrades the creative joyfulness of the proletarian party that is building socialism."[84]

Although the struggle to define Ioffe's suicide took place within the common conceptual framework of party health, Ioffe and his supporters were at a rhetorical disadvantage because Ioffe was beset by a real illness of the body and mind. He had had a long history of sickness prior to his suicide in 1927, having been diagnosed with so-called Korsakov's psychosis, polyneuritis, and an incurable morphine addiction.[85] This background allowed Iaroslavskii to challenge the opposition's representation of the suicide with a powerful counternarrative that blurred the boundaries between physical and political health. He listed the vast sums of money and expert care expended on Ioffe, which included a stint with the psychoanalyst Viktor Adler in Vienna, as proof that the opposition's charges of neglect were untrue. Moreover, he highlighted Ioffe's drug addiction and medical reports of hallucinations to call into question Ioffe's various assertions as well as his motivations for committing suicide.[86] Iaroslavskii, in

83. Iaroslavskii, "Filosofiia upadochnichestva," 138.

84. Ibid., 142–43 (my emphasis).

85. RGASPI, f. 82, op. 2, d. 189, l. 98; and Iaroslavskii, "Filosofiia upadochnichestva," 138–39.

86. For example, he questioned Ioffe's claim that he had personally heard Lenin say that Trotsky had correctly assessed the situation in 1905. Iaroslavskii asked, "Could not such a hallucination have arisen in the fantastical imagination of the morphine addict?" In addition, Iaroslavskii also sought to undermine Ioffe's complaints about his treatment by suggesting that these were the product of his condition, not the reality of the situation. "This sickness," wrote Iaroslavskii, "made him [Ioffe] not only irritable but, as it so often does with

other words, challenged Ioffe's sense of reality. His inability to recognize the incorrectness of his position and, conversely, the correctness of the party, was akin to mental illness, a chilling intimation, given the later role of psychiatry in suppressing alternative views in the Soviet Union.

SUICIDE AND THE SOVIET SUBJECT

The debates about suicides in the Bolshevik Party reveal the Soviets' quandary regarding individuality and autonomy. In their encouragement of personalized care and their attention to the particular elements of the suicide's story, the Bolsheviks acknowledged the individual as a distinct product of different elements, including specific histories, environments, and even biology. Nevertheless, this recognition sat uncomfortably with their rejection of liberal assumptions about the autonomous subject who operated independently of society. Igal Halfin, in fact, has gone so far as to argue that joining the Bolshevik Party was itself a form of suicide since it required the death of "an autonomous, self-sufficient individual."[87] Consequently, the challenge facing the Bolsheviks was how to promote individual development without also promoting individualism. Or, in other words, how should they calibrate their efforts to bring about a landscape where individuals, freed from the false consciousness of capitalism, were finally able to realize their true potential as social beings?

These concerns about the social nature of the individual were not unique to the Bolsheviks. Social scientists in Europe had for many decades been framing suicide primarily as a matter of alienation in the modern industrial world. Thus we see a strong affinity between Bolshevik and non-Bolshevik narratives of failed or incomplete integration, where the isolated individual finds physical or metaphorical death beyond the bonds of society. What stands out in the Bolshevik versions of this narrative is their radical vision of personal transformation and social inclusion. In particular, responses to suicide articulated a fundamental Marxist belief: the postcapitalist social order would function through genuine internal unity among individuals rather than through the external bonds that once held societies together.[88]

---

sick people, also *unfair* to those around him." Iaroslavskii, "Filosofiia upadochnichestva," 138, 142 (emphasis in the original).
    87. Halfin, *Terror in My Soul*, 283.
    88. Hellbeck, *Revolution on My Mind*, 86.

The formation of collective opinion and the promotion of mutual surveillance were therefore creative as well as disciplinary endeavors. Collective opinion promoted a particular form of subjectivity by providing the framework for self-expression while also encouraging individuals to become self-regulating, fully participating members of society. Simultaneously, the practice of mutual surveillance involved horizontal forms of control organized through the continuous interaction among the collective's individual members. Indeed, Bolshevik responses to suicide recognized that threats could come from within the group, an awareness that deepened fears of internal corruption and furthered the trend toward seeing life outside the group in pathological terms. As Martyn Liadov proclaimed in 1924, "It will hurt me to violate these [common] interests, and in the future society they will look upon the person who has violated these interests as a sick person who needs to be cured."[89] Accordingly, when Soviet individuals transgressed society, they also transgressed themselves, since their interests and the interests of society were the same. Defense of the group was in this manner intimately tied to the protection of the individual.

It is perhaps ironic, then, that some of the key measures of the Bolshevik Party's fight against internal illness—notably purging and mutual surveillance—could also incite antisocial acts within the party. Throughout the 1920s, the practice of expulsion occasioned both threats and actual instances of suicide. Moreover, as the assault on communism intensified toward the end of the decade with the abandonment of the NEP in favor of collectivization and rapid industrialization, the party observed a growing number of suicides associated with the exposure, or "unmasking," of class aliens among it ranks. By 1930, in fact, the Main Administration and Political Administration of the Red Army had created an entirely new statistical category for suicides—"discharge from the army and hiding alien origins." Suicides placed in this group were said to be a "reflection of the great sense of urgency and watchfulness that has accompanied the process of intensifying the class struggle in the country." Given the possible lethality of this campaign, some party leaders worried about the careless and arbitrary application of the collective's defensive measures, a concern

---

89. Liadov, *Voprosy byta*, 23. At least one early commentator recognized the danger of such thinking for the autonomous being. Evgenii Zamiatin's dystopian novel *We* (1920) satirizes the total merger of the part and the whole in the nightmarish vision of the One State. In the end, the complete union of the two is possible only through an act of therapeutic violence carried out against the individual—the so-called great operation, which removes the person's imagination.

similar to the one expressed by Trotsky after Mikhail Glazman's suicide in 1924.[90]

Although cause for unease, the suicides brought about by the party's attempts to maintain its revolutionary purity did not necessarily cause regret. Many of these individuals, especially oppositionists, were already politically dead in the eyes of leading Bolsheviks and thus did not merit consternation. Emel'ian Iaroslavskii, ever on the attack against apostasy, argued for this way of thinking at the Second Plenum of the Central Control Commission in 1924. Alluding to Glazman, whom he criticized for not taking his case to the TsKK, Iaroslavskii conceded that the party needed to exercise its powers judiciously and called on those accused of wrongdoing to redeem themselves in the eyes of the party. However, he also suggested that some party members were simply beyond redemption and thus fully deserving of the party's strictest disciplinary measures. He cited the example of a Bolshevik who remained in the ranks despite the fact that he had openly joined another (unnamed) organization and worked against the party. Now facing expulsion, this individual was said to be on the verge of suicide. Iaroslavskii coldly remarked, "So, let him commit suicide. It would be the best way out for him because he has already killed himself [*ubil sebia*] politically."[91]

The blurring of the boundary between murder and suicide demonstrates that Bolshevik attitudes toward suicide were based on historically and culturally specific assumptions about the self. Where the individual is conceived as an autonomous being, murder can be thought to reflect the love of the self, while suicide suggests a desire to destroy it.[92] By contrast, the Bolsheviks' understanding of the individual as a social being made suicide appear the result of an excessive love and concern for oneself that conflicted with the interests of the larger collective. In fact, two interchangeable notions of the individual are visible in the debate about suicide and opposition—the person struggling to realize a collective self and the person fully enmeshed in the collective. Oppositionists and loyalists

---

90. "Statisticheskii ezhegodnik za 1928/29 god.," ll. 49–49ob.

91. E. M. Iaroslavskii, "O partetike. Doklad na II pleniume TsKK RKP(b) 5 oktiabria 1924 g.," in *Partiinaia etika*, 195. Interestingly, the version of Iaroslavskii's talk published in *Pravda* omitted his oblique reference to Glazman and his comments regarding the opposition member's suicide. Perhaps this omission reflected the editors' desire to limit public discussion of Glazman's death. For the edited version, see "Nuzhno surovo osudit'," 4.

92. Researchers today still view suicide and murder as two distinct forms of violence, with suicide being aggression turned inward while murder is aggression turned outward against another human being. See N. Prabha Unnithan et al., *The Currents of Lethal Violence: An Integrated Model of Suicide and Homicide* (Albany, 1994), 7–34.

alike were simply unable to think of the individual without the collective and its life-giving force. Both sides equated an existence outside the party with death. Whereas the opposition essentially accused the party leadership of murdering its most revolutionary members by depriving them of their political lives, Iaroslavskii could rationalize and perhaps even welcome acts of suicide among the opposition as putting an end to the danger they posed to the kollektiv. Irredeemably lost both to themselves and to the party, these individuals had effectively opted for death when they made the conscious decision to stand against the proletarian dictatorship and outside its life-giving force.

Iaroslavskii's response to the young communists cited at the opening of the chapter thus becomes more comprehensible when interpreted in terms of the Bolshevik discourse about the collectivist individual. It would appear on the surface that his argument against expelling the suicide went against his severe and reproachful attitude toward self-killing. On closer inspection, however, the advice he gave was consistent with his role as guardian of the party's ideological health. Iaroslavskii and the Central Control Commission were chiefly concerned with looking into the soul of the individual in order to determine innocence or guilt before the party. A successful suicide, however, meant that the party's diagnosticians had a victim but no perpetrator, since the latter had escaped with the very commission of the crime. In his absence, there was no way to establish the political state of the accused, which was necessary to establish grounds for excommunication from the party. This left only the memory of the dead through which the collective looked at itself, and a corpse whose story awaited discovery in the hands of forensic-medical experts.

3

Suicide and Social Autopsy

In early 1926, the Komsomolist Grigorii Kopein hanged himself in his dormitory room, leaving behind a note that claimed he had done three stupid things in his life—he was born, he got married, and now he had committed suicide. Outwardly, he appeared an unlikely candidate for suicide from the standpoint of the Bolshevik Party. Although the child of well-to-do peasants (kulaks), he had broken off all relations with his politically suspect parents. He had married recently, was academically successful at the Bukharin workers' faculty (*rabfak*), participated frequently in social work, and was especially active in the Komsomol. An investigation therefore failed to uncover any "social causes that might have served as the reason [*povod*] for suicide." It turned out, however, that Kopein's degeneration was physiological rather than political, a condition that was not discovered until his autopsy. The physician who examined the corpse was said to have "established the degeneration [*degeneratsiia*] of the skull." He wrote, "In such illnesses, the person sometimes loses the instinct for self-preservation."[1]

Kopein was not unique. Doctors working in the Red Army also found telltale signs in the bodies of several soldiers who had taken their own

---

1. The same internal party publication also included a case where the doctors found "signs of congenital [*vrozhdennyi*] suicide." "Boleznennye iavleniia v organizatsii (informatsionnyi obzor)," RGASPI, f. 17, op. 85, d. 66, ll. 73–73ob.

lives. An autopsy performed on the Red Army man Ivan Chotur' in 1926, for example, revealed "a cranial structure and condition of the cerebral membrane indicating the psychopathological constitution of the suicide."[2] Moreover, the reader of the autopsy report on Kirill Vasil'ev underlined the finding "thymus gland is enlarged," which the author cited as one of the morphological signs of "severe pathological heredity" and "physical degeneration." The report concluded, "If to this we add the previously observed comblike growths in the cranium (these have been noted by many legal doctors during the autopsy of suicides), which can often irritate the brain mechanically as it fills up with blood and thus can have a harmful effect on the psyche, then we must conclude that in the person of the deceased we have a subject not only physically degenerated but also with a defect of the psyche. This, one must submit, is also the cause [*prichina*] of the suicide."[3]

The idea that suicide was the product of internal physiological changes, including the possibility that self-destructive tendencies were constitutional or inherited, made self-destruction into a biomedical problem that privileged the corpse and those who interpreted it, namely, forensic-medical doctors. Indeed, forensic experts pioneered the study of suicide after the Bolshevik Revolution. As early as September 1920, several speakers addressed the topic at the All-Russian Congress of State Medical Experts, the first major gathering of the forensic-medical community after the collapse of the autocracy. They included the country's chief medical examiner, Iakov L'vovich Leibovich, who urged doctors to be more attentive to the study and registration of suicides, and the forensic doctor Aleksandr Ivanovich Kriukov, who delivered a paper on the anatomical changes he had observed in the skulls of suicides. We lack a full record of these presentations, but the participants apparently heeded the advice of another presenter—the psychiatrist Leonid Prozorov, who called on physicians to take the matter of counting suicides "into their own hands." During the discussion that followed, they proposed the creation of a special commission to study suicides under Soviet power.[4]

Practitioners of a "boundary science" that straddled the fields of medicine and the law, forensic doctors were well positioned for such an

2. Report of February 2, 1926 from the Military-Sanitary Administration of the Ukrainian Military District to the Military-Sanitary Administration RKKA, RGVA, f. 34, op. 3, d. 42, ll. 182–182ob.

3. "Akt No. 1 Sudebno-meditsinskogo vskrytiia trupa kr-tsa Vasil'eva Kirilla," RGVA, f. 34, op. 3, d. 42, ll. 19–21ob.

4. "Vserossiiskii s"ezd gosudarstvennykh meditsinkikh ekspertov sozvannyi 20–25 sentiabria 1920 goda," GARF, f. 482, op. 1, d. 217, ll. 19ob–21ob.

investigation.[5] In particular, their concern with death made them valuable to knowledge-based governments that undertook the biological administration of the population. Modern definitions of death as a physiological process heightened the importance of the forensic doctors' expertise over the human body and deemphasized subjective experience in favor of the special cognitive skills required for establishing the cause and mode of death as dictated by law.[6] Moreover, the profession's abiding connection to "the most deformed pathological phenomena of...everyday life" created a potential space where the forensic-medical doctors could extend their expertise to the body politic, including the measurement of its injuries and mortality.[7] Forensic doctors in this way helped to make death and deviance meaningful for the rest of society.

From the outset there was a discernible tension in the way that the practitioners of Soviet forensic medicine framed the problem of suicide. Medical experts like Leibovich discussed self-destruction primarily in terms of its social character. In his address to the All-Russian Congress he spoke of general patterns, large numbers, and statistical laws. At the same time, Aleksandr Kriukov treated suicide as an individualized problem. His presentation emphasized the autopsy and the particular facts discovered through the postmortem examination of the corpse. The difference between the two approaches is neatly captured in the Russian language, which allows one to distinguish between the suicide as a distinct person (*samoubiitsa*) and suicide as an act or phenomenon (*samoubiistvo*). Accordingly, the relationship between the part (the individual) and the whole (the social organism) shaped forensic-medical debates about self-destruction and the discipline's role in the Soviet state. Those interested in the personality of the suicide (*lichnost' samoubiitsy*) emphasized the importance of heredity and biology in creating the mental and emotional states they associated with self-destruction. This necessitated a case-by-case search for the bodily signs that characterized the suicidal type. Supporters of the sociological approach countered that the primary sources of suicide were in the environment and that these external factors could be discerned only through the statistical aggregate. The end result was an

5. On forensic medicine as a boundary science, see Ia. Leibovich, "Sudebno-meditsinskaia ekspertiza pri NEP'e," *Ezhenedel'nik sovetskoi iustitsii,* January 23, 1923, 37.

6. Ian A. Burney, *Bodies of Evidence: Medicine and the Politics of the English Inquest, 1830–1926* (Baltimore, 2000), 2, 11.

7. "Gubernskoe soveshchanie sudebnomeditsinskikh ekspertov Riazanskoi gubernii pri uchastii predstavitelei iustitsii i organov doznaniia. (g. Riazan', 2–4 fevralia 1929 g.)," *Sudebno-meditsinskaia ekspertiza,* no. 13 (1930): 80.

overlapping series of investigations, with anatomical explorations existing alongside quantitative studies.

The coexistence and interpenetration of these two outlooks provide further evidence that the biological was compatible with the environmentalist leanings of Bolshevik Marxism. Daniel Beer, for instance, has demonstrated the continued relevance of a biological perspective to understandings of social experience during the 1920s. Bolshevik leaders as well as Soviet professionals accepted the notion that class consciousness, instincts, and other environmental influences could be passed on from one generation to the next. This biopsychological model provided a powerful explanation for the failure of certain individuals to adapt to the new circumstances of Soviet power and increasingly shaped policy by suggesting that there were limits to the state's ability to reshape some individuals.[8] Similarly, Narkomzdrav, which one scholar has described as a loose "professional network encompassing divergent agendas," supported both hereditarian and environmentalist programs. These included a popular form of eugenics designed to strengthen the population through the regulation of marriage as well as the patronage of biological studies of sex that reaffirmed the norm of heterosexuality.[9]

This chapter argues that the deeper tension in forensic medicine was instead over the question of the individual as an object of sociomedical study. Forensic-medical investigations took place within a fluid institutional environment where different disciplines and programs competed for patronage; indeed, forensic doctors during the 1920s lacked a uniform vision of their discipline and were challenged to make it relevant to the new governmental project. As a result, the work on self-destruction is in part a reflection of their efforts to flesh out the role of scientific expertise under Soviet power. Understandings of suicide and other forensic-medical objects helped to define the profession, determined research strategies, privileged certain types of knowledge, and delineated possible sites of intervention in the everyday life of Soviet citizens. Most notably, forensic doctors assumed the individual to be a complex personality formed through the interplay of biological and social factors. Where they differed among themselves—and with others in the scientific community—was

8. Daniel Beer, *Renovating Russia: The Human Sciences and the Fate of Liberal Modernity, 1880–1930* (Ithaca, 2008), 200–201.

9. Mark B. Adams, "Eugenics as Social Medicine in Revolutionary Russia: Prophets, Patrons, and the Dialectics of Discipline-Building," in *Health and Society in Revolutionary Russia*, ed. Susan Gross Solomon and John F. Hutchinson (Bloomington, 1990), 200–201; and Frances Lee Bernstein, *The Dictatorship of Sex: Lifestyle Advice for the Soviet Masses* (DeKalb, IL, 2007), 54, 172–73.

regarding the relative weight to be given the place of nature and nurture in human development.[10] The choice between these two factors helped to determine the social meaning of suicide, whether as a comparable unit of statistical information or an irreducible personal history. Rather than a monolithic imposition of a single social science model, the forensic-medical explorations into suicide suggest a series of intellectual and professional negotiations along the boundaries of the part and the whole. They reveal the problematic nature of the individual in Soviet medical discourse and demonstrate how partitive definitions of the personality helped to rationalize the overlapping, and somewhat competing, investigations into suicide as a social and biological phenomenon. Delineating their spheres of action in Soviet life, forensic doctors, no less than the ruling Bolsheviks, were engaged in a dialogue about and with the individual.

FORENSIC MEDICINE AND THE SOVIET SOCIAL ORDER

Suicide was formally decriminalized after the revolution of 1917. Still, the postrevolutionary state remained interested in the act. Article 148 of the 1922 Russian criminal code made it a punishable offense to assist or compel a suicide by a minor or any persons deemed incapable of understanding the meaning of their actions. In the revised criminal code of 1926, article 141 mandated a five-year prison term for anyone found guilty of driving to suicide someone found materially or otherwise dependent, whether through cruel treatment or by similar means.[11] These statutes emphasized the state's paternalistic role by protecting the most vulnerable members of society, in particular women, children, and the mentally ill. They also continued the prerevolutionary approach of prosecuting

10. On the nurture-nature debates regarding crime and homosexuality see, Sharon A. Kowalsky, "Who's Responsible for Female Crime? Gender, Deviance, and the Development of Social Norms in Revolutionary Russia," *Russian Review* 62 (July 2003): 366–86; and Dan Healey, *Homosexual Desire in Revolutionary Russia: The Regulation of Sexual and Gender Dissent* (Chicago, 2001), 126–51.

11. Ia. Leibovich, "Sovremennye samoubiistva v Sovetskoi Rossii," in *Trudy II Vserossiiskogo s"ezda sudebno-meditsinskikh ekspertov. Moskva, 25 fevralia–3 marta 1926 g.*, ed. Ia. Leibovich (Ulyanovsk, 1926), 208; D. P. Kosorotov, *Uchebnik sudebnoi-meditsiny*, 2nd ed., ed. Ia. L. Leibovich (Moscow-Leningrad, 1926), 499; and Kosorotov, *Uchebnik sudebnoi-meditsiny*, 3rd ed., ed. Ia. L. Leibovich (Moscow-Leningrad, 1928), 290. On the legal history of suicide in Russia, see especially P. F. Bulatsel', *Samoubiistvo s drevneishikh vremen do nashikh dnei. Istoricheskii ocherk filosoficheskikh vozzrenii i zakonodatel'stv o samoubiistve*, 2nd ed. (St. Petersburg, 1900); and A. F. Koni, *Samoubiistvo v zakone i zhizni* (Moscow, 1923).

individuals who instigated suicide, but with the key difference that they removed the burden of criminal responsibility from the main actor—the suicide.[12] Accordingly, members of the Soviet militia were instructed to inform the nearest criminal-investigative unit whenever they encountered a suicide and to fill out a special form (*oprosnyi list*) to provide information that could help to establish the presence of a murder masked as a suicide.[13] A 1924 review of these forms raised questions about the willingness of the police to fulfill their tasks in this realm. Its author called on investigators to pay greater attention to suicides and cited a number of cases where there were grounds to suspect the responsibility of outsiders. In particular, he urged them to consider the less obvious signs of external pressure or influence, giving examples of suicides among women neglected by their spouses and lovers as well as acts committed by depressed or mentally ill individuals who were left unattended despite the risk they posed to themselves.[14]

Soviet forensic-medical experts (*sudebno-meditsinskie eksperty*) also showed a deep interest in self-destruction as both a legal and medical problem. Beginning in 1919, all instances of suicide, as well as murder and suspicious or sudden death, fell within the jurisdiction of a newly created apparatus of forensic medicine. In that year, Narkomzdrav established the Department of Forensic-Medical Expertise and began to organize throughout the Russian Republic a centralized system of full-time forensic-medical examiners.[15] With headquarters in Moscow and branches in major cities, provincial centers, and local districts, the new apparatus was intended to eliminate the accidental character of forensic medicine under the Old Regime by placing it in the hands of specially trained physicians and by

12. Susan Morrissey discusses law and responsibility before 1917 in "Patriarchy on Trial: Suicide, Discipline, and Governance in Imperial Russia," *Journal of Modern History* 75 (March 2003): 23–58.

13. For example, the form asked about the presence of bodily injuries delivered by another person, whether the suicide had been coerced or talked into the act, whether someone else had supplied the instrument of death, and whether the suicide had suffered torment or beating. See "Oprosnyi list," GAIaO, f. 844, op. 1, d. 2, ll. 93–93ob.

14. A. Uchevatov, "Samoubiistva i organy doznaniia," *Raboche-krest'ianskaia militsiia*, nos. 7–8 (July–August 1924): 21–23. On suicides and Soviet investigative organs see also V. Ignat'ev, "Militsiia kak organ doznaniia," *Raboche-krest'ianskaia militsiia*, no. 1 (November 1922): 40; and V. Khalfin, "Samoubiistvo. (Po materialam TsAU NKVD)," *Raboche-krest'ianskaia militsiia*, no. 1 (January 1924): 17–20.

15. The organization of this apparatus actually began the previous year, with the creation of the subdepartment of forensic medicine under Narkomzdrav's Department of Civilian Medicine. During a general reorganization of Narkomzdrav in 1919, this subdepartment was upgraded to the status of an independent department.

giving greater initiative and deference to the scientific expert.[16] Building Soviet forensic medicine therefore entailed more than the creation of the necessary institutional infrastructure. It was also a process of self-definition that centered on the discipline's spheres of activity in the Soviet state and among the public more generally.

Leadership of the new forensic-medical apparatus belonged to Iakov Leibovich, a forensic gynecologist from Odessa who had helped to build the medical and university systems in Smolensk before coming to Moscow. Active throughout the decade of the 1920s, Leibovich is credited by historians and his peers with providing Soviet forensic medicine with its necessary professional accoutrements, including the founding of specialized laboratories, organizing professional conferences, translating and writing key instructional texts, and resolving a wide variety of scientific and practical questions related to the field. Most notably, according V. A. Rozhanovskii, the chronicler of early Soviet forensic medicine, Leibovich strove to connect the discipline to the masses in order to "extricate it from the walls of the morgue" and gain it the "right of citizenship" as a "social science."[17]

Soviet visions of forensic medicine communicated the rather utopian aspirations of total surveillance, complete transparency, and the hegemony of scientific knowledge. Ideally, in the not-so-distant future not a single case of sudden, violent, or suspicious death would escape the medical experts, who would examine and interpret the physical evidence with their specially trained minds. This would bolster the causes of science and justice in Soviet society, as knowledge of death deepened and the objective truth in criminal matters was discovered. However, forensic medicine's ambiguous position between the medical and legal worlds sometimes complicated the delineation of its role within the Soviet state. During the 1920s its practitioners were dogged by questions about the field's areas of competency, its precise relationship to the new judicial system, and even its place within the medical profession. Indeed, some of the discipline's greatest skeptics were fellow doctors who believed that virtually any

---

16. V. A. Rozhanovskii, "Sudebno-meditsinskaia ekspertiza v dorevoliutsionnoi Rossii i v SSSR," *Sudebno-meditsinskaia ekspertiza,* no. 6 (1927): 10. The growth of Soviet forensic medicine was a gradual process. According to one summary, there were ninety-three trained forensic experts in 1919; by 1925 this number had risen to three hundred experts and thirty-three legal chemists. Ia. Leibovich, "Itogi deiatel'nosti sudebno-meditsinskoi ekspertizy za 7 let i ee zadachi," in Leibovich, *Trudy II Vserossiiskogo s"ezda,* 5.

17. On Leibovich and his activities, see Iu. A. Nekliudov, "Iakov L'vovich Leibovich— vidnyi deiatel' otechestvennoi sudebnoi meditsiny," *Sudebno-meditsinskaia ekspertiza,* no. 5 (2003): 48–49; and Rozhanovskii, "Sudebno-meditsinskaia ekspertiza," 56–57.

physician could carry out the duties of the legal doctor, as had often been the case during the prerevolutionary era.[18]

The organizers of early Soviet forensic medicine disavowed any legacy from the Old Regime, although this rhetoric ignored the continuity of personnel as well as their pursuits across the revolutionary divide.[19] In particular, they cast the nascent forensic-medical apparatus as a fundamentally new enterprise born out of the Bolshevik Revolution and the imperatives of constructing a new society, which would require its own legal structure and generate its own unique forms of justice and criminality. Forensic-medical experts, for instance, trumpeted their participation in the creation of the 1922 Russian criminal code, which they claimed sought to cure rather than punish social illnesses. Moreover, speaking at the First All-Russian Congress of State Medical Experts in 1920, Leibovich sought to link the discipline with the fields of eugenics, criminal anthropology, and psychology and to highlight its pertinence to the fight against alcoholism and other social problems.[20] In a regime where individual health and heredity were governmental matters, forensic-medical experts saw themselves in an excellent position to provide the state with the information, advice, and practical skills needed for population management.

Under Leibovich's leadership, forensic-medical experts strove to integrate their profession more fully into the larger project of investigating and transforming the Soviet body politic after the revolution. As Leibovich argued in a 1920 circular to provincial departments of medical expertise, "Forensic medicine should not limit itself to the autopsy of dead bodies and the investigation of injured ones, but to a proper degree contribute its share toward the study and construction of social life."[21] He emphasized, for example, that forensic doctors were involved in the discussions

---

18. On Russian forensic medicine before 1917, see Elisa M. Becker, "Judicial Reform and the Role of Medical Expertise in Late Imperial Russian Courts," *Law and History Review* 17, no. 1 (Spring 1999): 1–26; A. A. Solokhin and Iu. A. Solokhin, *Sudebno-meditsinskaia nauka v Rossii i SSSR v XIX i XX stoletiiakh* (Moscow, 1998); and Rozhanovskii, "Sudebno-meditsinskaia ekspertiza," 7–37.

19. Such claims to novelty were an important source of legitimacy and self-understanding in early Soviet medicine. See, for example, Susan Solomon, "David and Goliath in Soviet Public Health: The Rivalry of Social Hygienists and Psychiatrists for Authority over the *Bytovoi* Alcoholic," *Soviet Studies* 41, no. 2 (April 1989): 254–75.

20. Ia. Leibovich, "Tri goda sudebnoi meditsiny," *Izvestiia narodnogo komissariata zdravookhraneniia*, nos. 1–2 (1922): 12–13; and "Tesizy doklada D-ra Leibovicha na temu: 'Polozhenie Gosudarstvennogo Meditsinskogo Eksperta, ego prava i obiazannosti i otnoshenie k sudo-sledstvennym i drugim organam i 'Organizatsiia Meditsinskogo Ekspertizy i ee blizhaishchiie zadachi,'" GARF, f. 482, op. 1, d. 217, l. 12.

21. Circular from Iakov Leibovich to the Provincial Subdepartments of Medical Expertise dated February 27, 1920, GARF, f. 482, op. 1, d. 208, l. 35.

about Soviet policy toward a number of pressing social questions, such as the legalization of abortion and the regulation of marriage as a means of preventing the transmission of venereal disease.[22] Moreover, the day-to-day responsibilities of the forensic-medical experts brought them into direct contact with the Soviet public. Forensic doctors were called upon to establish paternity and sexual maturity, confirm bodily signs of rape, evaluate the competency of suspected criminals, and perform a variety of examinations at the behest of both state officials and individual citizens.[23]

Many forensic doctors framed such activities within the state's concern for a robust and well-ordered population. Speaking at the Second All-Russian Congress of Forensic-Medical Experts held in Moscow in 1926, the medical expert Golitsyn made the connection explicit. He told his colleagues that the importance of their work stemmed from its implications for maintaining the health and size of the population:

> Considered only in terms of its influence on the decrease of the population as a result of murders, suicides, etc., criminality is no less a social evil and calamity than famine, war, epidemics, and so on. If infectious epidemics strike us every other decade and only for a relatively short time, then criminal epidemics brutally cut down the population day after day. Crime statistics speak to the fact that across the entire Union every year an entire army is counted consisting of hundreds of thousands of the murdered and self-murdered, as well as individuals maimed and imprisoned (who are also dead members of society). Therefore, we must spend no less energy and resources on the struggle against criminality than we do on the struggle against infectious diseases. The state receives a great benefit from this, since a highly developed criminality severely impedes all social construction, not to mention the loss of population.[24]

Such thinking aligned the discipline with the criminological theories of social defense, which emphasized the right of society to protect itself from deviant individuals. It also placed the medical expert at a critical position along the front lines of the struggle to build Soviet society. While other branches of Soviet medicine fought against infectious and epidemic disease, the task of forensic-medical expertise was said to involve

22. Ia. L. Leibovich, "Piat' let sudebnoi meditsiny," *Ezhenedel'nik sovetskoi iustitsii*, August 30, 1923, 777.

23. Dan Healey, "Early Soviet Forensic Psychiatric Approaches to Sex Crime, 1917–1934," in *Madness and the Mad in Russian Culture*, ed. Angela Brintlinger and Ilya Vinitsky (Toronto, 2007), 150–68.

24. Leibovich, *Trudy II Vserossiiskogo s"ezda*, 80.

the prevention of crime, which Golitsyn deemed "the most severe social illness."[25]

Leading forensic doctors therefore insisted that their discipline was a branch of Soviet "social medicine," with its strong emphasis on prophylaxis, the primacy of environmental factors in human health and disease, and its promotion of the physician as a kind of social investigator.[26] In fact, the image of the forensic-medical doctor as a "physician-sociologist" (*vrach-sotsiolog*) was essential to the self-identity of many practitioners in the 1920s. Whereas prerevolutionary legal physicians were commonly depicted as little more than functionaries working at the beck and call of tsarist officials, Soviet forensic experts were lauded for their activism and public-mindedness. Most notably, they were to display independent initiative, possess a strong "social streak," and, finally, apply their scientific knowledge to the benefit of all society. Leibovich himself implied that the Soviet social order had brought forth a new kind of legal doctor in Russia. "At the present time," he wrote, "the forensic-medical expert is not a bureaucrat, but a social worker [*obshchestvennyi rabotnik*], not a functionary, but a sociologist [*sotsiolog*]. If there are people who think differently, who are not in agreement with the new position of the physician-expert, then they are still living in the poisoned atmosphere of the past and do not understand the new social forms called to life by the revolution."[27]

The activist imagery was aimed partly at countering perceptions of the forensic doctor as an introverted anatomist whose world revolved around the corpse and thus had little to do with the living. Nevertheless, the practice of autopsy remained central to the identity of Soviet forensic-medical experts. Deemed their "fundamental and most crucial form of work" by participants at the Second All-Russian Congress, the postmortem examination set forensic doctors apart because it required special skills and cognitive abilities that other medical practitioners, not to mention laypeople, lacked.[28] Professor V. A. Rozhanovskii, who in 1927 published the first

25. Ibid., 80. Dr. V. P. Nikol'skii also argued that forensic medicine needed to adopt a "prophylactic bent [*uklon*]" under Soviet power. However, his understanding of prophylaxis extended beyond crime and included the prevention of miscarriages of justice. "Nauchnye zasedaniia Obshchestva Meditsinskoi Ekspertizy g. Leningrada i gubernii," *Sudebno-meditsinskaia ekspertiza*, no. 6 (1927): 68–69.

26. Representatives of Soviet medicine called on doctors to be trained not only in the biological and natural sciences but also in the methods and techniques of the social sciences. Sally Ewing, "The Science and Politics of Soviet Insurance Medicine," in Solomon and Hutchinson, *Health and Society*, 69–70.

27. Leibovich, "Sudebno-meditsinskaia ekspertiza pri NEP'e," 37.

28. "O poriadke issledovaniia trupov i o novykh pravilakh vskrytiia trupov," in Leibovich, *Trudy II Vserossiiskogo s"ezda*, 259. Medical experts, however, resisted the equation of legal

extensive history of the tsarist and early Soviet forensic-medical systems, posited a sharp distinction between pathological anatomists and forensic doctors in their dealings with the dead body. "For the pathological anatomist," he wrote,

> the final goal of autopsy is to determine the cause of death; for the legal physician the final goal of autopsy is to . . . find changes and signs on the body that could establish the character of the crime and to pass judgment on the figure who has committed the crime. Therefore, everything that leads to this—including the study and qualification of injuries, the timing of their origin and the sequence of their occurrence, the determination of the instrument of the crime or the agents that caused the poisoning, the establishment of either murder or suicide, etc.—is inaccessible to the pathological anatomist.[29]

Rozhanovskii's description neatly captured the distinctive, if sometimes ambiguous, character of forensic expertise. Poised on the border between medicine and law, the forensic-medical expert read the body as both anatomist and criminologist.

Forensic doctors often communicated their unique specialization through the language of revelation and illumination. When experts performed an autopsy, they functioned as a kind of medium for the dead by opening up the hidden recesses of the body and exposing them to the rational mind of the scientist. Peeling away layers of tissue and noting the condition of the organism, they looked for certain telltale signs that were accessible only to their specially trained eyes.[30] In this way, the forensic doctor was said to uncover hidden realities and thus promote justice in Soviet society. According to the Leningrad medical expert Mikhail Ivanovich Raiskii, all cases of suspicious death, even those whose nature appeared unambiguous, required a complete examination of the body. Citing instances where a murder was made to look like suicide, for example, he argued, "Clarity and definitiveness are revealed only through autopsy."[31]

---

medicine with the autopsy, arguing that opening the corpse was only one, albeit crucial, element among a much broader set of concerns and practices. See Leibovich, "Sudebno-meditsinskaia ekspertiza pri NEP'e," 37.

29. Rozhanovskii, "Sudebno-meditsinskaia ekspertiza," 8.

30. The word in Russian for autopsy—*vskrytie*—is derived from the verb *vskryt'*, which means to reveal, disclose, or open something. For a discussion of its symbolism see Irina Paperno, *Suicide as a Cultural Institution in Dostoevsky's Russia* (Ithaca, 1997), 33–36.

31. M. Raiskii, "Poriadok sudebno-meditsinskogo issledovaniia trupa," in Leibovich, *Trudy II Vserossiiskogo s"ezda*, 125.

Consistent with this understanding of the discipline, the forensic-medical doctors' role in the Soviet medical and legal system was predicated on their distinctive ability to discover the truths hidden in the body. "With knife in hand at the dissection table," proclaimed A. V. Parabuchev in an article on suicides, "the pathological anatomist and legal doctor have attempted to solve the mystery of death."[32]

Such evocations of death as a mystery, a common trope in the literature on suicide, highlighted the interpretative function of the forensic-medical doctor as well as the illuminative power of scientific expertise. In particular, they made the discovery of normal physiological and psychological states dependent upon knowledge of the abnormal or pathological, a suggestion that continued the move toward making suicide a regular, if undesirable, feature of modern existence. Aleksandr Kriukov, for example, argued that scientists "could not close their eyes" to the problem of suicide, which he listed among the "dark sides of life." Indeed, those who possessed special knowledge had a "sacred obligation" to "clarify the causes of these severe abnormalities and indicate the means and the path toward the improvement [*ozdorovlenie*] of humankind."[33] In other words, the key to transforming and bettering the living was contained in the dead and deviant members of society, precisely those objects that fell within the sphere of forensic-medical activity.

Forensic medicine's interaction with the dark sides of life also justified the profession's turn to the social in the 1920s. Forensic experts drew a strong connection between empirical sociology, as an organized system of knowledge concerned with the social order, and the study of social deviance or pathology. For decades the dominant example of sociological research in Russia and Europe had been moral statistics (*moral'naia statistika*), which were devoted primarily to the measurement of social facts like abortion, crime, murder, and suicide. Consequently, forensic doctors believed they were uniquely positioned for investigating society. According to Golytsin, the forensic doctor's practice was akin to a photographic negative that mirrored the shadowy side of Soviet life. It reflected, he argued, "all the hereditary, social, economic, psychic, everyday, and other ailments [*nedugi*] of society."[34] Leibovich similarly spoke of forensic doctors studying "society in the kaleidoscope of negative phenomena."

32. A. V. Parabuchev, "Status thymicus u samoubiits kak morfologicheskii pokazatel' rasstroistva inkretornoi sistemy (avtoreferat)," in *Vtoroi s"ezd khirurgov Severo-kavkazskogo kraia. 12–15 ianvaria 1927 g.* (Rostov-on-Don, 1927), 263.

33. A. I. Kriukov, "K voprosu o prichinakh samoubiistva," *Nevrologiia i psikhiatriia. Trudy gosudarstvennogo meditsinskogo instituta v Moskve* 1, no. 1 (1923): 295.

34. Leibovich, *Trudy II Vserossiiskogo s"ezda*, 80.

They could therefore play "an enormous role in sociology" because they were the closest of all medical workers to the "arena of human society's saddest facts."[35]

Ultimately, then, the intellectual content and professional position of Soviet forensic medicine reflected its status as a border discipline, running along the normative boundaries of legality/illegality, normality/abnormality, and health/pathology. Moreover, the discipline was poised at the axis between the individual (the part) and society (the whole), a position that found expression in the intertwined images of the Soviet forensic doctor as both an anatomist interested in the particulars of the human body and a sociologist concerned with the larger body politic. This duality is particularly evident in terms of the rhetoric and practices surrounding suicide and its place within the discipline. Truth, it seems, was waiting to be found through the autopsy—literal as well as metaphorical—of the human and social organisms.

Surveying Suicide

The tensions in Soviet forensic medicine were hardly unique, and in many ways they echoed long-standing debates over the nature of knowledge and facts. With the rise of statistical thinking in the early nineteenth century, physicians in Europe and elsewhere split over the relative value of individual particularities and larger aggregates. Some practitioners held firm in their belief that scientific truth could be established only through the careful observation of particular signs. This Enlightenment-era outlook privileged physicians' encounters with their individual patients and made direct experience the basis of reality. By contrast, proponents of a statistical approach offered a different way of thinking about individuals. They looked to large numbers rather than minority facts in order to establish broad patterns of causation, with the cumulative effect being that individual actions lost their particular qualities and were seen to have implications for the rest of the nation.[36]

Soviet forensic medicine's shift toward the social was structured around this process of transposing individual objects into larger statistical truths

35. Leibovich, "Piat' let sudebnoi meditsiny," 775; and "Tesizy doklada D-ra Leibovicha," l. 12.

36. Joshua Cole, *The Power of Large Numbers: Population, Politics, and Gender in Nineteenth-Century France* (Ithaca, 2000); Alain Desrosières, *The Politics of Large Numbers: A History of Statistical Reasoning*, trans. Camille Naish (Cambridge, MA, 1998); and Theodore M. Porter, *The Rise of Statistical Thinking 1820–1900* (Princeton, 1986).

that spoke more directly to the interests of the state and the public. Most notably, beginning in mid-1920 the Department of Forensic Medicine organized the scientific (*nauchnyi*) study of suicide around the survey method, a highly popular and rather inexpensive means of information gathering during the 1920s.[37] For each suicide examined by a forensic-medical doctor (or by an attending physician in the localities, since there were few trained experts outside the major population centers), a specially formulated *anketa o samoubiistvakh* (questionnaire on suicides) was to be completed.[38] The ankety were then sent to Leibovich in Moscow, with copies going to the respective provincial medical departments, which would use them to compile quarterly summaries (*svodki*). Needless to say, this was a rather ambitious program even in the best of times. It was especially so in 1920 given the upheavals of the civil war, the embryonic nature of the forensic-medical apparatus, and the general preoccupation with more pressing public health threats such as infectious disease and famine. Indeed, Leibovich acknowledged that he did not receive all the ankety he expected and that many of the forms were completed either incorrectly or in a cursory fashion.[39] Nevertheless, he justifiably called the nationwide registration system of suicides in Russia a pioneering effort and believed that it would not only provide information about a variety of social problems but also shape the discipline by awakening the interest of forensic-medical experts in a wider range of scientific questions.[40]

The questionnaire on suicides facilitated a potentially broader vision of forensic medicine by forming a bridge between two different texts and the two types of knowledge that they represented—the narrative forensic-medical report (*protokol* or *akt*) and descriptive statistics. In fact, the desire of forensic doctors to preserve the particular amid the aggregate informed their early debates about the statistical tabulation of

37. Mark Adams notes that the survey method was a relatively low-cost way to gather data and conduct research amid the difficult economic conditions of the early Soviet period. See "Eugenics in Russia 1900–1940," in *The Wellborn Science: Eugenics in Germany, France, Brazil, and Russia,* ed. Mark B. Adams (Oxford, 1990), 168. On the history of the social survey see, Martin Bulmer, Kevin Bales, and Kathryn Kish Sklar, eds., *The Social Survey in Historical Perspective* (Cambridge, 1991).

38. This arrangement obviously privileged the counting of *completed* suicides. Ankety were also filled out by the local investigating authorities (police, criminal investigators, etc.) and by mental hospital personnel, with the goal of including attempted suicides in the overall count.

39. Leibovich therefore supplemented the ankety with data from statistical cards that registered the general activities in the sphere of forensic medicine (which included the number of bodies autopsied and their manner of death).

40. Leibovich, "Piat' let sudebnoi meditsiny," 777.

practitioners' everyday activities. Among his many projects, Leibovich pushed throughout the 1920s for improved accounting (*otchetnost'*) in the Department of Forensic-Medical Expertise, which would provide a clearer picture of the discipline to those within Narkomzdrav who were responsible for allocating resources to its various branches. Some forensic doctors were wary of this effort, expressing the concern that by counting the number of autopsies, examinations, and chemical tests performed, they would obscure what made each intervention distinctive. A special commission at the First Congress of State Medical Experts in 1920 therefore argued for preserving the traditional forensic-medical report along with the introduction of registration cards, contending that the former represented the "individual particularities" (*individual'nye osobennosti*) of the given case and could not be replaced by a generic form that stressed standardization and uniformity.[41] Being the product of the interaction between forensic-medical examiners and their objects, the narrative report was valued as much for capturing the exercise of scientific expertise as it was for describing the details of an individual case. It therefore remained an essential feature of forensic-medical practice alongside the move toward quantification.

A statistical picture of Soviet suicide gradually emerged out of the information gathered through the questionnaire, thereby fulfilling the hopes of prerevolutionary physicians for a national accounting of the people's self-destructive tendencies. Between 1920 and 1929, forensic doctors compiled a series of quantitative studies that covered the Russian Republic, including a specialized investigation into self-poisoning and regional examinations of Leningrad, Tomsk, and Kazan.[42] By far the most prolific writer was the chief forensic-medical expert himself, who produced a number of publications and scholarly papers on the subject throughout the decade.[43] Leibovich's prominence in this particular area of research

---

41. GARF, f. 482, op. 1, d. 217, ll. 8–9. The commission called for the registration cards themselves to contain space for information about the deceased individual, the relevant elements of the case, the objective data found during autopsy, and the conclusion of the medical expert.

42. I. Ia. Bychkov and S. Ia. Rachkovskii, "Samoubiistva v RSFSR posredstvom otravleniia za 1920–1924 gg," in Leibovich, *Trudy II Vserossiiskogo s"ezda*, 222–38; P. A. Maskin, "Samoubiistva v Leningrade s 1922 g. po 1925 god (Avtoreferat)," *Sudebno-meditsinskaia ekspertiza*, no. 6 (1927): 71–75; A. A. Vongrodskii, "Samoubiistvo v Tomske po anketnym dannym," *Trudy pervogo s"ezda vrachei Sibiri. Tomsk, 23–27 aprelia 1926 goda* (Tomsk, 1927), 291; and O. I. Korchazhinskaia, *Samoubiistva v Kazani v 1921 godu* (Kazan, 1922).

43. Many of Leibovich's works, however, were little more than reformulations and redactions of his two most complete studies: Ia. Leibovich, *1000 sovremennykh samoubiistv. (Sotsiologicheskii ocherk)* (Moscow, 1923); and "Sovremennye samoubiistva v Sovetskoi Rossii," GARF,

is further evidence of his pivotal role in organizing the entire research program. Since he was the primary spokesman and lobbyist for forensic medicine within the People's Commissariat of Public Health, his promotion of the anketa method was an important part of his efforts to situate the discipline within the larger framework of Soviet social medicine.[44] V. A. Rozhanovskii, for one, included the "detailed registration and analysis by medical personnel of all cases of suicide" among the forensic-medical activities that aimed to "resolve questions that have great social significance."[45]

Quantification shifted focus from the individual to the body politic. Unlike the forensic doctors who prioritized narratives that captured the careful, firsthand observation of particular signs through autopsy, the sociologically inclined experts opted for the broader truths revealed through statistical aggregates. Large numbers were their primary means for representing what was otherwise an abstract, even imaginary phenomenon—society. Leibovich hinted at the invented nature of the social order when he employed the analogy of the paleontologist to describe the sociologist's work on suicide. Both extrapolated from the part to get a sense of the whole. He wrote, "In the same way that the paleontologist can reproduce in his imagination an entire antediluvian animal on the basis of a single part of a skeleton, for example, a femur, or that a chemist on the basis of just a single structural formula can determine a range of properties for a substance that he has never seen in his life, so too the sociologist, on the basis of a single group of phenomena or one link in the chain of social facts, is often capable of providing the characterization of the given society. This is why suicide interests us."[46] Statistics, in other words, proved the social nature of suicide and, in turn, confirmed the existence of society as a distinct entity that could be diagnosed and administered. They also allowed the metaphor of autopsy to be transferred to the social body, but as Irina Paperno notes, the statistical exploration into society was more akin to vivisection—cutting

---

f. 482, op. 1, d. 596, ll. 211–21. His other publications include Ia. Leibovich, "K kharakteristike sovremennykh samoubiistv v Sovetskoi Rossii," *Ezhenedel'nik sovetskoi iustitsii*, April 12, 1923, 315–17; "Zhenskie samoubiistva," *Rabochii sud*, nos. 8 and 9 (April and May 1926): 551–59, 623–32; "Sovremennye samoubiistva v Sovetskoi Rossii," in Kosorotov, *Uchebnik sudebnoi meditsiny*, 295–307; and the contribution to "O samoubiistve. Nasha anketa," *Vecherniaia Moskva*, January 7, 1926, 2.

44. The archival record confirms this impression of Leibovich's role. See, for example, letter of April 26, 1920, from Leibovich to the provincial subdepartments of Medical Expertise, GARF, f. 482, op. 1, d. 208, ll. 38–39.

45. Rozhanovskii, "Sudebno-meditsinskaia ekspertiza," 103.

46. Leibovich, *1000 sovremennykh samoubiistv*, 3.

open a living organism to see how it works and to establish its normal and pathological states.[47]

The statistical dissection of Soviet society also resembled an autopsy in the sense of being an act of visualization. At the same time that it provided a picture of the social order, it also allowed the forensic-medical doctors to envisage a role for themselves in caring for the population. In particular, forensic-medical experts would use the numbers to map out the sources of deviance with the eventual goal of their elimination. Statistics in this way created a link between the individual objects of forensic-medical practice and the preventative goals of Soviet social medicine. Speaking to his colleagues in 1929, Dr. Ia. N. Iavorskii argued that experts who studied alcoholism and other everyday factors in the etiology of suicide placed the "accent on prophylaxis" and "elevated their significance as prophylacticians and social workers."[48] Leibovich similarly used his statistical analyses to warn readers of some potentially menacing trends. In particular, he raised the specter of an increase in suicides among young people unless something was done to improve their lot during the New Economic Policy. Evoking memories of the post-1905 suicide epidemics, he cited a number of developments that portended a similar experience at the present time: rising social dislocation, the growing oppression of family and school discipline, and the general problem of youth homelessness. "The first ominous signs," wrote Leibovich, "are already visible!"[49]

Statistics also offered a powerful means to overcome the individuality of suicide. Iakov Leibovich claimed that the persistent interest in suicide stemmed from that fact that seemingly random acts displayed a certain unity when placed together in the aggregate.[50] He and other authors routinely cited European scholars like Enrico Morselli and Émile Durkheim, who emphasized the lawlike nature of self-destruction and established a variety of correlations between rates of suicide and such factors as sex, age, marital status, and time of the year. In particular, fluctuating rates of suicide during the turbulent period 1914–21 were regarded as empirical evidence that the true sources of suicide existed outside the individual. Forensic-medical experts repeatedly cited the apparent decline in suicides beginning with the onset of the First World War and the subsequent rise following the end of the civil war. For them, this was direct confirmation

47. Paperno, *Suicide as a Cultural Institution*, 33–36.

48. "Nauchnoe soveshchanie pri kafedre sudebnoi meditsiny leningradskogo instituta dlia sovershenstvovaniia vrachei," *Sudebno-meditsinskaia ekspertiza*, no. 14 (1930): 157.

49. Leibovich, *1000 sovremennykh samoubiistv*, 8.

50. Ibid., 3.

of Durkheim's theory that suicide rates fall during periods of deep social crisis as personal interests are displaced by collective feelings, resulting in greater levels of social cohesion and fewer suicides. Dr. N. I. Izhevskii, for instance, explained that the rise of suicides in Leningrad province during the early 1920s was not simply the result of population growth; rather, it fit the general pattern for suicides to increase "with the calming of the country following major wars and following great political revolutions."[51] Moreover, the medical experts I. Ia. Bychkov and S. Ia. Rachkovskii, who carried out a study of self-poisoning in Russia, claimed that the decline in suicides during war and revolution undermined anthropological theories that "the causes of suicide are inside us, in our individual particularities, and that there exist special suicidal types [*osobye typy samoubiits*]."[52]

Nevertheless, the statistical narrative of suicide ultimately relied on particular facts. The forensic doctors' primary tool for gathering information about suicide—the anketa o samoubiistvakh—was a one page, single-sided printed sheet that contained eighteen questions and a brief space for remarks. Its formulation reveals the assumptions behind the survey as well as the larger goals set for the project.[53] Clearly, the creators of the anketa recognized the individual as a social being and sought information about the suicide's birthplace, place of residence, education, profession, nationality, religion, material condition, military service, political activity, and family status. It also cataloged the life according to several key markers in the development of the Soviet project, noting for example the person's occupation before and after 1917.[54] This biographical information provided context for data gathered about health and physiology, which

51. N. I. Izhevskii, "Osnovy organizatsii otdeleniia sudebno-meditsinskoi i trudovoi ekspertizy Leningradgubzdravotdela i statisticheskii otchet za poslednie piat' let," *Sudebno-meditsinskaia ekspertiza*, no. 1 (1925): 104. For similar interpretations of the forensic-medical data see Leibovich, *1000 sovremennykh samoubiistv*, 4–5; Leibovich, "Sovremennye samoubiistva v Sovetskoi Rossii," 295–96; V. A. Giliarovskii, "K psikhopatologii detskikh samoubiistv," in *Psikhopatologiia i psikhoprofilaktika detskogo vozrasta. Sbornik rabot sotrudnikov Detskogo otdeleniia Donskoi nervno-psikhiatricheskoi lechebnitsy—psikhiatricheskoi kliniki 2 MGU*, ed. V. A. Giliarovskii (Moscow, 1929), 66; and N. Semashko, "Ugrozhaet li nam epidemiia samoubiistva?" *Izvestiia TsIK Sovetov*, January 22, 1926, 5.

52. Bychkov and Rachkovskii, "Samoubiistva v RSFSR," 234–35.

53. Mikhail Nikolaevich Gernet, whose Department of Moral Statistics in the Central Statistical Administration produced its own questionnaire on suicides in 1922, described the forensic-medical ankety as an attempt to collect data of both a sociological and a medical character. *Samoubiistva v SSSR 1922–1925* (Moscow, 1927), 9.

54. This was a broader and distinctive feature of Soviet questionnaires. See Peter Holquist, "State Violence as Technique: The Logic of Violence in Soviet Totalitarianism," in *Landscaping the Human Garden: Twentieth-Century Population Management in a Comparative Framework*, ed. Amir Weiner (Stanford, 2003), 35.

reflected the investigators' equal interest in the individual as a biological being shaped by his or her past and family. In addition to questions about age and sex, the anketa contained entries about the suicide's heredity and previous illnesses and asked the compiler to indicate the presence of mental illness, alcoholism, syphilis, degeneration (*vyrozhdenie*), and menstruation. Specifics regarding the character (*kharakter*) of the suicide were also sought, including recent behavioral changes that attracted the attention of others, and there was even a line to note the right- or left-handedness of the individual. Of course, the survey form also provided space for information about the event itself—when and where the suicide had occurred, the condition in which the suicide was found (dress, location, etc.), the content of any suicide note, and the means as well as cause and motive. Finally, the survey concluded with several blank lines for entering the most pertinent pathological-anatomical data from the autopsy or medical examination.

In many respects, the questionnaire was a form of anamnesis, capturing the suicide's history as related by witnesses, friends and family, the criminal investigator, and the forensic examiner. Like the standard case history, each anketa involved an attempt on the part of the physician to impose order onto the patient's story so as to give it meaning within the framework of medical knowledge. However, this was a fragmented narrative, broken down according to the needs of quantification and reflecting ideas about the essential elements that composed a suicide as well as a Soviet individual. The anketa therefore captured the suicide with the intent of overcoming the limitations of its individuating circumstances. It was by means of the questionnaire that forensic-medical doctors prepared a suicide to become one with the statistical aggregate, an empirical medical and social fact that, in combination with others like it, could be used to explore the character of life and death in their world. The whole was in this manner constructed out of its individual parts.

The anketa o samoubiistvakh nevertheless retained a dialogic quality that belied the doctors' intent to impose a particular reading on the event. In the responses to the questions we see glimmers of the ways that the different actors—friends, families, attending physicians, etc.—viewed the suicide and contributed to the scientific narrative. Among the most notable qualities of extant questionnaires from the provinces of Tula and Iaroslavl', for example, is the lack of standardized nomenclature as well as inconsistencies in the amount and type of information they provide. Some respondents were rather laconic, entering just a few words per entry, while others went well beyond the allotted space in writing up their answers. The summary reports from Tula oblast in 1925 give a wide variety of responses to the question regarding the suicide's character and any noticeable changes in behavior before the act. They range from medicalized terms like "neurasthenia" and "inbecillitas" to commonplace descriptors such as "nervous," "melancholic," "short-tempered," "depressed," and "reserved." In addition, the responses vary according to gender, with women and girls more frequently labeled as excitable, impressionable, and changeable.[55] Great variation is also evident in the attributions of cause or motive. More generic categories include "mental illness," "family discord," "nervous-mental exhaustion," and the ubiquitous "dissatisfaction with life." Alongside these, however, are responses that summarize or retell the specifics of the case, sometimes in the form of a short narrative. One anketa lists the cause of a young man's suicide as "a dispute with the mother, who refused to allow his fiancé into the home due to her bad reputation." The anketa filled out for an eighteen-year-old female tells of the husband's discovery of her infidelity and his declaration of divorce, after which the young woman poisoned herself. Finally, the cause provided for a male also eighteen years of age recounts the tragic story of his suicide on the eve of marriage, tormented as he was by his incontinence.[56]

Such particularities receded during the process of constructing social types and transcribing the individual narratives into official categories. Bychkov and Rachkovskii, for example, blended the individual cases from the ankety to conclude that two distinct groups of self-poisoners existed in Soviet Russia: (1) those who grabbed whatever poison was available without concern about its potency, mostly workers, peasants, artisans, domestics, and young medical personnel; and (2) the better-educated (white-collar workers, doctors, lawyers, and other professionals, and students), who took more time preparing their deaths and selected more lethal chemical agents.[57] Leibovich, who believed that "every country has a certain propensity for suicide in a given historical epoch," devoted most of his accounts to analyzing the patterns found in the numbers, claiming in particular that the indicators of sex, age, and method revealed changing social conditions in Soviet Russia. As we shall see in the next chapter, his most notable discovery was the fact that women were killing themselves with much greater frequency after 1917, a shift that he attributed to their newly emancipated status in postrevolutionary society.[58]

55. GATO, f. 451, op. 1, d. 1791 and d. 2184, passim.
56. GATO, f. 451, op. 1, d. 1791, ll. 30, 110ob–11, 112ob–13.
57. Bychkov and Rachkovskii, "Samoubiistva v RSFSR," 232.
58. Leibovich, *1000 sovremennykh samoubiistv,* 4.

Rather tellingly, the voices of the suicides appeared only when investigators addressed the psychology or motives of self-destruction, which were realms that statisticians had difficulty accessing through numbers. In discussing the overall significance of mental illness, Leibovich noted that one frequently encountered indications of the suicide's nervous or depressed state, or a "special pensiveness" that attracted attention, clearly a determination that drew upon the information provided by witnesses. Motive, however, was often established on the basis of the explanation provided by the suicides in their notes. Leibovich recognized the researcher's dependence on this evidence and included brief illustrations for his readers. Some letters, he remarked, were simply a short statement, such as "I ask that no one be blamed for my death." Others expressed rage and frustration or were more philosophically inclined, including the individual who wrote, "The happy live. The weak perish. I submit to this merciless law."[59] In a similar fashion, Bychkov and Rachkovskii offered their readers fragments of suicide notes as illustrative of the thinking behind different types of self-poisoning. Thus, the words of "Suicide B," who described his desire to "die beautifully," were used to convey the deliberate planning and careful selection of poison that characterized the suicides of many Soviet white-collar workers and free professionals.[60] However, when inscribed into the standard nomenclature of causation—material need, physical suffering, troubles and insults, unhappy love, and so forth—the personalized features of these suicide notes and the responses described above disappeared. Concerned primarily with the aggregate picture, the sociological essays were mostly devoid of the individual details that were captured in the anketa.[61]

Still, there is some evidence that the generalizations produced on the basis of the anketa had a reverse effect and pointed investigators back to individuals and their bodies. In 1928, the medical expert D. I. Ziskind stated that his interest in the degenerate skulls of suicides was sparked by patterns he observed in the data collected through questionnaires from the Kursk region. Specifically, he was struck by both the insignificance (*nichtozhnost'*) of most motives and the unevenness of the suicides' character (they were generally explosive, withdrawn, sullen, etc.). Notably, Ziskind cited a list of original motives (theft of a hat, fear of imaginary

59. *Ibid.*, 14–15.

60. Bychkov and Rachkovskii, "Samoubiistva v RSFSR," 230–31.

61. At least one text based on the ankety preserved the individual by appending excerpts from suicide notes after the body of descriptive statistics. See Korchazhinskaia, *Samoubiistva v kazani*, 15–18.

arrest, fight with husband, etc.) *before* their transcription into general statistical categories; the latter, in his opinion, gave the motives a degree of
solidity that they lacked in reality. While Ziskind referred to suicide as a
"social phenomenon," his observations regarding the shared characteristics among suicides led him to hypothesize that answers to the mystery of
self-destruction must be contained within the human body. He therefore
moved from the whole to the part via the anketa and the individual story
captured within.[62]

SEEING THE SUICIDE INSIDE

Given the Soviet state's interest in establishing the cause and manner of
death among its citizens, the story of the suicide was also transcribed in
another type of narrative—the forensic-medical protocol or report. Here
the forensic doctor recounted the ritual of examining the body, first describing its exterior and then searching inside its cavities, according to a
set of prescribed rules and procedures. As V. A. Rozhanovskii noted in
his depiction of forensic doctors, the postmortem examination played
a significant role in the legal process by confirming or establishing the
fact of a suicide. Extant autopsy reports from Iaroslavl' Province show that
forensic-medical experts routinely provided a scientifically based conclusion (*zakliuchenie*) or opinion (*mnenie*) about the cause and manner of
death in the last section of their protocols. For example, they described
the indications of strangulation, summarized the characteristics of gunshots and other wounds, noted the smell of alcohol or other chemicals
inside the body, and provided the results from toxicology tests performed
on the tissues. They also remarked on the presence or absence of signs of
violence on the body.[63] Such determinations were critical for identifying
the existence of a crime and necessary for the interment of the corpse.

---

62. D. I. Ziskind, "Degeneratsiia cherepa kak faktor, pomogaiushchii stavit' differentsial'nyi
diagnoz mezhdu ubiistvom and samoubiistvom," *Sudebno-meditsinskaia ekspertiza*, no. 14
(1930): 48. Ziskind's move suggests some fluidity within the model of knowledge put forth
by Irina Paperno, who contends that performance of the autopsy involves moving from the
whole to the part, as the body is dissected and broken up into its constituent elements. By
contrast, statistics involves the creation of the whole—the social organism—out of its individual parts. See *Suicide as a Cultural Phenomenon*, 36.

63. GAIaO, f. 844, op. 1, d. 39, ll. 85–88, 117–117ob.; and f. 844, op. 1, d. 19, ll. 71–72.
The telltale signs of suicide were debated and outlined in journal articles, at professional conferences, and in forensic-medical textbooks. See, for example, Ia. L. Leibovich, *Prakticheskoe
rukovodstvo po sudebnoi meditsine* (Moscow, 1922), 101–3; A. P. Vladimirskii, "K voprosu o raspoz-
navanii ubiistva ili samoubiistva pri ognestrel'nykh povrezhdeniiakh," *Sudebno-meditsinskaia*

State regulations, for example, included suicide among the suspicious or violent deaths that demanded a forensic-medical examination before burial could take place.[64]

One of the curious facts that emerge from reading the extant ankety is the rather large number of suicides that were never autopsied (usually because the examiners deemed the external signs and available evidence sufficient to establish cause of death). When an autopsy was conducted, the investigator included only the primary facts describing the cause of death. For example, in cases of hanging, they noted the place and size of strangulation marks, cyanosis of lips and face, and the condition of the tongue. Similarly, the questionnaires for suicides from self-inflicted gunshots noted such details as the sites of entry and exit wounds, the size and shape of the wounds, and the damage done internally to the various organs and skeletal structure. This kind of information was fully consistent with the medical examiner's responsibility to render an objectively determined "differential diagnosis" about the cause and manner of death. However, it suggests a disconnect between the more practically minded experts, who were primarily concerned with carrying out their prescribed legal responsibilities, and the more theoretically inclined members of the discipline, who looked to the body for deeper answers about the nature of suicide.

In the 1920s a small but influential group of forensic-medical experts promoted a more expansive role for the autopsy within the realm of scientific work on suicide. Based primarily in university institutes of forensic medicine, these academic physicians believed that the human body was the primary venue through which a more profound understanding of suicide—and deviance more generally—could be obtained. Specifically, they argued that anatomical particularities were vital to explaining the individuality of self-destruction, or why only certain people in society opted to lay hands on themselves. In 1929, for example, the forensic doctor V. P. Gavrilovskii contended, "It is impossible to explain satisfactorily by the social factor of suicide why between two people who are of the same age, sex, and nationality, who are living in the same climate and under identical conditions, and who are physically healthy and equal under all visible circumstances, one commits suicide, while for the other the very idea of suicide is offensive and completely out of character." According to Gavrilovskii, the answer to this riddle rested within the human organism.

---

ekspertiza, no. 7 (1928): 40–41; and S. N. Matveev, "Ubiistvo ili samoubiistvo?" *Arkhiv kriminologii i sudebnoi meditsiny* 1, nos. 2–3 (1927): 781–88.

64. Raiskii, "Poriadok sudebno-meditsinskogo issledovaniia trupa," 124.

"The researcher," he continued, "is sometimes forced to search for the cause of suicide not outside the person, but inside of him, in the tissues and organs of his body, in the biological functions of his body."[65]

The search for the biological key to suicide predated the Bolshevik Revolution and built on mechanistic understandings of human psychology. Legal physicians in Europe and Russia privileged the concreteness of the body in order to understand self-destructive behavior. Both Ivan Ivanovich Neiding and Petr Andreevich Minakov, who were on the faculty at Moscow University, explored the relationship between the mental state of suicides and the anatomical changes they found during multiple forensic-medical autopsies.[66] Most notably, Ivan Gvozdev, professor of forensic medicine at Kazan University, published an extensive work in 1889 based on twenty years of clinical observations. Gvozdev was convinced that suicidal tendencies, like mental illness, had a physical basis, and he devoted himself to its discovery through autopsy. However, while he found that the dura mater (the outermost membrane surrounding the brain) often adhered to the skull of suicides, he was unable to establish a precise causal link between this anatomical condition and suicidal tendencies. Gvozdev and others nonetheless remained unshaken in their belief that the secret to understanding suicide existed somewhere beneath the surface and that its discovery was only a matter of time and improved technology.[67]

Soviet forensic doctors, led by Aleksandr Ivanovich Kriukov, continued the emphasis on the body's concrete materiality, focusing their work on the brain and cranium of self-destructive individuals. Director of Moscow University's Department of Forensic Medicine, Kriukov claimed that over the course of his career he regularly observed signs of degeneration in the bodies of suicides, which in his mind were clear evidence of an improper correspondence between brain size and cranial capacity. Among the indicators were the swelling of the brain, sharp crests and unevenness at the interior base of the skull, the premature adhesion of the cranial sutures, severe tension in the dura mater, and greater brain mass than that of non-suicides of similar age, sex, and intellect. These morphological changes all suggested that the brain of the suicide was compressed from a lack of sufficient space. As a consequence, argued Kriukov and his supporters,

---

65. V. P. Gavrilovskii, "K voprosu ob anatomicheskikh izmeneniiakh na trupakh samou-biits," *Sudebno-meditsinskaia ekspertiza*, no. 11 (1929): 59.

66. P. Minakov, *Ivan Ivanovich Neiding (nekrolog)* (Moscow, 1905), 3–4.

67. Paperno, *Suicide as a Cultural Institution*, 88–90. A similar refusal to accept the invisibility of physical signs characterized the American scientific community. See Howard I. Kushner, *American Suicide: A Psychocultural Exploration* (New Brunswick, 1991), 49.

the normal circulation and nourishment of the brain was disrupted, leading not only to the starvation of brain cells but also to their pollution from the buildup of cellular waste products. This in turn produced a broad set of symptoms that included headaches, vision problems, fits, and cognitive impairment.[68]

A second line of research engaged developments in the emergent fields of constitutional disorders and endocrinology, both of which achieved wide popularity during the 1920s as potentially revolutionary methods for uncovering the sources of human identity.[69] Forensic-medical experts paid particular attention to the thymus gland, the exact function of which was the source of much conjecture at the time. A. V. Parabuchev, for example, found that the thymus gland in suicides did not shrink and disappear with the onset of puberty, indicating the hyperfunctioning of the thymus and the improper functioning of the gonads. He linked these changes to the constitutional disorder known as status thymicolymphaticus, a highly contested and ambiguous cluster of symptoms that European scientists had associated with sudden death, particularly among infants, since its discovery in 1889.[70] Some Soviet physicians thought the condition to be the direct cause, or culprit (*vinovnitsa*) of suicide.[71] Others, however, suggested that status thymicus was only an indirect factor and linked it to the morphological changes observed by Kriukov in the head of the suicide. Whatever the causal interpretation, the dysfunction of the endocrine system was understood as a constitutional anomaly that weakened individuals and predisposed them to illness.[72]

The body, in other words, was deemed the seat of the suicidal personality, a complex amalgam of experiences, physical states, and behavioral characteristics that produced an imbalanced individual who could no longer contain "the psychopathic tendencies slumbering within."[73] Forensic-medical experts framed suicide in terms of physiological impairment, hypothesizing the suppression of the otherwise natural instinct for

---

68. A. I. Kriukov, "O degeneratsii cherepa u samoubiits," *Sudebno-meditsinskaia ekspertiza,* no. 1 (1925): 18–24; and Kriukov, "O degeneratsii cherepa," *Arkhiv kriminologii i sudebnoi meditsiny* 1, nos. 2–3 (1927): 705–14.

69. Bernstein, *Dictatorship of Sex,* chap. 2; and Eric Naiman, *Sex in Public: The Incarnation of Early Soviet Ideology* (Princeton, 1997), 143–47.

70. Ann Dally, "Status Lymphaticus: Sudden Death in Children from 'Visitation of God' to Cot Death," *Medical History* 41 (January 1997): 70–85.

71. Parabuchev, "Status thymicus u samoubiits," 263–67.

72. T. A. Sharbe, "Sudebnyi medik i Status Thymico-Lymphaticus," *Sudebno-meditsinskaia ekspertiza,* no. 7 (1928): 68–72; and Leibovich, *Prakticheskoe rukovodstvo,* 100.

73. G. S. Belen'kii and E. V. Eremeeva, "O sotsial'no-bytovykh motivakh samoubiistva zhenshchin," *Leningradskii meditsinskii zhurnal,* no. 4 (April 1928): 3.

life and emphasizing the perturbations associated with certain developmental periods, notably puberty and old age, and with the sexual life of women, notably during their menses, pregnancy, and postpartum condition (hence question thirteen of the anketa asked about menstruation, signs of degeneration, and previous illnesses). Although suicides were assigned a range of contradictory character traits (some were described as reserved, solitary, and morose, still others as sociable, hot-tempered, and high-strung), what they all shared was a high degree of emotional and psychological instability that prevented them from properly filtering their experiences and checking their reactions to events in daily life. This did not mean that they were seen as suffering from an organic mental illness. The psychiatrist Vasilii Alekseevich Giliarovskii, for example, wrote that suicide could result from a "temporary disturbance of mental balance" brought on by "severe shocks" in people suffering from nervous exhaustion and physical debility.[74] Still, the psychopathologist Nikolai Pavlovich Brukhanskii, who conducted a detailed study of some 350 suicides in Moscow, concluded that he could not find a single example of an "average, sufficiently stable, and healthy individual." "All suicides," he summarized in his major work *Suicides* (1927), "are psychopathic personalities or are acting in a psychotic state."[75]

The elements deemed significant in the makeup of the suicidal personality are visible in the case of "Anna S," whose story was published by N. V. Popov and O. V. Krasovskaia in *The Russian Eugenics Journal* (1925). Their report tellingly began at the corporal level, which provided the material foundations for explaining the young woman's life and death. An autopsy reportedly uncovered multiple signs of a constitutional predisposition to suicide as outlined by Aleksandr Kriukov and the Viennese physician Julius Bartel, including the telltale indications of brain compression and the atrophying of the ovaries and other glands. These anatomical data were then followed by a lengthy description of the suicide's personality. Popov and Krasovskaia covered her childhood, her relationships with husband and friends, her physical health and sexual life, and her general demeanor. In particular, they highlighted examples and possible causes of destabilization: mood swings, bouts of fainting and hysteria, earlier threats of suicide, menstrual problems, and an abortion that had ended the deceased's only pregnancy. Ultimately, Popov and Krasovskaia concluded that Anna S. was both victim and manifestation of her family's progressive degeneration, a pattern that fit Bénédict-Augustin Morel's

74. "O samoubiistve. Nasha anketa," *Vecherniaia moskva*, January 7, 1926, 2.
75. N. P. Brukhanskii, *Samoubiitsy* (Leningrad, 1927), 23, 32.

vision of generational decline. Their partial reconstruction of the family's genealogy found the presence of alcoholism, psychopathy, and cycloidal and schizoid personality traits, all of which had shaped the constitution of Anna S. and predisposed her toward self-destructive behavior. The general lesson taken from the case history reinforced Popov and Krasovskaia's eugenics message: everyone needed to thoroughly investigate the health and heredity of his or her potential spouse before entering into marriage.[76] Otherwise, the past would continue to haunt society in the form of individuals who were mentally and physically maladapted to the existing environment.

The challenge facing the scientific community was how to access and "shed light on the still dark personality of the suicide."[77] In his study *Suicides*, for example, Nikolai Brukhanskii proposed a biosocial model of individual development that emphasized the dynamic relationship between the body and its surroundings. "Suicide," he wrote, "is the changing dialectic of life, of the personality. For us as natural scientists, there are no distinctions between biological and social factors in the same way that there are no distinctions between material and spiritual phenomena." This line of reasoning won official praise from the chief physician, Nikolai Semashko, who lauded Brukhanskii as a dialectical materialist. It also framed Brukhanskii's calls for a multidisciplinary approach that would overcome the false divisions between the anthropological, sociological, and psychiatric schools. In conceptualizing the formation of the suicide, he argued for the presence of a strong biological component—a so-called physical preparedness (*fizicheskaia gotovnost'*)—that made the individual vulnerable to external shocks. The environmental "irritant" that sparked the "affective tendencies" toward self-destruction, Brukhanskii concluded, "has an effect only where there exists *suitable ground in the psychophysical organization* of the individual."[78]

The reference to the preparatory ground or soil (*pochva*), a common metaphor in Russian and Soviet discourse on suicide that emphasized depth or rootedness, helps us to better comprehend the forensic doctors'

76. N.V. Popov and O. V. Krasovskaia, "Sluchai samoubiistva v degenerativnoi sem'e," *Russkii evgenicheskii zhurnal* 3, no. 1 (1925): 67–71. A contemporary study of female suicides in Leningrad also drew a strong connection between women's hereditary "neuro-psychopathic constitutions" and unfavorable conditions in their everyday life. See Belen'kii and Eremeeva, "O sotsial'no-bytovykh motivakh," 3–15.

77. Ia. I. Stal'nov, "Puti bio-khimicheskogo analiza lichnosti samoubiitsy," *Sudebno-meditsinskaia ekpsertiza*, no. 5 (1927): 11.

78. Brukhanskii, *Samoubiitsy*, 6, 14–5, 31–32 (emphasis in the original).

interest in the body.[79] Even though Brukhanskii lumped them together with the anthropological school and its deterministic theories of race and heredity, Kriukov and others recognized the complexity of suicide and called for a multidisciplinary approach to the suicidal personality. Moreover, their work did not necessarily contradict the theories of Durkheim that shaped the investigations of the sociologically inclined forensic doctors. Durkheim, after all, had acknowledged that the psychopathic states associated with degeneration could make individuals more apt to contemplate an ending to their lives.[80] Nevertheless, supporters of the somatic approach were at odds with other researchers in terms of their vision of causation. Whereas Durkheim believed that degeneration itself could not be considered a *cause* of suicide, limiting it solely to a potentiality, Kriukov and his followers made the body—and not the social milieu—the defining element in the causational chain that set off the suicidal drama. Most notably, they framed the primacy of biology over the environment in terms of the theoretical distinction between cause and motive or reason. For them cause was something deep and essential; it suggested a predisposition to certain forms of behavior that was embedded in the material reality of body. Motive, by contrast, was considered a much more fleeting and superficial factor in shaping human action. This distinction allowed forensic doctors to claim that their work on the body aimed to reveal the underlying causes of suicide while preserving a dynamic understanding of self-destruction. Kriukov, for example, contended that "the root cause of suicides lies in the physical organization of the subject, who for the time being copes with the conditions of life, but in whom can just as easily arise such perturbations in the psyche that he becomes capable of an awful deed like taking his own life or the life of others (like him). However, external causes sometimes, though not always, can play merely the role of a spark or a stimulus."[81]

Consequently, the forensic doctors offered a mechanistic understanding of human behavior that made anatomical changes both sign and source of the suicidal personality. These alterations were purported to cause the disequilibrium, most notably in the nervous system, that made the individual unstable, impulsive, and prone to overreaction. D. I. Ziskind explained, "The pathological significance of this degeneration [of the skull] finds

79. On the metaphorical as well as literal uses of "soil" in Russian discourse, see Paperno, *Suicide as a Cultural Institution*, 87–88.

80. Émile Durkheim, *Suicide: A Study in Sociology*, trans. John A. Spaulding and George Simpson (New York, 1951), 81.

81. Kriukov, "K voprosu o prichinakh samoubiistva," 295. In the same article, Kriukov also stated that in a majority of cases the "main and root cause is in the brain."

expression in the great sensitivity of such people to all kinds of harmful influences and emotional tribulations."[82] Kriukov referenced Ivan Pavlov's "reflex of purpose" and the wider instinct of self-preservation to suggest that the disruption of such a "delicate machine as the human brain" could increase the likelihood of the individual's losing interest in life.[83] In addition, those working on the body's internal secretions connected their dysfunction to highly affective behavior and a general deficiency in the larger struggle for existence. The forensic doctor Iakov Ivanovich Stal'nov, for example, regarded the emotional swings and asocial tendencies associated with cycloid and schizoid personalities as the product of physiological disruption: "The contemporary scientific researcher, while delving analytically into the mechanically ruined system of the suicide's organism, is obligated to devote significant attention to the constitution of the organism and its biochemical components, with the goal toward finding the correlation between them and the mental symptom-complexes that suppress the powerful force of the instinct for self-preservation."[84]

While placing the forensic-medical experts in the mainstream of Soviet thought about human psychology for much of the 1920s, mechanistic understandings of suicide had serious implications for thinking about the individual and volition.[85] In particular, making self-destructive tendencies into a reactive disorder seemingly removed agency and responsibility from the suicide, who acted under the temporary affect caused by a mental "short circuit" (*korotkoe zamykanie*).[86] Kriukov himself recognized the possible repercussions of his work in dealing with criminals, suicides, and other deviants. In an article on the causes of suicide, he alluded to the possibility that all people were potential suicides depending on the

82. Ziskind, "Degeneratsiia cherepa," 49.

83. Kriukov, "O degeneratsii cherepa u samoubiits," 18–19, 24.

84. Stal'nov, "Puti bio-khimicheskogo analiza," 7–8.

85. On the dominance of objective psychology, particularly in the scientific-medical community, until the later part of the decade, see Raymond A. Bauer, *The New Man in Soviet Psychology* (Cambridge, MA, 1952), chap. 5; David Joravsky, *Russian Psychology: A Critical History* (Oxford, 1989), pt. 3; and Jaromír Janoušek and Irina Sirotkina, "Psychology in Russia and Central and Eastern Europe," in *The Cambridge History of Science*, vol. 7, *The Modern Social Sciences*, ed. Theodore M. Porter and Dorothy Ross (Cambridge, 2003), 434–35.

86. On some suicides as the product of a mental short circuit see Brukhanskii, *Samoubiitsy*, 32–33. Opponents of this view cited examples where the suicide spent days or weeks thinking about and planning his or her death. See P. V. Serebrianikov, "Neskol'ko zamechanii k stat'e prof. Kriukova 'O degeneratsii cherepa u samoubiits,'" *Sudebno-meditsinskaia ekspertiza*, no. 7 (1928): 83. According to Igal Halfin, the so-called solar eclipse defense, which emphasized the commission of a criminal or antisocial act under temporary affect, was used to explain moral lapses among Bolshevik Party members during much of the 1920s. *Terror in My Soul: Communist Autobiographies on Trial* (Cambridge, MA, 2003), 92–95.

circumstances and their organisms: "Perhaps people who kill themselves, or who kill those like themselves, are not as culpable for their acts as is customarily believed. Perhaps there are only sick and healthy people who happen to be in unfortunate or unfortunate conditions."[87] Nikolai Brukhanskii, moreover, argued that it was impossible to talk about the suicide as either a strong or weak person. When it came to self-destruction there were only individuals with an "abnormal, sick will." Suggestions for combating suicide therefore included the promotion of psychohygienic knowledge among the masses along with the increased integration of citizens through social work and heightened feelings of collectivism.[88]

Making suicide the product of a disordered personality also overrode individual subjectivity in favor of the doctor's objective reading of the body. Indeed, the significance of the forensic-medical autopsy only increased in the absence of a clear or compelling motive. A. V. Parabuchev confessed that his interest in studying the relationship between the body and suicidal behavior stemmed partly from his deep concern over young and healthy people who killed themselves for seemingly trivial reasons.[89] Only developments hidden inside the body, argued the forensic-medical expert D. I. Ziskind, made "the high frequency of suicides incited by insignificant causes" comprehensible to the normal observer.[90] Gavrilovskii went even further, claiming that morphological variations were most sharply expressed in the bodies of suicides who acted without any apparent reason. "The most vivid and consistently similar changes," he stated, "are found in the corpses of individuals whose suicide, from the point of view of the inquiry and investigation, was without motive [*ne motivirovalos'*]."[91] Such formulations deepened the perception of suicides as individuals who lacked any sort of control over their emotional and psychological responses to external stimuli.

Perhaps the most reductive expression of the belief in expert knowledge was the argument put forth by some forensic doctors: when faced with a lack of other evidence the expert could make a differential diagnosis (i.e., distinguish between a murder and a suicide) solely on the basis of morphological indicators. In fact, at the Second All-Russian Congress of Forensic-Medical Experts, Kriukov claimed that signs of cranial degeneration were serving as the "guiding principle" for some local experts

87. Kriukov, "K voprosu o prichinakh samoubiistva," 295.
88. "O samoubiistve. Nasha anketa," *Vecherniaia moskva*, January 9, 1927, 2; and Brukhanskii, *Samoubiitsy*, 33.
89. Parabuchev, "Status thymicus u samoubiits," 263.
90. Ziskind, "Degeneratsiia cherepa," 49.
91. Gavrilovskii, "K voprosu ob anatomicheskikh izmeneniiakh," 60.

in cases where the line between murder and suicide was blurred.[92] Looking to the future, the medical expert Iakov Stal'nov prophesied that one day they might be able to identify the suicidal personality simply by assaying the individual's blood chemistry. Because a disruption in the functioning of different glands produced specific alterations in the blood's composition, he speculated that the presence or lack of certain chemicals by itself distinguished a suicide from a nonsuicide. Thus the suicide was potentially visible at the molecular level.[93]

A potential bridge therefore existed between the autopsy of the body and the Soviet regime's revolutionary politics, for the corporeal self could now be disassembled in the search for broader truths about human subjectivity and behavior. Indeed, the atomized vision of the individual fit exquisitely with the transformative inclinations and hopes of the broader scientific community, which aimed to refashion the personality through a mixture of education, health care, and disciplinary measures. This aspiration was evident in the ongoing work on the human glands and reflexes and in the special institutes devoted to the study of Soviet criminals during the 1920s. Epitomized by the State Institute for the Study of Crime and the Criminal Personality established by the People's Commissariat of Internal Affairs in 1925, these interdisciplinary centers included the forensic-medical community and promoted the clinical observation of criminals through a combined program of psychological evaluations, anthropometric examinations of the body, and survey studies.[94] The wide range of biosocial material gathered through such efforts—including biometric data and information on heredity, childhood experiences, reading habits, and notions of morality—indicated various points of intervention by the state's experts. It also solidified the centrality of the individual suicide or criminal, who was at once outside society yet also reflective of its features, as a means of accessing the social world.[95]

While opening up possibilities for Soviet forensic medicine, however, the anatomical model also made the university-based forensic experts

---

92. A. I. Kriukov, "O znachenii degeneratsii na opredelenie prichiny skoropostizhnoi smerti," GARF, f. 482, op. 1, d. 596, l. 181. He also claimed in 1926 that his laboratory was being bombarded with requests for microscopic analyses of biological material taken from suicides. "Zasedanie Moskovskogo sudebno-meditsinskogo obshchestva 28/IV-26 goda," *Sudebno-meditsinskaia ekspertiza*, no. 4 (1926): 158.

93. Stal'nov, "Puti bio-khimicheskogo analiza," 7–11.

94. On forensic medicine's close relationship with these institutes, see Rozhanovskii, "Sudebno-meditsinskaia ekspertiza," 74–77. The history of the criminological institutes is explored in L. O. Ivanov and L. V. Il'ina, *Puti i sud'by otechestvennoi kriminologii* (Moscow, 1991), 127–43.

95. Beer, *Renovating Russia*, 115–18.

vulnerable to charges of deterministic fatalism. In particular, they were linked to the Italian criminologist Cesare Lombroso, whose theories of degeneration and atavism posited the existence of inborn criminals and suicides.[96] Taking advantage of this association, opponents rhetorically sharpened the social-biological binary in order to portray the university-based experts as out of step with the dominant sociological paradigm. This was apparent in the efforts of some forensic doctors, including the chief medical examiner, Leibovich, to limit the influence and scope of the anatomical approach. An editorial note accompanying Kriukov's 1925 article in the flagship journal *Forensic-Medical Expertise* strongly disavowed his contention that degenerative transformations of the cranium were the primary cause of suicide in particular and criminality in general. "Socioeconomic conditions," it argued, were the fundamental source of self-destructive behavior.[97] Several years later, the journal editors included another disclaimer that warned against providing a differential diagnosis based solely on anatomical changes. To do so, they stated, would ignore the fact that suicides were "almost exclusively the result of socioeconomic conditions."[98]

Faced with the challenge of making their work socially relevant, the adherents of the somatic model confronted a number of obstacles. The fact that internal truths contained in the body were seen only after death raised the thorny problem of how to identify and treat suicidal citizens *before* they harmed themselves. After all, Kriukov and others cited cases where the individual was physically beautiful and appeared outwardly normal until the moment of the suicide, a situation that undercut the possibility of prevention through visual diagnostics alone. However, more fundamental disagreements over the precise morphological indicators of suicide, their specific role in the formation of the suicidal personality, and their very existence seriously diminished the diagnostic potential of the biological paradigm. Petr Minakov, who was Kriukov's mentor at Moscow University, made this point when he criticized status thymico-lymphaticus

---

96. Kriukov's tendency to see the early adhesion of the cranial sutures as a sign of pathology is at least consistent with the work of the Italian anthropological school. Israel Hershkovitz et al., "Why Do We Fail in Aging the Skull from the Sagittal Suture?" *American Journal of Physical Anthropology* 103, no. 3 (July 1997): 394.

97. Kriukov, "O degeneratsii u cherepa samoubiits," 18n. The editorial comment stated that Kriukov's views were his alone and noted that the very concept of degeneration had been called into question by recent studies.

98. Ziskind, "Degeneratsiia cherepa," 50. Ziskind's colleagues also rejected this idea after his presentation before the scientific meeting of the Department of Forensic Medicine at the Leningrad Institute for the Upgrading of Physicians. See *Sudebno-meditsinskaia ekspertiza*, no. 14 (1930): 156–58.

as a jack-of-all-trades. In his view, the lack of consensus over its meaning deprived the condition of any real explanatory value within forensic-medical practice.[99] Similar problems plagued the forensic-medical studies of the cranium. While not disputing the underlying importance of biology to the self-destructive personality, one of Kriukov's former pupils claimed that he was simply unable to find the degenerative changes described by Kriukov and Minakov.[100] Equally significant was the fact that forensic-medical experts could not even decide on a basic definition of degeneration, let alone its diagnostic relevance for suicide.[101] Claims to possess special visual and interpretive skills were thus bedeviled by the continued illegibility of the body.

In the final analysis, Soviet forensic-medical experts experienced the same frustrations faced by researchers looking into the biological origins of homosexuality and criminality. Although the search for deviant types promised transparency and control, the opposite resulted as the border between the normal and the pathological became less and less certain.[102] Kriukov himself was forced to admit that signs of degeneration could be found in virtually every person and that their presence did not necessarily translate into pathological behavior. In fact, geniuses were said to share specific physiological traits with idiots, criminals, and prostitutes.[103] The apparent ubiquity of degeneration therefore raised questions about

99. "Zasedanie Moskovskogo sudebno-meditsinskogo obshchestva," 158. Kriukov, who staked much of his intellectual authority upon his work on the degeneration of the skull, also contended that an enlarged thymus gland was by itself insufficient evidence upon which to make a diagnosis of either suicide or sudden death. "Piatyi rasshirennyi s"ezd sudebno-meditsinskikh ekspertov, 15-17 sentiabria 1927 g.," *Sudebno-meditsinskaia ekspertiza*, no. 7 (1927): 157.

100. Serebrianikov, "Neskol'ko zamechanii," 81–84. Dr. Ivan Mikhailovich Leplinskii also attempted to duplicate the work of Kriukov in his clinic at Azerbaijan State University but claimed that he was able to find the signs of suicide described by Kriukov in only three out of the fifty cases he autopsied. I. M. Leplinskii, "K voprosu o samoubiistvakh v Azerbaidzhane," *Zhurnal teorii i praktiki meditsiny* 2, nos. 1–3 (1926): 281–82.

101. Kriukov, "O znachenii degeneratsii," l. 178; Kriukov, "O degeneratsii cherepa u samoubiits," 21, 23; and "Zasedanie Moskovskogo sudebno-meditsinskogo obshchestva," 157–58.

102. See, for example, David G. Horn, "The Norm Which Is Not One: Reading the Female Body in Lombroso's Anthropology"; and Jennifer Terry, "Anxious Slippages between 'Us' and 'Them': A Brief History of the Scientific Search for Homosexual Bodies," both in *Deviant Bodies: Critical Perspectives on Difference in Science and Popular Culture*, ed. Jennifer Terry and Jacqueline Urla (Bloomington, 1995), 109–28, 129–69.

103. In the face of criticism, Kriukov likened degeneration to the potentiality of tuberculosis. Many people had TB within them, but relatively few of them actually died from the disease. Kriukov, "O degeneratsii cherepa u samoubiits," 23–24; and Kriukov, "O degeneratsii cherepa," 712. On the deep interest among Soviet psychiatrists in the link between genius and mental illness, see Irina Sirotkina, *Diagnosing Literary Genius: A Cultural History of Psychiatry in Russia, 1880–1930* (Baltimore, 2002).

the very existence of the suicidal type while also sowing doubts among forensic doctors about differentiating suicides from murders solely through autopsy. These concerns came to the fore during a 1926 meeting of the Moscow Forensic-Medical Society, where Kriukov delivered a paper on the link between degeneration and sudden death. Suggesting the lack of consensus over the morphological signs of self-destruction, for example, the forensic doctor Esaulov asked whether it was sufficient to write in the official protocol that "changes characteristic of a suicide" had been found. Kriukov conceded in his response that "the entirety of signs speak to a suicide," not just a single one like the degeneration of the skull. The critical issue, concluded Petr Minakov, was not the existence of degenerative changes, which he took for granted. It was establishing their source and their causal meaning. In a statement that tellingly revealed the connection between particular facts and broader truths, Minakov declared, "It is still too early to draw general conclusions from our observations of suicides. We are only registering them, and they need to be studied."[104]

Thus it comes as little surprise that there is mixed evidence of a broad search for the physiological signs of the suicidal personality. Many of the suicides autopsied as part of Nikolai Brukhanskii's Moscow study were said to display the key morphological conditions outlined by Kriukov and his supporters, a possible indication of this group's influence among the capital's scientific community. However, outside Moscow the story appears quite different, despite claims by Leibovich in 1926 that the provinces were showing a heightened interest in the question of physiological degeneration. The lack of anatomical information in the questionnaires suggests a split among forensic doctors between the theoretical inclinations of the clinicians and the more practical concerns of practitioners in the field. In fact, among the available ankety surveyed for this study there are only two instances where the forensic-medical expert went beyond the formal application of his knowledge to show a specific interest in the internal structure of the suicide. Both cases involved children (age fourteen) and lacked clear motives. In the first, the forensic doctor noted a large thyroid, irregularity in the thickness of the skullcap with some translucence, and

---

104. Kriukov agreed that it would take several generations and countless more autopsies before a firmer understanding of suicide could be achieved. "Zasedanie Moskovskogo sudebno-meditsinskogo obshchestva," 157–58. Similar issues and doubts about the degeneration model were raised during a session of the forensic-medical department of the Leningrad Institute for the Upgrading of Physicians. See "Nauchnoe soveshchanie na kafedre sudebnoi meditsiny leningr. instituta dlia usovershenstvovaniia vrachei 16-19 marta 1929 g.," *Sudebno-meditsinskaia ekspertiza*, no. 14 (1930): 156–58.

protuberances on the anterior and middle fossae of the cranium.[105] In the second case, which involved a young girl, the investigator found protuberances and spines at the cranial base as well as asymmetry between the two halves of the skull, growth of the mammary glands with little development of the labia minora (*malye polovye guby*), and menstrual hyperemia of the "sexual tract." Here a link was drawn between the anatomical observations and the cause of the suicide. The anketa stated that although the cause had not been established, the girl's suicide was probably the result of "nervous mental depression in the period of menses during puberty."[106]

These two cases highlight once more the persistence of individual particularities amid the desire for generalized truths. In fact, one could argue that the suicides stood out precisely because they were viewed against a normative background constructed on the basis of multiple observations, conventional wisdom, and statistical patterns. When forensic-medical doctors shared remarkable cases during their professional gatherings or in published articles, they were drawn, almost involuntarily, to suicides that seemed out of the ordinary, whether in terms of their age, their family history, or the manner in which they had killed themselves.[107] Something similar was going on with the explorations inside the body. There the forensic doctors hunted for signs of difference in the hopes of establishing a kind of universality among all suicides. One only needed the desire to see them. For example, Kriukov's articles are rife with the imagery of perception, both willful and unintentional. Describing the spines encountered in the cranial base of suicides, for example, he warned that they sometimes made themselves known by pricking one's fingers during the brain's removal from its cavity. He also recounted the medical world's encounter with the degenerative skull as a story of enlightenment born of multiple exposures: "Looking more attentively at the anatomical structure of suicides, several anomalies of the cranial bones instinctively [*nevol'no*] caught the eye. At first they did not attribute a vital significance to these changes, considering them to be random; but over time, in proportion to the accumulation of experience and observations, they began to explain many phenomena associated with suicide by these changes

---

105. GATO, f. 451, op. 1, d. 2184, l. 44.
106. Ibid., ll. 71ob–72.
107. See, for example, the discussion of a suicide that combined hanging with the ingestion of turpentine. "Nauchnoe soveshchanie," *Sudebno-meditsinskaia ekspertiza*, no. 14 (1930): 156–57. Moreover, as noted above, inexplicable cases of suicides among children and young people were cited as reasons for looking to the body for answers. See, for example, Parabuchev, "Status thymicus," 263.

[in the cranium]."[108] In the world of Soviet forensic medicine, the part and the whole remained inexorably intertwined in the search for truth. It was a mutual relationship that went all the way down to the bone.

SUICIDE AND MEDICAL THERAPEUTICS

Never far from the surface of the forensic-medical debates over suicide was the pressing question of the discipline's role within the Soviet governmental project. The answer depended in large measure on how forensic doctors viewed the objects that fell by law within their jurisdiction. Environmental explanations of suicide and other forms of deviance created common ground among the forensic-medical community, law enforcement officials, and other social scientists, while biological theories carved out a more specialized sphere of influence for the discipline.[109] However, it would be incorrect to assume that the majority of forensic-medical doctors saw an absolute dividing line between the two schools of thought. Although somatic models of deviance came under increasing attack toward the end of the 1920s, forensic-medical theory was sufficiently flexible to acknowledge an interdependent relationship between the individual and society, thereby positioning the expert as concerned with both. Kriukov, after all, could refer to suicide as a "horrible social phenomenon" while simultaneously urging his colleagues to look more attentively for signs of physiological degeneration.[110] Similarly, opposition to the somatic approach did not mean the complete rejection of biology's role in creating the suicide. Leibovich certainly denigrated the anthropological school for its racial and deterministic overtones, but he also lauded the work being done in the field of endocrinology as creating a potential explanatory bridge between mental and physical illnesses. Nevertheless, he asked his readers to consider the possibility that the environment was the ultimate cause of glandular pathology and thus the

---

108. Kriukov, "K voprosu o prichinakh samoubiistva," 288.

109. For example, the political leadership of the Red Army acknowledged that suicides related to degeneration were beyond their control. "Statisticheskii ezhegodnik za 1928/29 god. Politiko-moral'noe sostoianie RKKA. (Sostoianie distsipliny i distsiplinarnaia praktika, samoubiistva, chrezvychainye proisshestviia)," RGVA, f. 54, op. 4, d. 64, l. 45ob.

110. Kriukov, "K voprosu o prichinakh samoubiistva," 295. In his review of child suicides, Vasilii Giliarovskii contended that there were no contradictions between the anthropological and social theories of self-destruction. Both, he suggested, approached the same "biological phenomenon" but from different angles. Giliarovskii, "K psikhopatologii detskikh samoubiistv," 69.

unstable personalities associated with it. To Leibovich, then, the issue was primarily about emphasis. The social milieu, and not biology, had to be the dominant factor. By the mid-1920s, for example, he concluded several articles on suicide by suggesting a path of investigation constructed on a causational hierarchy sharply at odds with that of Kriukov and his allies: "social-economic conditions—internal secretions—somatic phenomena—reactive psychosis—suicide."[111]

The challenge facing forensic-medical experts was how to demonstrate the broader relevance of their work to others. At various gatherings, they urged one another to become more visible in the community through enlightenment work among the people. They discussed, for example, the value of performing public autopsies and making use of their periodic forays into the remote countryside to lecture and hold discussions about different medical topics, such as venereal disease and alcoholism.[112] To raise their profile among physicians and criminal investigators, forensic-medical experts held joint meetings and conferences to encourage mutual understanding and coordination among the different professionals. They also used the information gathered through statistical cards to publicize their collective activities, including the number and type of bodily examinations and chemical analyses annually performed. This enabled Leibovich in 1929 to tout the increasing percentage of corpses that had undergone autopsy since 1924, a success that in his opinion "even the Germans envy."[113] Still, the forensic-medical experts had difficulty overcoming perceptions that they practiced a discipline without much relevance for the living. During a 1926 gathering of the Leningrad Society of Medical Expertise, a criminal investigator challenged the contention that the forensic-medical study of criminality and other social anomalies would

111. Leibovich, "Sovremennye samoubiistva," 221.
112. Attendance at autopsies was also considered a good way of raising the interest of policemen and criminal investigators in the work of forensic-medical experts. Moreover, one medical expert called for performing public autopsies on alcoholics in order to educate the population about alcohol's harmful physiological effects. "1-i Sibirskii kraevoi s"ezd medekspertov sovmestno s deiateliami suda i sledstviia," *Sudebno-meditsinskaia ekpsertiza*, no. 15 (1931): 71. See also the discussions of cultural-enlightenment work in "Gubernskoe soveshchanie," 82–83; "Donskoe okruzhnoe soveshchanie po voprosam sudebnoi meditsiny, vrachebnoi ekspertizy i kriminalistiki," *Sudebno-meditsinskaia ekspertiza*, no. 8 (1928): 192; Leibovich, "Itogi deiatel'nosti sudebno-meditsinskoi ekspertizy," 14; and the various responses to N. N. Esaulov's "Material'noe i pravovoe polozhenie sudebno-meditsinskikh ekspertov RSFSR," in Leibovich, *Trudy II Vserossiiskogo s"ezda*, 39–40.
113. Leibovich framed such numbers in terms of forensic medicine's contributions to the national economy and the construction of the state. Its practitioners annually examined over sixty thousand corpses, over five hundred thousand living persons, and up to thirty thousand pieces of physical evidence. "1-i Sibirskii kraevoi s"ezd," 71.

prevent acts of deviance. How was this possible, he asked, when crime is a social phenomenon and only a change in the country's social structure would diminish it? His skepticism suggests not just the power of sociopolitical explanations during the 1920s but also the persistence of perceptions that forensic medicine "deals only with corpses."[114]

Noteworthy therefore was the resolution passed in 1926 at the Second All-Russian Congress of Forensic-Medical Experts, which called for the creation of a permanent central commission to coordinate the nationwide study of the suicidal personality. Criticizing the state of current investigations in the USSR, the resolution cited the pressing need for an "authoritative scientific plan," asked the commission to invite representatives of other disciplines, and emphasized the importance of approaching the problem "not just from the social-everyday and prophylactic perspective, but also from the clinical, biochemical, pathological-anatomical, and other perspectives."[115] Although the commission never came to fruition, the proposal was significant as an expression of the desire for a holistic approach to suicide, one that sought to overcome the tensions between particularistic and generalized understandings of the individual. In addition, it was another manifestation of the attempts to bring forensic-medical expertise closer to other disciplines and medical specialties while also promoting greater coherency within the discipline itself.[116]

Considered more broadly, the forensic-medical investigations into suicide tapped into debates about human nature, its transformability, and the power of state-sponsored experts to control it. While privileging the specialized knowledge of medical practitioners, the somatic understanding of suicide and deviance suggested a troubling degree of permanence, whether from a hereditary taint that would take generations to eradicate or a pathological conundrum that would require decades to solve. Until then, Soviet Russia would continue to be threatened by dangerous persons whose containment depended on a program of therapeutics directed at the individual. "At the present time," stated Dr. P. A. Maskin in a 1927 talk on suicides in Leningrad, "every suicide must be looked upon as a socially

---

114. "Nauchnye zasedaniia Obshchestva meditsinskoi ekspertizy g. Leningrada i gubernii," *Sudebno-meditsinskaia ekspertiza*, no. 6 (1927): 69–70; and "1-i Sibirskii kraevoi s"ezd medekspertov," 71.

115. GARF, f. 482, op. 1, d. 585, l. 131. It was agreed that an invitation would be extended to Commissar of Health Semashko.

116. In 1927, Dr. Iakov Stal'nov also called for a multidisciplinary effort, bringing together sociologists, forensic doctors, psychiatrists, and histologists in an effort to understand the hereditary and physiological sources of the suicidal personality. See "Puti biokhimicheskogo analiza," 7.

sick element, harmful to society." Citing recent scientific opinion that all suicides have a "psychically abnormal constitution," he believed that suicides might disappear only in the future after the implementation of eugenic policies "under the ideal order of human society."[117] Similarly, the Moscow psychiatrist Leonid Prozorov called for a combination of eugenics and social hygiene to reduce the number of suicides linked to heredity, degeneration, and alcoholism. This meant prohibiting marriages with the mentally ill, epileptics, and extreme alcoholics, as well as a broader fight against venereal disease, tuberculosis, and other social illnesses. Both Prozorov and the health commissar, Nikolai Semashko, cited the importance of the new system of psychiatric dispensaries that was gradually coming into existence in Moscow and other major urban centers. Prozorov, in particular, believed that these outpatient clinics would catch potential suicides through their daily "supervision [*nadzor*], care, and guardianship [*opeka*] of all inferior, unstable, feeble individuals [*lichnosti*]." Moreover, he envisaged that psychiatrists working among the people would provide psychotherapy and generally help reconnect them to the "living collective," which remained the main defense against suicidal inclinations.[118] "The filling of the personality with the interests of society," argued Bychkov and Rachkovskii, "is the fundamental path toward the prophylaxis of suicide."[119]

Of course, suicides were practicing their own form of social therapeutics in the sense that they revealed themselves as maladapted to the new conditions of postrevolutionary life and eliminated themselves as potential threats to others. Toward the end of the 1920s, the rhetoric of personal responsibility became sharper as Soviet psychological theory shifted to more subjective understandings of human behavior. The added emphasis on volition empowered the Bolsheviks in carrying out their plans to remake the social landscape and suggested that individuals were the authors and not simply the objects of revolutionary change.[120] Those left behind or standing outside the Soviet collective were increasingly understood in class terms

117. Maskin, "Samoubiistva v Leningrade," 71. Maskin also spoke of the desirability of creating a standardized all-Union survey that would isolate the "biosocial personality" of the suicide. "Nauchnoe soveshchanie," *Sudebno-meditsinskaia ekspertiza,* no. 14 (1930): 158.

118. L. A. Prozorov, "Profilaktika i terapiia samoubiistva," in *Nevrologiia, nevropatologiia, psikhologiia, psikhiatriia. Sbornik posviashchennyi 40-letiiu nauchnoi, vrachebnoi i pedagogicheskoi deiatel'nosti Prof. G. I. Rossolimo 1884–1924* (Moscow, 1925), 51–55. On the role of psychiatric dispensaries, see also Semashko, "Ugrozhaet li nam epidemiia samoubiistv?" 5; and Stal'nov, "Puti bio-khimicheskogo analiza," 11.

119. Bychkov and Rachkovskii, "Samoubiistva v RSFSR," 238.

120. On this important cognitive shift and its broader implications for notions of guilt and innocence, see Halfin, *Terror in My Soul,* 179–92.

that suggested the enduring power of ingrained instincts or worldviews. For example, at a February 1929 gathering of medical experts and legal personnel in Riazan', S. V. Bakshev, a member of the provincial courts, claimed that suicides came mostly from "alien" social classes that were cut off from the rest of society. He explained, "They lack prospects, they don't participate in socialist construction, their life lacks social content, from which we have the preconditions for despondency [*upadochnichestvo*]."[121] Writing that same year about the psychopathology of child suicides, the psychiatrist Vasilii Alekseevich Giliarovskii argued that issues usually plaguing the suicidal individual—material difficulties, mental disturbances, insecurity, and the feeling of losing the ground under one's feet—could now be studied in connection with a broader "pathology of classes and social groups." However, he warned against the tendency to overemphasize social-environmental factors at the expense of the foundation that "was placed [*zalozheno*] in the person at birth."[122]

Such thinking reflected a medical politics that was growing increasingly ideological and reshaping the traditional concerns of investigators with class or social position. As Soviet Russia moved toward socialism, went the logic, the economic, cultural, and social transformations that would bring about improved health and well-being for the masses would also increase morbidity among the dispossessed classes and their representatives. Notions of social integration (or alienation) merged with theories of the suicidal personality to suggest that one could—indeed, should—expect higher rates of self-destruction among individuals whose biological-class makeup assumed a degree of fixedness that prevented them from adapting to the new order of things. This understanding of the pathological individual was both reassuring and anxiety-provoking. On the one hand, it separated the sick from the healthy social body by stamping them as products of the past, a social anomaly that was unreflective of the emergent socialist reality. On the other, it acknowledged the continued existence of déclassé individuals, like the poet Sergei Esenin, whose psychological deterioration posed a larger threat to the public.[123] This state of affairs presented political leaders as well as physicians with an interpretative and therapeutic challenge not unlike the one facing the forensic-medical experts. Specifically, how were dangerous members of society to be identified

121. "Gubernskoe soveshchanie," *Sudebno-meditsinskaia ekspertiza*, no. 13 (1930): 95.

122. Giliarovskii, "K psikhopatologii detskikh samoubiistv," 70.

123. On references to Esenin as a "declassed peasant" suffering from mental problems, see Semashko, "Ugrozhaet li nam epidemiia samoubiistv?" 5; and I. B. Galant, "O dushevnoi bolezni S. Esenina," *Klinicheskii arkhiv genial'nosti i odarennosti (evropatologii)* 2, no. 2 (1926): 115–32. Galant attributed Esenin's mental illness to his alcoholism.

before causing harm to themselves and/or others when, as Aleksandr Kriukov told one of his audiences, a simple look around revealed signs of degeneration on virtually everyone? Like the anatomical deformations of the skull, the suicidal personality was at once everywhere and nowhere, a group of signs whose variability and indeterminacy reflected the tenacious presence of the individual in Soviet life.

4

Markers of Modernity

Moral Statistics and the Making of Soviet Suicide

In his introduction to Nikolai Pavlovich Brukhanskii's *Suicides* (1927), Nikolai Aleksandrovich Semashko, head of the People's Commissariat of Public Health, reiterated the general belief that the revolution had altered patterns of self-destruction in the country. He praised the work not only for its methodology and rich material but also for studying suicides "committed under...the Soviet system." According to Semashko, "new living conditions never before seen in history" were finding expression in the kinds of people who were killing themselves, in the motivations that led them to act on their impulses, and in the "technology" (*tekhnika*) they selected to carry out their suicidal objective. In particular, he highlighted the "generally accepted fact" that more women were killing themselves as a result of their greater activity in public life and that changes in the family and marital relations during the "transition period" were influencing the pattern of self-destruction. Suicide, in other words, was different because Russia was different. "Without exception," declared Semashko, "investigators of suicide in recent years unanimously attest to the fact that the Soviet system has introduced something truly new into the statistics of suicide."[1]

Semashko's statement about Soviet suicide statistics can be read in several ways. His obvious intention was to emphasize the fact that political,

---

1. Nikolai Semashko, introduction to *Samoubiitsy*, by N. P. Brukhanskii (Moscow-Leningrad, 1927), 5.

economic, and social changes instituted after 1917 were now finding reflection in the data about suicide. This line of thinking echoed the widely shared idea that the state of society could be read through the aggregate behavior of its individual members. However, one can also choose to read Semashko's words as an oblique commentary on the fundamentally changed nature of statistics under the Bolsheviks. Alain Blum has argued that after 1917, nation building and modern statistics finally converged in Russia, whereby statistics became vital for the achievement of uniformity and standardization as well as for the fulfillment of the regime's desire to know about the people within its borders.[2] Statisticians, who before the revolution had labored outside the autocratic state, whether in the local zemstvos, city dumas, or professional societies, now had the opportunity to carry out their activities within a centralized apparatus—the Central Statistical Administration—that was helping to construct a coherent social and political order. One could therefore argue, to paraphrase Semashko, that the Soviet system "introduced something truly new into the statistics of suicide" through the very mechanisms of their production. Postrevolutionary suicide statistics were Soviet not simply in terms of the reality they were said to reflect but in terms of how statisticians captured and portrayed this reality.

The process by which the Soviet Union became statistical during the 1920s is encapsulated in the work of moral statisticians who began a national registration of suicides in February 1922. Their main institutional base—the Department of Moral Statistics in the TsSU—lacked any equivalent under the autocracy and was itself emblematic of the new regime's interest in statistical knowledge. In fact, Soviet moral statisticians consciously distanced themselves from the prerevolutionary past in order to highlight the progressive qualities of their efforts. To these professionals, moral statistics were a necessary activity of the modern state, which had to know as much about social phenomena like suicide as it did about economic life. With the implementation of their nationwide registry, they began the process of promoting a standardized accounting of self-destruction across the entire territory of Russia and the USSR. This involved the creation of an apparatus for gathering information, the inscription of suicides into a single grid of classification, and the production of a statistical aggregate within a shared interpretive framework.

2. About this process, Blum writes, "The ambition of statistics is not simply to count, but to achieve a uniform description, and hence representation, of society through censuses, surveys, and the regular collection of information from the entire territory. The understanding of the social at the heart of the nation implies the uniformization, the objectivization of the interpretative grid." Alain Blum, "Society, Politics and Demography: The Example of Soviet History," *Czech Sociological Review* 4, no. 1 (1996): 86.

An exploration into Soviet moral statistics reveals the relationship among suicide, social knowledge, and identification in postrevolutionary Russia.[3] First and foremost, suicide statistics were a vital part of the moral statisticians' self-understanding as professionals engaged in both the Soviet state-building project and the pan-European debate about suicide, crime, and society. Keenly aware of this dual commitment, they inscribed themselves within a teleological narrative that emphasized the country's move from a state of statistical silence and ignorance to one of enumerated enlightenment. At the same time, the moral statisticians contributed to the formation of the Soviet social order by inscribing suicides into a narrative of national development that captured the emergence of new living patterns amid the dissolution of old ones. Framed within a comparative, and highly gendered, discourse of progress and civilization, their statistical representations brought into vivid relief assumptions about the country's historical trajectory—past, present, and future. The story of how Soviet Russia became statistical is therefore a story of rhetorical moves, professional identities, institution building, and the construction of meaning through classification and the language of numbers.

Moral statistics' rise and fall during the 1920s also allow us to consider the politics of social science in the Soviet regime. Behind the different sources of information about suicide were a number of assumptions about what could be known through statistics and, in turn, what should be done on their basis. Soviet forensic experts, for example, regarded quantification as the basis for specific medical interventions in the population, an understanding that allowed them to speak about themselves as activist physician-sociologists. By contrast, moral statisticians in the Central Statistical Administration had a more circumspect vision of their enterprise. They saw the professional statistician primarily as a producer of empirical information that captured external realities and made visible the laws of the social world; it would be left to the politicians and other experts to decide whether and how to act upon these data. The result is a rich set of statistics that is highly descriptive but mostly devoid of overt judgments and theoretical debate. Such scientific modesty, which rationalized the production of information for its own sake, fit uncomfortably with the totalizing nature of Soviet politics and with instrumentalist views of

3. Here I use the term "identification" rather than "identity" in order to emphasize the reciprocal process of identifying or categorizing oneself and others. It is a process that involves not just individuals but "the modern state's efforts to inscribe its subjects onto a classificatory grid." See, for example, Rogers Brubaker and Frederick Cooper, "Beyond 'Identity,'" *Theory and Society* 29, no. 1 (February 2000): 14–17.

numbers as a tool for remaking reality. By the late 1920s, statistics and social knowledge could no longer be divorced from the Soviet state's primary purpose—which was to act upon and transform its citizenry according to the Bolshevik vision of the future.

DEFINING MORAL STATISTICS

"Moral statistics" (*statistique morale*), which explore human or social phenomena as opposed to physical and natural facts, were part of the "avalanche of printed numbers" that swept across Europe during the early part of the nineteenth century.[4] They originated with the work in the 1830s of the Parisian lawyer André-Michel Guerry, who observed an uncanny regularity in crime statistics, and the Belgian mathematician and astronomer Adolphe Quetelet, who revolutionized statistics with his concept of the "average man."[5] Both men helped to advance the idea that by looking at statistical aggregates one could strip away the particularities of the individual personality and come face to face with the essential properties of society. Quetelet, in particular, is credited with the construction of the individual as a social being who carried parts of society within. By effectively ending the direct correspondence between numbers and objects, he made statistically based abstractions "real" and set the foundations for governmental policy focused on regulating the population rather than the individual.[6]

Soviet moral statisticians placed themselves squarely within this intellectual tradition. Their primary advocate was Mikhail Nikolaevich Gernet, a noted jurist and educator whose early career was limited by his public stance against the death penalty and the tsarist regime's encroachment on university autonomy.[7] Prior to 1917, Gernet taught criminology in the law faculty at Moscow University before moving on to Vladimir Bekhterev's

---

4. Ian Hacking discusses the "avalanche of printed numbers" in *The Taming of Chance* (Cambridge, 1990).

5. Theodore M. Porter, *The Rise of Statistical Thinking 1820–1900* (Princeton, 1986), 49. Some authors attribute the origins of moral statistics to Johann Peter Süssmilch, who in the eighteenth century gathered data about births and deaths in order to prove the divine order of things. Guerry, however, is credited with being the first among Belgian-French scholars to apply the term to his work. See Piers Beirne, *Inventing Criminology: Essays on the Rise of Homo Criminalis* (Albany, 1993), 104 n. 56.

6. Joshua Cole, *The Power of Large Numbers: Population, Politics and Gender in Nineteenth-Century France* (Ithaca, 2000), 78–85; and Hacking, *Taming of Chance*, 107–9.

7. "Avtobiografiia," Otdel rukopisei RGB, f. 603, k. 1, d. 1, ll. 3–4; and M. N. Gernet, *Izbrannye proizvedeniia* (Moscow, 1974), 8–37.

renowned Psychoneurological Institute in St. Petersburg. Both in the classroom and in numerous writings, he emphasized social factors in the genesis of crime while criticizing the anthropological school's strong focus on the human body. Although never a Marxist, Gernet was sympathetic toward the socialist interpretation of criminality as the product of economic inequalities in bourgeois society. In his major work *The Social Causes of Crime* (1906), for example, he called for more humane policies that fought crime by reducing its underlying causal factors instead of using traditional forms of punishment, such as imprisonment and the death penalty.[8]

The October Revolution of 1917 afforded Gernet and other like-minded criminal scientists the opportunity to enter the state and put their progressive ideas about law and justice into effect. Indeed, Gernet was part of a sizable cohort of prerevolutionary experts who dominated the nascent Soviet legal and statistical apparatus during the decade of the 1920s.[9] He participated as an educator, organizer, researcher, and moral statistician. In 1919, Gernet resumed his teaching duties at Moscow State University, first within the newly formed Faculty of Social Sciences (FON)[10] and later in the Faculty of Soviet Law, where he was responsible for conducting seminars on moral statistics as part of the department's mission to prepare specialists for the country's new judicial administration.[11] In addition to teaching, he also ran the university's criminological laboratory (*kabinet*), which contained a library, museum, and special auditorium for lectures conducted by faculty and outside experts. Gernet oversaw the collection of special teaching materials—including prison tattoos, the personal papers and effects of criminals and suicides, and a variety of charts that diagrammed crime and suicide in the USSR and abroad—and made a

8. M. Gernet, *Obshchestvennye prichiny prestupnosti. Sotsialisticheskoe napravlenie v nauke ugolovnogo prava* (Moscow, 1906). Gernet's Soviet-era biographer gave him credit for helping to acquaint prerevolutionary Russian society with the "social concepts of crime and punishment." See Gernet, *Izbrannye proizvedeniia*, 21–22.

9. See, for example, Alain Blum and Martine Mespoulet, *L'anarchie bureaucratique: Pouvoir et statistique sous Staline* (Paris, 2003); and Peter H. Solomon, Jr., "Soviet Criminology: Its Demise and Rebirth, 1928–1963," *Soviet Union/Union Sovietique* 1, no. 2 (1974): 122–40.

10. The Faculties of Social Science were part of the ideological struggle over the social sciences after 1917. They were created during the civil war by the People's Commissariat of Enlightenment to replace the old university faculties of law, history, and philology. Originally conceived as the bases for new centers of Marxist social science, they were gradually shut down in the early 1920s as a result of the continued predominance of non-Marxist professors within them. See Michael David-Fox, *Revolution of the Mind: Higher Learning among the Bolsheviks, 1918–1929* (Ithaca, 1997), 76–79.

11. "Avtobiografiia," l. 5; and "Kratkie vospominaniia o moei universitetskoi rabote posle oktiabr'skoi revoliutsii," Otdel rukopisei RGB, f. 603, k. 1, d. 16, ll. 1–3.

concerted effort to acquire foreign books and journals, which had become extremely scarce in the years immediately following the revolution.[12]

Gernet's research centered around two institutions that he helped to found—the State Institute for the Study of Crime and the Criminal under the People's Commissariat of Internal Affairs (NKVD) RSFSR and the Department of Moral Statistics in the Central Statistical Administration. As we have seen, the State Institute brought together representatives of various disciplines (medicine, criminal law, anthropology, psychology, etc.) to formulate a unified, scientific approach to crime and the treatment of the criminal. Noteworthy in this respect was the desire to develop a methodology that emphasized social factors without ignoring the particularities of the criminal personality. It was an approach that promoted investigations into crime as both an aggregate and an individual phenomenon. Statistical studies of crime rates, punishments, and the workings of the judicial administration were complemented by survey and psychological research done on criminal subjects.[13]

The Department of Moral Statistics, by contrast, focused solely on the aggregate study of the population and the social phenomena of crime and suicide. It was organized in November 1918 by M. F. Zamengof, with the assistance of Gernet and Evgenii Nikitich Tarnovskii, the former head of statistics for the tsarist Ministry of Justice who in the 1920s became a leading statistician for the new Commissariat of Internal Affairs. Located in Moscow, the Department of Moral Statistics was originally tasked with setting up the collection of criminal statistics (*ugolovnyie statistiki*) for the new state and working through undigested data that had been gathered during the war.[14] It soon came under Gernet's personal direction and gradually expanded its scope to encompass a wide variety of investigative areas: criminal statistics (crimes, court statistics, penal statistics, and specialized studies on such problems as youth homelessness); different facets of "the sexual life" (prostitution, abortion, and divorce); alcoholism; and suicides.[15] However, the collection of information about crime and suicide,

12. "Otchet po kabinetu kriminologii i ugolovnoi politiki," TsAGM, f. 1609, op. 7, d. 104, ll. 15–21; and "Otchet po Muzeiu i Kabinetu Kriminologii i Ugolovnoi Politiki za 1924 god," TsAGM, f. 1609, op. 7, d. 7, ll. 9–12.

13. For the history of the State Institute see Louise Shelly, "Soviet Criminology: Its Birth and Demise, 1917–1936," *Slavic Review* 38, no. 4 (December 1979): 614–28; and L. O. Ivanov and L. V. Il'ina, *Puti i sud'by otechestvennoi kriminologii* (Moscow, 1991), 179–99.

14. "Kratkii otchet o deiatel'nosti Otdela Moral'noi Statistiki," *Vestnik statistiki*, nos. 1–4 (January–April 1921): 279.

15. D. Rodin, "O moral'noi statistiki," *Vestnik statistiki*, nos. 9–12 (September–December 1922): 105–6.

which were deemed "the two most important segments of moral statistics," always remained at the center of the department's efforts.[16]

The department's sphere of activities was a matter of some dispute. Above all, Gernet and his colleagues battled perceptions that several facets of moral statistics belonged more properly within other branches of the Central Statistical Administration or even other state institutions. Suicide statistics, for example, could be housed in the demography section because of its interest in mortality rates and the "movement of the population," while the numbers on abortion could be considered to fall more accurately within the purview of public health statistics. According to an internal memorandum that noted these alternative viewpoints, some inside the TsSU opposed the expansion of the Department of Moral Statistics over the course of the 1920s as "an encroachment on someone else's domain [*chuzhaia oblast'*]."[17] Partly turf wars, these objections also reflected a broader set of negotiations regarding the nature of social statistics. As Alain Blum and Martine Mespoulet suggest, with the rise of "social facts" in the nineteenth century the statistician was entrusted with the job of describing the state of society and outlining possible routes toward the resolution of its ills; however, it was the politician who decided what curative measures to take. Thus, the collection of abortion statistics by the Department of Moral Statistics rather than the Commissariat of Public Health suggests that the project was more about having the information available for analysis than about establishing control over the population.[18] The creation of a specific department devoted to moral statistics was in this respect an intellectual and political move within the wider struggle to define the nature of knowledge in the Soviet regime.

Mikhail Gernet acknowledged the lack of consensus over the content and purpose of moral statistics. In *Moral Statistics*, a textbook written in 1922 and used in the courses taught at Moscow State University, he sought to clarify his understanding of the discipline through a short history of the field. Gernet rejected the idea of simply renaming moral statistics "cultural statistics," an alternative proposed by several European scholars and supported by the eminent Russian statistician Aleksandr Aleksandrovich

16. Letter of January 11, 1922, from the Department of Moral Statistics TsSU, RGAE, f. 1562, op. 31, d. 61, l. 5. Gernet also stressed the centrality of crime and suicide statistics in his survey of the discipline. M. N. Gernet, *Moral'naia statistika (ugolovnaia statistika i statistika samoubiistv)* (Moscow, 1922), 19.

17. "Perspektivnyi 5-letnyi plan rabot po sotsial'noi statistike TsSU SSSR (1928/9–1932/3 g.)," RGAE, f. 1562, op. 1, d. 490, l. 131ob.

18. Blum and Mespoulet, *L'anarchie bureaucratique*, 218–21.

Chuprov in the late nineteenth century.[19] Proponents of the cultural statistics model hoped to break the association between moral statistics and ethics. They noted, for example, that moral statisticians had also begun to gather data about literacy, reading patterns, education, and religion in addition to their earlier focus on crimes, suicides, and other asocial phenomena. Gernet, however, believed that the "cultural statistics" label was much too expansive and failed to capture the traditional concerns of moral statistics. It could be for this reason that he opted to use the Russian *moral'naia statistika,* which more closely mirrored the original French, rather than *nravstvennaia statistika,* an alternative variant whose root—*nravy*—conveyed a wider concern with ways of life.

At the same time, Gernet also rejected the commonplace assumption that moral statistics were primarily a tool for measuring a society's level of morality. Revealing his socialist sympathies, he claimed that the inherent relativism and class contingency of all social norms made it difficult to compare data gathered in different places and at different times. Even evaluating data from within a society was problematic, since the meaning ascribed to human actions depended on the individual's position inside the social structure. More important, Gernet believed that statistics were unable to capture human subjectivity and thus could not establish the inherent morality or immorality of any act deemed criminal by society.[20] He was supported in this opinion by his chief assistant and former university pupil Dmitrii Petrovich Rodin.[21] Statistics, claimed Rodin, could detect only the "mental [*dushevnye*] 'moral' phenomena" that manifested themselves externally, and it was almost impossible to isolate moral causes from the many possible factors behind these objective facts. Motive, conscience, and the "human soul" were thus deemed beyond the grasp of statistical knowledge.[22]

The idea that numbers could reveal neither morality nor human subjectivity raised serious questions about the epistemological value of moral statistics and modern sociological knowledge more generally. In-

---

19. A. A. Chuprov, "Nravstvennaia statistika," *Entsiklopedicheskii slovar' F. A. Brokgauz i I. A. Efron,* vol. 21 (St. Petersburg, 1897), 403–8.

20. Gernet, *Moral'naia statistika,* 6–12.

21. Dmitrii Petrovich Rodin studied criminal law before the revolution and completed his studies in the Law Faculty of the FON at Moscow University. There, he took courses in criminology and completed a study of suicides in Moscow before World War I. See his university record and materials in TsAGM, f. 1609, op. 7, d. 1629, ll. 2–17ob.

22. Rodin, "O moral'noi statistike," 105–6; and Gernet, *Moral'naia statistika,* 11. This did not, however, stop the moral statisticians from attempting to measure the causes behind crimes and suicides.

deed, Gernet sought to limit the meaning of the numbers to an objective correspondence between the actions committed and the actions counted. He wrote, "When the moral statistician presents figures on crime, suicide, divorces, and so forth, we will learn not so much about the level of morality in the country as about its criminality, the durability of its marriages, the mortality in the population from suicide, and about their connection with various social conditions."[23] This limited definition of moral statistics as a factual enterprise concerned with general laws and patterns shaped understandings of the moral statisticians and their work on suicide during the 1920s. In the view of the moral statisticians, it was only natural that a modern state, especially one with a socialist economy and centralized system of health care, would want to possess full knowledge of its population.[24] This ethos, however, did not answer the question of how the information would translate into action. It suggested a potential disconnect between social knowledge and governance as well as a rather restricted role for the moral statistician. Unlike other social investigators, the moral statisticians implied that when it came to suicides, their job was to describe and analyze but not manage the population.[25]

Ultimately, the arguments in favor of moral statistics as a distinct discipline rested heavily on history and tradition. Gernet concluded his review section of *Moral Statistics* by suggesting that the only way to abandon the name "moral statistics" was to break the field down into its constituent parts and refer individually to each of them—crime statistics, suicide statistics, and so forth. However, he argued against this move since the name "moral statistics" had become so widely used and consolidated.[26] By the same token, Dmitrii Rodin conceded that there were grounds to question "the name and content of moral statistics," but he countered that "in statis-

23. Gernet, *Moral'naia statistika*, 11. In the same passage, Gernet continued, "The vast majority of suicides are neutral from a moral standpoint and provide material more for judging the suicide's level of disenchantment with his fate than the moral state of society."

24. D. Rodin, "O postanovke statistiki samoubiistv v Rossii," *Vestnik statistiki*, nos. 5–8 (May–August 1921): 94. During a reorganization of the Central Statistical Administration in 1926, the TsSU's collegium argued that moral statistics should be preserved in the new plan because of their relevance to tasks pursued by "state statistics" (*gosudarstvennaia statistika*). "Plan rabot Tsentral'nogo Statisticheskogo Upravleniia Soiuza SSR na 1926/27 god," RGAE, f. 1562, op. 1, d. 423, l. 5.

25. This understanding was formally confirmed in the plan submitted by the TsSU for the years 1928–29. The work of the Department of Moral Statistics on suicides was said to have a mostly "cognitive [*poznavitel'nyi*] purpose, although various departments and institutions use these analyses (but here too largely for scientific purposes)." "Svodnyi plan statisticheskikh rabot (TsSU RSFSR i vedomstv) na 1928/29 g. Po sotsial'noi statistike," RGAE, 1562, op. 1, d. 490, l. 9ob.

26. Gernet, *Moral'naia statistika*, 11–12.

tical practice this concept has achieved the right to exist."[27] Such thinking apparently prevailed within the Central Statistical Administration during its reorganization in middle of the 1920s. Explaining the position of the Department of Moral Statistics within the Social Statistics Sector, Mitrofan Pavlovich Krasil'nikov stated in 1927 that owing to broad understandings and the lack of a clear scientific definition, the TsSU had "technically" (*tekhnicheski*) included the registration of crime, suicides, and abortions in the field of moral statistics.[28] Hardly the most positive endorsement of moral statistics' "right to exist," this instinctive approach nevertheless recognized the field's historical connection to certain types of quantification and helped sanction the work of the Department of Moral Statistics until its closure in 1931.

Notions of history also played an important role in the moral statisticians' self-understanding and self-representation. When surveying their field in the years following the revolution, Gernet and Rodin told a story of Russia's troubled and rather belated entry into the world of suicide statistics. They depicted Imperial Russia as being virtually speechless when it came to the language of numbers. Blame for this sad state of affairs was placed squarely on the autocratic regime's hostility to progress and unwillingness to allocate the governmental and scientific resources needed to study the population. In fact, Mikhail Gernet suggested that the obscurantism of the old regime had deprived the country of an important opportunity to distinguish itself in the field of moral statistics. Alongside Adolphe Quetelet, the "father of moral statistics," he placed the academician Karl Hermann of the Russian Imperial Academy of Sciences, who in 1830 published a work on suicide that presciently noted the "regularity" (*zakonomernost'*) and "causality" (*prichinost'*) of human actions that on the surface appeared the products of free will.[29] However, further publication of such research was thwarted by the tsarist government, which found Hermann's efforts threatening and of little practical value. The result, argued Gernet,

27. Rodin, "O moral'noi statistike," 105.
28. "O rabote Sektora Sotsial'noi Statistiki," RGAE, f. 1562, op. 1, d. 498, l. 3ob.
29. Ch.-Th. Hermann, "Recherches sur le nombre des suicides et des homicides commis en Russie pendant les années 1819 et 1820," *Mémoires de l'Academie impériale des sciences de S. Petersbourg* 6, no. 1 (1830), 3–20. Hermann first presented his data in 1823, which meant that it predated the work of both Quetelet and Guerry by almost a decade. In fact, Quetelet cited Hermann's data in his 1835 work *Sur l'homme*. See Irina Paperno, *Suicide as a Cultural Institution in Dostoevsky's Russia* (Ithaca, 1997), 70–71; Susan K. Morrissey, *Suicide and the Body Politic in Imperial Russia* (Cambridge, 2006), 86–89; and Vladimir Evgen'evich Kuznetsov, "Etapy razvitiia otechestvennoi dorevoliutsionnoi suitsidologii: Psikhiatricheskii i mezhditsiplinarnyi aspekty" (candidate diss., Moscow Scientific-Investigative Institute of Psychiatry, 1987), 29.

was the "fully conscious and determined silencing [*zamalchivanie*]" of the suicide problem in Russia.[30]

Both Gernet and Rodin lamented the subsequent fate of Russian suicide statistics after the original promise of Hermann's work. Because the tsarist regime was largely uninterested in the problem of suicide, much of the statistical information gathered before 1917 was characterized as "disorganized," "fragmentary," and generally unreliable.[31] To be sure, the moral statisticians recognized the work of individual researchers and local governments, praising in particular the detailed studies of specific population groups (especially the Ministry of Education's work on suicides among Russian students) or within individual cities (notably St. Petersburg, Moscow, and Odessa). However, the significance of these efforts was diminished in their eyes by their unsystematic character and the lack of involvement on the part of the government's main statistical bodies. They were seen as the work of amateur "theorists" who relied on demographic and police data as well as newspaper reports, a clear reference to people like the physicians Dmitrii Zhbankov and Grigorii Gordon. Moreover, the only two government sources covering the entire territory of the empire—the annual reports of provincial governors and regular statistical compilations of crime, both of which counted suicide together with other illegal acts—were said to contain such limited information that working with them was virtually impossible. Thus, with the exception of a few large cities, Russia remained unexplored territory when it came to suicide. It was all but absent from Gernet's 1922 textbook on moral statistics.[32]

The statistical void continued in the period immediately following the October Revolution. Not only had materials been destroyed during the sacking of government ministry buildings, but the state organs responsible for data gathering in the old regime had been swept away by the currents of the revolution. Their replacements in turn suffered from a dearth of funding, trained personnel, and interagency cooperation. Local organs in major urban centers like Petrograd and Odessa continued to gather information about suicides, but this meant that Russia continued to lack a national accounting of deaths due to self-destruction. Moreover, the moral statisticians were critical of the forensic-medical anketa and skeptical about the forensic doctors' attempt to create an effective system of registration.

---

30. *Samoubiistva v SSSR 1922–1925* (Moscow, 1927), 5–6.
31. Gernet, *Moral'naia statistika,* 226–28; Rodin, "O postanovke," 89–92; and E. N. Tarnovskii, "Svedeniia o samoubiistvakh v Zapadnoi Evrope i v RSFSR za polednee desiatiletie," *Problemy prestupnosti,* no. 1 (1926): 192.
32. Gernet himself made note of this absence in *Moral'naia statistika,* 228.

Dmitrii Rodin therefore bemoaned the fact that the most basic information about suicide was still nonexistent inside the young Soviet state. "At
the present time," he wrote in 1921, "the statistics of suicide in Russia are
found in an even more pitiful condition than prior to the revolution.... Even
the number of suicides committed today in Russia is unknown."[33]

Whatever its factual discrepancies, the prestatistical world conjured up
by the moral statisticians had immense rhetorical appeal and allowed them
to dramatize their contribution toward Russia's maturation as a political and
scientific power. Within their teleological narrative, the implementation of
TsSU's national suicide registry in February 1922 represented an end to
silence and disorder as Russia finally acquired its statistical voice on the subject. An internal summary of the department's activities for that year was cate-
gorical in its representation of the program as a historical break. "Suicide
statistics," it stated, "which enter into the plan of the department's work,
were not carried out in the prerevolutionary period. Only now have such
statistics been organized and will information come into the department."[34]

Five years later, Mikhail Gernet was equally resolute in declaring the publication of suicide statistics for the period 1922–25 an unprecedented act in
his country. He wrote, "We are completely justified in speaking so decisively
and unconditionally when using the expression 'never before existed,' since
that branch of moral statistics which bears the name 'suicide statistics' only
appeared for the first time in our country in 1922."[35] Gernet here was referring to the introduction of the "questionnaire on the suicide" (*oprosnyi listok
o samoubiitse*), a special survey form developed by the Department of Moral
Statistics and completed by a variety of government agencies responsible for
keeping track of demographic trends in the population.

The year 1922 therefore became a special date in the writings of the
Soviet moral statisticians. It heralded a new era in the study of suicide in
Russia, a virtual divide between the imposed ignorance of the autocracy
and the enlightened actions of the Soviet regime. In a reference to the
long time period that had elapsed between the academician Hermann's

---

33. Rodin, "O postanovke," 92–94. In his survey of suicide statistics, Rodin argued that
the forensic-medical anketa was poorly organized and formulated. As an example of its shortcomings he cited the plethora of questions and the fact that age, sex, and nationality were
collapsed into a single entry. He also noted the lack of an entry for information regarding
the structure and size of the suicide's family.

34. "Protokol zasedaniia kollegii Tsentral'nogo Statisticheskogo Upravleniia. No. 241,"
RGAE, f. 1562, op. 1, d. 282, l. 77.

35. *Samoubiistva v SSSR 1922–1925*, 5. At the same time, Gernet referred to the TsSU's
program for criminal statistics as the restoration of efforts that had been halted by the
First World War. M. N. Gernet, *Prestupnost' i samoubiistva vo vremia voiny i posle nee* (Moscow,
1927), 4.

pioneering work and the organization of suicide statistics under the Department of Moral Statistics, Gernet wrote, "If one recalls that the attention of Russian theoreticians to the statistics of suicide revealed itself some one hundred years ago…, then the organization of such statistics only since 1922 speaks not just to the astonishingly long patience of Russian science, but to the even more astonishing century-long ignorance of leading administrative circles toward the proper accounting of a phenomenon possessing the deepest social significance and interest."[36] Consistent with such a vision of history, the moral statisticians understood their efforts as the much-delayed fruition in Russia of a Europe-wide endeavor. And when Gernet later revised his textbook on moral statistics, he no longer had to pass over the question of self-destruction in Russia. The second edition (1927) now included a section entitled "Suicide Statistics in the USSR," which drew upon a vast body of data produced under Gernet's guidance at the Department of Moral Statistics.[37]

MAKING MORAL STATISTICS

The moral statisticians, who judged themselves against prerevolutionary and European investigators, saw their efforts as giving Soviet Russia a distinctive and unitary voice when it came to the study of suicide. In particular, the tsarist past served them as a valuable foil for self-representation within their historical narrative. It was the reverse image of the ideal attributes the moral statisticians assigned to their own investigations and methods. Whereas prerevolutionary suicide statistics were represented as fragmentary, disorganized, and incomprehensible, the Department of Moral Statistics' centrally coordinated program conveyed the ideals of rationality, uniformity, and comprehensiveness. For the moral statisticians, the way that the numbers were being created mattered as much as the reality they reflected.

To be sure, becoming statistical was more than just a rhetorical move. The Department of Moral Statistics also faced the particularly daunting challenge of organizing a reliable, nationwide registration of suicides virtually from scratch.[38] Rather than build an apparatus devoted solely to

---

36. *Samoubiistva v SSSR 1922–1925*, 5.

37. Gernet, *Prestupnost' i samoubiistva*, 221–29. This work was labeled as the second edition of *Moral'naia statistika*.

38. Originally a stand-alone entity within the TsSU, the Department of Moral Statistics was housed in the Social Statistics Sector as part of the reorganization of "state statistics" in 1926. The Social Statistics Sector also included departments devoted to demography,

moral statistics, the department's organizers instead chose to gather information through existing government agencies, notably the network of civil registry bureaus commonly known by their acronym ZAGS (*otdely zapisi aktov grazhdanskogo sostoianiia*). The ZAGS, which were run by the People's Commissariat of Internal Affairs RSFSR, were responsible for recording all births, marriages, and deaths, and since no burial could take place without permission of the local registry bureaus, the moral statisticians believed they were the ideal mechanism through which to count completed suicides. This strategy meant the exclusion of attempted suicides from the registration, a lacuna that the moral statisticians and others openly acknowledged.[39] Moreover, a certain percentage of deaths, notably those occurring among the military and prison populations, bypassed the civilian registration agency altogether. Suicides committed by soldiers and prisoners were therefore registered separately by the governmental agencies charged with their care.[40]

Lacking branches outside Moscow, the Department of Moral Statistics worked with the provincial statistical bureaus or departments (*gubstatbiuro* or *gubstatotdely*) to implement its program throughout the country. Local statisticians, usually employed in the demographic sections of the provincial apparatus, distributed the questionnaire on the suicide to the appropriate agencies in their area and then monitored their completion and return. The completed forms were forwarded on a monthly basis from the localities to the provincial statistical agencies, which were encouraged to use the data for their own regional statistical profiles before sending the questionnaires on to Moscow for integration into the national statistical picture. Moral statisticians in the capital believed that allowing the provincial bodies to utilize the information would foster greater oversight and result in more accurate and complete data from the localities.[41]

---

education, public health, and housing. See "Plan rabot Tsentral'nogo Statisticheskogo Upravleniia Soiuza SSR na 1926/27 god," l. 5 (l. 16 within original document); and "Protokol zasedaniia kollegii Tsentral'nogo Statisticheskogo Upravleniia. No. 8 (7–9 iiunia 1926 g.)," RGAE, f. 1562, op. 1, d. 408, l. 25ob.

39. See, for example, the statistical variations linked to the inclusion or exclusion of attempted suicides in Skliar, "K voprosu o chisle samobuiistv v nostoiashchee vremia," *Vlast' sovetov,* nos. 8–9 (August–September 1923): 95–99.

40. Examples of completed questionnaires from the prison system are housed in the archives of the Main Prison Administration. GARF, f. 4042, op. 2, d. 346, ll. 3–3ob, 19–9ob, 32–32ob.

41. Nikolai Nikolaevich Visherskii of Iaroslavl' and Sergei Aleksandrovich Novosel'skii of Leningrad are two noteworthy examples of local demographers who helped to organize moral statistics and made use of the department's program to publish studies about suicides within their respective regions. For biographical information see "Kratkaia avtobiografiia zaveduiushchei demograficheskoi st-ki N. N. Visherskogo," GAIaO, f. 548, op. 1, 339, ll.

The success or failure of Soviet moral statistics depended heavily on a diverse group of government officials ranging from the police to the heads of rural soviets, some of whom lacked formal education, let alone training in the proper collection of statistical data. This was especially the case in the more remote localities of the USSR. Provincial statisticians in Ukraine, for instance, complained that the lack of competent personnel was hindering their efforts to follow the movement of the population. In particular, they noted that rural officials did not fully comprehend the importance of registering basic demographic information and were often indifferent to the matter.[42] To help remedy the situation, statisticians in some regions worked with law enforcement representatives to verify and supplement the suicide questionnaires completed by the civil registries. Police in Iaroslavl' Province, for example, were asked to telegraph brief reports that contained information about the suicide's name and sex, permanent place of residence, residence at the moment of the suicide, and the month, date, and time when the suicide occurred. In addition, criminal investigators, who completed their own forms when looking into cases of suicide, were requested to provide the provincial statistical bureau with copies.[43]

Mikhail Gernet and Dmitrii Rodin did their part to strengthen the statistical apparatus by familiarizing Soviet legal workers with the basic goals and techniques of their discipline. Most significantly, criminal law students at Moscow University took classes on moral statistics as part of their general curriculum, usually in their second or third year of study. In both lectures and more specialized seminars, Gernet and Rodin discussed the formulation and analysis of statistical forms, taught the proper way to construct statistical tables, trained students to conduct research on living subjects, and generally introduced their pupils to the work of state

---

47–48ob; and L. E. Poliakov, "Kratkii ocherk zhizni i deiatel'nosti S. A. Novosel'skogo," in S. A. Novosel'skii, *Demografiia i statistika (Izbrannye proizvedeniia)*, ed. L. E. Poliakov (Moscow, 1979), 7–15.

42. See, for example, the correspondence from 1923 between TsSU Ukraine and its provincial statistical bureaus. TsDAVO, f. 582, d. 274, ll. 101–101ob, 197, 284–284ob. As late as 1928, complaints were still being generated about deficiencies in the work being done by rural ZAGS. One study found that almost half the statistical forms submitted from the remote regions of Siberia contained some sort of defect, including the listing of "tired of life" and "old age" as causes of death. "Statistika i ZAGS'y," *Statisticheskii vestnik*, 29, no. 1 (May 1928): 172.

43. Copy of letter from the heads of the provincial statistical bureau and its demography section to the administrative department of the Iaroslavl' executive committee, GAIaO, f. 548, op. 2, d. 619a, l.8; and letter from the head of the demography section to the director of the Iaroslavl' provincial department of criminal investigation, GAIaO, f. 548, op. 2, d. 619a, l. 15.

organs involved in gathering data about so-called social anomalies.[44] Gernet also sought to demonstrate the practical side of moral statistics. He directed several firsthand explorations of the Moscow criminal world as well as the 1924 citywide study that formed the basis of Nikolai Brukhanskii's *Suicides*.[45] The ultimate goal of these educational efforts was to prepare students for their future role as "criminalist-sociologists" (*kriminalisty-sotsiologi*).[46] They aimed to make information gathering a constituent element of Soviet legal workers' everyday responsibilities and to make these workers conscious of the need to take such responsibilities seriously. For Russia to become statistical it was necessary for people to think statistically, a point made by the physician Grigorii Gordon in his prerevolutionary critique of the tsarist system.

As the central oversight body, the Department of Moral Statistics looked for signs of indifference within the statistical apparatus. In particular, its leaders made note of extended periods of silence from particular regions or provinces. To the moral statisticians in Moscow, a lack of completed survey forms did not necessarily equate with a lack of suicides; rather, they read it as indicating the breakdown of the statistical network. For example, a July 1922 letter regarding the state of affairs in Perm expressed skepticism about the work being carried out there. Gernet confessed that it was "difficult to imagine that over the course of five months there were no cases of suicide in the province."[47] Such silence threatened the vision of a unitary statistical voice and the ultimate goal of the moral statisticians, which was to have as complete a picture as possible of suicides. A circular sent out to all the provincial statistical bureaus just before the start of the registration program in February 1922 stressed the importance of counting every case. "The provincial statistical bureaus," read the circular, "should take measures so that not a single completed suicide (i.e., with a fatal outcome) inside the boundaries of the province remains without

---

44. See, for example, "Programma seminarskikh zaniatii po kursu moral'noi statistiki," TsAGM, f. 1609, op. 7, d. 95, l. 119; "Programma seminarii po moral'noi statistiki," TsAGM, f. 1609, op. 7, d. 120, l. 25; and "Programma seminariia po moral'noi statistike," TsAGM, f. 1609, op. 7, d. 182, l. 49.

45. The results of these efforts were published in a single edited volume. M. Gernet, ed., *Prestupnyi mir Moskvy* (Moscow, 1924).

46. "Programma seminariia prof. M. N. Gerneta po ugolovnomu pravu (na tret'em kursu)," TsAGM, f. 1609, op. 6, d. 102, ll. 27–28; M. N. Gernet, "Kratkie vospominaniia," l. 2; and *Samoubiistva v SSSR 1922–1925*, 11.

47. Letter of July 14, 1922, from the Department of Moral Statistics to the Perm Provincial Statistical Administration, RGAE, f. 1562, op. 31, d. 61, l. 209. The absence of any forms on suicide was also noted in a letter to the statistical bureau in Penza Province. See the letter of the same date, RGAE, f. 1562, op. 31, d. 61, l. 210.

a completed registration card." Moreover, the circular stressed that the relatively small number of suicides meant that their "exhaustive registration" would not pose a burden to the local agencies and provided "grounds to demand the completeness and accuracy of the reported information."[48]

The suicide questionnaires therefore acquired significance beyond the basic information contained within them. Besides serving as a means for evaluating the workings of the statistical apparatus beyond the capital, they were critical to the moral statisticians' ideal of creating a uniform system of information gathering across the entire country. Just prior to the start of the registration drive in 1922, Gernet and Rodin sought to enlist the statistical authorities in Armenia, Belorussia, Turkestan, Azerbaijan, Georgia, and the Far East by offering to supply them with the questionnaire on the suicide. Rodin, in particular, stressed the enormous benefits derived from a common approach. "Without a doubt," he wrote, "the scientific and practical significance of all these materials grows if they are gathered according to a single program and identical methodology, and are worked out uniformly in all the republics within the borders of the RSFSR."[49] Full implementation of the program meant that every suicide would be recorded in the same manner regardless of time and location. Each would become Soviet in the sense that it had been identified, broken down, and represented according to a single cognitive and institutional framework.

The questionnaire helped to standardize Soviet suicide by shaping the information provided by the respondents. Moral statisticians extolled the form for its clear and concise formulation. In contrast to the unwieldiness of the forensic doctors' survey, for example, the Department of Moral Statistics' questionnaire was said to break down the information into more discrete units that facilitated the construction of statistical tables. Moreover, several questions included a set of possible answers to be selected and underlined by the respondent, an organizational scheme that was intended to keep variation to a minimum. At the same time, the Department of Moral Statistics attempted to shape the responses by providing

48. Circular of January 1922 from the Department of Moral Statistics to all provincial statistical bureaus, RGAE, f. 1562, op. 31, d. 61, l. 29. The provincial bureaus were instructed to consult with the local departments of criminal investigation in the event that ZAGS failed to provide sufficient information about a suicide.

49. At the time when Rodin was writing, these territories were still connected with the Russian Federation, their status being altered with the creation of the federated USSR in December 1922. RGAE, f. 1562, op. 31, d. 61, l. 5. Mikhail Gernet made an offer of assistance to the Central Statistical Administration of the Armenian Republic in a letter of July 26, 1922. RGAE, f. 1562, op. 31, d. 61, l. 224.

detailed instructions along with the questionnaires. These guidelines explained many of the questions on the form and told respondents how to properly determine nationality, native language, marital status, education level, and occupation. Uniformity was desired even when information was lacking. In such instances, the respondent was asked to simply write "unknown" (*neizvestno*) in the appropriate blank space.[50]

The kinds of information being gathered through the questionnaire reflected the moral statisticians' membership in the larger Soviet and international statistical communities. Keenly aware of the way that other nations gathered information, they sought to collect facts that were deemed generally accepted for the characterization of suicides: the sex, age, and occupation of the suicide; the mode of suicide; and the underlying cause of the act. In addition to these universal elements, the questionnaire contained other entries that reconstructed the social and personal biography of the deceased, including nationality, marital status, number of children, education, and place of residence. Their inclusion enabled the Soviets to engage the larger debates about the social factors that shaped suicides among different groups and populations.[51]

While reflecting the broader field of suicide studies, the questionnaire also had several distinctive features that mirrored its Soviet context. The first edition issued in early 1922 contained an entry asking for the suicide's religious beliefs (*veroispovedovanie*), and respondents were instructed to indicate the deceased's faith or to label him or her as indifferent. However, the question on religion was soon removed and never appeared among the department's tabular analyses of the data. The decision to delete this entry was confirmed at the March 9, 1922, meeting of the Central Statistical Administration's collegium, a collective body that governed all scientific and scholarly matters inside the TsSU.[52] Its reasoning is not made

---

50. "Instruktsiia po zapolneniiu 'Oprosnogo listka o samoubiitse,'" RGAE, f. 1562, op. 1, d. 261, ll. 28–28ob; and the later, slightly amended version, "Instruktsiia po zapolneniiu 'oprosnogo listka o samoubiitse,'" RGAE, f. 1562, op. 1, d. 458, ll. 12–12ob.

51. Rodin, "O postanovke," 95–97. With an eye toward achieving uniformity within the larger Soviet statistical community, the selection of classifications for such factors as occupation, age groups, and nationalities was made in consultation with other members of the TsSU. See, for example, "Protokoly zasedaniia Kollegiia Ts.S.U.," TsGA SPb, f. 164, op. 18, d. 10, l. 102; and "Protokol zasedaniia kollegii Tsentral'nogo Statisticheskogo Upravleniia. No. 250 (15 iiunia 1922 g.)," RGAE, f. 1562, op. 1, d. 282, l. 167.

52. Several weeks later the collegium instructed the Department of Moral Statistics not to carry out any analyses of the suicide data in combination with the factor of religion (*religiia*). "Protokol zasedaniia kollegii Tsentral'nogo Statisticheskogo Upravleniia. No. 236 (9 marta 1922 g.)," RGAE, f. 1562, op. 1, d. 282, l. 45; and "Protokol zasedaniia kollegii Tsentral'nogo Statisticheskogo Upravleniia. No. 250," l. 167. A small sample of extant questionnaires from Iaroslavl' Province suggests that the original version of the questionnaire, which included

clear in the existing documents, but the collegium's move to exclude religion is doubtless an example of the intersection of ideology and social knowledge during the 1920s. This is suggested by the decision taken in 1926 to *add* a question about the suicide's political status (*partiinost'*). The redacted version of the questionnaire now asked whether the suicide had been a Bolshevik Party member, candidate member, a member of the Komsomol, or nonparty.[53] Although the Department of Moral Statistics never published any of the data gathered about party affiliation, the inclusion of the question about political status was another manifestation of a revolutionary politics concerned with the development of the person as a fundamentally political being. At least in the world of Soviet suicide, politics had replaced religion as the key indicator of the individual's beliefs, loyalties, and worldview.

Overall, then, the questionnaire on the suicide both reflected and shaped the character of Soviet suicide during the 1920s. In breaking down the suicide and framing the information provided by respondents, it promoted a common classificatory grid across the country. At the same time, the questionnaire was a form of self-representation that expressed the moral statisticians' understanding of their place within the larger community of social researchers. Gernet and Rodin both lauded their questionnaire for the fact that it contained the essential questions for studying suicide while also providing information not seen elsewhere in the world. Most notably, they emphasized their concern with previous suicide attempts as well as the precise time and location of the act. This meant that statisticians in other countries could not reproduce the variety of data found in Russia. An early publication by the moral statisticians trumpeted this difference, stating, "The questionnaire on the suicide in the RSFSR contains, compared with similar forms abroad, much wider information. And here the opportunity presents itself for the construction of new and original [statistical] tables."[54] Indeed, the richness of statistical

---

the entry on religion, was in use as late as 1924–25. GAIaO, f. 584, op. 2, d. 892, ll. 86, 87, 111, 115, 126. On a broader level, the use of the original form reflects the continued absence of complete uniformity and coordination within the Soviet statistical apparatus. Moreover, economic factors were probably at work here. A large portion of the Department of Moral Statistics' budget went to cover printing costs, which might have made it too costly to replace the older forms with new ones.

53. It also requested information about party members' length of involvement in the organization. See "Oprosnyi listok o samoubiitse," RGAE, f. 1562, op. 1, d. 458, l. 11ob; and *Samoubiistva v SSSR 1922–1925*, 10.

54. M. N. Gernet and D. P. Rodin, "Statistika osuzhdennykh v 1922 g. i statistika samoubiistv v 1922–23 gg.," *Biulleten' Tsentral'nogo statisticheskogo upravleniia*, no. 84 (1924): 114.

information was hailed as a distinctive hallmark of Soviet moral statistics.[55] Although Gernet admitted as late as 1927 that the new statistical apparatus was still a work in progress, he nevertheless claimed that it was making an important contribution that merited attention outside the USSR. "In view of the absence of information about suicides in our country over the preceding years," he explained, "and in view of the fact that the tables contained within this publication are novel in their construction, the latter are printed with headings and graphs translated into French." Now that they had a statistical voice and the capacity to make moral statistics, the Soviets desired to speak to as broad an audience as possible.[56]

FRAMING SOVIET SUICIDE

Suicides in the USSR 1922–1925, which appeared in 1927 with an introductory essay by Mikhail Gernet and an analytical summary by Dmitrii Rodin, marked the first major publication of suicide data gathered through the Department of Moral Statistics. Writing with pride over the accomplishment, Gernet proclaimed that the "broadly conceived and executed strategy of analysis [*plan obrabotki*] constitutes the exceptional distinctiveness of suicide statistics in the USSR."[57] However, suicide was becoming Soviet not only in terms of the way that it was being made known to Russia and the world but also in the statistical patterns and regularities that were being revealed through the numbers. Soviet moral statisticians, who saw their role primarily as informational, shared the widespread belief that different countries and population groups displayed particular tendencies when it came to self-killing. Given their understanding that Russia had never before possessed accurate, comprehensive data about suicide, as well as their faith in the historical uniqueness of the Soviet experiment, they were keen to establish the precise character of suicide in the postrevolutionary social order. This meant that much of the material produced

55. "Our suicide statistics," wrote Gernet, "present special interest because they have brought together information that is not available in any other country, and the tables are noteworthy for the variety of data in a wealth of combinations." Prof. M. Gernet, "Statistika samoubiistv v SSSR," *Administrativnyi vestnik*, no. 3 (1927): 17.

56. *Samoubiistva v SSSR 1922–1925*, 12. According to one internal memorandum, foreign scholars had in fact noticed the moral statisticians' work on suicide. "As a work of science," it stated, "this [effort] has also received recognition abroad." "Svodnyi plan statisticheskikh rabot (TsSU RSFSR i vedomstv) na 1928/29g.," l. 9ob.

57. *Samoubiistva v SSSR 1922–1925*, 10.

by the moral statisticians during the 1920s was descriptive in nature, with the bulk of their two major publications consisting of numerical tables in a variety of combinations. However, it would be wrong to see their efforts merely as a passive reflection of reality. For when they composed their statistical portraits, the moral statisticians were helping to flesh out the physiognomy of the postrevolutionary body politic. In this sense, they were active participants in the ongoing construction of the Soviet nation, both real and imagined.

Historians have shown the link between moral statistics and the formation of national identities in the nineteenth and early twentieth centuries. Elites who interpreted data on crime, suicide, and other social phenomena did so within the framework of the pan-European debate about the nature of civilization and progress. Moral statistics provided them with an instrument for ranking both peoples and states along a continuum of development according to levels and types of criminal activity, with different forms being labeled more or less "modern." At the same time, the numbers were a means of defining who belonged within the nation. Moral statistics helped to establish and reinforce internal boundaries as much as they provided a framework through which a state could be delineated against the rest of Europe. Numbers on crime and suicide were therefore both a domestic enterprise and a means of communicating across national borders and between intellectual communities.[58]

When viewed against this larger historical context, Soviet moral statistics are not overly remarkable in terms of their purpose and structure. Gernet and Rodin had been trained within the European intellectual tradition, and they worked hard to maintain relationships with their counterparts abroad, publishing comparative data, producing bibliographies of foreign scholarship, and paying visits to Germany and elsewhere.[59] Moreover, in their desire to engage the wider debates about suicide, the Soviets employed an interpretative framework used by social researchers outside the USSR. The moral statisticians asked the same questions of

---

58. In the case of Italy, for example, these sorts of statistics were an essential part of the debates about nationhood. See Silvana Patriarca, *Numbers and Nationhood: Writing Statistics in Nineteenth-Century Italy* (New York, 1996), chap. 6.

59. Gernet traveled abroad at least twice, including trips to France, Germany, and England, in order to gather updated material for his books on moral statistics. Rodin, meanwhile, visited Germany in 1924 and reported his observations about that country's statistical system. Speaking of suicide statistics, he noted that materials in Germany were much more decentralized and "analyzed in greater detail than in our country." In particular, he noted that in Saxony the information was broken down according to nine combined tables. "Protokoly zasedaniia Kollegiia Ts.S.U.," l. 101.

their data, used similar categories of analysis, and were interested in discovering whether postrevolutionary Russia adhered to the statistical laws established by scholars over the past century. In their analysis of the data, for example, they often referred (positively and negatively) to the formulations of such European scholars as Quetelet, Durkheim, Enrico Morselli, and the Italian criminologists Enrico Ferri and Cesare Lombroso. As a consequence, the work of the Soviet moral statisticians reads much like that of their European colleagues and was accessible to investigators outside the USSR.[60] It was focused on establishing general suicide rates (usually calculated per hundred thousand in population) as well as rates of suicide broken down according to a variety of factors such as sex, age, marital and family status, social class, time, and method.

Comparing national rates of suicide, Soviet moral statisticians confirmed perceptions of Russia's overall backwardness vis-à-vis the West. They found that levels of suicide in the USSR were still much lower than for most other European countries. The rate of 8.6 suicides per 100,000 population in 1925 and 7.8 suicides in 1926, for example, paled in comparison with Germany's coefficients of 24.5 and 26.2 for the same years.[61] Within these national figures, Soviet investigators noted regional variations, which they attributed to specific economic, cultural, and social factors. Vladimir Solomonovich Khalfin, a moral statistician with the Moscow provincial statistical department, attributed the spike and subsequent decline in suicide rates in southern Russia to the onset and abatement of famine in the early 1920s, while he explained a surge in suicides in the central industrial region as reflecting the large migration of people into the capital, Moscow.[62] Looking more broadly, the moral statisticians assumed that rates of suicide within the USSR reproduced the historical link between suicide and levels of socioeconomic development. In his com-

60. See, for example, the review by I. M. Rubinow of Gernet's *Prestupnost' i samoubiistva vo vremia voiny i posle nee* in the *Journal of the American Institute of Criminal Law and Criminology* 18, no. 4 (February 1928): 607–9. The reviewer noted the attempt to reach a foreign audience through the inclusion of French in the statistical charts but claimed that knowledge of Russian was needed in order to fully grasp the book's content.

61. *Samoubiistva v SSSR v 1925 i 1926 g.g.* (Moscow, 1929), 9. Soviet statisticians ranked Russia alongside such countries as Spain and Italy, which had a suicide rate of approximately 8.3 per 100,000. Gernet, "Statistika samoubiistv," 18; and *Samoubiistva v SSSR 1922–1925,* 14–15.

62. V. Khalfin, "Samoubiistvo (Po materialam TsAU NKVD)," *Raboche-krest'ianskaia militsiia,* no. 1 (1924): 17–18. A regional breakdown provided by the Department of Moral Statistics showed that in 1922 the Moscow industrial region had the highest rate of suicide in the country (28.8 percent of all suicides). *Samoubiistva v SSSR v 1925 i 1926 g.g.,* 8. Similarities and variations between national and local rates of suicide are also discussed in N. N. Visherskii, "Samoubiistva v Iaroslavskoi gubernii," *Sotsial'naia gigiena,* no. 1 (1929): 90–96.

ments on the different rates among European states and his country's relatively low position, Dmitrii Rodin confirmed the view that high numbers of suicide were a largely modern, urban phenomenon. "Just as it was prior to the war," he wrote, "suicides in our country stand in one of the last places according to their intensity. This is explained by the agricultural and rural character of the country."[63]

Russia did contain several islands of modernity within its borders—notably the capital cities Moscow and Leningrad (formerly Petrograd and St. Petersburg). Both urban centers were distinguished for their high suicide rates in comparison with those of the rest of the country. According to *Suicides in the USSR 1922–1925*, for the year 1925 there were approximately 31.8 and 17.5 suicides per 100,000 population in Leningrad and Moscow, respectively, which contrasted sharply against the national average of only 8.6 per 100,000.[64] Not surprisingly, because of their high rates, Moscow and Leningrad occupied a special place in the literature on Russian suicide both before and after the revolution. They were more heavily studied than other parts of the country, had more extensive statistical coverage, and were often compared with major European cities, with Leningrad in the 1920s being said to occupy a "middle position" between the high of Budapest (56.3) and the low of Amsterdam (7.1).[65] In addition, the Department of Moral Statistics provided separate headings in all its statistical tables for the data from Leningrad and Moscow, thereby representing them as distinct geographic and social spaces within the Russian body politic.[66]

Surprisingly little was published about the variation of Soviet suicide according to nationality. The moral statisticians attributed this lacuna to the lack of reliable census data, which made it impossible to calculate

63. *Samoubiistva v SSSR 1922–1925*, 15. The presumed difference between the city and rural areas was written into the moral statisticians' questionnaire. According to Rodin, the inclusion of the question on place of residence reflected their interest in determining the "influence of the city" on suicide. Rodin, "O postanovke," 96. Soviet criminologists interpreted the data on crime within a similar conceptual framework organized around the urban-rural dichotomy. See, for example, Sharon A. Kowalsky, "Who's Responsible for Female Crime? Gender, Deviance, and the Development of Social Norms in Revolutionary Russia," *Russian Review* 62 (July 2003): 366–86.

64. *Samoubiistva v SSSR 1922–1925*, 13–14.

65. S. Novosel'skii, "Samoubiistva v Leningrade," *Statisticheskii biulleten'*, no. 24 (1930): 67.

66. The moral statisticians organized their data into three spatial groupings: (1) Moscow and Leningrad, (2) other cities, and (3) rural areas (*sel'skie mestnosti*). See, for example, the charts in Gernet and Rodin, "Statistika osuzhdennykh," 122; *Samoubiistva v SSSR 1922–1925*; and *Samoubiistva v SSSR v 1925 i 1926 g.g.*

coefficients for different national or ethnic groups.[67] Moreover, despite their desire to establish a uniform system of information gathering across the entire USSR, many regions and republics began the registration of suicides at different points throughout the decade. Ukraine, for example, had yet to join the national program as late as 1926, the same year that the Autonomous Republic of Iakutiia in Siberia started to collect moral statistics.[68] Other researchers, however, used forensic-medical and police reports, as well as ZAGS materials, to examine suicides in Azerbaijan, Georgia, Uzbekistan, Ukraine, and Kazan, the center of the Tartar Autonomous Republic.[69] Ol'ga Ivanovna Korchazhinskaia, the investigator in Kazan, examined limited forensic-medical data to establish that rates of suicide were higher among the Russian population in the region. She tellingly employed a sociocultural rather than racial framework to explain the lower rates among native Tatars. As a whole, Korchazhinskaia speculated, the largely Muslim Tatar population was "less civilized" and therefore led a less demanding life that presented fewer opportunities for disappointment.[70] Thus the hierarchical interpretative grid that applied to the national figures was also at work when statisticians looked at the numbers for specific regions and populations. In this manner, moral statisticians and their contemporaries sketched out the contours of the Soviet social landscape according to a shared set of assumptions about the nature of suicide and historical development.

This interpretative framework, which was structured around the rural-urban divide, emphasized the social nature of suicide and applied to a variety of statistical factors. For example, not only were urban women said to kill themselves more often than rural women, a divergence that attested to the greater social pressures of the city, but the motives most commonly ascribed to female suicides—"love and jealousy" and "family troubles"—reportedly played a much smaller role in Moscow and Leningrad than in the less-populated cities and countryside. According to Mikhail Gernet,

67. *Samoubiistva v SSSR 1922–1925*, 29.

68. Ibid., 10; and D. Shepilov, *Samoubiistva v Iakutii (etiud)* (Yakutsk, 1928), 25.

69. A. S. Shaverdov, "K voprosu o samoubiistvakh v Tiflise," *Meditsinskii sbornik zhelezno-dorozhnykh vrachei Zakavkaz'ia*, no. 2 (April–June 1923): 153–74; S. A., "Samoubiistva na Ukraine," *Statisticheskoe obozrenie*, no. 9 (September 1928): 97–100; I. M. Leplinskii, "K voprosu o samoubiistvakh v Azerbaidzhane," *Zhurnal teorii i praktiki meditsiny* 2, nos. 1–3 (1926): 277–86; and I. I. Anosov, "Tashkentskie samoubiistva (1927–1929 g.g.) (po materialam rassledovanii militsii)," *Meditsinskaia mysl' Uzbekistana i Turkmenistana* 4, nos. 9–10 (June–July 1930): 101–10.

70. Ol'ga Ivanovna Korchazhinskaia, *Samoubiistva v Kazani v 1921 godu* (Kazan, 1922), 7. In a similar vein of interpretation, Shepilov linked the higher average of suicides among Russians in Iakutiia to their overwhelming residence in urban areas. *Samoubiistva v Iakutii*, 27.

"The more intense political and social life of Moscow and Leningrad, as well as their level of culture [*kul'turnaia uroven'*], decreases the role of these motives."[71] By the same token, levels of social development could be traced through the ways that people killed themselves. In particular, death by gunfire or poison was considered a more modern gesture than self-inflicted death by the noose or the knife, since both the gun and the chemical reagent were seen as products of an advanced society. Rodin wrote of these methods, "If it is possible to call poisons and firearms 'civilized' [*kul'turnyi*], and rope and cold weapons 'backward' [*otstalyi*], then through comparisons of old and current data it is possible to see that modes of suicide are evolving toward the side of 'civilized' methods at the expense of 'backward' ones." Such civilized methods were more prominent in urban centers, but figures for the nation as a whole suggested that "in comparison with other countries, civilized means—firearms and poison—play no less a role in contemporary Russian suicides."[72]

The moral statisticians' conceptual framework was therefore inherently comparative, and they tested their numbers against the statistical laws discovered by European social investigators. Like the forensic-medical doctors, they were particularly interested in determining the impact of the war and revolution on the population. They, too, believed that suicide rates had fallen in virtually all the combatant countries of World War I, even if they had doubts about the accuracy of the numbers collected during this tumultuous historical period.[73] The moral statisticians were far more certain that suicides in Russia, as elsewhere, had begun to rise with the cessation of hostilities. Nikolai Visherskii, for example, admitted that he lacked any data from Iaroslavl' Province for what he called the "military-revolutionary period." But thanks to the material gathered through the Department of Moral Statistics' questionnaire, he found that suicides over the years 1923–27 had more than doubled in the province compared with the average for 1908–12, a rapidly increasing incidence that far outstripped the rise in total population.[74] Leningrad was also displaying suicide rates that equaled or exceeded those calculated for the

71. *Samoubiistva v SSSR v 1925 i 1926 g.g.*, 12.

72. *Samoubiistva v SSSR 1922–1925*, 35–37. In his study of Iaroslavl' Province, the demographer Nikolai Visherskii claimed that civilized methods were most prominent among urban suicides. Visherskii, "Samboubiistva v iaroslavskoi gubernii," 95.

73. Gernet confirmed the sharp decrease in absolute numbers in a 1927 article, but he was rather skeptical about what questions the limited figures could answer. See his "Noveishie dannye statistiki samoubiistv za granitsei," *Administrativnyi vestnik*, no. 2 (1927): 6–7.

74. Visherskii, "Samoubiistva v Iaroslavskoi gubernii," 92–94.

prerevolutionary period. Making use of the moral statisticians' questionnaire, the noted demographer Sergei Aleksandrovich Novosel'skii established that the average suicide rate in Leningrad for the years 1925–28
was 33.7 per 100,000, a figure that was slightly higher than the 30.1 average for 1911–13 (but still lower than the peak of 38.5 in 1911).[75]

Time, which figured prominently in the comparisons of historical and
national development, was another central category of analysis in the
literature on Soviet suicide. As mentioned above, the moral statisticians
included a number of questions regarding the temporal nature of suicide in their questionnaire and stressed its potential to provide a wealth
of new information. In particular, they sought to provide a more precise
accounting of suicides according to the hour of day, rather than simply
days of the week or months of the year. They concluded early on that
Soviet Russia largely adhered to the "calendar of suicides" established
by researchers in other countries, with suicides rising until the summer
months and then decreasing toward winter, at which time the cycle repeated itself. Moreover, the daily distribution displayed a certain statistical regularity. Monday claimed the most lives from suicide and Thursday
or Friday the least.[76] In terms of the data regarding the hourly breakdown
of suicides, which were considered "unknown in foreign statistics," the
moral statisticians found a relatively stable pattern for the years 1922–26.
The highest number of suicides occurred during daytime (10:00 a.m. to
3:00 p.m.), followed by evening (4:00 p.m. to 9:00 p.m.), night (11:00 p.m.
to 3:00 a.m.), and morning (4:00 a.m. to 9:00 a.m.).[77] Getting even more
specific, Gernet claimed that the most "lethal" hour for both men and
women was two o'clock in the afternoon.[78]

Soviet moral statisticians adopted a deeply sociological explanation
for these temporal regularities. Taking their cue from Durkheim, they rejected the theories of the Italian school of criminology, which posited a
connection with higher or changing temperatures or even greater levels
of sexual feeling. Instead, self-destruction had to be a barometer of social

---

75. Novosel'skii, "Samoubiistva v Leningrade," 67; and Novosel'skii, "Samoubiistva, ubiistva i smertel'nye neschastnye sluchai v Leningrade," *Biulleten' Leningradskogo gubstatotdela*,
no. 14 (July–September 1925): 118. See also the comparative rates established for Moscow
and Leningrad in Skliar, "K voprosu," 97–98.

76. Visherskii, "Samoubiistva v Iaroslavskoi gubernii," 95; *Samoubiistva v SSSR 1922–1925*,
30; and *Samoubiistva v SSSR v 1925 i 1926 g.g.*, 13–14.

77. However, when the numbers were broken down by individual hours, no clear pattern emerged. See *Samoubiistva v SSSR v 1925 i 1926 g.g.*, 13.

78. Gernet, *Prestupnost' i samoubiistva*, 227.

involvement: since rates of suicide were related to the intensity of social life, suicidal tendencies rose and fell along with the degree of social activity. Thus, they were most common during the daytime and in those months, such as May and June, with the longest periods of daylight.[79] Dmitrii Rodin took pains, however, to point out that the length of day could not itself be considered a cause of suicide in the same way that material deprivation or jealousy could be. "It is more accurate," he wrote, "to state that the more intensive activity occurring during long days delivers a greater number of minor blows, which overflow 'the cup of patience.'" The question of time, he concluded, only helped to explain the psychology of carrying out suicidal intentions and, like the selection of method, was ultimately dependent on a host of social factors.[80]

Social factors were also deemed critical in the distribution of Soviet suicides according to class and occupation. Although the moral statisticians recognized problems with categorization and accurate census data, they deemed social position to be one of the most important areas of investigation. In particular, they found that Soviet suicides largely adhered to theories about the relationship between rates of suicide, mental activity, and public participation. Limiting themselves to the urban population, for which there existed more precise census material, the moral statisticians found that "dependents" (*nesamodeiatel'nye*)—those over the age of ten who were living on the support of others—had the lowest coefficient of suicide, which was said to reflect their lack of involvement in the economy. Conversely, the free professions (doctors, lawyers, etc.) displayed the highest rates along with white-collar employees and the unemployed, although the reasons behind their suicidal tendencies were said to vary. Whereas the unemployed killed themselves because of material hardships, members of the free professions and white-collar employees committed suicide because of the "mental" and "nervous activity" associated with their work. This pattern held true when the moral statisticians broke down white-collar employees into their specific occupations. Rodin summarized the results as follows: "Standing out are workers in the organs of public security and administration, whose activity demands more energy and is more

79. *Samoubiistva v SSSR 1922–1925*, 29–30.

80. Ibid., 33. Within all these figures regarding the timing of suicides, the moral statisticians noted differences between the cities and the countryside, which they believed were a reflection of the particular "tempo of social life" in these different areas. For example, the monthly "calendar of suicides" was said to express itself less sharply in the urban centers, where "the perturbational factors of the intense social life obscure [*zatushevyvaiut*] the influence of factors associated with the length of day." Gernet and Rodin, "Statistika osuzhdennykh," 122.

nervous and intense, which finds expression in the higher suicides among them."[81] These findings dovetailed with studies conducted elsewhere. Tarnovskii, in particular, claimed that the statistical data about social position once more demonstrated the distinctive, even salutary, qualities of life in the countryside. "The statistics of suicide not just in Russia, but in other countries," he wrote, "prove that the generally slow, quiet tempo of country life, with its stable physical health, constitutes an undeniable guarantee against the heightened urge to 'move on to a better world.'"[82]

Such a positive portrayal of rural life vis-à-vis the urban environment seems rather discordant given the Soviet leaders' agenda of industrialization and proletarianization. So, too, does the absence of the class rhetoric that emblazoned the work of other Soviet investigators, including references to the "class contradictions" of capitalism that one sometimes finds in discussions of urban suicides.[83] Dmitii Rodin, for example, characterized the prevalence of the motive "material deprivation" among suicides of the unemployed as being "entirely natural," just as that factor was virtually absent among soldiers, who had better material support.[84] Such neutral language was in keeping with the primary philosophy and purpose behind the Department of Moral Statistics: interested more in information about the population rather than control over it, Gernet and Rodin were content to describe and analyze the observable trends, posit causal relationships, and highlight those places where their data diverged from the conventional wisdom of the scholarly community.[85] The fact that they were able to operate in such a fashion is indicative of the continued negotiation over the content and form of quantification during the formative stages of the Central Statistical Administration. At least during the early to middle years of the 1920s, the moral statisticians were more or less left alone to pursue their own vision of the social science state.

---

81. *Samoubiistva v SSSR 1922–1925*, 21–25. The relational pattern between suicide and mental labor also held true when measured according to rates of literacy, with higher numbers of suicide seen among the more literate members of society.

82. Tarnovskii, "Svedeniia o samoubiistvakh," 207–9. Tarnovskii specifically noted the calming effects of the countryside on the nerves of city folk.

83. See, for example, I. Z. Kovalenko, "Opyt izucheniia pokushenii i zakochennykh samoubiistv sredi gorodskogo naseleniia," *Profilakticheskaia meditsina*, no. 10 (1926): 46.

84. *Samoubiistva v SSSR 1922–1925*, 24–25.

85. On the distinction between gathering data for information and gathering it for control see Alexandre Avdeev, Alain Blum, and Irina Troitskaya, "The History of Abortion Statistics in Russia and the USSR from 1900 to 1991," *Population: An English Selection* 7 (1995): 39–66. The authors see strong similarities between the Department of Moral Statistics' work on suicide and its 1927 publication of abortion statistics, which were gathered to understand the "social nature of this practice." The collection of both sets of data served solely as a means to analyze postrevolutionary society (42–43).

INTERPRETING SOVIET SUICIDE

Much of the moral statisticians' focus was on the key facets of everyday life that had been altered by the revolution, notably the family, marriage and gender relations, and youth. These were the areas most heavily explored by other social investigators during the 1920s as part of the wider effort to understand and transform the way people lived and interacted after the revolution.[86] In addition, they were among the elements of social life most frequently examined in the scientific literature on suicide. Thus there was an easy correspondence between the discourse of revolutionary social change and the European tradition of social investigation, an affinity that facilitated statistical comparisons of Soviet life with both prerevolutionary society and capitalist countries. As with investigations into the individual personality, Soviet Russia's distinctive features were cast as the product of its past, present, and possible future.

One "distinctive feature" (*osobennost'*) of Soviet suicides was their "different distribution according to age groups."[87] European investigators had long before established that, with minor exceptions, rates of suicide rose along with age. They were extremely rare among children and most common among the elderly.[88] However, Soviet statisticians found that suicides throughout their country occurred most frequently during the so-called peak age (*tsvetushchyi vozrast*) of twenty to twenty-four.[89] With some variation according to sex and place of residence, the national pattern also held true in other locations like Leningrad, although there the trend toward younger suicides actually predated the revolution.[90] Writing in 1924,

86. On the intense interest in everyday life see, for example, Gregory Carleton, *Sexual Revolution in Bolshevik Russia* (Pittsburgh, 2005); Tricia Starks, *The Body Soviet: Propaganda, Hygiene, and the Revolutionary State* (Madison, 2008); Frances Lee Bernstein, *The Dictatorship of Sex: Lifestyle Advice for the Soviet Masses* (DeKalb, IL, 2007); and Natalia Borisovna Lebina, *Povsednevnaia zhizn' sovetskogo goroda: Normy i anomalii: 1920–1930 gody* (St. Petersburg, 1999).

87. Gernet, *Prestupnost' i samoubiistva*, 224; *Samoubiistva v SSSR 1922–1925*, 18; and *Samoubiistva v SSSR v 1925 i 1926 g.g.*, 9–10.

88. Durkheim, for example, cited this pattern as additional proof that suicide could not be considered an organic or hereditary characteristic. See his *Suicide: A Study in Sociology*, trans. John A. Spaulding and George Simpson (New York, 1951), 100–102.

89. *Samoubiistva v SSSR 1922–1925*, 18; and Gernet, "Statistika samoubiistv v SSSR," 19. According to the data for 1926, the suicide rate for this age group was 14.4 suicides (per 100,000 of the respective age group) followed by 12.4 for ages eighteen to nineteen and 9.7 for ages twenty-five to twenty-nine, each of which was higher than the national average of 7.8. See *Samoubiistva v SSSR v 1925 i 1926 g.g.*, 9.

90. M. Gernet, "Vozrast samoubiits v SSSR," *Statisticheskoe obozrenie* 6 (June 1927): 93; and Novosel'skii, "Samoubiistva, ubiistva i smertel'nye neschastnye sluchai," 121–22. Novosel'skii calculated a rate of 68.7 suicides per 100,000 males aged twenty to twenty-four and 54.5 suicides per 100,000 women aged twenty to twenty-four. For the period 1925, he found a slightly

Gernet and Rodin linked the new statistical "regularity" to the inability of youth to withstand the pressures of life. They remarked, "If we keep in mind that statistics usually show the strengthening of suicide's intensity with age (toward old age), then today we come to the opposite conclusion: that in the current conditions youth, having yet to be toughened up [*ne okrepshaia*] in the struggle of life, are quite often defeated and unable to bear the burdens of life."[91]

Evgenii Tarnovskii likewise grappled with the question of age in his comparative study of suicides in Russia and Western Europe. He noted that only Japan displayed a similar age pattern and questioned whether the predominance of youth among Russian suicides was a temporary phenomenon brought about by recent events and current conditions or a more lasting phenomenon. Citing earlier data for Moscow, Tarnovskii was inclined to see the roots of suicide in prerevolutionary soil, although he pointed out that the tsarist school system blamed for so many student suicides was now only a memory. Moreover, he theorized that the age distribution of suicide was shaped by both social and individual or anthropological factors. Elderly persons, for example, were more likely to commit suicide out of illness, fatigue, feelings of uselessness, and the sense of loneliness that came from losing friends and loved ones. Youth, by contrast, was deeply affected by the "sexual moment" during puberty. But how, asked Tarnovskii, was the anomalous situation in Russia to be explained?

Tarnovskii believed that the answer could be traced to the historical and economic conditions prevailing in Russia and Japan. Both nations were economically behind Europe and had devoted an immense amount of capital and energy to overcoming their backwardness. This partly involved a profound ideological and cultural break with tradition. "Out of this," wrote Tarnovskii, "unavoidably flows the stormy, revolutionary mood of youth, especially student youth, and their hostility toward the past, including its representatives and forbearers." The result was a deepening struggle between old and new, and between "fathers and children," that extended to the October Revolution, "when the past was decisively broken and put away in the archives." Exacerbating this ideological struggle was a deep economic "break" (*perelom*) that affected the entire population and strained everyone's "living resources." However, according to Tarnovskii, it was Russia's young people who experienced the greatest difficulties ideologically as well as economically. The suicides among them were the

---

different pattern, with the highest average for men aged twenty-five to twenty-nine (65.3) and women aged twenty to twenty-four (63.7). Novosel'skii, "Samoubiistva v Leningrade," 68.

91. Gernet and Rodin, "Statistika osuzhdennykh," 122.

"sacrificial victims" demanded by the struggle to modernize the country and catch up to the West.[92]

In addition to their age distribution, Soviet suicides also displayed a distinctive pattern when broken down according to sex. As early as 1920, the chief forensic-medical expert Iakov Leibovich detected a rise in the relative incidence of suicides among women after the October Revolution. Speaking at the First Congress of State Medical Experts, Leibovich told the audience that according to his calculations the ratio of female to male suicides in 1920 was approximately 2:3 as compared with a ratio of 1:4 prior to 1917.[93] He elaborated upon these preliminary findings a few years later in his major work *1,000 Contemporary Suicides (A Sociological Study)*, which was based upon data gathered from the forensic-medical survey forms for 1920 and 1921. Leibovich argued that the number of female suicides relative to male suicides had roughly doubled from prerevolutionary levels, a figure that he confirmed in a more detailed review of women's suicide published in 1926.[94]

With few exceptions, Leibovich's discovery of a rapidly changing gender balance was repeated by other researchers, including the moral statisticians, and became an almost canonical truth within the Soviet literature on suicide.[95] To be sure, social investigators found that men continued to outnumber women when completed suicides were tabulated. However, they argued that the gap between the sexes was closing and that Russian women were committing suicide more often than women in Western Europe. Dmitrii Rodin, for example, went as far back as the data gathered by the academician Hermann to construct a table showing the steadily increasing rate of female suicide in Russia over the previous century.

92. Tarnovskii, "Svedeniia o samoubiistvakh," 196–204. Gernet repeated Tarnovksii's argument in the revised edition of *Moral Statistics* and sought to test it by comparing rates over time and by looking at the distribution of motives among different age groups. However, the foreign data needed for such comparisons were either lacking or inconclusive (for example, the figures for the revolutionary year 1919 in Prussia actually showed a drop in the percentage of young suicides). See his *Prestupnost' i samoubiistva*, 224.

93. "Vserossiiskii s"ezd gosudarstvennykh meditsinskikh ekspertov sozvannyi 20–25 sentiabria 1920 goda (protokol)," GARF, f. 482, op. 1, d. 217, l. 19; and "Pervyi Vserossiiskii s"ezd sudebno-meditsinskikh ekspertov 20–25 sentiabria 1920 g.," *Izvestiia Narodnogo Komissariata Zdravookhraneniia,* nos. 1–4 (1921): 13–14.

94. Ia. Leibovich, *1000 sovremmenykh samoubiistv (Sotsiologicheskii ocherk)* (Moscow, 1923), 5–6; and Leibovich, "Zhenskie samoubiistva," *Rabochii sud,* no. 8 (April 1926): 555. Observations about the rising rates of suicide among urban Russian women actually began prior to 1917. See Morrissey, *Suicide and the Body Politic,* 316.

95. See, for example, Gernet and Rodin, "Statistika osuzhdennykh," 121; *Samoubiistva v SSSR 1922–1925,* 15–16; and Khalfin, "Samoubiistvo," 19–20. For a more skeptical attitude toward Leibovich's numbers, see Skliar, "K voprosu," 95–99.

According to his data, the female to male suicide ratio had jumped from 21:100 in 1821–22 to 32:100 in 1891–99 and finally to 49:100 in 1924. Moreover, Rodin presented his readers with a comparative chart illustrating the higher rate of female suicide in Russia compared with that in other European nations.[96]

Interpretations of the changing calculus of despair among the sexes reflected the widespread belief that suicide was essentially a male act. The historian Howard Kushner has traced the rise of this idea over the course of the nineteenth century and demonstrated how it profoundly shaped the entire medical and sociological corpus on suicide, including Durkheim's *Suicide*. Gendered assumptions about motivations and sexual-social roles, coupled with an exclusive focus on completed suicides that skewed the data heavily in favor of men, resulted in the definition of suicide as the product of stresses and strains inherent in male activities outside the home. Men, went this line of thinking, were active participants in the struggle for existence and thus killed themselves more frequently than women, who committed fewer suicides thanks to the family and home, which provided a shield against the suicidogenic currents buffeting individuals in the public sphere.[97] This overwhelming emphasis on social factors further deprived female suicides of agency. In the descriptive statistics of self-destruction, they were commonly portrayed as victims, be it of circumstance or of the cruelty and misdeeds of others.[98]

Soviet moral statisticians were unanimous in their belief that social factors explained the differential rates of suicide between men and women, although their emphasis on the "struggle for existence" also implied that women were intrinsically less equipped to survive its challenges. Mikhail Gernet, for example, claimed that the sheltering qualities of the home and family explained the lower levels of suicide and crime generally observed among women. Describing the relationship between a woman's milieu

96. The table also showed that Japan had a much higher rate, 66 female suicides per 100 male in 1918. *Samoubiistva v SSSR 1922–1925*, 15–16. Using the data for 1922–24, Gernet provided a ratio of 36 women for every 100 male suicides, which was higher than that for England (29), Denmark (28), Germany (27.4), Italy (26.9), and Holland (26.3). *Prestupnost' i samoubiistva*, 222.

97. Howard I. Kushner, "Women and Suicide in Historical Perspective," *Signs* 10, no. 3 (Spring 1985): 537–52; and Kushner, "Suicide, Gender, and the Fear of Modernity in Nineteenth-Century Medical and Social Thought," *Journal of Social History* 26, no. 3 (Spring 1993): 461–90.

98. On gender, suicide, and agency within the sociological discourse of suicide, see Susan K. Morrissey, "Suicide and Civilization in Late Imperial Russia," *Jahrbücher für Geschichte Osteuropas* 43 (1995): 201–17; and Lisa Lieberman, *Leaving You: The Cultural Meaning of Suicide* (Chicago, 2003), 67–94.

and the likelihood of killing herself, he wrote, "The circle of petty interests where she is born, lives, and constantly returns, keeps her away from the disturbances associated with life and work in the public eye [*u vsekh na vidu*]. It reduces the depth and force of mental shocks from failures in the arena of political and economic struggle that are little known to her but which befall the man."[99] D. Shepilov concurred with this explanation in his 1928 sketch of suicide in the Autonomous Republic of Iakutiia. Posing the question of why women committed fewer suicides than men, he answered, "The causes, no doubt, lie in that sociolegal position which a woman occupies in society. Involved to a lesser degree in the process of production and in social and official activity, she is therefore less subject to the vicissitudes of life borne by the man, who takes a more active part in both the struggle for existence and the political arena."[100] A statistician writing about Ukrainian suicide echoed these ideas and predicted that sometime in the future the number of suicides among the sexes would be equal as women became more directly involved in "the difficult conflicts connected with the independent struggle for existence."[101]

The moral statisticians used the question of female suicides to further refute the anthropological school's emphasis on biology in its explanation of suicide and crime. Where men and women were essentially equals, they argued, there should be little or no difference in their respective rates of suicide. In their study of the data for 1922–25, for example, the moral statisticians highlighted social and occupational groups in which the position and activities of men and women were deemed similar—such as cultural-enlightenment workers and medical personnel—and found that the frequency of suicide in these groups did not differ greatly by sex. To Dmitrii Rodin, the figures demonstrated that the lower rate of suicides observed for women "[did] not depend on the distinctiveness of their organism, but on the distinctiveness of their social position, and change[d] together with its alteration."[102]

Within this explanatory framework, the fact that growing numbers of women in Soviet Russia were taking their own lives was interpreted as a sign of women's altered position in postrevolutionary society. Leibovich was perhaps the most insistent in attributing the higher rates of female

99. Gernet, *Moral'naia statistika*, 232.

100. Shepilov, *Samoubiistva v Iakutii*, 13.

101. S. A., "Samoubiistva na Ukraine," 97–98. The same author provided the following explanation for lower rates of female suicide before 1917: "In the prerevolutionary period, a woman, being absorbed to a greater degree than today in the interests of her family, was relatively protected from the unfavorable influences of the external environment."

102. *Samoubiistva v SSSR 1922–1925*, 17, 23–24.

suicide to the progressive transformations wrought by the revolution. Commenting on this increase, he wrote, "The rise of female suicides is highly indicative and characteristic for the current epoch. But nowhere else does the woman enjoy such absolute equality as she does in Russia. Nowhere else does she participate so intensely in social life. Only a social revolution that has turned the old world upside down, carried out a reevaluation of all values, and made human labor the cornerstone of all interrelations could provide such equality."[103] Others joined Leibovich in linking women's higher suicide rates to their emancipation from the burdens of traditional, patriarchal life. Shepilov, for one, contended that the significant growth of female suicides after the October Revolution appeared "to be the result of the immensely increased participation (in comparison with prerevolutionary times) of emancipated women in productive and sociopolitical activity."[104]

Mikhail Gernet also recognized the growth of female suicides after 1917, but he offered a somewhat different perspective on its meaning. In his early work *Moral Statistics,* he pointed out that high rates of suicide among women did not always correlate with increased social freedoms. Countries like India, where the legal and social status of women was exceedingly low, also tended to have elevated levels of female suicide, which in Gernet's opinion could only be interpreted as a form of escape.[105] Similarly, Gernet wrestled with the apparent contradiction between high rates of female suicide and the fact that most peasant women in Soviet Russia continued to live rather traditional lives outside the public sphere. "What then explains," he pondered, "the higher percentage of suicides among Russian women compared with women in England, Germany, France, Denmark, etc.?" His response to this interpretative dilemma was to label both female suicide and crime as protests that signaled the weakening of the patriarchal order amid a growing struggle for emancipation. "From our point of view," he wrote in 1927, "even suicides committed on the grounds of jealousy and family troubles, when it would appear that the woman does not exist beyond the narrow circle of sexual and family life, become possible only when the foundations of family life and women's

103. Leibovich, "Zhenskie samoubiistva," 555. This is a slightly amended version of the claim made earlier in his *1000 sovremennykh samoubiistv,* 6.

104. Shepilov, *Samoubiistva v Iakutii,* 13. On expectations that rates of crime among Soviet women should also increase along with their greater participation in social life, see Kowalsky, "Who's Responsible for Female Crime?" 377.

105. Gernet, *Moral'naia statistika,* 233. Leibovich made note of Gernet's observations regarding the high rate of female suicide in India but did not apply them to the Soviet figures. See his "Zhenskie samoubiistva," 554–55; and *1000 sovremennykh samoubiistv,* 5 n. 2.

insularity [*zamknutost'*] have begun to shake." Gernet then summarized his argument through the analogy of slave revolt: "Before he becomes a citizen, the slave becomes an unruly slave, a rebel, and a 'criminal.' Woman, before she escapes from the position of being the reproducer of the species [*samka-proizvoditel'nitsa*] and the obedient housemaid, also moves along a lengthy path of struggle."[106]

Accordingly, higher rates of suicide among women directed the attention of social investigators to the status of marriage and the family in Russia, which were under attack in the decade following the October Revolution. Soviet law, in particular, sought to promote sexual equality by recognizing out-of-wedlock births, decriminalizing abortion, simplifying divorce, and giving full legal status to nonregistered marriages, i.e. cohabitating partners. Given the broad conviction that marriage and children acted as brakes on suicide, especially among women, this assault on the traditional social structure raised questions about the effects of the family in Soviet Russia. Leibovich, lacking any data, speculated in 1923 that the "lability" (*labil'nost'*) of contemporary marriage meant that it no longer possessed the same "preservative force about which [Enrico] Morselli, Durkheim, and [Alexander von] Oettingen spoke in their day."[107] Several years later, Dmitrii Rodin was able to test some of these hypotheses. Using the first set of complete data from the Department of Moral Statistics, he found that the presence of children continued to have a dampening effect on women's suicide rates, while women in unregistered marriages (especially divorcees, single women, and married women living with another man instead of their lawful husband) had a higher level of suicide. Rodin's analysis also highlighted the elevated rates of suicide observed among single women with children and noted that the rate of suicide in this group was much lower in the capital cities than elsewhere. Unmarried women in Moscow and Leningrad, he speculated, were not stigmatized as heavily for being pregnant; moreover, they had easier access to abortions, presumably reducing the number of unwanted children, who were a burden rather than a boon to the unwed mother. Finally, the data suggested that entering into an unregistered marriage seemed to soften the blow of pregnancy for single women and reduced their rate of suicide.[108]

106. This, to him, explained why there were fewer suicides among rural Russian women and why the absolute number of female suicides due to "jealousy" and "family troubles" was nearly identical for urban and rural women, even though the latter greatly outnumbered the former. Gernet, "Statistika samoubiistv v SSSR," 18; and Gernet, *Prestupnost' i samoubiistva*, 222–23.

107. Leibovich, *1000 sovremennykh samoubiistv*, 9.

108. *Samoubiistva v SSSR 1922–1925*, 27–28.

Implicit in the work of the statisticians was the idea that women in Soviet Russia had achieved, or would achieve, equal status both socially and in terms of suicide by acting like men. Gernet was rather explicit in this regard when he discussed the factors behind the rising rates of female suicide observed in all combatant nations during World War I. As part of the total mobilization campaigns, women in these countries had assumed a greater role in the labor force, many of them replacing male factory workers who had gone to the front. This, in Gernet's view, had resulted in greater levels of both female criminality and female suicide. By the same token, the ratio of female to male suicide in the European nations decreased after the cessation of hostilities, as both sexes returned to their traditional roles and places.[109] In Soviet Russia, by contrast, the number of women who were taking their own lives continued at a higher pace into the 1920s, which suggested to the moral statisticians and other investigators that the social changes brought about by the October Revolution were deeper and more lasting.

In fact, Soviet investigators working in the 1920s believed that the revolution had also imprinted itself on the modes of suicide. It was an axiom among researchers that distinctive patterns of preference could be discerned in the data for a nation or specific population groups. "Without exaggeration," wrote Leibovich, "every people of a certain epoch has its favorite forms of death and the order of their preference rarely changes. Sex, occupation, profession, place of residence, motives, and particularities of character all influence the modes of suicide."[110] Employing a very similar formula, Mikhail Gernet contended, "Without a doubt every country has its favorite [*izliublennyi*] methods of suicide: rope, poison, revolver and other modes play their own special role in each country, but this role changes depending on the place where the suicide is committed (cities of various populations), the sex of the suicide, his profession and age, etc."[111]

Interpretations of suicide methods were highly gendered and overlapped with the broader debate about the relationship between sex and suicide. Soviet moral statisticians approached the data from the viewpoint

---

109. Gernet, *Moral'naia statistika*, 248. When he wrote this text in 1922, Gernet posited that these patterns might be further confirmation of Durkheim's sociological theories. However, he acknowledged that any firm conclusions would have to await the availability of greater statistical evidence. Several years later, he adopted a much more skeptical attitude about the meaning of the data. See his "Noveishie dannye," 6–7.

110. Ia. Leibovich, "Zhenskie samoubiistva (Okonchanie)," *Rabochii sud*, no. 9 (May 1926): 624–25.

111. Gernet, *Moral'naia statistika*, 240.

that men and women, by virtue of their social position and nature, killed themselves in different ways. With some minor variation, men were more violent and resolute in their desire to die, thus resorting most frequently to so-called heavy methods such as side arms (knives, razors, etc.), self-strangulation (hanging), and firearms. Women, on the other hand, were thought ruled by moods and emotions, displaying the opposite traits of reaction, spontaneity, and passion in the way they committed suicide. This usually meant opting for the most readily available and less lethal or "light methods," such as poison and drowning.[112] Gernet summarized the difference between men and women as follows: "The means of suicide that demand several preparatory actions (the loading of the revolver, the strengthening of the rope) are apparently more foreign to a woman: she prefers to throw herself from the apartment window, to jump into the water, or to drink poison."[113]

Moral statisticians claimed that this universal picture continued to hold true after the revolution. Several researchers, however, found that suicides from gunshot wounds among both sexes had increased, a trend that was thought to reflect the greater availability of weaponry and the loss of respect for life resulting from the country's prolonged encounter with war and social strife.[114] Moreover, according to the demographer Novosel'skii, the "technology of suicides" in Leningrad changed over the course of the 1920s. The number of suicides due to gunshots declined dramatically in the second half of the decade, while hangings rose among males and poisonings among females. Novosel'skii found that vinegar essence had returned to its previously dominant position, accounting for 49.2 percent of all self-poisonings for 1925–28 compared with 13.7 percent for 1922–24. Believing that the selection of the poison depended heavily on what was available in the household, he resurrected the prerevolutionary call to

112. On the difference between "heavy" and "light" methods see I. Z. Kovalenko, "Opyt izucheniia pokushenii i zakochennykh samoubiistv sredi gorodskogo naseleniia (okonchanie)," *Profilakticheskaia meditsina*, no. 11 (1926): 53. Also at work here were highly gendered notions of female psychology. It was presumed that women, because of their emotional nature, often used suicide as a ploy to get attention and thus selected less lethal methods. See, for example, the discussion of suicides due to poisoning in I. Ia. Bychkov and S. Ia. Rachkovskii, "Samoubiistva v RSFSR posredstvom otravleniia za 1920–1924 gg.," in *Trudy II Vserossiskogo s"ezda sudebno-meditsinskikh ekspertov. Moskva, 25 fevralia–3 marta 1926 g.*, ed. Ia. Leibovich (Ulyanovsk, 1926), 222–23.

113. Gernet, *Moral'naia statistika*, 242.

114. Kovalenko, "Opyt izucheniia pokushenii i zakochennykh samoubiistv," 53–54; S. N., "Samoubiistva v Petrograde," *Biulleten' Petrogradskogo gubstatotdela*, no. 3 (June 1923): 64; S. A. Novosel'skii, "Estestvennoe dvizhenie naseleniia v Petrograde v 1920 godu," *Materialy po statistike Petrograda i petrogradskoi gubernii*, vol. 5 (Petrograd, 1921): 43–44. On the continuity of the general pattern among the sexes see *Samoubiistva v SSSR v 1925 i 1926 g.g.*, 14.

limit the sale of vinegar essence. Novosel'skii, however, recognized that this prohibition would influence only those suicides carried out "under the influence of short-term affect." It was a formula that applied particularly to women, given the highly gendered discourse that continued to shape interpretations of suicide well after the revolutionary events of 1917.[115]

SOCIAL PATHOLOGY OR SOCIAL PROGRESS?

The published works of the Department of Moral Statistics seem almost anomalous given the ideologically charged environment in which they were produced. Particularly noteworthy are their lack of theoretical controversy, overt political content, and prescriptive commentary. Such an approach was fully in keeping with the guiding principles of Mikhail Gernet and his followers, who gathered information for its own sake in the position of scientific observers of the social world. It also reflects the continued negotiation within Soviet Russia over the nature and purpose of statistical knowledge, which for most of the 1920s allowed multiple understandings to coexist within the institutions of state. Several scholars have in fact referred to the years 1926–27 as the apogee of sociological analysis in the Soviet period, a time frame that corresponds to the publication of the first major study on suicide in the USSR. They have in mind a "pure" form of social investigation where the data were privileged over ideology and a time in Soviet history when demography was not yet the sensitive issue it would become once the population had been buffeted by the collectivization and industrialization drives of the late 1920s, the great famine of the early 1930s, and the Stalinist terror that followed later in the decade.[116] Nevertheless, in a regime that made everything and everyone political, the stance assumed by the moral statisticians was also a form of politics that expressed a particular view of social knowledge and its role in Soviet power.

Even without overt statements of opinion, the moral statisticians could not help but comment on Soviet life. By framing their studies of self-destruction against the past and against the rest of Europe, for example, they questioned the nature and benefits of the postrevolutionary changes in people's everyday life. Within the gendered discourse of self-destruction,

115. Novosel'skii, "Samoubiistva v Leningrade," 70–71. Novosel'skii also commented on a recent decision to ban the free sale of potassium chloride, which led him to anticipate a drop in suicides using this poisonous reagent.
116. Blum and Mespoulet, *L'anarchie bureaucratique,* 221.

female suicides in particular functioned as a measure of the nation and its development. They were a sign of modernity and the breakdown of tradition in the face of industrialization, urbanization, and the rise of mass politics. Indeed, the fact that women were seen as essentially backward in comparison with men, a belief seemingly confirmed by their preference for less-civilized modes of suicide as well as their lower suicide rate, only made their growing propensity for self-destruction after 1917 into a more potent symbol within the debates about social change.

Of course, there was a potential paradox in linking rising rates of female suicide to the country's transformation under Soviet power. Suicide, as we have seen, continued to be understood as a social illness during the 1920s despite the fact that it had been decriminalized. Whether viewed in the political-class terms of the Bolsheviks or the sociological theory of Durkheim, the act of killing oneself was regarded as a potentially ominous sign of breakdown and its attendant social costs. For example, when referring to the skewed age pattern in Soviet Russia, Mikhail Gernet confessed that in terms of the "interests of the nation and the national economy," it was easier to accept the greater propensity toward suicide among the elderly than the high rates of self-destruction among citizens possessing "youth and full power."[117] By the same logic, higher rates of female suicide could have been interpreted as an indication of social pathology, or at least the worsening of conditions for women, many of whom found themselves abandoned, unemployed, and without a social safety net as a result of the conditions fostered by the New Economic Policy.[118] The psychopathologist Nikolai Brukhanskii, to take one example, connected higher rates of female suicide to the increased complexity and strains of women's lives, especially in the spheres of sexual and family relations. In the same breath, he also attacked Durkheim's argument that suicides were the product of increased social activity, since in his view such activity was a sign of health, not sickness. Brukhanskii instead attributed suicide to the urbanization process and its legacy of nervous-psychological injury.[119] Most social investigators, however, either ignored the multivalent nature of their data on female suicide or elected to read those data as a sign of positive changes in the country's social and political order.

The will to believe in the progressive effects of the revolution is particularly clear in the case of D. Shepilov and in his study of the Autonomous

117. Gernet, "Vozrast samoubiits v SSSR," 93.
118. See, for example, the linkage of suicide and women's continued dependence on men in Lev Semenovich Fridland, *S raznykh storon: Prostitutsiia v SSSR* (Berlin,1931), 77–78.
119. Brukhanskii, *Samoubiitsy,* 17.

Republic of Iakutiia. Basing his views on an admittedly small sampling, Shepilov maintained that the statistical picture in Iakutiia was the reverse of that in the rest of Russia: female suicides there had been higher *before* the revolution than afterward, accounting for only 22 percent of suicides during the 1920s. He attributed the high rates in prerevolutionary times to women's extremely degraded status and cited Gernet's theory about female suicides in India to support his case. The subsequent decrease, therefore, was a product of the revolution. Shepilov claimed that although Iakutiia had not seen a "broad entrance of women into the arena of political struggle and social-productive activity," the economic, cultural, and legal status of women living there had improved since 1917. "This," he concluded, "was a major step forward toward undoing the unbearable atmosphere in which the woman lived and which had given rise to the mass character [*massovnost'*] of female suicides. Only this could explain the variation in the correlation of the sexes among the cadres of suicides in postrevolutionary Iakutiia."[120] Thanks to the flexibility of the explanatory framework, both lower and higher rates of suicide among women could be cast as the consequence of progressive developments occurring after 1917.

The inclination toward a positive interpretation of the data was not the result of blind faith alone. Rather, it can also be understood in terms of the cross-cultural reception of symbols and knowledge. As noted earlier, representations of suicide as both male and a key barometer of modernity were first constructed within the context of Western Europe. They were part of a cultural imagination that posited the West as the epitome of progress, and at the same time, they articulated deep fears about the dysgenic effects of industrialization and urbanization. In fact, most investigations into suicide during the nineteenth century were motivated by the desire to prove that modernity itself was the cause of self-destructive behavior.[121] Soviet investigators certainly shared the view that suicide was a genuine social illness as well as some of the ambivalence toward the chaotic urban world that bred it. However, they were interpreting the data as citizens of a country deemed backward by the standards of the general discourse and as participants in a forward-looking regime that promised completely new forms of social and economic relations. Soviet investigators therefore were not inclined to fear the loss of tradition inherent in the patriarchal family. Instead, they were predisposed to see female suicide as an encouraging

120. Shepilov, *Samoubiistva v Iakutii*, 13–15, 27–29.
121. Kushner, "Suicide, Gender, and the Fear of Modernity"; and Kushner, "Women and Suicide in Historical Perspective."

sign of the old order's breakdown, the precise effects of which were still unknown and deserving of scientific study.

A key factor shaping Soviet discourse on suicide and mediating some of its potentially negative implications was the teleology implicit in the work of social investigators whose view of the data was animated by the idea of Russia's move toward socialism. This is most apparent in the case of the NKVD statistician Evgenii Tarnovskii, who reconciled the apparent contradiction in representing social illness as a sign of social progress by making the former a precondition of the latter. Tarnovskii sharply framed the problem of suicide within a narrative of modernization and socialist construction. Russian women, like Russian youth, were paying a steep but necessary price for overcoming the country's centuries of backwardness. Freed by the October Revolution, Soviet women were now an active force in Soviet life, helping to build the new society and fulfill its enormous promise. Those among them who took their own lives were the "unavoidable victims of the transition period" and the struggle to make Russia an industrial nation. Tarnovskii, in other words, overcame the contradictions of modernity by placing female suicides within a model of historical development that justified their sacrifices. "These victims," he contended, "will be compensated for a hundred times over when new forms of everyday life are embodied in existence, forms free from all remnants of the dark, burdensome past." Suicides, then, were symptoms of a temporary illness that would only make the social organism stronger and healthier.[122]

The concept of the transition period, which suggested the passage from Russia's autocratic past to its socialist future, allowed for the presence of suicide without calling into question the fundamental health of the Soviet social order. It implied a lack of internal stability as the social organism moved from one stage of development to the next, which in effect made suicides and other social problems a product of the disequilibrium inherent in the transformational process, much in the same way that the human body and mind became unbalanced during puberty. Shepilov, who asserted that the revolution had had a positive therapeutic effect in terms of this "destructive illness," could therefore warn simultaneously of continued suicides in the immediate future as people continued the struggle to escape the "inheritance of the past." "Iakutiia," he wrote, "is still experiencing an era of the transition period filled with the trials, contradictions,

---

122. Tarnovskii, "Svedeniia o samoubiistvakh," 196. The forensic-medical experts Bychkov and Rachkovskii made a similar claim in their study of suicides from poisoning. They stated that women were "paying" for their greater involvement in Soviet society and the construction of socialism. See "Samoubiistva v RSFSR," 222.

and difficulties of building a new society.... Over the course of a definite period, the difficulties of the struggle which are characteristic for our time might still generate a penchant for suicide, but this is an unavoidable 'cost of the revolution.'"[123]

In Evgenii Tarnovskii's study, the transition period was constructed around two distinct visions of Russia—an older Russia disfigured by its uphill struggle to catch up to the West and an imagined socialist Russia that did not yet exist but would inevitably achieve a unique form of modernity. By adapting the social criticism of Émile Durkheim to the Soviet experiment, Tarnovskii found a way to overcome the political sensitivities of his data and thus create a bridge to the Marxist world of the future. He believed that the great French sociologist's ideas led to one logical conclusion, even if Durkheim himself did not realize this: "[T]he main cause of the development of suicides in contemporary society is the anarchic state of production and distribution, i.e. the bourgeois or capitalist system in general." Therefore, the basic "medicine" (*lekarstvo*) against this "social illness" was socialism. In contrast to the anomie of capitalism, individuals living under socialism would become conscious of their organic link to the larger collective and seek integration within it, as class struggle and individual competition ceased to exist. "Here," wrote Tarnovskii, "there can be no place for depression, apathy, or aversion to life. The value of life, as a whole, rises by necessity, since the sum of cheerful, pleasant impressions it affords exceeds the sum total of contrary thoughts and feelings." However, he acknowledged that the ideal socialist society, with all its internal "harmony" and "equilibrium," was still a "matter of the future."[124]

The utopian optimism expressed in such visions suggested that Soviet Russia's arrival at communism would be met with a return to statistical silence. For although suicides might increase during the transition period, they were heralding the death of the old world and the elimination of the conditions that drove people to kill themselves or commit crimes and other asocial acts. "These phenomena," wrote Tarnovskii, "are essentially vestiges of old forms of life that have yet to finally disappear, and of an old psychology and ideology that have yet to adapt to the new order of economic and political relations. However, this adaptation is occurring gradually and should end with the complete triumph of communist bases

---

123. Shepilov, *Samoubiistva v Iakutii*, 29.
124. Tarnovskii, "Svedeniia o samoubiistvakh," 212–14. Tarnovskii, it should be noted, expressed complete faith in Soviet Russia's ability to reach the communist utopia. "Our country," he stated, "finds itself on the true path toward the achievement of this ideal, although this path is made difficult by countless and arduous obstacles."

of life, under which there will be no place for either crime or suicide."[125] Thus, unlike the statistical silence decried by the moral statisticians in their representations of the prerevolutionary past, the absence of numbers in the communist future would be an affirmation of the country's historical uniqueness and progressiveness.

The irony, however, was that moral statistics disappeared from the Soviet scene before its objects did. In 1931 the Department of Moral Statistics was closed amid the assault on prerevolutionary specialists and positivist social science during the so-called Cultural Revolution (1928–31). The available evidence provides few clues as to the precise reasons behind the department's closure, but no doubt it was severely weakened by the growing emphasis put on practical over theoretical knowledge, the limitations placed on sociological criminology in general, and the attempts to purge non-Marxists from the universities and state agencies. Mikhail Gernet, the department's director, had himself come under criticism two years earlier for being a "representative of the petit bourgeois wing of the Russian school [of criminology]."[126] Dmitrii Rodin, moreover, was dismissed from Moscow University after the academic year 1929–30.[127] Such moves signaled the end to the laissez-faire attitude of the Bolsheviks, who endeavored to impose greater ideological control over social research and its practitioners. They also signaled an end to the transition period associated with the New Economic Policy as the regime began the final push toward socialism through forced collectivization of agriculture and the rapid industrialization of the country. In terms of suicide, these developments brought a halt to the planned publication of several works on the topic and generally made suicide a taboo subject rarely discussed publicly within the USSR.[128] To be sure, suicides continued to be counted

125. Tarnovskii, "Svedeniia o samoubiistvakh," 214.

126. Solomon, "Soviet Criminology," 125 n. 15. Gernet's work with the Department of Moral Statistics may also have been affected by health problems. According to his autobiography, in 1930 he began receiving a personal pension due to the deterioration of his eyesight, which eventually resulted in blindness. That same year Gernet also traveled to Germany, England, France, and Belgium to collect statistical material that appeared in his *Prestupnost' za granitsei i v SSSR* (Moscow, 1931), a work that contained an editorial introduction critical of Gernet's positivistic outlook. "Avtobiografiia," 1, 7; and Gernet, *Izbrannye proizvedeniia*, 26–28.

127. Personnel list for the Faculty of Soviet Construction and Law as of October 1, 1930, TsAGM, f. 1609, op. 7, d. 248, ll. 22–23.

128. According to the research plan for the social statistics sector, which housed the Department of Moral Statistics, the compilation and analysis of data on suicides in the USSR for 1929 were to be carried out in late 1930 and early 1931. A follow-up report also listed work on suicide statistics for the years 1929–30. RGAE, f. 1562, op. 1, d. 631, ll. 64, 77. In addition, the project schedule for the "Moral Statistics Section" mentioned the preparation

by the Central Statistical Administration, but they were now part of its general interest in demography and remained unpublished secret data as the population question grew politically sensitive.[129] More significantly, the diagnostic apparatus of the Bolshevik Party, particularly its Political Administration in the Red Army, continued to study suicides as a sociopolitical problem well into the 1930s. In the hands of the Political Administration, suicide statistics became a tool of both information and control as part of the regime's efforts to govern the population and monitor the country's move toward socialism.

The fate of moral statistics therefore offers an object lesson in the nature of social knowledge and politics in Soviet Russia. Increasingly, the passive observational stance of moral statistics was untenable within an activist regime whose raison d'être was the radical transformation of everyday life according to a specific and ever more rigid ideology. For the early to middle part of the 1920s, at least, there existed a kind of truce between the two impulses, as the commonalities of Marxist and non-Marxist visions of statistics and the social order prevailed. In particular, both were constructed on the notion that social laws governed the individual and that these laws were discernible through large numbers. But whereas prerevolutionary liberal critics of the law of large numbers highlighted its diminution of the individual, Bolshevik critics were uneasy with its implicit fatalism and chafed at the suggestion that the Soviet state was powerless to alter the course of society. The result toward the end of the 1920s was the expansion of an instrumentalist view of numbers whereby "the logic of social statistics was replaced by the logic of accounting and policing."[130] Moral statisticians, who sought to capture the present reality, failed to articulate a vision of the future as it would be and thus wrote themselves out of the revolution's grand narrative. It was not simply that their numbers revealed truths that were not to the liking of the country's leaders; rather, the ethos behind them made politics potentially impotent, a damning suggestion given the Bolsheviks' belief in their ability to bend history and society to their will. With the onset of Stalinism, the moral statisticians were in no position to dictate what made suicide and its statistics Soviet.

---

of suicide statistics for publication among its goals for the period 1929–30. RGAE, f. 1562, op. 1, d. 595, 91.

129. See, for example, "Godovye svodki TsSU soiuznykh respublik dannykh ob umershikh po polu, vozrastu i prichinam smerti po otdel'nym gorodam RSFSR i g. Alma-Ate Kazakhskoi SSR za 1934 god," RGAE, f. 1562, op. 29, d. 33a; and "Svedeniia ob umershikh po polu, vozrastu i prichinam za 1937 g.," RGAE, 1562, op. 20, d. 93.

130. Blum and Mespoulet, *L'anarchie bureaucratique*, 202–5, 227.

5

Suicide and Surveillance

Medicopolitics in the Red Army

In 1914, the Moscow psychiatrist Leonid Alekseevich Prozorov wrote of the enormous potential for surveillance within the Russian army. He argued that the military provided a discrete and ordered population readily accessible to scientific investigation. In particular, he believed that acts of suicide and the complicated psychology behind them could be observed more easily inside the army. "Up to the last minutes of their lives," wrote Prozorov, "military suicides are normally found in the company of comrades under the vigilant tutelage [*opeka*] of the command. This presents an opportunity for gathering material about the personality of the soldier or officer who has killed himself or attempted suicide, as well as the causes and reasons for this sad fact."[1] The organized and communal character of the barracks, in other words, promoted a degree of openness not found in the civilian world, where the private apartment or home formed a shield against the prying eyes of outsiders. As a result, the critical last days, hours, and minutes of the civilian suicide often went unobserved, hidden from potential witnesses and, consequently, from the investigator.

Prozorov was not alone in seeing the military as an ideal site for implementing scientific and governmental schemes. After the 1905 revolution, the Imperial Russian Army became a key instrument of socialization and

---

1. L. Prozorov, *Samoubiistva voennykh* (Moscow, 1914), 1.

nation building as the autocratic regime sought to ensure greater loyalty and unity among its subjects.[2] The military was also a means to overcome the tsarist state's limited ability to intervene in the daily lives of the population. Most notably, during the crisis years 1914–21 the Russian army increasingly became a surrogate for missing state and civil institutions. It offered both the autocracy and the subsequent revolutionary governments the organizational structure and techniques for mass mobilization, which eventually expanded beyond the military population toward the larger goal of reordering society as a whole. Particularly under the Bolsheviks, the technocratic ideals of modern government fused with the revolutionary ethos around the dual practices of surveillance and enlightenment. Aiming to reshape human nature and cultivate a loyal citizenry, the Soviet party-state created a vast system of information gathering in order to know, and ultimately transform, the daily lives and thoughts of the Red Army soldier and commander. The result was a distinctive exercise in social science and psychology.[3]

This changed political and ideological landscape helps to explain why a comprehensive and centrally coordinated investigation into military suicides was organized in Russia only after the establishment of Soviet power. Prozorov's expression of technocratic idealism was predicated on the centrality of the physician, whose role as caregiver to the men would make him an excellent observer of military life.[4] However, a new type of social investigator—the political worker—played the lead role in Soviet-era studies of military suicides. Neither physician nor psychiatrist, the political

2. Joshua A. Sanborn, *Drafting the Russian Nation: Military Conscription, Total War, and Mass Politics, 1905–1925* (DeKalb, IL, 2003).

3. Peter I. Holquist, *Making War, Forging Revolution: Russia's Continuum of Crisis, 1914–1921* (Cambridge, MA, 2002), 232–40.

4. On the centrality of the physician to his research program, see Prozorov, *Samoubiistva voennykh*, 17–18. Physicians did play a key role in producing information about suicides in the imperial army. Several military doctors undertook their own independent investigations, producing an interesting but small body of work. Moreover, physicians were also responsible for producing the only official statistical material published on self-destruction in the Imperial Russian Army. Numbers of suicides were regularly grouped among "sudden deaths" in the annual reports on the "sanitary condition" of the army. See, for example, the yearly *Otchet o sanitarnom sostoianii russkoi armii* (St. Petersburg), published by the Chief Military-Medical Administration as a supplement to the journal *Voenno-meditsinskii zhurnal;* N. M. Bekker, *Samoubiistvo v Russkoi Armii. Statisticheskii ocherk* (Kiev, 1914); E. V. Erikson, "O samoubiistvakh v armii," *Voenno-meditsinskii zhurnal* 242, no. 3 (March 1915): 336–48; D. P. Nikol'skii, "O samoubiistvakh uchashchikhsia v voenno-uchebnykh zavedenii," *Prakticheskii vrach,* April 15, 1912, 262–66; V. A. Bernatskii, "Samoubiistva sredi vospitannikov voenno-uchebnykh zavedenii," *Pedagogicheskii sbornik,* nos. 8–9 (August–September 1911): 99–125, 238–81; and R. I. Gaikovich, "Samoubiistva v voiskakh russkoi armii za 15 let," *Russkii vrach,* March 10, 1907, 344–45.

worker was instead an expert in the care of the political self. He was responsible for promoting proper revolutionary consciousness while also working to ward off a variety of threats to the ideological health of the troops. Thus, the political worker's interest in suicide was an extension of the regime's broader concern with the "political-moral condition" (*politiko-moral'noe sostoianie*) of the Workers' and Peasants' Red Army (RKKA).[5]

Within the Red Army, surveillance, suicide, and political enlightenment all fell under the purview of its primary political organ—the Political Administration. Beginning in 1923–24, PUR spearheaded a collaborative effort to catalog and analyze all acts of self-destruction within the military.[6] Considered by many a "second Commissariat of Enlightenment," the Political Administration was a semiautonomous agency established in February 1919. It oversaw the Bolshevik Party's military wing as well as general political and cultural education inside the Red Army.[7] PUR was also part of a broader network of institutions responsible for the comprehensive care of the military population. In studying suicides, PUR worked closely with medical personnel in the Military-Sanitary Administration (VSUpr), legal officials working under the Military Procurator of the Supreme Court, and general administrators in the Main Administration (GURKKA). Furthermore, the Special Department of the State Political Directorate (OOGPU), the military branch of the Soviet state's secret police, also got involved in the investigation of suicides. Together, these various agencies produced a wealth of material that included general statistical surveys, periodic informational summaries, secret political reports, and forensic-medical protocols.

5. The duties and position of political workers, including their focus on morale and discipline, are described further in Roger R. Reese, *Red Commanders: A Social History of the Soviet Army Officer Corps, 1918–1991* (Lawrence, KS, 2005), 111–15.

6. According to a 1927 memorandum, the Political Administration began to "systematically" study suicides in early 1924. However, another memorandum cites 1923 as the starting point for its investigations. See the report of April 1927 from PUR's Infstatodtel to Mikhail Markovich Landa, assistant director of PUR, RGVA, f. 9, op. 26, d. 429, l. 1; and the October 24, 1925, *Spravka* from the head of the Infstatotdel Chernevskii, RGVA, f. 9, op. 28, d. 794, l. 106.

7. The Political Administration grew out of the political department of the Revolutionary Military Council of the Republic (RVSR). This latter institution was established at the Eighth Party Congress to direct party and political work inside both the army and the navy. In May 1919, the political department was reconstituted as the Political Administration RVSR, which consisted of three departments: political, enlightenment, and literary-publication. The Political Administration's formal association with the Communist Party was not officially confirmed until 1925. On the history of the Political Administration, see Mark von Hagen, *Soldiers in the Proletarian Dictatorship: The Red Army and the Socialist State, 1917–1930* (Ithaca, 1990); Francesco Benvenuti, *The Bolsheviks and the Red Army, 1918–1922*, trans. Christopher Woodall (Cambridge, 1988); and I. Petukhov, *Partiinaia organizatsiia i partiinaia rabota v RKKA* (Moscow-Leningrad, 1928).

The Political Administration's work on suicide illustrates most vividly the expansive social and political terrain upon which the Soviet social science state operated. Its efforts to sculpt the military population combined an abiding interest in groups and aggregates with an understanding of the individual personality that opened up each soldier to scrutiny. Statistics and survey information were routinely used to monitor the condition of the military organism and to identify the presence of disease within it. This epidemiological approach emphasized the role of the environment in shaping the individual and was the basis for policies designed to ameliorate the sociopolitical conditions that fostered suicidal and other unhealthy moods. At the same time, the Red Army was deeply interested in the psychology of the individual. Consistent with the ethos of mutual surveillance, political workers, as well as commanders and medical personnel, were encouraged to get closer to the soldiers in order to really know them as persons. They were to be aware of their thoughts and feelings, their strengths and weaknesses, their everyday life inside and outside the unit. In this sense, political workers performed a dual function within the military apparatus. They were both gatherers and producers of information and social workers responsible for coordinating the various resources that existed to support the Red Army man.

The Soviets' insistence on accessing the social organism and the individual soul was predicated on an unprecedented degree of transparency and legibility. It required the continuous production of detailed information within an analytical framework shaped by the needs and desires of the Red Army's political leadership. Primary responsibility for creating such material fell to the Political Administration's Informational-Statistical Department (Infstatotdel) under the leadership of Vsevelod Nikolaevich Chernevskii. Among its various duties, the Informational-Statistical Department was charged with the "systematic notification of the central organs of the RSFSR about the political condition of the Red Army."[8] This included the biweekly summaries (*svodki*) compiled for a very select group of military, governmental, and political leaders.[9] The breadth of their content suggests the extensive social space that was open to study and deemed critical for understanding the political situation inside the military. They covered living conditions, the status and health of new recruits,

8. "Polozhenie o politicheskom upravlenii revoliutsionnogo voennogo soveta respubliki (18 oktiabria 1922 g.)," in *Partiino-politicheskaia rabota v Krasnoi Armii: Dokumenty 1921–1929 gg.* (Moscow, 1981), 110.

9. Only thirty-seven or thirty-eight copies of each summary were produced for an audience that included Stalin, Roshal' (head of the Central Control Commission), and Genrikh Iagoda.

the contents of personal mail, the state of discipline, the reactions of the troops to different political events or international happenings, as well as the family life and leisure-time activities of the soldiers and officers. Particular attention was devoted to criminal or deviant activities occurring both on and off duty, among them drunkenness, thefts, self-mutilations, card playing, sexual assaults, and general "debauchery." Suicides were also a regular feature of the secret summaries throughout the 1920s; moreover, they were described and analyzed in a number of special surveys (*obzory*) devoted solely to the topic of self-destruction.[10]

These reports and summaries present us with a wealth of facts for reconstructing lived experience and Soviet subjectivity. However, when viewed as a form of knowledge about the social world, they also reveal the meaning and expectations ascribed to the information by its creators and consumers. The political-military leadership was certainly interested in empirical data and thus displayed a highly positivistic outlook. Yet the Red Army's information also exhibits a deeply analytical and speculative quality indicative of its central role in the revolutionary project.[11] In fact, the practices surrounding the gathering and production of information helped to constitute Soviet reality on a number of levels. They formed the basis of various policies, expressed certain values, and shaped the character of the political workers' interactions with the troops. Moreover, when Red Army political workers went about constructing their narratives, they articulated and promoted a particular vision of suicide and the social world. This outlook included a general theory of the suicidal personality as well as a range of signs that indicated self-destructive mental states and made their existence comprehensible, if not condonable.

MAPPING ILLNESS IN THE MILITARY ORGANISM

According to one internal assessment, information was nothing less than "the eyes and ears of the Red Army." It was the basis of military preparedness and effective command and key to the proper functioning of the

---

10. According to an April 1927 summary of its activities, the Political Administration's Informational-Statistical Department circulated at least eight of these topical surveys between 1924 and 1926. RGVA, f. 9, op. 26, d. 429, ll. 1–1ob.

11. On the importance of surveillance for the transformation of individuals as well as society, see Peter Holquist, "'Information Is the Alpha and Omega of Our Work': Bolshevik Surveillance in Its Pan-European Context," *Journal of Modern History* 69, no. 3 (September 1997): 415–36; and Vladlen Semenovich Izmozik, *Glaza i ushi rezhima: Gosudarstvennyi politicheskii kontrol' za naseleniem Sovetskoi Rossii v 1918–1928 godakh* (St. Petersburg, 1995).

internal "political organs." Responsibility for collecting and reporting information rested with communists, political instructors, and political workers, who served as informants (*informatory*) in addition to performing their other duties. These informants played a vital role in maintaining the health of the Red Army by reporting on, and thus helping to eliminate, the "harmful phenomena" in their units or cells. The same internal report summarized their larger importance as follows: "Information puts in motion not only the entire organism of the Red Army, but also the entire organism of the vast Soviet Republic. Information is used so that all deficiencies and imperfections detected by it are immediately eliminated."[12]

The Red Army's information on suicide shared much with the social sciences of the time. Its investigators adopted analytical categories that were quite similar to those used by Soviet moral statisticians, forensic-medical doctors, and European sociologists. They employed corporeal metaphors to represent the military population and its condition and used theories of crowd psychology to explain and manage the troops' behavior. Moreover, they broke down the experience of suicide according to such personal indicators as age, occupation, and family status; such environmental determinants as geography and season; and such causal factors as romance, fear of punishment, incurable illness, material want, family squabbles, and the ubiquitous "disappointment with life."[13] Use of this standardized nomenclature and common discourse allowed military investigators to juxtapose their data with other materials to construct an aggregate picture that revealed the temporal, spatial, and causal dimensions of self-destruction.

The recognizable features of the Red Army studies are suggestive of the broader ecology of social knowledge at work during the 1920s. They speak to the continuity of personnel and practices across the revolutionary divide of 1917. Moreover, on a practical level they reflect the dialogue between representatives of different state agencies, who required a shared set of categories to achieve the goal of gathering comprehensive data about the

---

12. "Nuzhno osnovatel'no priniatsia delo (Kak proizvodit' sobiranie informatsionnykh svedenii)," RGVA, f. 9, op. 17, d. 72, ll. 209–22.

13. The Political Administration, however, did not analyze the methods of military suicides, which were a staple of medical and sociological investigations. PUR's interest in suicide as a political problem may have reduced the importance of methods. Moreover, the overwhelming prevalence of suicides due to firearms in the Red Army probably made the study of methods seem superfluous. A report stated, "There is only one means of suicide in the army's party organization. This is, 'He shot himself.'" "O samoubiistvakh sredi chlenov RKP(b) v partorganizatsii krasnoi armii i flota. (Po skheme Orgotdela TsKKRKP(b) i dannym Partkomissii)," RGVA, f. 9, op. 28, d. 736, l. 4ob.

population. The Department of Moral Statistics, to take one example, relied on the military's informational branches to furnish it with statistics on
suicides among the troops.[14] More generally, the common features of the
military materials reveal the wide currency of sociomedical explanations
regarding human behavior. As Daniel Beer has demonstrated, the human
sciences became a dominant tool in Russian culture for comprehending
the challenges and potentialities of modern life, and they proved remark-
ably adaptable to the radical policies of the Bolsheviks. This facilitated the
interpenetration of certain theories (such as degeneration) and language
(such as organic metaphors of the social body) with the class-based politics of the party, which in turn fused the practices of social investigation
with the goals of administration and transformation.[15]

The fusion of Bolshevik ideology, social science, and revolutionary politics produced a particular form of medicopolitics that sought to control
ideological, rather than infectious, disease. Operating according to an assumption that all citizens were potential political actors, not to mention
an understanding of everyday life that blurred the boundaries between
the personal and the political, the Political Administration approached
self-destruction from the standpoint of "political information."[16] In other
words, suicides were read along with a host of other social facts expressly
for what they revealed about the population's mood and the ideological
state of affairs inside the military.[17] This political definition of suicide led
to the construction of some rather idiosyncratic statistical categories—
such as "lack of a firm worldview or principles" and "disappointment in
the prospects of world revolution and hopes for the rapid establishment
of a socialist life"—that diverged from the canonical nomenclature. It also
lent a distinctive coloring to the purpose and form of the Red Army's
information, the dissemination and gathering of which was essential for
creating a dialogic relationship between the Soviet state and its citizens.[18]

14. The Department of Moral Statistics is listed among the recipients of a study released
on military suicides for the period 1924–25. "Spisok eksempliarov 'Samoubiistva v RKKA
za 1924/25 god,' vydannykh na ruku (iz ostatki ottiskov No. 37–50)," RGVA, f. 54, op. 6,
d. 462, l. 2.
15. Daniel Beer, *Renovating Russia: The Human Sciences and the Fate of Liberal Modernity,
1880–1930* (Ithaca, 2008), esp. chap. 5.
16. PUR's study of suicide as "political information" was highlighted in a summary report on self-destruction among party members in the Red Army and Navy. See "Kratkii obzor
o samoubiistvakh v Krasnoi Armii i vo Flote za 1924–1925 gody," RGASPI, f. 17, op. 85,
d. 126, l. 97.
17. Izmozik, *Glaza*, 95–99.
18. Peter Holquist, "Anti-Soviet *Svodki* from the Civil War: Surveillance as a Shared Feature of Russian Political Culture," *Russian Review* 56, no. 3 (July 1997): 446.

The Political Administration's interest in suicide grew out of its primary responsibility for the so-called political-moral condition of the troops. Viewed by the Soviet leadership as a school of socialism, the military was a key site of socialization and acculturation in the revolutionary project. Indeed, the Red Army as a whole and the Red Army man in particular assumed increased importance during the 1920s as "key agents" in the establishment of Bolshevik hegemony.[19] Confronted with an alarming diminution of the working class and finding itself surrounded by an unreliable peasantry, the party anxiously sought to identify a more secure base of social support.[20] Eventually it was the Red Army soldier who came to fill the social and political void. He was a surrogate for the proletarian, his loyalty to the Soviet state being equated with that of the worker. Furthermore, after their demobilization from the military, many veterans continued to serve as representatives of the party and the state in the countryside, where they carried the Bolshevik vision to the outlying villages and towns of the Soviet Union. Given their crucial role in the defense and spread of the revolution, it was vitally important that soldiers and officers be inculcated with the proper political beliefs and worldview during their time in the military.[21]

Within the context of its enlightenment duties, the Political Administration was truly practicing a form of moral statistics when it measured rates of suicide and other "negative" or "anti-moral phenomena."[22] Unlike the moral statisticians, who limited themselves to measuring observable phenomena, political workers vigorously sought to access the interior psychology and beliefs of individuals. They routinely interpreted outward behavior as indicative of attitudes toward the revolution and the fulfillment of one's military responsibilities. To be precise, the Political Administration portrayed suicide as a social fact that could be used to measure levels of morality, ideological belief, and cohesiveness. In a 1924 circular

19. von Hagen, *Soldiers,* 5–6.

20. On the Bolsheviks' obsession with identifying social support in the aftermath of the civil war, see Sheila Fitzpatrick, "The Bolsheviks' Dilemma: The Class Issue in Party Politics and Culture," in *The Cultural Front: Power and Culture in Revolutionary Russia* (Ithaca, 1992), 16–36; and Fitzpatrick, "Ascribing Class: The Construction of Social Identity in Soviet Russia," *Journal of Modern History* 65, no. 4 (December 1993): 745–70.

21. For example, social policies originally meant to discriminate in favor of the working class, including special access to education and favorable criteria for membership in the Bolshevik Party, were extended to soldiers and veterans. See von Hagen, *Soldiers,* passim.

22. Among these were crime, disciplinary infractions, drinking, desertions, hunger strikes, and "peasant moods." See, for example, "Opis' materialov doklada t. Bubnova na RVS 25/VI-28 g.," RGVA, f. 9, op. 28, d. 587, ll. 257–59; and "Materialy ob otritsatel'nykh iavleniiakh v politiko-moral'nom sostoianii RKKA," RGVA, f. 9, op. 28, d. 587, ll. 260–86.

to A. Krylov, head of the Political Administration's Conflict Commission (KK), the Military Procurator of the Supreme Court stated explicitly, "As a symptomatic phenomenon, suicide very clearly reflects the moral condition [*moral'noe sostoianie*] of the Red Army."[23] For this reason, the Moscow Military District asserted that the political organs examined suicides "as factors influencing the political-moral condition of the given unit."[24]

Of course, the study of military suicides also reflected the character of the Red Army, with its unique structure, purpose, and overwhelmingly masculine composition.[25] Red Army political leaders viewed the Soviet armed forces as part of the larger "political-economic organism of the country" and conceded that the army reflected broader developments under the New Economic Policy. However, they also considered the army "an organizational whole composed of separate elements—the Red Army, political, and command staff." Its "political-moral condition," in the leadership's view, was in no small measure determined by "the social, political, and cultural-everyday quality of these elements."[26] This way of looking at the Red Army meant that internal investigations were also, by extension, an exploration into the broader state of affairs in the country. It was not enough to know what was going on inside the barracks and different units; the political and military leadership also had to concern itself with external influences that were shaping the troops both before their induction and during their service.

Local and district political workers served as the main suppliers of the leadership's information about the troops. In terms of suicide, for example, they furnished reports that included a recounting of the suicide's personal history, a description of the suicide or suicide attempt, a discussion of reactions to the suicide, and, whenever possible, some conclusions about the cause or motive behind the incident. Copies of suicide notes,

23. Circular of early December 1924 from Kuz'min, the military procurator of the Supreme Court SSSR to Krylov, executive secretary KK PUR, RGVA, f. 9, op. 28, d. 738, l. 36.

24. "Samoubiistva v chastiakh M.V.O. (Obzor za 1923 i 24 g.g. po dannym Prokuratory MVO)," RGVA, f. 9, op. 28, d. 739, l. 44. According to another report, the "most characteristic" cases of suicide were studied according to the "line of PUR, as political information." "Kratkii obzor o samoubiistvakh," l. 97.

25. Here it should be noted that social scientists routinely treated the civilian and military populations as separate entities, with different levels and types of social forces at work within them. Typically, rates of suicide were thought to be higher in the military population. Émile Durkheim explained this higher rate in terms of what he called altruistic suicide, which involved the loss of individuality resulting from overintegration in the group. See *Suicide: A Study in Sociology*, trans. John A. Spaulding and George Simpson (New York, 1951), 228–39.

26. "Politiko-moral'noe sostoianie okruga i blizhaishchie zadachi," RGVA, f. 9, op. 10, d. 29, l. 59.

autopsy reports, criminal investigations, or any other official proceedings were also appended to the reports. These local accounts were then sent up the institutional hierarchy to the appropriate military district's political administration (*puokr*), which used the information to describe the political situation in the district or to compile statistical analyses specifically devoted to the problem of suicide. Finally, the central Informational-Statistical Department processed both the local and district materials to create the regular summaries and surveys mentioned above.

The Red Army's attentiveness to suicide was partly the product of its own informational loop. Beginning in 1923, the Political Administration and its investigators noted the increasing frequency of suicides in the military. Despite being categorized among "extraordinary events" (*chrezvychainye proisshestviia*), suicides were quickly becoming a "fact of everyday life" (*bytovoe iavlenie*). According to a secret publication printed jointly by PUR and the Main Administration in 1931, the annual rate of suicides among all servicemen in the Red Army observed the following trend: 8.3 cases of suicide per 10,000 population in 1925–26; 10.7 in 1926–27; 11.5 in 1927–28; 11.2 in 1928–29; and 9.8 in the latest period, 1929–30.[27] In addition, there were periodic reports of epidemic suicide coming from the localities, while members of PUR remarked with particular concern that suicides had taken on a "mass character" in some party organizations.[28] Reports compiled for the Main Administration and Bolshevik Party added to the growing sense of crisis by highlighting the fact that rates of suicide in the Red Army exceeded those for the Imperial Russian Army before 1914.[29] Amid the growing perception of a general outbreak of self-destruction, the desire for additional information among Soviet military and political authorities only intensified.[30]

27. The pamphlet also noted a decline in absolute numbers. Cases of suicide reportedly fell from a total of 715 in 1927–28 to 689 in 1928–29, and finally to 609 in 1929–30. "Statisticheskii ezhegodnik. Politiko-moral'noe sostoianie RKKA. (Sostoianie distsipliny, samoubiistva, chrezvychainye proisshestviia). 1929/30 god.," RGVA, f. 54, op. 4, d. 69, l. 29.

28. "Ob uchastivshchikhsia sluchaiakh samoubiistv sredi chlenov partii i RLKSM," RGVA, f. 9, op. 28, d. 739, l. 126–27; "Material'noe polozhenie i nastroeniia komvzvodov RKKA (23 iiunia 1923 g.)," RGVA, f. 9, op. 3, d. 195, l. 106ob; and "Svodka daniia o politiko-moral'noi sostoianii v Krasnoi Armii za ianvar' 1923 g.," RGVA, 9, op. 48, d. 417, l. 8. Significantly, the military procurator's office complained that local political organs took an interest in suicides only once they assumed a "mass character." "Obzor 'Samoubiistva v krasnoi armii i flote' (avgust'–dekabr' 1923 g.)," RGVA, f. 9, op. 28, d. 738, ll. 12–12ob.

29. "Samoubiistva v RKKA za 1924/5 god," RGVA, f. 54, op. 6, d. 462, ll. 9–9ob; and "Kratkii obzor," ll. 100ob–101.

30. See, for example, the calls for more frequent reportage in the letter of June 9, 1926, from PUR's Infstatotdel to the Administration on Military Orders and Statistics, RGVA, f. 54,

To fulfill this growing need for information, the Political Administration created a series of descriptive statistical portraits over the course of the 1920s. Consistent with the image of the Red Army as a single organism composed of different elements, most surveys of self-destruction provided a total picture of the data and then compared suicide rates according to the factors of geography (military districts and territorial units), military formation (infantry, artillery, headquarters, etc.), and service group (commanders, Red Army men, political workers, and medical personnel). Variations were thought to reflect the particular makeup or prevailing conditions of the different elements. For example, the Political Administration's study of the military districts followed the urban-rural dichotomy seen in other works on suicide. Investigators found higher totals of suicide in the Leningrad, Moscow, and Siberian military districts during the first three months of 1925 and attributed them to the "influence of large cities" as well as the difficult material conditions in these regions. Previous data from the Ukrainian Military District, where the majority of cases came from Khar'kov, Kiev, and Odessa, also confirmed the dangers posed by the city. The report's authors wrote, "The closer contact with the NEP world and the petit bourgeois milieu, the larger number of criminal temptations, the more frequent instances of infection with syphilis, which sometimes lead to suicide, and similar such causes can truly find reflection in the number of suicides."[31]

In terms of the different service groups, the Red Army found that suicide rates were highest among the more responsible and educated members. This was particularly the case with the officer corps, whose condition was the object of much consternation throughout the 1920s. Periodic investigations, as well as regular political reports, highlighted officers' extremely poor material situation, their lack of suitable housing, and the greater percentage of physical and nervous illnesses among them. These factors found partial expression in higher rates of suicide and other amoral actions, most notably among junior officers and those who were on extended tours of duty.[32] Despite some overall improvement, as late as 1930 "nightmarish" living conditions were still being blamed for pulling officers

op. 6, d. 462, l. 41; and "Svodka dannykh o politiko-moral'nom sostoianii v Krasnoi Armii. Za fevral' 1923 goda," RGVA, f. 9, op. 48, d. 417, l. 35.

31. "Samoubiistva v krasnoi armii i flote. Za Ianvar'–Mart 1925 g.," RGVA, f. 9, op. 28, d. 739, ll. 64–65; and "Obzor 'Samoubiistva v chastiakh UVO v period ianvar'–iiun' 1924 g.,'" RGVA, f. 9, op. 28, d. 738, l. 37.

32. For the period 1926–27, the rate of suicide per 10,000 had the following distribution: (1) middle command staff—25.3 (with 34.7 among platoon commanders); (2) medical personnel—20.7; (3) political staff—15.1; (4) junior command staff—14.2 (24.6 among

away from the army and inciting suicides among the "weakest." In fact, only 49 percent of officers were deemed healthy, with some 41 percent considered severely in need of rest and treatment.[33] As we shall see below, these physiological and material factors were deemed highly significant in shaping the political outlook of the officers, not just their emotional and psychological stability.

A review of the Political Administration's work on the seasonal variability of suicide rates shows most clearly the epidemiological logic that animated its approach. PUR's statisticians broke down the aggregate of suicides in the Red Army according to the winter, spring, summer, and fall quarters. In a report covering the period 1924 to 1925, the investigators claimed to have uncovered a distinct pattern in the seasonal distribution of military suicides. For both years the winter period produced the greatest total number of cases (167 in 1924; 172 in 1925), followed in descending order by the spring quarter (142 and 135), summer quarter (98 and 111), and fall quarter (81 and 80).[34] To explain the apparent "regularity" (*zakonomernost'*) of these distributions, the analysts argued for a causal relationship between levels of suicide and the different living and working conditions associated with each particular time period. Their interpretations clearly emphasized the power of external surroundings to affect the physical well-being of the individual and, in turn, to shape political consciousness in either a positive or a negative manner.

According to the Political Administration's representations, service in the Red Army was a highly cyclical experience. Every season brought important changes to the way the commanders and Red Army men lived, worked, and interacted, and the effects of one season carried over into the next. Winter (January–March), for example, was characterized as a time of stationary living, mental labor, and indoor existence. Bad weather forced soldiers and officers to spend a large amount of time inside. Here they concentrated on individual instruction and learning while also preparing for

---

extended tour officers); and (5) general ranks—7.6. "Materialy ob otritsatel'nykh iavleni-iakh," l. 273.

33. "Nedochety material'nogo polozheniia nachsostava RKKA (svodka)," RGVA, f. 9, op. 28, d. 161, ll. 75–76.

34. "Kratkii obzor o samoubiistvakh," ll. 97–99. Apparently this regularity did not maintain itself over the long term. A study of military suicides for the period 1928–29 revealed a slightly different distribution of suicides. Compared with earlier trends, for example, the expected upward spike of suicides occurred in February rather than in December, with further growth over the spring months. The authors of this survey attributed the changes to both the overall decline in the number of suicides and the greater fitness of the servicemen. "Statisticheskii ezhegodnik za 1928/29 god. Politiko-moral'noe sostoianie RKKA," RGVA, f. 54, op. 4, d. 64, l. 41ob.

maneuvers in the spring. Springtime (April–June) involved the organization and outfitting of outdoor encampments, as well as the onset of group
training exercises amid improved weather conditions. Summer months
(July–September) were noteworthy for the large amount of time spent
outside in the field, the completion of military training, and heightened
expectations (as well as anxieties) among the troops about the possibility
of demobilization from the Red Army. Finally, the fall quarter (October–
December) was a period of maneuvers and field trips, the transition back
to the barracks, the issuing of discharges and leaves, and the induction of
new recruits. Thus completed, the circle of military life began anew.

Red Army investigators assumed that along with these seasonal lifestyle
changes also came variations in the self-destructive forces at work upon
the troops. Summaries of the first-quarter numbers focused on the heightened influence of living conditions and the cumulative effects of previous seasons on the physical and mental state of the individual. Because
servicemen were forced to spend more time indoors during the winter,
everyday life within the home or barracks presumably assumed its greatest significance at this time of the year. For some soldiers and officers this
could have negative consequences. Indoor living not only meant an intensification of the Red Army's nagging housing problem but could also en-
tail a heightened and prolonged exposure to unhealthy environments.[35]
Indeed, statisticians attempting to explain the rise of suicides during the
winter period emphasized "the insufficient organization of barracks life,
the lack of leaves, the heightened influence of the housing question for
the command-political staff... [and] the greatest influence of the petit
bourgeois milieu and of the cities in general." These harmful influences
were exacerbated by a high level of "fatigue" among the troops as a result
of the previous months' intensive fieldwork. "In both the third and fourth
quarters," wrote the report's authors, "the grounds [*pochva*] for suicides
are less fertile, but both of these periods seriously overexhaust [*pereutomli-
aiut*] the command personnel and the Red Army men who remain in the
army. Thus, the ground is prepared for the new, periodic rise of suicides
in the next year. This condition is then further stimulated by the conditions of the first quarter cited above."[36]

When viewed as a form of social scientific knowledge, the Red Army's
calendar of suicide stands out for its comprehensiveness as well as the

---

35. Conversely, investigators attributed the lower rates of suicide during the summer period in part to "a more diverse life (in particular with the departure from the cities)," which
had a "salubrious effect on the servicemen." "Samoubiistva v krasnoi armii i flote," l. 66.

36. "Kratkii obzor o samoubiistvakh," ll. 98–99. The link between suicide, fatigue, and
winter course work is also made in "Samoubiistva v krasnoi armii i flote," l. 66.

underlying desire to move from description to prescription. Looking at the aggregate picture, for example, Red Army investigators highlighted the convergence of personal, political, and social factors to account for the greater rates of suicide in the winter period. A susceptible population group—commanders exhausted from the preceding months of fieldwork—coupled with the highest levels of negative conditions in the military, provided a compelling explanation for the upward spike observed during these months. This conclusion was seemingly confirmed when the data were further broken down. Suicides due to nervous illness or exhaustion were at their highest levels during the winter period and the group of servicemen deemed most threatened by pathological living conditions—command and political personnel—also provided its largest number of cases at this time.[37] The identification of the forces behind the formation of vulnerable individuals led the authors of one report to recommend a set of preventative measures. Among their proposals for fighting against future cases of suicide was the following: "Give attention to repairing the health of the command-political staff during the summer period. Allow, as an exception, the [early] discharge from the Army of individuals with especially severe nervous illness."[38]

The Red Army's diagnostics were shaped by broader concerns over the ideological compromises of the New Economic Policy. Scholars of the 1920s increasingly characterize the decade as a period of high anxiety for the Bolsheviks and their supporters. Eric Naiman in particular has explored different levels of Soviet culture to demonstrate how such unease was expressed through corporeal images of collective breakdown, misogynistic attitudes toward women, and nightmarish visions of bodily defilement and penetration. The New Economic Policy itself was conceived in terms of inoculation and the dangers that this practice entailed: while capitalism was injected back into the body politic with the intent to overcome and destroy it through socialism, the fear always lingered that the foreign substance would prove too formidable and end up disfiguring its host.[39]

Statistical epidemiology therefore functioned as political information because the Political Administration conceived of ideological threats in

37. "Kratkii obzor o samoubiistvakh," ll. 99ob, 100ob. On the general preponderance of suicides among members of the command personnel see "Samoubiistva v krasnoi armii i flote," l. 67.

38. "Samoubiistva v krasnoi armii i flote," l. 75. Another report for 1924–25 similarly called for the "physical repair of the command personnel" in addition to "sanitary-enlightenment propaganda" (which encompassed the creation of "collective opinion" around suicides). "Kratkii obzor o samoubiistvakh," l. 101ob.

39. Eric Naiman, *Sex in Public: The Incarnation of Early Soviet Ideology* (Princeton, 1997), 262–66.

terms of contagion. Reports on suicide and other forms of asocial behavior routinely spoke of individuals having been tainted by a variety of pathological outlooks, including "Eseninism," "despondency," "the pessimism of the intelligentsia," "demobilization moods," and the generic "suicidal moods."[40] More generally, depictions of the Bolshevik Party and the military were infused with obsessive references to infection, pollution, and decomposition, as well as endless diagnoses of organizational and individual health. In his comments on the Twelfth Party Congress of 1923, A. Krylov employed the imagery of contagion to conceptualize the challenges facing the military wing of the party during the NEP. He suggested that ideologically tainted individuals could infect others with their philistine worldviews through daily interactions or indirectly through literature and other reading material.[41] At the same time, the Political Administration also practiced a spatial diagnostics that focused on the transmission of unhealthy ideas and lifestyles from the surrounding milieu. Individual contamination in this sense was imagined in terms of contact with the remnants of the old, decaying prerevolutionary social body. Private apartments and businesses, places of prostitution, taverns, or any other space where noncommunist lifestyles were still being practiced all represented pockets of prerevolutionary life that had yet to be excised from the body politic. Prolonged exposure to these realms, or to their living representatives, could have a corrosive effect upon the individual's political consciousness, which in turn only increased the danger to the rest of the military population.

Labeled an "illness of everyday life" (*bolezn' byta*), suicide provided the Red Army leadership with a window into the ideological state of affairs among the troops. It was at once its own disease, with the potential for causing additional self-destructive acts and fostering an unhealthy political situation, and a product of other negative phenomena in the military environment. In 1924, the authors of a survey on suicides in the Red Army and Navy argued that the study of suicide was a means for uncovering other social problems:

> Suicides in the Red Army..., while having a negative effect on the servicemen, are also one of the most visible indicators of the illnesses of everyday

40. See, for example, "Moskva. 1-go aprelia 1927 g. Svodka Politicheskogo Upravleniia Raboche-Krest'ianskoi Krasnoi armii i flota. No. 357," RGASPI, f. 17, op. 85, d. 127, l. 65; and K. Vasil'ev, "Bor'ba za novyi byt," *Voennyi vestnik,* July 2, 1923, 43–44.

41. A. Krylov, "Boleznennye iavleniia v partorganizatsii krasnoi armii i flota," *Politrabotnik,* nos. 4–5 (April–May 1924): 47.

life that exist in the Red Army: the difficult material condition of servicemen, especially those with families; the limitations of solidarity among the
command-political staff; the clumsy relations of commanders toward the
Red Army men; abnormalities of sexual life; the severe shattering of nerves
and overexhaustion among old fighters in the Red Army, etc.[42]

In another evaluation of the military's political-moral condition, every
case of suicide was said to signal a "defect" (*nedochet*) in the unit or party
cell.[43] As stated in a 1924 report on the suicide of Georgii Torgashev and
the attempted suicide of the instructor Suderevskii, these acts were "not a
chance occurrence [*iavlenie nesluchainoe*], but ones that characterize the
general moral condition, in particular [that] of the middle and junior
commanders."[44]

Suicide statistics were therefore a powerful tool for mapping the ideological state of affairs inside the military. As a type of political information,
they represented unhealthy environments, suspicious beliefs and everyday
practices, or even dangerous people among the ranks. Not surprisingly,
the apartment and bedroom of the Red Army commander caused political workers the greatest degree of consternation. These areas were already
marked within Soviet discourse as threatening because of their direct association with privacy and individualism. Moreover, the isolated apartment
served as a telling reminder of the poor material conditions in which the
officer corps was often forced to live and work. Party activists and other
servicemen complained bitterly about the Red Army's continued inability
to provide adequate housing for its commanders, who in many instances
had to find separate lodgings for themselves and their families in the nearest city or among a local population that was suspect from a social and ideological standpoint. However, conditions inside the home posed the most
insidious threat to the ideological well-being of the command personnel.
It was here, at the spatial center of family and personal life, that officers
and political workers experienced the negative influence of dangerous
class elements most acutely.

42. "Obzor 'Samoubiistva v Krasnoi Armii i Flote za ianvar'–aprel' 1924 goda,'" RGVA,
f. 9, op. 28, d. 738, l. 53.

43. "Statisticheskii ezhegodnik za 1928/29 god," l. 44.

44. Attached material to a report from the Special Department (OO) of the ChK,
RGVA, f. 9, op. 17, d. 186, l. 116. A memorandum from the central Political Administration
also directed the attention of the political administration in the Belorussian Military District
(BVO) to three cases of suicide within a single division, arguing that they "signal trouble."
Letter of November 14, 1929, from PUR to the director of Puokr BVO, RGVA, f. 9, op. 26,
d. 461, l. 28.

Within the Red Army reports, "socially distant" women acted as the new "Eves" by tempting males and threatening their entry into the earthly paradise being constructed in Soviet Russia. Specifically, the military's investigations into suicide highlighted the role of petit bourgeois or philistine women (*meshchanki*) who, according to one local political report, constituted an alarmingly high proportion of the officers' wives.[45] These were the offspring of the previous ruling elites and the currently disenfranchised (*lishentsy*) and were considered apolitical, religious, deeply materialistic, and generally hostile to the regime. Once under the woman's influence, the Red Army commander withdrew from social work and became isolated from the collective. He began to think more about satisfying personal needs and attaining the trappings of middle-class comfort than he did about sacrificing for the Soviet cause. According to Krylov, the end result of the petit bourgeois wife's influence on her husband was "alienation…from party work and from the nonparty masses, as well as the opposition of personal interests to the interests of the party and the working class."[46]

In terms of suicide, the Political Administration established a causal link between self-destruction and the servicemen's exposure to dangerous women. A review of suicides among party members in the military, for example, noted the high percentage of suicides committed on the grounds of "family squabbles." Many of these cases involved the demoralizing influence of a "domestic everyday life" that could be traced back to the presence of a socially suspect wife. Its authors wrote:

> We must pay attention to the negative consequences for the party member that can sometimes result from a thoughtless and flippant attitude toward marriage to a woman from an alien background. If the "romantic" in well-known cases shoots himself because a woman of easy virtue, the daughter of a trader or a nobleman, or the former wife of a White Army officer does not reciprocate his love, then the family man in some cases shoots himself because marriage to a woman from an alien background subsequently led to his complete moral decomposition and final isolation from the party.[47]

A pamphlet surveying the overall political-moral condition inside the military for the period 1928–29 came to a similar conclusion. During their

---

45. "Vypiska iz protokola VPS 9 otdel'noi Dalne-Vostochnoi kavbrigady ot 13/I-1928 goda," RGVA, f. 9, op. 28, d. 587, l. 318.

46. Krylov, "Boleznennye iavleniia," 50.

47. "Obzor 'Samoubiistv sredi chlenov i kandidatov partii v armeiskikh partorganizatsiiakh (Po materialam OPK za 1925 g., 1926 g., i 1-iu polovinu 1927 g.),'" RGVA, f. 9, op. 28, d. 73, l. 2.

analysis of suicides categorized under the motive "discord in the family," the report's authors stated:

> In the last year, the study of a number of units located in minor garrisons revealed with utmost clarity the influence of the petit bourgeois environ-ment, the social pollution of the commanders' wives, and the utterly inad-equate social-political envelopment of the command staff's off-duty life by party-political influence and work. Without a doubt, gossiping and squab-bles in the dormitories, ties to the milieu of the petite bourgeoisie and, at times, to those deprived of voting rights—were the basis for this entire group of suicides.

While these clusters of suicides signaled an imbalance between the forces of revolution and those of counterrevolution, they also suggested a pos-sible direction for therapeutic interventions into the military population. As stated in the same report, "The strengthening of work in remote, non-industrial garrisons, the sharper class education of the commanders, and the improvement of work with families will doubtless result in a decrease of this group of suicides."[48]

On the basis of its statistical and anecdotal information, the Political Administration identified Red Army commanders as particularly vulner-able to ideological contagion. As noted earlier, officers routinely had the highest suicide rate of any class of servicemen when levels of suicide were measured as the number of cases per ten thousand of the particular ser-vice group.[49] Moreover, the data also suggested that motives associated with the petit bourgeois milieu were most frequent among suicides from the officer corps. The 1929 PUR study of everyday life, for example, con-cluded that suicides of commanders predominated among those linked to dissension and discord within the family.[50] In addition, a survey on suicides in the Red Army during the first quarter of 1924 found that command-ers constituted a rather large percentage of those cases motivated by "ro-mantic" situations (eleven cases out of twenty-seven). Commenting on the pattern, the report's authors remarked that this type of suicide reflected

---

48. "Statisticheskii ezhegodnik za 1928/29 god," l. 51.

49. See, for example, ibid., l. 43; "Samoubiistva i pokusheniia sredi voennosluzhash-chikh RKKA za 1927–28 god," RGVA, f. 9, op. 28, d. 115, l. 293; and "Kratkii obzor o samou-biistvakh," ll. 99ob, 101.

50. According to the report, most suicides in this group "were explained by a 'fight with the wife,' 'infidelity of the wife,' 'divorce,' 'family troubles,' etc., that is, by the general distor-tions of the servicemen's domestic life." "Melko-burzhuaznoe okruzhenie i byt nachsostava," RGVA, f. 9, op. 28, d. 115, l. 257.

the "petit-bourgeoisification" (*omeshchanivanie*) of the individual. They explained, "The enthusiasm frequently noted by the political organs of the commanders and cadets with 'courting and making the acquaintance of young ladies of the philistine cut [*pokroi*]' often leads to corresponding moods, to the appearance of 'disenchantment,' and then to suicides due to 'ill-fated love.'"[51]

Investigators also discerned a geographic pattern to ideological infection. In addition to the nefarious temptations offered by the city, they found that troops stationed in outlying regions or remote garrisons were highly exposed to the influences of the local petite bourgeoisie. The command staff in these areas was threatened by its cultural isolation and its need to find lodging among the population, which frequently lacked any real working-class representation and could offer precious little in terms of healthy entertainment and social interaction.[52] Red Army investigators in the Turkmenistan front contended that suicides with a "romantic lining" (*romanicheskaia podkladka*) were connected to the "abnormalities of sexual life" created by local conditions. Frustrated over their inability to have a normal family life or to live comfortably, some commanders committed crimes of passion, pursued the wives of other officers, and generally fell apart morally under the "influence of the surrounding petit bourgeois milieu."[53]

The ideological vulnerability of some commanders as well as the formation of suicidal tendencies was seen as having economic roots. Especially during the middle years of the 1920s, political workers cited the preponderance of suicides motivated by "lack of material security" to argue that the impoverishment of officers was a primary reason behind the degenerative influence of petit bourgeois women (as well as other NEP-era social elements).[54] They contended that because of their very low wages,

51. "Obzor 'Samoubiistva v Krasnoi Armii i Flote za ianvar'–aprel' 1924 goda,'" l. 54.

52. "Melko-burzhuaznoe okruzhenie i byt nachsostava," l. 256.

53. The almost total lack of any "European women" (i.e., Russians) in many garrison towns apparently created abnormal sexual situations, including at least one case where a soldier committed suicide out of remorse over raping his comrade's wife. "Obzor-direktiva. O samoubiistvakh v chastiakh Turkfronta za vremia avgust–dekabr' 1924 g.," RGVA, f. 9, op. 28, d. 781, l. 83ob. Another survey on suicides among party members in the military also remarked on the extremely difficult material situation of commanders' families in the territorial units. See "O samoubiistvakh sredi chlenov RKP(b)," l. 3ob.

54. An early study of junior platoon commanders suggested that their mood was directly determined by their poor material situation. Drinking was depicted as a means for some to forget about their dire straits; moreover, the impoverished commander was thought to fall more easily under the influence of female company and other temptations that were emerging along with the NEP. "Material'noe polozhenie i nastroenie komvzvodov," ll. 105–7.

many officers were simply unable to fulfill a woman's desire for even the most minimal creature comforts. This led them to break down under the pressure and shame of their failure to fulfill the role of husband. A report on suicides during the first quarter of 1925, which directed the reader's attention to the large number committed "on romantic grounds," cited material insecurity as a key factor behind such acts. Among the examples provided was the suicide of a platoon commander, who shot himself after his betrothed insisted that he remain in the service. He reportedly fell into despair because he could not support a family on his military pay. In another case, the woman refused marriage unless her fiancé resigned from the army, since she deemed his wages insufficient for raising a family. This matter similarly ended in the serviceman's suicide.[55] Finally, a number of officers resorted to embezzlement or theft of military property in order to satisfy the material needs of their wives or lovers, which in turn fed into another category of suicide: those committed as a result of "moral oppression" (*moral'noe ugnetenie*) and the fear of being punished for one's misdeeds.

Still, the Political Administration never envisaged the fight against suicides and degenerative influences as simply a matter of improving the material conditions in which the commander and his family lived. Military investigators and leaders certainly used the problem of suicide to lobby for the amelioration of the servicemen's most immediate troubles.[56] However, recognition of poor material conditions did not relieve individuals of responsibility for their actions. After all, soldiers and officers who succumbed to the temptations of petit bourgeois women showed themselves to be fundamentally lacking as party members or Soviet citizens. In the final analysis, they did not have the requisite ideological strength and political maturity to endure their present circumstances and to resist the negative influences of their surroundings.[57] The special commission investigating the 1924 suicide of the military commissar Maklashev emphasized

---

55. "Samoubiistva v Krasnoi Armii i Flote," l. 71. For a more general suggestion of the connection between the lack of material well-being and suicides motivated by romance see "Kratkii obzor o samoubiistvakh," l. 100ob. Toward the end of the decade, the compilers of one report claimed that the motive "could not get married because of poverty," a common problem in the tsarist army, was no longer much of a factor in the Soviet military. "Statisticheskii ezhegodnik za 1928/29 god," l. 52.

56. "Vypiska iz protokola Politsoveshchaniia ot 6 maia s/g po voprosu o samoubiistvakh," RGASPI, f. 17, op. 84, d. 953, l. 35.

57. For an argument against reducing the problem of ideological wavering to the commanders' difficult material circumstances see Terent'ev et al., "Eshche o 'byte komsostava,'" *Voennyi vestnik*, February 23, 1924, 53. Using a similar logic, the authors of a joint GURKKA-PUR report stated that although suicides due to bureaucratic distortions were a sign of

not only the unhealthy circumstances in which he found himself but also his lack of proper political development. Its report summarized, "Maklashev, an immature young man who had not gone through the demanding school of Bolshevism, who was deprived of party leadership and firm influence, and who lacked self-control, found himself in a rotten petit bourgeois setting, of which he became a victim. The lack of any healthy political-enlightenment work, as well as the absence of the influence of any real party organization, disfigured Maklashev, having turned him into a sentimental romantic who whines over the divided love of a prostitute and kills himself while half-drunk in the style of a 'heartrending' drama."[58]

Suicide statistics were in essence a map of "influence" according to which the Political Administration and the Red Army could visualize the ongoing struggle between the forces of revolution and counterrevolution. The distribution of suicides suggested the relative strength of the collective's regenerative force and exposed those areas where the "the sores of everyday life" threatened the regime's enlightenment project in the military.[59] Like the epidemiological study of infectious disease, the Red Army's informational reports marked the high-risk groups, charted the spread of illness, hypothesized about modes of transmission, and provided the basis for preventative or therapeutic measures. However, this was done primarily in the service of understanding and promoting the ideological health of the troops. As the 1930 PUR and GURKKA joint report on suicides concluded, "The activation of party work, the greater supervision [*bol'shii okhvat*] of the servicemen's off-duty life, and the involvement of every single serviceman in public life will no doubt decrease the number of those individuals who feel most sharply the influence of petit bourgeois waverings, which are the result of our decisive assault upon capitalist elements."[60]

Soviet information therefore had a sharply self-reflexive quality. The reports themselves became an important indicator of the level and quality of surveillance existing throughout the military population. Rates of explained and—sometimes more important—unexplained suicides were used to evaluate the political workers' attitude toward the specific problem of self-destruction and, more generally, the life of the troops. Early on, there were suggestions that the local political workers were not fulfilling

---

genuine problems in the military, they could never be excused as a valid response to those problems. "Statisticheskii ezhegodnik za 1928/29," l. 47.

58. Report to the commander of the Turkestan Infantry Division from the commission investigating the suicides that took place in the Fifth Infantry Regiment, RGVA, f. 9, op. 28, d. 781, l. 85ob.

59. A. Karpov, "Kak lechit' boliachki byta," *Voennyi vestnik*, September 1, 1928, 48.

60. "Statisticheskii ezhegodnik za 1928/29 god," l. 52.

their assigned tasks in this area. Arguing that that it was "necessary in the future to bring the number of unexplained cases to zero," the authors of a 1924 report on suicides in the Ukrainian Military District criticized the lack of attention given by political workers to suicide and their formal approach to the specific problem of causation.[61] Several years later, a general survey of party suicides lamented the fact that district political commissions often passed over the question of suicide "in silence."[62] By the late 1920s, however, military and political authorities were touting their improved ability to analyze the information about motives and causation: the percentage of unexplained cases had declined from 44.8 percent in 1924 to 9.5 percent in 1927–28 and 7.9 percent in 1928–29.[63] The achievement of increased legibility was regarded as an important step in the Red Army's ability to fight against the scourge of self-destruction. "Thanks to this [higher percentage of explained cases]," stated the authors of a joint PUR-GURKKA survey, "we have a much wider opportunity for studying suicides, and so it facilitates the possibility of finding a path toward eliminating one of the most negative phenomena in the political-moral condition of the army."[64]

Conceived in such terms, the very act of collecting information became part of the Red Army's arsenal against suicide and other illnesses. Among the prescriptions offered by the Central Military Political Meeting (TsVPS) for fighting suicides was a deceptively simple recommendation: "Study and examine every case of suicide."[65] Various circulars and reports exhorted the political workers to delve deeply into each act. For example, a 1924 Political Administration survey admonished, "The simple 'registration' of suicides in local reports is meaningless [*bessmyslenna*]. Every case must be illuminated as fully as possible. We must make it a rule to collect materials in all cases of suicide without exception."[66] Above all, this meant conducting an exhaustive investigation, compiling a thorough report, and providing superiors with a clear idea of the underlying circumstances and

61. "Obzor 'Samoubiistva v chastiakh UVO,'" l. 38ob.

62. "Obzor 'Samoubiistv sredi chlenov i kandidatov partii,'" l. 1. This dissatisfaction extended to the civilian apparatus of the Bolshevik Party. In Leningrad, the Komsomol instructor Gaitskhoki expressed frustration over the lack of materials gathered by local party organs and suggested that this was a sign of their lack of attention to the problem. "V sekretariat leningradskogo gubkoma VLKSM," TsGAIPD (SPb), f. 601, op. 1, d. 735, l. 1.

63. "Statisticheskii ezhegodnik za 1928/1929 god," l. 44.

64. "Samoubiistva v RKKA za 1926/27 god. Obzor sostavlen glavnym i politicheskim upravleniiami RKKA," RGVA, f. 9, op. 28, d. 73, l. 12ob.

65. "Proekt rezoliutsii TsVPS o samoubiistvakh," RGVA, f. 9, op. 28, d. 1175, l. 42.

66. "Obzor 'Samoubiistva v krasnoi armii i flote (avgust–dekabr' 1923 g.)," RGVA, f. 9, op. 28, d. 333, l. 49ob.

motivations. The political officer, in other words, could not limit himself to a straightforward rendering of events. He had to take a personal interest in the individual suicide as an extension of his broader responsibility to "know about everything that goes on in his company or brigade."[67] Otherwise, the self-corrective power of the Red Army organism remained in stasis rather than in motion.

Indeed, when the Political Administration mapped suicide, it was ultimately visualizing the effectiveness of its own enlightenment efforts. Just as a lower percentage of unexplained cases suggested greater attentiveness on the part of political workers, so too a reduction in suicides could be interpreted as a sign of success in cultivating a more salubrious political-moral atmosphere. In 1930, a joint statement published by PUR and the Main Administration made this relationship explicit: "We cannot separate the tasks of the struggle against suicides in the military from the general tasks standing before the Red Army in the realm of strengthening the political-moral condition. Each case of suicide is a concrete signal that the matter of realizing these general tasks goes unfavorably."[68] Using similar logic, an earlier review of military suicides interpreted the decline of suicides related to living and working conditions as evidence that the localities were getting more serious about ameliorating these causal factors. Still, the authors warned against complacency since the overall number of suicides remained high.[69]

In many respects, then, the work of the Political Administration can be seen as expanding and transforming the panoptic ideals expressed in Leonid Prozorov's prerevolutionary vision. The goal of total transparency around and through the individual resonated with particular force inside the Red Army, given the Bolsheviks' resolve to create a social order where everyone and everything were open to scrutiny. This aspiration was manifest in the relentless promotion of mutual surveillance and in the concomitant hostility toward private life and spaces as barriers to the "eyes and ears of the Red Army." The threat posed by the latter was vividly exposed in the dual suicide of two junior commanders in the Moscow Military District. Not only had they shot themselves outside the barracks in one of their residences, but the subsequent investigation also established that "neither the party organization nor the leading staff knew the lifestyle of the junior commanders, who lived in a private apartment." Tellingly, the

---

67. "Nuzhno osnovatel'no priniatsia delo," l. 211.
68. "Statisticheskii ezhegodnik za 1928/29 god.," l. 45ob.
69. "Samoubiistva v RKKA za 1926/1927 god," l. 14.

reporting of this case in the Political Administration's regular summary only provoked the desire for more information. Andrei Bubnov, head of PUR, scrawled in frustration across the margins of the report: "It is unclear what our organizations in the localities are doing." Reaffirming the intrinsic relationship between self-diagnostics and social diagnostics, he went on to write Chernevskii, director of the Information-Statistical Department, and instructed him that in the future all summaries should "indicate not only the facts but what was done about them."[70]

MAPPING THE WORLD OF SOVIET SUICIDE

Never a passive affair, the gathering of information about military suicide was always tied to the mission of sculpting the social environment and shaping the psychology of those living within it. Knowledge of the psychological states associated with suicide was based on the reports of the political workers in the field, who were tasked not just with reporting facts but also with explaining them. Suicides in the Red Army demanded explanation because they transgressed boundaries of ethical and political conduct, violated codes of military discipline, indicated abnormal states of mind, and defied assumptions about the individual self as continuously moving forward toward future completion. Such expectations most certainly reflected the universal belief that the instinct for life is a natural, and therefore normal, condition of human existence. However, they also reflected beliefs about the revolutionary regime and the kind of person it was bringing into existence. Specifically, the act of suicide violated visions of the ideal Soviet citizen as strong-willed, optimistic, and politically conscious. Through their narratives, the Red Army's investigators helped to build a conceptual bridge between the disturbing reality of suicide and these idealized traits. In so doing they created a "possible world" where unexpected and deviant actions were made comprehensible.[71]

The Red Army narratives offer a window into their authors' understandings of human psychology and suggest the construction of a shared intellectual framework for explaining why some members of the Soviet

70. "Svodka Politicheskogo Upravleniia Raboche-Krest'ianskoi Krasnoi Armii. Moskva, 12 aprelia 1928 g.," RGVA, f. 9, op. 28, d. 587, l. 100; and "Rezoliutsiia t. Bubnova na svodke PU RKKA za No. 376 ot 21/IV-28 g.," RGVA, f. 9, op. 28, d. 587, l. 97.

71. The idea of a "possible world" is developed in Jerome Bruner, *Acts of Meaning* (Cambridge, MA, 1990), 43–50.

military succumbed to thoughts of self-destruction. For example, they express ideas about the general conditions that produce a suicide, involve reconstructions of the suicidal state of mind, and manifest assumptions about the types of people who take their own lives. They also involve more specific notions of causation, motivation, and desire, as well as expectations about situated behavior. Thus, narratives of suicide in the Red Army reflect the ideals and values championed by representatives of the new regime as well as the particularities of the military. They tell us as much about the investigators as they do about the suicide.

Explaining suicide presented Red Army investigators with a number of cognitive challenges. Primary among them was the matter of how to determine internal, and therefore hidden, motivations, states of mind, beliefs, and emotions. To be sure, the suicide might have left behind some evidence in the form of a written note, words spoken to friends and acquaintances, recent behavior, or even the physical condition of his body. Still, as one report cautioned, these facts had to be treated with care and could not be taken at face value.[72] The political workers were therefore left to untangle the available evidence in order to develop a plausible explanation for the individual's actions. Above all, the search for motivation and cause meant constructing a believable narrative that told the story of how a specific individual ended up a suicide. This is why each act of self-destruction required a separate investigation and why Vsevelod Chernevskii, head of PUR's Informational-Statistical Department, could assure Andrei Bubnov in 1929 that the figures for suicides were "absolutely trustworthy." For each incident, he claimed, the Political Administration possessed a "precise description."[73]

The military leadership devoted much attention to shaping the narrative information flowing from the localities. It was not enough for political workers to simply create a report; they also were judged according to the content and form of their account. For example, the 1924 report on suicides in the Ukrainian Military District argued that a lack of interest found expression in the way that reports were written up for individual cases. It stated, "We must *eliminate* the formal attitude toward suicide, which, in the best case, expresses itself only in laconic announcements about causes."[74] Another report from the same military district interpreted the incomplete

---

72. Specifically, the report cited instances when suicides had sought justification by blaming punishments in their farewell notes. Military officials, however, deemed punishment to be a stimulating factor and not the underlying cause. RGVA, f. 9, op. 28, d. 239, l. 51ob.

73. Informational letter of June 19, 1929, from Chernevskii to Bubnov, director of the Political Administration, RGVA, f. 9, op. 28, d. 587, l. 29.

74. "Obzor 'Samoubiistva v chastiakh UVO,'" l. 38ob (emphasis in the original).

information to reflect the generally poor state of suicide studies in the region. "So far," contended its authors,

> the study of suicide has not even reached a primitive level; the localities, reporting laconically, don't even bother to conduct inquiries. All divisional political officers and political secretaries must eliminate this by conducting a detailed investigation into every suicide on the basis of all possible materials and by presenting this material to the Political Administration of the Ukrainian Military District.[75]

As these different statements indicate, writing about suicide performed a disciplinary and integrative function that went beyond the simple production of a report. In carrying out an investigation and writing up a proper narrative, the political workers showed their superiors that they grasped the full significance of suicide and their own role as informants. Otherwise, terse and unsupported reports were taken as tangible evidence of lack of interest on the part of local commanders and political personnel. For this reason, the Political Administration in 1924 gave "a push to the localities toward increasing attention to the question of suicides."[76]

In particular, the central leadership worried that its informants would be too easily satisfied with the most obvious and superficial explanation of suicide, thereby confusing the direct reason or motive with the predisposing cause of the suicide. For example, political workers reportedly overlooked nervous illness as the cause in many instances of suicide because they focused instead on the more easily recognizable motives that had incited the act.[77] Or, to cite an opposite tendency, they attributed virtually every suicide to a case of nerves and thus ignored the specific circumstances.[78] As described by the Military Procurator's office of the Moscow Military District, a careful and thoughtful interpretation of suicide required the ability to "distinguish the final cause, as the causal stimulus [*prichina-vozbuditel'*] of the suicide from the entire chain of causes, which frequently relate to the distant past. Within the series of causes the causal stimulus plays only one role—that of bringing the given individual to the resolution to kill himself."[79] Confusion of these different causal

---

75. "Obzor samoubiistv po ukrainskomu voennomu okrugu," RGVA, f. 9, op. 28, d. 738, l. 44.

76. "Obzor 'Samoubiistva v Krasnoi Armii i Flote za ianvar'–aprel' 1924 goda,'" l. 53.

77. "Kratkii obzor o samoubiistvakh v Krasnoi Armii i vo Flote za 1924–25 gody," l. 100ob.

78. "Samoubiistva v RKKA za 1926/27 god," l. 13.

79. "Samoubiistva v chastiakh M.V.O.," ll. 46ob–47.

elements led to the omission or muddling of key details in the suicide's story, thereby limiting its possible interpretations and the prescriptions that could be drawn from it.

To illustrate the problem, the Moscow procurator provided an example of an "incorrect" approach. Korneev, a party member and military commissar (*voenkom*) of the Seventeenth Division's Forty-ninth Regiment, committed suicide in February 1925.[80] According to the procurator, an initial inquiry resulted in the isolation of two basic causes. First, the original investigators concluded that on the eve of his suicide Korneev had been offended by a public rebuke issued by the divisional military commissar. When Korneev admitted that he had not read newspapers in two weeks because he was "overloaded" with work, the divisional commissar pointed out that the regimental commissar who failed to keep up with the newspapers eventually became alienated from international politics. Korneev was said to have replied, "Then go after such a military commissar." Second, the investigators also noted that Korneev had lost his brother and sister at the hands of the Whites during the civil war, apparently concluding that deep feelings of personal loss had pushed him toward suicide.

In its review of this case, the Moscow prosecutor's office criticized these initial conclusions as being highly superficial and failing to explicate the suicide. According to the prosecutor, those who first looked into Korneev's death had been "captivated" by the encounter between the deceased and the divisional commissar and therefore decided that the latter's remark had to be the "primary cause" (*pervoprichina*) of the suicide. The investigators seized upon the most obvious reason for suicide—the presumed feelings of shame or indignation that flowed from being chastised in front of one's colleagues—and thus failed to look any further into Korneev's circumstances and life history. At first glance, then, the suicide appeared to have resulted from the expectation of a diminished standing in the Red Army and the party. In fact, Korneev's death was classified in one general study as a suicide caused by "loss of prospects in future work."[81]

However, the divisional political meeting (*politsoveshchanie*) rejected the initial conclusion and instructed the district procurator to revisit the matter. This time an exhaustive study revealed a number of crucial facts that had been either ignored or overlooked by the first investigator. Primary among these was the fact that several hours prior to the suicide Korneev

---

80. The following discussion is based on "Samoubiistva v chastiakh M.V.O.," ll. 47–47ob; and "Samoubiistva v M.V.O. za 1923 i 1924 goda," RGVA, f. 9, op. 28, d. 739, l. 5.

81. The report's author, P. Tsel'min, suggested that Korneev feared being demobilized from the Red Army. "O samoubiistvakh sredi chlenov RKP(b)," l. 1ob.

brought home a bottle of sweet-grass vodka and drank it with a companion. On the basis of this and other new evidence the district procurator offered a different story of Korneev's death. First of all, he sought to establish an underlying cause that would help to explain Korneev's behavior prior to committing suicide. A forensic-medical autopsy revealed that Korneev's skull was misshapen, the parietal bones of his cranium being improperly joined. This was thought to have created periodic pressure on the brain and frequently conditioned a "state of depression" (*upadochnoe sostoianie dukha*), a conclusion that fully "corresponded to comrade Korneev's character." Thus, the forensic-medical doctor had located the internal or somatic origins of the deceased's outward personality.

Once the source of Korneev's underlying character had been established, the rest of his actions became more meaningful, or at least appeared more comprehensible. His family history now acquired a greater significance, since it was during the fits of depression caused by his preexisting physical abnormality that he fixated on the deaths of his siblings. Moreover, any intake of alcohol would have had a profound effect when Korneev was in such a state of mind, and the district procurator concluded that the vodka consumed prior to the suicide had helped to build up the inner resolve needed to commit such an act. Finally, the added significance of these causal factors sharply decreased the importance of the public reprimand. Within the new narrative constructed by the district procurator, the remark made by the divisional commissar was said to have had some influence within the chain of events, but it could not have been the primary cause, let alone an "essential" one. To corroborate this conclusion, the district procurator noted that Korneev had reportedly discussed the event with his comrades, had recognized the correctness of the divisional commissar's statement, and had already begun to devise plans to improve the political situation in the regiment. These words and actions were interpreted as proof that Korneev still thought in terms of an open-ended future for himself as a participant in the military and the party.

We clearly see in this case the importance of narrative to understandings of Soviet suicide. The district military procurator who reexamined Korneev's suicide had composed a more convincing story that reinforced key signifiers and offered a plausible explanation for the commissar's death. In contrast to the primary investigator, who advanced several possible motives but made no conjecture about why these particular factors had had such a pathological effect on Korneev (after all, not every person who received a reprimand or lost relatives in the civil war committed suicide), the district procurator's account contained a theory about the deceased's character and state of mind. Once an underlying cause was discovered (the degenerative skull producing a moody nature), such seemingly innocuous happenings as getting drunk with friends, reflecting upon departed loved ones, or being reprimanded by a superior became, in retrospect, surprisingly deadly ones. This is not to suggest that Korneev's suicide was justified or vindicated by the new narrative, only that the district procurator's account seemed to provide a more powerful explanatory bridge between expected behavior and its violation by Korneev.

The Red Army reports are thus organized around the identification and interpretation of external or physical signs that conveyed instability and crisis. These included words, actions, and gestures that seemed to reveal certain intentions and outlooks. In particular, the Red Army investigators scoured the suicide's record for outward indications of despair, alienation, ideological confusion, or a general loss of interest in life and work. They looked for sudden changes in behavior and for other signs that indicated a sense of finality or a preoccupation with death. Their identification made it possible to isolate the specific incidents that had set off the suicidal drama. These might be the receipt of a letter with bad tidings from home, a woman's refusal of marriage, the failure to receive a promotion, or the discovery of an incurable illness. Throughout, interpretations of such signs were shaped by the investigators' class-based understanding of the individual psyche.[82]

The signs of suicide were interpreted according to a linear understanding of personal development. Red Army narratives routinely included information about the suicides' past (their medical history, family background, education, and previous work experience); present (their occupation and family life, living conditions, state of health at the time of the suicide); and future (their career outlook or possible social roles as husbands, fathers, lovers, party members, etc.). All three of these elements in combination were thought to play a role in creating the personality and producing the suicide. A person like Korneev, for example, might be predisposed to certain states of mind because of his biological organization or social origins, which in turn made him extremely vulnerable to the destabilizing effects of present conditions. Moreover, the current circumstances of the suicide might have fatal consequences to the extent that they prevented individuals from realizing their potential future selves. In the words of the military procurator, the suicide killed himself because he believed that he had reached a "dead end."[83]

---

82. The sources of this class-based psychology are examined in Igal Halfin, *Terror in My Soul: Communist Autobiographies on Trial* (Cambridge, MA, 2003), esp. chap. 3.

83. "Samoubiistva v chastiakh M.V.O.," l. 51.

Linear notions of development reinforced the image of the personality as a dynamic and highly plastic entity. While Red Army investigators were suspicious of free will, they rejected the possibility of an "inborn suicide," a deeply deterministic concept that posited a hereditary predisposition for self-destruction that was passed on from one generation to the next.[84] Biological and hereditary factors were instead interpreted within a framework that suggested the suicide was made over time, not fated from birth. In this respect, the Red Army investigators' understanding of the personality resembled the doctrine of "sociobiology," a popular scientific approach of the period that tried to take into account the biological components of social behavior and customs. As discussed earlier, Nikolai Semashko, head of the People's Commissariat of Public Health, argued that the personality of the suicide was the result of the continuous "interaction and counteraction" between the internal self and its environment.[85] Such an understanding implied that health was itself a fluid condition and left open the possibility that the propensity for suicide might be reversed if those who displayed it were treated in a timely manner and placed in a healthier environment.

The mutability of the personality helped to explain the process of individual degeneration and fed into broader anxieties about the health of the troops. In particular, Soviet notions of psychological well-being were premised on a certain degree of internal equilibrium and on the congruence between interior states and the external environment. Red Army reports therefore highlighted the precarious status of the least seasoned members of the military—namely, the young soldiers and officers who composed a rather large percentage of the Soviet armed forces. Still developing mentally and physically, the military's youth were also maturing politically. This malleability represented an enormous opportunity for shaping the personality through political education and training; however, it also entailed great danger since the young person was extremely vulnerable to destabilizing forces in both himself and his environment. One Red Army investigator, for example, emphasized the "relatively low age of most junior officers" when he explained the predominance of suicides among this group of servicemen in the Western Military District. He wrote that at this young age "they have not yet managed to form a fundamental, clear worldview and a firm view of life."[86] Not surprisingly,

84. On the rejection of biological determinism see, for example, the circular of early December 1924, l. 36ob; and "Samoubiistva v chastiakh M.V.O.," l. 46ob.

85. Nikolai Semashko, introduction to *Samoubiitsy*, by N. P. Brukhanskii (Moscow-Leningrad, 1927), 5–6.

86. Report of Assistant Military Procurator Dobronravov to the military procurator of the Western Military District (January 14, 1925), RGVA, f. 9, op. 28, d. 781, ll. 71–72.

the youth were therefore considered the segment of the military popula-tion most susceptible to the corruptive effects of decadent literature, petit bourgeois lifestyles, and difficult material conditions, all factors that could not only undermine a person's commitment to the revolution but also lead to crisis and a suicidal state of mind.[87]

The central character of the Red Army narratives—the suicide—was conspicuous for his imbalance, lack of firmness, and high degree of im-pressionability. Political officers frequently referred to a suicide's "weak will" (*slabovolie*) and "instability" (*neustoichivost'*), characterizations that suggested the self-destructive personality was highly reactive rather than proactive. Significantly, this hypersensitivity was thought to reflect the individual's state of physical, psychological, and political development. As elaborated in the report on suicides in the Western Military District, the largest percentage of suicides among the junior command staff fell "on the element lacking firm ideological principles, the least developed mentally in general, lacking firmly formed views about life, in terms of age the youngest, the most impressionable, and the most distracted."[88] Such descriptions reinforced the idea that the suicidal personality was notable for its absent qualities; quite simply, it lacked the components necessary to process and deal with the vicissitudes of everyday life. As a result, reality conquered the individual instead of the other way around.

The class-based reality of Soviet life also shaped the narratives of Red Army suicides. Reflecting the Marxist interpretative framework in which they operated, political workers treated class as both a social and a bio-psychological signifier. In their analyses, a person's instinct and conscious-ness depended heavily on his class origins, which imprinted themselves on the individual and could even be passed on from one generation to the next.[89] Members of different classes, in other words, developed dif-ferent sets of cognitive and reflexive tools that shaped their understand-ings of life as well as their ability to navigate within certain environments. This accounts for the frequent discussions about peasant moods among Red Army men from the villages as well as the fear of ideological threats stemming from petit bourgeois women and private traders (Nepmen). Moreover, because mental health was deemed contingent upon the con-gruence between a person's internal essence and his surroundings, the

---

87. On the link between the loss of faith in oneself and the loss of faith in the revolution, see "Samoubiistva v chastiakh M.V.O.," l. 48.

88. Report of Assistant Military Procurator Dobronravov, l. 72.

89. On the significance of instinct more generally in Marxist and Bolshevik thought, see Anna Krylova, "Beyond the Spontaneity-Consciousness Paradigm: 'Class Instinct' as a Prom-ising Category of Historical Analysis," *Slavic Review* 62, no. 1 (Spring 2003): 1–23.

significance of the Bolshevik Revolution depended on the individual's socioeconomic background. Whereas the working class could expect improvement in its psychological health under Soviet power, the country's past elites were primed for an increase in nervous and mental disorders.[90] So-called former people, to put it another way, were more vulnerable to thoughts of self-destruction because they could never achieve full mental (or social) integration into the collective.[91]

The result was a distinctively Soviet version of the alienation story commonly associated with modern suicide. A special commission studying suicides in the Western Military District represented the death of a twenty-two-year-old cadet of the Third Infantry Reserve School as "characteristic for people who have left one class but have not yet merged with another." The son of a wealthy businessman, the cadet had demonstrated a lack of commitment to the new regime by resigning from the Komsomol over a disagreement about the New Economic Policy. In addition, his "loose lifestyle" (*razgul'naia zhizn'*) and general lack of interest in cultural-enlightenment work indicated a preoccupation with private life at the expense of obligations to the larger collective. The special commission also identified several elements in the cadet's suicide note that conveyed feelings of alienation and uselessness, including the phrase "All my ideals have long ago been crushed, and with a devastated soul, with nothing to believe in, it is impossible to live."[92]

The suicide of the teacher Antonov similarly revolved around the idea of the alienated class personality. A veteran of Kolchak's White Army, Antonov wrote to his mother (described in the Red Army report as a *meshchanka*)

90. The physician and psychoneurologist Aron Borisovich Zalkind believed that the uncertainty and dislocation caused by the revolution had resulted in widespread nervous and mental disorders, especially among the old ruling classes. Changes in social structure caused the "repression of neuropsychological processes" and the "perversion of their normal aspirations [*ustremleniia*]." For this reason, he claimed, former tsarist officers and former members of the nobility serving in the Red Army during the civil war suffered a greater number of nervous illnesses than did their social counterparts fighting with the Whites. A. B. Zalkind, *Revoliutsiia i molodezh'* (Moscow, 1925), 26–27.

91. Conversely, the proletariat was commonly assumed to experience fewer suicides because of its innate character and its greater hopes for the future (although the data did not always support such expectations). Also at work here was the long-standing belief among social scientists that causation varied among different social groups. Whereas suicides among the upper classes and intelligentsia were often linked to a disturbance of the person's mental faculties, workers were assumed to kill themselves primarily as a consequence of socioeconomic factors (unemployment, poverty, etc.). Thus several commentators contrasted the higher rate of suicide among workers in capitalist Europe with the lower figures for their Soviet brethren.

92. "Samoubiistva v voiskakh Zapadnogo Voennogo Okruga," RGVA, f. 9, op. 28, d. 781, l. 67.

that he had grown pessimistic and disenchanted with life because of his poor material condition. In one of his poems Antonov declared, "If I cannot succeed in life, then I will succeed in death." Summarizing their reading of Antonov's suicide, the political workers who examined his death concluded, "An obviously fainthearted element from a petit bourgeois milieu, who had dreamed in his childhood of perhaps working in a state-bureaucratic field. But then, having fallen into a working-class and peasant milieu and having seen himself maladjusted to the difficulties of proletarian struggle, he felt himself a small, useless [*nikchemnyi*] person."[93]

In many respects, the feelings conveyed by such suicides were universal expressions of internal crisis and anomie. Within the framework of the country's move toward socialism, however, the Red Army's investigators read them as indicators of a particularly Soviet form of self-destruction. This understanding certainly applied to a related group of suicides—those among class aliens who sought to mask their true selves from others. The double life led by these people violated assumptions about the need for a genuine harmonization between one's internal self and the social milieu. In addition to the stress created by the fear of being unmasked, keeping up a social façade prevented any true sense of belonging in Soviet society. Over time this limbolike status took a heavy toll on the individual. In the most extreme cases it could even lead to suicide. For example, Sizikov, a nonparty Red Army man, hid his social origins from others (he was the son of a large landowner). The brief summary of his death stated, "Fearing responsibility for his deception, having been unmasked—he shot himself."[94]

Thus, the different temporal elements of the Red Army narratives—past, present, and future—overlapped and reinforced one another. Exposure as an alien element in the Red Army, given the regime's class-based system of rewards and punishments, meant a sudden and premature end to one's vision of the future. The past in this way came back to haunt the individual. Its discovery spelled the loss of potential self-realization in the Bolshevik Party or the Red Army and so sharply altered life's trajectory that some people preferred suicide. For example, the section commander Riabov of the Siberian Military District got drunk and shot himself after he had been expelled from the party and discharged from the Red Army upon the unmasking of his kulak origins.[95] Similar stories of revelation and despair were recorded in the 1930 report on the political-moral condition

---

93. "Obzor samoubiistv po ukrainskomu voennomu okrugu," l. 42ob.
94. "Statisticheskii ezhegodnik. Politiko-moral'noe sostoianie RKKA," l. 33.
95. Ibid.

of the military. The Red Army man Shkilondze shot himself after his removal from the army for being the son of a noble-landowner; the cadet Gorodetskii did the same after he was transferred out of flight school as an alien element; and the section commander Paprits reportedly attempted suicide because of his dismissal from the Red Army as a disenfranchised person (*lishenets*).[96]

Reports of suicides among social aliens highlighted the historical contingency of suicidal individuals and placed their actions firmly within the larger narrative of the Soviet Union's move toward socialism. As we have seen, the continued presence of suicides was often attributed to the transition period, which suggested a kind of instability in the social organism that found expression in the moral and psychological instability of its weakest and least mature members. Toward the end of the 1920s, with the abandonment of the New Economic Policy in favor of a more aggressive campaign to build socialism and destroy the remnants of capitalism, a new wave of suicides was predicted. According to the 1930 report cited above, the number of suicides linked to the exposure of the individual's social background was increasing along with the implementation of party purges and the heightening of class warfare that accompanied the collectivization and industrialization drives of the late 1920s. The Main and Political administrations confirmed such expectations by creating a new statistical category in their summaries—"discharge from the army and hiding alien origins."[97] Paradoxically, the intensification of mutual surveillance, which was seen as a way to combat self-destruction in the military, could under certain conditions have the opposite effect, as more and more individuals became unhinged when they were found out. Delving into and opening up the individual therefore posed risks. For this reason the authors of the 1930 report expressed concern over the careless and arbitrary unmasking of individuals. Indeed, the suicide note left behind by the Red Army man Kulakov suggested both the internalization of the party's language of social class and a keen awareness of the way that class identity affected integration within the Soviet order. It stated simply, "I don't want to be an alien element in the Red Army in view of my father's kulak standing."[98]

Class-based understandings of imbalance and instability were interwoven with physiological readings of the suicidal personality. Especially

---

96. "Statisticheskii ezhegodnik za 1928/29 god.," ll. 49–49ob.
97. Ibid., ll. 44ob, 49–49ob. This category was included in the following year's report as well. See "Statisticheskii ezhegodnik. Politiko-moral'noe sostoianie RKKA," ll. 32ob–33.
98. "Statisticheskii ezhegodnik za 1928/29 god," l. 49.

during the early part of the 1920s, political workers and other military officials saw a strong connection among exhaustion, nervousness, and suicide. The wearing out of the troops was partly attributed to the conditions currently prevailing inside the military. Reports on suicide emphasized such aggravating factors as abominably poor housing conditions, low levels of material support, prolonged separation from loved ones, and a general state of "overloading" (*peregruzka*), especially among the officer corps and political workers.[99] One survey of the military's "political-moral condition" in 1923 pointed out that "nervous overstraining" sometimes led to full-blown cases of mental illness, insanity, and suicide.[100] At the same time, nervous illness and fatigue were seen as the cumulative product of past experiences. Most representative in this respect were the discussions about former members of the political underground or veterans of the imperialist and civil wars. For example, the higher rates of suicide in the Red Army in comparison with those in the Imperial Russian Army were attributed to the severe "exhaustion" (*iznoshennost'*) of the troops resulting from famine and continuous fighting between 1914 and 1921.[101] Similarly, another survey listed the "severe shattering [*izdergannost'*] and overexhaustion of the old fighters of the Red Army" as one of the "illnesses of everyday life" indicated by acts of suicide.[102]

Signs of nervousness also wrote the suicide into the larger story of the epic struggle to create socialism. In fact, nervous suicides were considered a product of their time. Life in Soviet Russia during the 1920s often was portrayed as particularly nerve-racking given the demands of building socialism and the myriad social and cultural changes to which people were forced to adapt. "Nervous people" were a common feature of Soviet literature, and the potential for widespread "neurasthenic malaise" raised concerns among both Bolshevik party leaders and the medical community.[103] Nikolai Semashko, who was otherwise quite sanguine about the problem of self-destruction, conceded that the Soviet people were living

99. On suicide and the overloading of individuals see the report of April 1927 from Chernevskii, head of PUR's Infstatotdel, RGVA, f. 9, op. 26, d. 429, l. 1ob; and "Protokol No. 3: Zasedaniia tsentral'nogo politsoveshchaniia 24 marta 1926 g.," RGVA, f. 9, op. 28, d. 1175, l. 50.

100. "Obzor material'no-bytovogo i politiko-moral'nogo sostoianiia krasnoi armii na I–VIII 1923 goda," RGVA, f. 9, op. 26, d. 111, l. 49.

101. "Samoubiistva v RKKA za 1924/25 god," l. 9; and "Kratkii obzor o samoubiistvakh v Krasnoi Armii i vo Flote za 1924–25 gody," ll. 100ob–101.

102. Obzor 'Samoubiistva v Krasnoi Armii i Flote za ianvar'–aprel' 1924 goda,'" l. 53.

103. Frances Lee Bernstein, *The Dictatorship of Sex: Lifestyle Advice for the Soviet Masses* (DeKalb, IL, 2007), 88. Bernstein notes that suicide was part of the symptomology of male sexual dysfunction, which in turn was linked to a variety of nervous disorders.

"under exceptional nervous strain."[104] Writing at the end of the decade, a pair of authors also linked suicides to the nervous confusion of the individual amid the particular challenges of the day. They opined, "Such is the influence of our stormy revolutionary era on the physically and mentally weakest, that amid the furious tempo of work the nerves of the individual—especially the most active builder of socialism—the communist—demand maximum exertion."[105]

Whether innate or recently acquired, the condition of nervousness became one of the key signs of Soviet suicide. Nervous persons were thought to display behaviors that communicated a lack of emotional and psychological balance. They were prone to irritability, agitation, preoccupation, crying bouts, excitability, and explosive outbursts of anger. Nervousness, in other words, was internal disorder written on the body. As described in one report, the suicide "literally appeared a bundle of nerves [*komok nervov*]."[106] Significantly, the signs associated with nervousness allowed for the possibility of restoring a person to equilibrium. Once identified, the individual could be physically "repaired" through an extended period of rest, the regular practice of physical culture, or the introduction of a more rational schedule of daily activities. For those soldiers and officers most severely affected, the recognition of their nervous condition might even lead to their early discharge from the Red Army, as the military strove to eliminate the potential for suicide and other illnesses from its ranks.[107]

Nevertheless, there was a danger in using the trope of the nervous suicide too often. The perceived ubiquity of nervousness among suicides threatened to drain the condition of any explanatory power. One particularly detailed discussion of causation noted that nervous (and thus psychological) instability was present in almost every case, a fact confirmed by studies in the USSR and elsewhere. The challenge for investigators, it concluded, was to uncover the true part played by the nerves in bringing about the suicide. According to the report's authors, "If we were to assign to the category 'on the grounds of nervous illness' all cases of suicide in

---

104. He therefore emphasized the importance of improving living and working conditions in order to prevent the waste of "nervous and mental energy." N. Semashko, "Ugrozhaet li nam epidemiia samoubiistv?" *Izvestiia TsIK Sovetov,* January 22, 1926, 5.

105. M. Dubrovskii and A. Lipkin, "O samoubiistvakh," *Revoliutsiia i kul'tura,* March 15, 1929, 35.

106. "Obzor-direktiva. O samoubiistvakh v chastiakh Turkfront," l. 83ob.

107. "Samoubiistva v krasnoi armii i flote," l. 75; and "Kratkii obzor o samoubiistvakh v Krasnoi Armii i vo Flote za 1924–25 gody," l. 101ob. For examples of the Red Army's campaign to "unburden" the officer corps and political workers see "Peregruzka aktiva i nashi zadachi," *Krasnaia zvezda,* February 18, 1925, 3; and "Nevrasteniki ne nuzhny," *Krasnaia zvezda,* April 4, 1925, 4.

which the element of nervous instability is present, then we would not make any progress toward resolving the question of the roots that nourish suicides in the army and could not illuminate those paths to be followed in the fight against suicides."[108] In fact, the interpretative challenge was severe enough that several surveys complained that the concept of nervousness was losing its meaning because of overuse and imprecision in the political workers' reports.[109]

Political workers therefore looked for other signs of the serviceman's inability to cope with the world around him. They ascribed particular importance to indications that he had become introverted and isolated from the collective. According to one Political Administration report, the tendency to turn inward was an external manifestation of "the rather long internal struggle" prior to the act of suicide. Rather than go to others for help or advice, the individual who withdrew into himself looked only to "settle accounts with life."[110] Officers were therefore told to look out for loners (*odinochki*) who did not actively participate in their unit's social life. In the retrospective reading that followed the suicide of the Black Sea Fleet sailor Nikiforov, for example, we see how the move away from others provided an important marker for interpreting his death. Nikiforov shot himself to death some thirty minutes after his commanding officer denied his request to visit a dentist in the port city. He apparently left the officer in tears and killed himself upon returning to his quarters. According to the investigating political officer's report, most sailors and political personnel on the ship considered the cause of the suicide to be "Nikiforov's depressed moods [*upadochnicheskie nastroeniia*], which lately had expressed themselves in self-isolation [*zamknutost'*] and his strong urge to read works of literature that spoke of death and suicides."[111] These external gestures—social withdrawal and a general interest in the question of

---

108. "Samoubiistva v RKKA za 1926/27 god," l. 13. Despite these concerns, the authors of the report concluded that any study of causation must take into account the mutual relationship between the nervous system and external factors or motivations.

109. For example, one survey included a list of "unconvincing conclusions" reached by military procurators during their investigations into suicide. These included "psychical disorder," "mental abnormality," "psychosis," "psychopathic condition," "hysteria," "melancholy," "nervous depression," "morbid mental condition," "lack of balance," "neurasthenia," "nervous instability," and "insufficient mental development." These diagnoses were contrasted in the survey with cases where the presence of a "graver" illness was indicated: "illness of the cerebrum," "epilepsy," "degeneration" (*degeneratsiia*), "persecution complex of mental illness," and "improper joining of the skull." "Statisticheskii ezhegodnik za 1928/29 god," l. 53.

110. "Obzor 'Samoubiistva v chastiakh UVO,'" l. 37ob.

111. "Svodka Politicheskogo Upravleniia Raboche-Krest'ianskoi Krasnoi Armii. No. 367," RGASPI, f. 17, op. 85, d. 127, l. 22ob.

death—shaped the reading of Nikiforov's conflict with his commanding officer. Although a minority of Nikiforov's fellow sailors sought to blame the commander for the suicide, the signs of a preexisting psychological instability undermined this explanation in favor of one that centered on the suicide himself.

Evaluations of the suicide's conduct on the job or as a party member also drove the Red Army narratives. The failure to fulfill military duties, poor attendance at party meetings or instructional classes, and a general abandonment of "social work" were all construed as indicators of mental states and attitudes. In particular, they suggested a pathological focus on personal problems, moral degeneration, and alienation from the collective. For example, the sharp change noticed in one political instructor's attitude toward work was traced to his marriage to a petit bourgeois woman, an event that investigators described as a turning point in his life. Prior to his marriage the political instructor had reportedly displayed the proper interest in his duties and was "earnest" in developing both his political and his intellectual self. However, after the nuptials "he quickly fell under the influence of his wife and began to disengage from party work." The resulting "moral crisis" drove the political instructor to shoot himself. For those investigating and interpreting the suicide, the instructor's sudden loss of interest in his work and political self not only violated assumptions about how the ideal Bolshevik should act but also contradicted understandings of his normal behavior. Hence, his suicide was assigned to the category of motives "due to romance, family squabbles, and a difficult family situation."[112]

Political workers organized their diagnoses around a repertoire of observable signs that to them suggested personal crisis. These included frequent outbursts of anger, mood swings, weepiness, or even a total abandonment of concern for one's personal appearance. Each of these connoted a general departure from normal codes of conduct, but they assumed special significance if they violated others' expectations based on their everyday observations of the individual's character. This was particularly the case with morally dissolute acts committed by an individual who had previously presented an upright and responsible face. In particular, bouts of heavy drinking, the frequenting of prostitutes, and sexual debauchery all suggested a loss of concern about the future since the person

---

112. "Obzor 'Samoubiistv sredi chlenov i kandidatov partii,'" l. 2. For another suicide where a connection was made between loss of interest in party work and marriage to an alien social element see "Obzor 'Samoubiistva v chastiakh UVO,'" l. 38. Here too the suicide was listed under the category "family causes."

risked his professional, social, and domestic position by carrying on in this amoral manner. Here the suicide of Iablokov is particularly instructive. Iablokov was an assistant platoon commander in the Twenty-fifth Division who had established rather good political credentials through his lengthy service in the Red Army. Although he reportedly had difficulty adjusting to the stricter discipline of the peacetime military, he managed to "correct himself" and petitioned for entrance into the Bolshevik Party. The battalion party cell approved his application, but the regimental bureau later denied it after looking deeper into Iablokov's life. According to the official account of Iablokov's suicide, "the refusal of entrance into the party obviously had a negative effect on him. He changed [*peremenilsia*], began to carouse, got involved with petit bourgeois girls, and, when they failed to reciprocate, he went on a drinking spree that intensified to the point of selling all his belongings." By focusing on the sudden transformation in Iablokov's behavior and its apparent coincidence with the party's rejection, the district political administration arrived at a conclusion regarding the cause of Iablokov's suicide. His action was assigned to the group of suicides motivated by "dissatisfaction with service."[113]

Interpretations of the individual's inability to deal properly with Soviet reality always had a strong political tinge to them. This was certainly the case with the stories of suicides placed under the categories "disappointment with life" and "without prospects." These narratives centered on the future self and the sense that circumstances had conspired to prevent the individual from achieving certain professional or political goals. For example, some commanders and political officers were said to suffer from "demobilization moods" as a result of the military's downsizing in response to the country's pressing economic problems. The fear of being let go from the Red Army, coupled with concerns about finding employment outside the military and sustaining a family, could provoke feelings of resignation, resentfulness, anger, and despair. When in the grip of this mental state, the affected officer might talk negatively about the Soviet regime, fail to carry out his duties, go on drinking sprees, or even kill himself.[114] At the same time, the Red Army linked the category "disappointment with life" to personal shortcomings and a "pathological undervaluing of one's

113. "Obzor samoubiistv po ukrainskomu voennomu okrugu," ll. 42–42ob.

114. For a discussion of the formation of demobilization moods and their effect on the servicemen's behavior see "Moskva, 23 iiulia 1926 goda. Svodka Politicheskogo Upravleniia Raboche-Krest'ianskoi Krasnoi Armii i Flota. No. 340," RGASPI, f. 17, op. 85, d. 127, l. 166; and "Moskva, 4-go oktiabria 1926 goda. Svodka Politicheskogo Upravleniia Raboche-Krest'ianskoi Krasnoi Armii i Flota. No. 346," RGASPI, f. 17, op. 85, d. 127, l. 148ob.

abilities."[115] These suicides violated expectations that the Soviet male was to be optimistic, disciplined, and unbending no matter the difficulties before him. They included the party cell secretary Frank, who shot himself when he failed to pass the entrance examination for an advanced training school; the cadet Georgii Smolin, who killed himself after a rebuke from his party cell; and the teacher Gil'ferding of the Military-Technical Academy, who hanged himself "after his unsuitability as an instructor was exposed at an educational conference."[116]

Suicides linked to the question of the individual's "prospects" conveyed a sense of finality sharply at odds with the futurist orientation of the Soviet experiment. Specifically, they suggested a lack of political consciousness and education. One summary report claimed that suicides related to uncertainty about life were born of the individuals' failure to know their rights as soldiers, since all members of the Red Army had "firm prospects, not only during the period of service in the army, but also following discharge."[117] Red Army officials, moreover, expected the servicemen to fight off feelings of rejection and pessimism, criticizing in particular the suicides, or threats of suicide, that followed disciplinary action or suspension/expulsion from the party organization. Although investigators formally considered the rebuke given to cadet Smolin as the motive for his suicide, they also noted that he suffered from a "loss of work prospects and ideological hopelessness, as well as the inability to sort himself out [*nevozhmnost' razobrat'sia s samim soboiu*]." In this manner, they rejected the belief expressed in Smolin's diary that "for a Komsomolist 'expulsion' means execution."[118]

Verbal threats of suicide and other signs of the individual's preoccupation with death were also highlighted in the Red Army narratives, since they communicated a closed rather than open-ended life. Investigators pored over the individual's words, both written and oral, for an indication of why and when he began to contemplate his mortality. In addition to open warnings, there were less obvious declarations indicating mental preparation for death. A report on a series of suicides in the Ukrainian Military District criticized the lack of attention given to servicemen who had "openly displayed a tendency toward suicide." It gave the example of an eventual suicide who reportedly gave numerous (but unspecified) hints

115. "Statisticheskii ezhegodnik za 1928/29 god," l. 51ob.
116. "O samoubiistvakh sredi chlenov RKP(b)," ll. 1–1ob; and "Statisticheskii ezhegodnik za 1928/29 god," l. 48.
117. "Statisticheskii ezhegodnik za 1928/29 god," l. 48.
118. "O samoubiistvakh sredi chlenov RKP(b)," l. 1.

about his desire to kill himself. The situation was the same with Iuzkov of the cavalry battalion, who on the day of his suicide announced, "Well, I'm cleaning my rifle for the last time."[119] Once placed into the retrospective narrative of the political officer, Iuzkov's statement possessed a clarity and power that it lacked when originally made. The challenge facing the Political Administration was getting people to recognize such warning signs in order to anticipate and forestall the end point that ultimately gave them such grave meaning.

Other forms of nonverbal communication highlighted in the narratives included the kinds of literature that attracted the suicidal individual. Red Army investigators continued the prerevolutionary practice of seeing literature as a potential source of self-destructive tendencies. They looked in particular for a fascination with works marked in Soviet culture as politically and morally threatening. Stories dealing with topics such as hooliganism, suicide, sexual debauchery among young people, and other examples of so-called decadence were all thought to have a negative effect on the impressionable reader.[120] Once under the influence of this material, which reinforced feelings of revolutionary drift, the weak individual was destabilized by its conflicting depictions of Soviet reality, sometimes to the point of contemplating an early end to life. For example, an April 1927 investigation into the political-moral condition of the Baltic Sea Fleet concluded that two suicides had been committed because of "degenerate moods," which partly expressed themselves in the distribution of poems that idealized hooliganism, drunkenness, and pornography.[121]

Not surprisingly, the most dangerous form of literature was the poetry of Sergei Esenin. The practice of reading Esenin's poetry, quoting from his work, or even mimicking his writing style in diaries and letters transmitted ideas about a number of mental or emotional states, among them pessimism, apathy, and alienation. Leukhin, a suicide in the Black Sea Fleet in February 1927, wrote in the letters he left behind that he was tired of living and, according to the political worker's report, concluded one with a "Eseninist phrase": "Well, so what, my love, so what." He was described as having been "unsociable" (*neobshchitelen*), sullen, and indifferent to almost everything. The official diagnosis of the suicide suggests that Leukhin's interest in Esenin only reinforced this common perception

119. "Moskva. 1-go aprelia 1927 g. Svodka Politicheskogo Upravleniia Raboche-Krest'ianskoi Krasnoi armii i flota. No. 357," RGASPI, f. 17, op. 85, d. 127, l. 63.

120. On the perceived threat posed by such literary works, see Gregory Carleton, *Sexual Revolution in Bolshevik Russia* (Pittsburgh, 2005).

121. "14-go aprelia 1927 g. Svodka Politicheskogo Upravleniia Raboche-Krest'ianskoi Krasnoi Armii i Flota. No. 358," RGASPI, f. 17, op. 85, d. 127, l. 60.

of his nature and mental state. "We consider," stated the summary, "the cause of the suicide to be Leukhin's apathetic mood under the influence of the Eseninist literature in which he became engrossed."[122]

The case of Nikolai Lavrov, a political instructor at the Tiflis Infantry School, provides another example of the assumptions routinely made on the basis of the kinds of literature read by the suicide. Lavrov, who killed himself in March 1926, was said to be hot-tempered (*vspyl'chivyi*), removed (*zamknutyi*), and extremely nervous. He reportedly began to contemplate taking his own life because of romantic problems and unhappiness with his work. Witnesses claimed that not long before the suicide he began to associate his own mood with that of Esenin, an affinity that was confirmed by his purchase and reading of Esenin's poetry. In addition, the decorations in his room also "began to reflect his mood." Lavrov hung a black towel above his bed and tacked on the portraits of Esenin and Larisa Reisner, a writer, Bolshevik, and former naval commissar who died of typhus in February 1926 at the young age of thirty. Nearby he posted another picture, this one of Trotsky, who had written a eulogy for Esenin, with his hand outstretched and pointing in the direction of the other portraits.[123]

Lavrov's case vividly demonstrates that the signs of Soviet suicide were not unidirectional in their meaning and usage. Because suicides were enmeshed within the same symbolic system as their observers, they too had to draw upon the possible world of Soviet suicide to make sense of their personal condition and to convey this understanding to others. They selected from a common set of coded objects, words, gestures, or even situations that communicated a range of ideas, feelings, conditions, or psychological states. For example, the black banner that Lavrov draped over his bed had associations with death and rituals of mourning. Similarly, the purchase and reading of Eseninist literature resonated among friends and fellow soldiers precisely because of the public discussion of Eseninism and its implications for the country's youth. Even his choice of Trotsky's portrait was politically significant in light of the ongoing struggle in the party leadership and Trotsky's growing association with the opposition. At the same time, the adoption of certain phrases and explanations in suicide notes suggests that a common interpretative framework shaped

122. The sailors who later met to discuss Leukhin's suicide characterized his act as a "desertion from life and from the honored post of Red Fleet sailor and commander" and condemned Eseninism as "poeticized vulgarity." "14 marta 1927 goda. Svodka Politicheskogo Upravleniia Raboche-Krest'ianskoi Armii i Flota. No. 356," RGASPI, f. 17, op. 85, d. 127, ll. 69–69ob.

123. "Moskva 22-go maia 1926 goda. Svodka Politicheskogo Upravleniia Raboche-Krest'ianskoi Krasnoi Armii i Flota. No. 334," RGASPI, f. 17, op. 85, d. 127, l. 201.

both the readings of the Red Army investigators and the object of their inquiries. Suicides' own representations of their behavior often touched upon issues of party ethics, personal failings as a Bolshevik, difficult material circumstances, and a host of causal factors that both reflected and reaffirmed the common analytical categories. The authors of the Red Army reports, in narrating the story of Soviet suicide, were therefore helping to shape the concrete and subjective world of everyday life in the military.[124]

Viewed together, the Red Army narratives presented a mirror image of the ideal Soviet male. Suicides were deemed inherently unstable individuals whose pathological sensitivity made them susceptible to the pressures of Soviet life and military service. Feelings of alienation and insecurity were portrayed as an excessive concern for one's personal affairs and a failure to understand the role one played in the larger scheme of the revolution. Furthermore, ideas about the sources of this instability reflected the political workers' particular role as caretakers of the military's "political-moral condition." The result was a flexible explanatory framework that contained theories about the states of mind and motives behind suicide, the types of people who were prone to self-destruction under Soviet power, and the circumstances that frequently occasioned their desperate acts. In the process of constructing their reports, the Red Army's investigators also formulated a common vocabulary for representing the internal thoughts and feelings of others. This included a range of signs that helped to make the suicidal personality visible to the rest of the collective.

The stories of Soviet suicide therefore reinforced the importance of information to the revolutionary project. A major implication of the various signs of suicide, especially from the standpoint of prevention, was the need for Red Army commanders and political officers to know the daily lives and personality of the individual serviceman. In order to detect the development of suicidal or other unhealthy moods, they had to establish what kinds of people he was associating with, what he was saying to others, the contents of his books or personal letters, the condition of his mental and physical health, his work habits and approach to political questions, and finally the state of his family and sexual life.[125] Each of these areas contained important bits of information that could be used to divine inner

---

124. Irina Paperno develops the argument for a hermeneutic circle around suicide in *Suicide as a Cultural Institution in Dostoevsky's Russia* (Ithaca, 1997).

125. A regional commission organized to study suicides emphasized the profound effect that letters from home had on the soldiers and instructed commanders and political officers to pay attention to those individuals who became depressed upon hearing bad news from their family. "Moskva 22-go maia 1926 goda. Svodka Politicheskogo Upravleniia Raboche-Krest'ianskoi Krasnoi Armii i Flota. No. 334," ll. 204–204ob.

thoughts and feelings. Furthermore, the Red Army's interest in fostering and maintaining a healthy serviceman created a demand for an archive of knowledge, in both written and unwritten form, about the personality of the individual. This personalized information served as a baseline against which to judge subsequent behavior, in particular any sudden or sharp alterations that might indicate individual crisis or disintegration. The proper functioning of the military organism, in other words, rested on the study of individuals and their life stories.

MEDICOPOLITICS AND SOVIET SURVEILLANCE

The Red Army can be read as a kind of laboratory where the Soviet regime experimented with various technologies of government upon a discrete, accessible population. Indeed, given their dual authority as both party members and military officials, its political workers operated with greater latitude and upon a wider canvas than many other social investigators during the 1920s. The end result was the development of a distinctive medicopolitics that eventually applied to the entire Soviet population. As evident in the efforts to study and prevent suicide, the Political Administration and its fellow military agencies elaborated a vision of the individual as a highly plastic being who could be remade through the interventions of the state and various disciplinary experts. They treated the personality as the product of various elements—including biology, heredity, environment, occupation, and social class—and regarded suicide as the consequence of disharmony between external reality and the interior self. Notions of health, most significantly, were cast in the broadest of terms, whereby the boundaries between the medical, sociological, and political spheres blurred to the point of nonexistence. In the hands of the political workers, an individual's physical, emotional, and psychological conditions all became signifiers of his commitment to the revolution as well as the regime's level of success in bringing the socialist future closer to fruition. It was a sociopolitical definition that dramatically opened up the state's therapeutic reach into the lives of its citizens.

The response to suicide was part of a continuous diagnostic regime that worked through the individual. In his pioneering study of the individual and collective in Russia, Oleg Kharkhordin suggests that the Soviet regime's focus on the personality achieved prominence during the 1930s, whereas before that the relative emphasis had been on the collective. Thus, the party cell, and not the individual, was being purged in the era of the New Economic Policy. After 1931, however, the individual approach dominated, as the party began to search more insistently for personal deeds and other external signs that could reveal subjective motives and authentic identity.[126]

This examination of the Red Army investigations into suicide during the 1920s shows that the turn toward the individual and the subjective world was well under way before the tumultuous decade that followed. The Soviet state's growing claim on its citizens as political actors, coupled with the discourse of ideological pathology, translated into an increasingly widespread system of information gathering and tutelage. Offering a rather ordered and manageable population, the military served as the incubator for the new citizen and, not surprisingly, became the site where many of the aspirations for total knowledge and social work found their most concrete expression. A resolution on suicide proposed by the Red Army's Central Military-Political Meeting in 1926, for example, emphasized both broad measures to improve the condition of servicemen and the opportunity for soldiers and officers to realize themselves as individuals while constructing the collective: "The system of political work combined with the cultural-enlightenment and social organizations provides enormous opportunities for servicemen to fulfill their spiritual needs [*dukhovnye zaprosy*], to display initiative, and to resolve abnormalities of everyday life, etc."[127] Within the military, suicides therefore became a specific type of indicator in the hands of the political workers. Their responses to acts of self-destruction are further confirmation of the fact that the Soviet polity was shaped in no small way by conceptions of the individual.

Key here was the complete absence of boundaries separating the physical, the moral, and the political realms of existence. Attributes assigned to the suicidal personality—notably weakness, instability, unsociability, and obsessive self-interest—applied equally as well to the politically suspect individual. Such overlap made the care for one's physical and mental health a component of political consciousness while also adding a strong moral dimension to virtually every action (or inaction). The result was a medicopolitics that promoted the comprehensive care of the individual as an integral component of the collective's existence and well-being. Those servicemen recognized as being physically impaired or psychologically unstable would be placed in the hands of doctors and psychiatrists in the Military-Sanitary Administration, who would oversee a therapeutic regimen to repair their bodies and minds. At the same time, political workers

126. Oleg Kharkhordin, *The Individual and the Collective in Russia: A Study of Practices* (Berkeley, 1999), esp. chap. 5.
127. "Proekt rezoliutsii TsVPS o samoubiistvakh," l. 42.

would cultivate politically healthy citizens by attempting to cure the ideo-logically infected and strengthen the resistance of the ideologically weak through a combination of political education courses, cultural programs, and environmental change. "One of the primary obligations and tasks of all leadership personnel," stated the Main and Political administrations in 1930, "is the elimination of [the] 'objective' causes [of suicide] (through the treatment of the nervously ill, work on ordering everyday life in the family, the inclusion of all servicemen in healthy social work, etc.) and the creation of the conditions that eliminate suicides as a means for service-men to resolve their agonizing dilemmas [*boleznennye voprosy*]."[128] When such ameliorative efforts failed, the Political Administration, the Military Procurator's Office, and/or the Special Department of the GPU would seek to isolate, and potentially reform, the recalcitrant individual through a series of disciplinary and exclusionary practices that included temporary suspensions, expulsions, corrective labor, and confinement.

The information on Red Army suicides therefore cannot be read as mere summaries of reality but must instead be interpreted within the larger framework of the revolutionary effort to achieve the dream of collec-tive harmony. Suicide statistics and other social data were, in this respect, part of an effort to measure the assimilation of new values, to identify and eradicate remaining pockets of illness, and to generally know how far away the Soviets remained from achieving the socialist utopia. After all, ill-nesses or bourgeois vestiges like suicide were supposed to disappear once the new society was created. Narrative accounts of self-destruction also reinforce the fact that the various actors in the suicidal drama were cultur-ally embedded and thus had a role to play in shaping the meaning of self-destruction. They offer a window into the way that the Soviets interpreted these acts to stand as markers of social health and how they developed particular policies on the basis of such understandings.

Overall, the assumptions behind the early manifestations of Soviet medicopolitics left open the possibility for a radicalization and deep-ening of both social diagnostics and social therapeutics as the country moved closer and closer to socialism. Given the historical contingency of the individual's relationship to the collective, it was understandable that notions of deviance would change once the dream of a holistic society had been attained. Indeed, the deep awareness of time that animated the Bolsheviks' eschatological worldview heightened sensitivity toward recal-citrant types and realigned the significance of the various elements that

128. "Statisticheskii ezhegodnik za 1928/29 god," ll. 45–45ob.

composed the human (and the suicidal) personality. Always uneasy about the relative permanence of class outlooks and residual social habits, Soviet investigators began to treat nurture as akin to nature in their haste to create the socialist utopia. Such inclinations gave a push toward methods of completely excising from the body politic the diseased members, who were now considered irredeemable and thus a more profound threat to others.[129]

In the Red Army's reactions to self-destruction, then, we come face-to-face with the expansiveness of the social science state's purchase on the individual. Seeing the soldier or officer solely as an object of study undermined the humane aspirations behind the Soviets' desire to promote comradely relations based on close attention to the specific needs and character of the personality. What seemed a means of promoting more intimate relationships between people actually created distance between the observer and the observed as mutual surveillance threatened to become mutual suspicion. Moreover, the objectification of the Soviet subject did not lead to uniformity and homogenization in terms of the possible world that framed understandings of the individual. But it did produce a distinct system that placed prescribed limits on individual potentiality, beyond which the collective had almost unlimited powers to defend itself. In the push for creating the conditions deemed necessary to bring about personal emancipation and happiness under socialism, the Soviet party-state would stop at nothing, including violence—provided, of course, that this violence was dispensed by society and not by individuals against themselves.

129. The historical development of this more pessimistic potentiality is a central theme in Daniel Beer's *Renovating Russia*.

Epilogue

Suicide and Stalinism

Beginning in 1928–29, the Soviet regime opened up a broad economic and ideological offensive that spelled the end of the New Economic Policy. Together with the collectivization of agriculture, the programs of mass industrialization enshrined in the First Five-Year Plan (1929–34) produced an extremely fluid society that challenged the state's ability to see and manage the population. About the same time, the Cultural Revolution (1928–31) unleashed a wave of attacks against the remnants of the prerevolutionary professional and intellectual elites, thereby unsettling the governmental and educational apparatuses. The results were dramatic: the countryside was transformed with the routing of the kulaks or better-off peasants, "bourgeois" specialists began to be replaced by "red" experts trained under Soviet power, a new set of political and social elites ascended to positions of authority, and the nation overall took a great leap toward becoming an urban, industrial polity. Indeed, by 1934 Joseph Stalin and other Bolshevik leaders felt confident enough to declare the construction of socialism completed and thereby begin the process of consolidating the gains of the previous years. One byproduct of such expectant victory was a sharpening of attitudes toward antisocial elements and a heightened reliance on the state's diagnostic and disciplinary apparatuses.[1] Even though the

1. See, for example, Paul M. Hagenloh, "'Socially Harmful Elements' and the Great Terror," in *Stalinism: New Directions (Rewriting History)*, ed. Sheila Fitzpatrick (New York, 2000), 286–308.

so-called Stalin Constitution of 1936 proclaimed an end to class struggle in the USSR, the regime remained on the lookout for enemies, who faced exposure through the cleansing of the party-state apparatuses and eventually isolation and destruction during the Great Purges of the late 1930s.

A study of the practices surrounding suicide in the 1920s allows us to consider the origins and nature of the political, cultural, and social terrain that emerged under Stalin's leadership. The diverse forms of social investigation that arose during the New Economic Policy provided the instruments and outlooks that ultimately helped to create a state with enormous powers to promote and defend its interests. This involved the creation of healthy individuals, the therapeutic treatment or segregation of transgressors, and the development of a continuous diagnostic regime that operated through and around the individual. The various processes of promotion and containment were always intertwined. Medical studies, political education, disciplinary measures, and the active formation of "collective opinion" all encouraged the formation of a desired Soviet subject by furthering a value system that denied any absolute distinction between the part and the whole. In the Soviet social science state, every form of thought and behavior was deemed socially as well as politically meaningful and thus open to scrutiny. As the Soviets got closer to their goal of creating a holistic society, the individual only became more significant.[2]

With the abandonment of the New Economic Policy, evolutionary assumptions about development finally gave way to the radicalism and impatience intrinsic to Bolshevism. Party members and young professionals, many of whom were educated in the Soviet era and resented the country's reliance upon prerevolutionary experts, clamored for their own revolution and an end to the stalemate of the transition period. They blamed the country's various problems on the compromises of the New Economic Policy and believed that such issues as unemployment, prostitution, and homelessness would all be solved once an industrialized society was created along noncapitalist lines. Rather than spell an end to revolutionary dreaming in Soviet Russia, the Stalinist "Great Break" meant the remobilization of the population toward a grand historical mission. It implied and indeed encouraged the idea that the Soviets could bend time according to their will.

2. The dual goals of promotion and containment regarding individuals were encapsulated in a 1935 study of child suicides. According to its author, a "collective upbringing" was effective at preventing suicide by both "raising self-worth" and "destroying egocentric inclinations [*ustanovki*]." I. N. Murakhovskaia, "K genezu detskikh samoubiistv," in *Problemy psikhiatrii i psikhopatologii*, ed. S. N. Davidenkov (Moscow, 1935), 575.

One effect of these moves was to bring out the utopianism always inherent in Soviet social investigation. During the 1920s, speculation about the future implied that suicides, crime, and other socially harmful activities would diminish and eventually disappear once collective harmony and happiness were achieved. Soviet social investigators theorized that after the end of class struggle and oppression the individual would achieve true integration, and thus genuine consciousness and emancipation, within the whole. "The task of socialist construction," proclaimed the physician Vladimir Velichkin in 1930, "consists of creating the person [*chelovek*] who sees the greatest freedom in giving himself up entirely to the service of his collective and who feels himself unfree [*nesvobodnyi*] to leave it without permission."[3] Several authors confirmed that the Soviet system under Stalin's leadership was in fact creating the conditions for such a person to be realized. They noted that suicides among schoolchildren had declined sharply since the tsarist period, attributing this decline to the improved environment now prevailing inside the classroom. Most notably, they claimed, the Soviet school catered to the individual. It promoted individual initiative, met the needs of the student through such organizations as the Young Pioneers, and, in the words of one researcher, no longer "look[ed] upon schoolchildren as an undifferentiated silent mass [*odnorodnaia bezotvetnaia massa*]."[4]

Millenarian expectations of conflict and violence coexisted alongside such optimism. Social and political commentators prophesied that as the Soviet Union moved closer to achieving the socialist dream, the country's class enemies—both internal and external—would make a last-ditch effort to derail the forces of history. "The more decisively the working class 'breaks the back' of the philistine throughout the Union," wrote Maksim Gorky in a 1930 discussion of suicides, "the shriller and more plaintively chirps the philistine, sensing that his final demise is approaching ever more quickly."[5] Those who studied suicide assumed that this sense of doom and estrangement from Soviet reality would find partial expression in the self-destruction of alien social elements. One of the same authors who touted the decrease in suicides among Soviet school youth, for example, noted that the propensity toward suicide depended heavily on the child's "class membership." Despite the improvements brought

3. V. Velichkin, "Pravo na smert'," *Sovetskii vrach*, nos. 17–18 (1930): 766.

4. I. V. Markovin, "Samoubiistvo sredi detei shkol'nikov," *Trudy sredneaziatskogo meditsinskogo instituta* 1, no. 1 (1935): 375; and V. M. Gur-Gurevich, "Samoubiistva sredi detskogo i iunoshevskogo vozrasta do i posle revoliutsii," *Pedologiia*, no. 1 (1930): 98–106.

5. M. Gor'kii, "O solitere," *Nashi dostizheniia*, no. 6 (June 1930): 3.

about by the revolution, adolescents from the bourgeois intelligentsia, who were thought to be experiencing a "moral-ideological crisis," continued to display old traits that accounted for their much higher rate of self-destruction than that of their proletarian counterparts.[6] Nevertheless, one fails to detect an obvious sense of relief or even acceptance when it comes to suicides committed by social aliens. Whereas the Nazis welcomed acts of suicide among Germans with illnesses or injuries as unburdening the nation and preserving racial health, the Soviets were discomfited by acts of self-destruction among their class enemies.[7] For although such violence confirmed their larger worldview, it also suggested that these individuals had escaped detection as well as justice. In a broader sense, suicides among class enemies added to the growing doubts that the regime could afford to reform the recalcitrant individual amid the accelerated tempo of building Soviet socialism that had been set off with the collectivization and industrialization drives of 1928–29. Seemingly mutable elements of the personality like social class now assumed the character of fixed qualities that demanded a firmer and more violent response on the part of society.[8]

The sense of urgency that accompanied the Stalinist revolution of the early 1930s only intensified the Soviets' Manichean worldview, which in turn amplified the desire to monitor the population through surveillance and to administer the individual through personalized measures. Indeed, the previous examination of responses to suicides inside the Red Army and Bolshevik Party suggests that one consequence of thinking in terms of corporeal metaphors was the unsettling realization that the defective or offending elements, like a cancer in the human body, could come from within the social organism. Such awareness deepened fears of corruption and furthered the trend toward pathologizing people who behaved in ways deemed threatening to the collective. Accordingly, when individuals transgressed society, they also transgressed themselves, since their interests and the interests of society were the same. Expectations about the

6. Gur-Gurevich, "Samoubiistva," 100–104. These characteristic traits were "heightened excitability, emotional thickening [*sgushchennost'*], sharply expressed sensitivity, and irritability, etc." They contrasted with the realism, practicality, and properly critical attitude toward life that supposedly characterized young proletarians.

7. Roísín Healy, "Suicide in Early Modern and Modern Europe," *Historical Review* 49, no. 3 (2006): 917.

8. On the slippage between social and biological theories see Eric D. Weitz, "Racial Politics without the Concept of Race: Reevaluating Soviet Ethnic and National Purges," *Slavic Review* 61, no. 1 (Spring 2002): 1–29; and Amir Weiner, "Nature, Nurture, and Memory in the Socialist Utopia: Delineating the Soviet Socio-Ethnic Body in the Age of Socialism," *American Historical Review* 104, no. 4 (October 1999): 1114–55.

imminent arrival of the socialist future therefore sharpened calls for citizens to reveal their true selves through deeds as well as words. Those who failed to fulfill their responsibilities or to demonstrate their unity with the collective were shown less and less mercy.

Suicides, seemingly as predicted, intruded on Soviet reality during the 1930s, particularly after the onset of the Great Purges in 1936. Rates of suicide in the Red Army kept rising, while inside the Bolshevik Party a series of prominent as well as lesser members opted to take their own lives before the state acted for them. These included the former oppositionist Mikhail Tomskii, the Central Committee member Panas Liubchenko, and the head of the Red Army's Political Administration Ian Borisovich Gamarnik, who had been implicated in the supposed "anti-Soviet conspiracy" led by Field Marshal Mikhail Tukhachevskii.[9] Self-destruction even reached the highest levels of power. In February 1937, Stalin's close friend and Georgian ally Sergo Ordzhonikidze shot himself; five years earlier Stalin's young wife Nadezhda had taken her own life after a party at the Kremlin. Stalin regarded these suicides as a personal betrayal, and he lashed out more generally against acts of self-destruction as willful attacks on the party. Some biographers suggest that Stalin was forever haunted by his wife's death and even speculate that her suicide may have contributed to his distrust of others and his callous attitude toward life more generally.[10]

Nevertheless, suicides also started to "disappear" in Soviet Russia. Amid the coalescence of Stalinist orthodoxies in the realm of culture, the act became an increasingly touchy, even taboo subject. Literary works that showed the negative side of contemporary life, including the despondency of young suicides, were gradually displaced by those that adhered to the officially sanctioned aesthetics of socialist realism, which aimed to show life as it should and would be under socialism.[11] In 1932, for example, Communist Party officials prevented Nikolai Erdman's satirical play *The Suicide* from going into production after some eighteen months of rehearsal at Vsevelod Meyerhold's theater in Moscow. The play depicted

9. Igal Halfin, *Terror in My Soul: Communist Autobiographies on Trial* (Cambridge, MA, 2003), 277; and O. V. Khlevniuk, *1937-i: Stalin, NKVD i sovetskoe obshchestvo* (Moscow, 1992), 196–207.

10. See, for example, Simon Sebag Montefiore, *Stalin: Court of the Red Tsar* (New York, 2004). There is some evidence to suggest that Stalin kept an eye on suicides across his country. For example, across the top of a report on suicides in the Kiev region is a handwritten notation that a copy was sent to Stalin on August 4, 1935. "Ob otdel'nykh faktakh samoubiistva molodezhi i detei kievskoi oblasti," RGASPI, f. M-1, op. 23, d. 1096, l. 113.

11. See, for example, Gregory Carleton, *Sexual Revolution in Bolshevik Russia* (Pittsburgh, 2005).

the story of Semen Semenovich Podsekal'nikov, an unemployed common man who contemplated suicide and was soon courted by representatives of various disaffected groups (the intelligentsia, NEPmen, clergy, etc.) asking that he kill himself in the name of their respective cause.[12] Potentially more troublesome for the regime was the suicide two years earlier of the revolution's greatest poet—Vladimir Mayakovsky. Given Mayakovsky's elevated status as the quasi-official poet of the revolution, Soviet officials had to tread carefully in their response to his death. His body lay in state at the writers' club, a mass funeral procession accompanied the corpse to the crematorium, and his gray matter was added to "the pantheon of Russian brains" being investigated at the State Institute of the Brain.[13] Initial newspaper announcements of Mayakovsky's suicide, moreover, made sure to separate his final act from his revolutionary biography. They attributed the suicide to causes of a "purely personal character" (primarily his lingering illness) and rejected the possibility that it had anything to do with his "social and literary activity."[14]

Suicide also disappeared in the scientific world. Beginning in the early 1930s, the open publication of suicide statistics ceased, and the two major scientific studies of self-destruction were brought to an end. The shift was part of the ideological offensive that involved the move to establish Bolshevik hegemony in the professions, universities, and government apparatus. Non-Marxist social science, in particular, came under attack for its failure to properly understand the laws of history and its preference for academic theorizing over practical utility. Furthermore, given the implicitly critical nature of much social investigation, the study of problems like suicide posed certain risks by suggesting flaws or unresolved problems in the sociopolitical order. Now firmly part of the Soviet state apparatus, doctors and statisticians exposed themselves to criticism since they were

---

12. Nikolai Robertovich Erdman, "Samoubiitsa," in *P'esy, intermedii, pis'm, dokumenty, vospominaniia sovremennikov* (Moscow, 1990), 82–164. In his capacity as the nation's primary censor and patron of the arts, Stalin himself became embroiled in the controversy over Erdman's play. See Katerina Clark and Evgeny Dobrenko, eds., *Soviet Culture and Power: A History in Documents, 1917–1953* (New Haven, 2007), 117–19.

13. Monika Spivak, *Posmertnaia diagnostika genial'nosti. Eduard Bagritskii, Andrei Belyi, Vladimir Maiakovskii v kollektsii Instituta mozga (materialy iz arkhiva G. I. Poliakova)* (Moscow, 2001), 5–8.

14. Aleksandr Mikhailov, *Zhizn' Maiakovskogo. Ia svoe zemnoe ne dozhil* (Moscow, 2001), 522–25. Mayakovsky's suicide also became an occasion to condemn suicides more generally. See Velichkin, "Pravo na smert'," 765–66. More recently, Grigorii Chkhartishvili, pseudonymous author of the Erast Fandorin novels, has explored the link between literary creativity and suicide. He includes Mayakovsky among the many Russian writers who ended their own lives as a result of the country's repressive politics. See *Pisatel' i samoubiistvo* (Moscow, 1999).

implicated as much in the regime's failures as in its successes.[15] Once the NEP was abandoned, the presence of suicides, criminals, and other asocial elements could no longer be explained away as a temporary and unreflective manifestation of the unsettling transitional period between the old and the new worlds. Now their existence could suggest that the move to socialism had not resulted in total victory over prerevolutionary vestiges or in the harmonious integration promised by the Bolsheviks' vision of history. Although a few articles were published on the topic in medical journals outside Moscow during the 1930s, it was not until 1970 that psychiatrists in the Soviet Union began to talk more openly about suicides in their country.[16]

Unfortunately, there is little evidence with which to reconstruct the exact circumstances surrounding the dissolution of the research programs organized in the name of Soviet forensic medicine and moral statistics. Both disciplines were vulnerable to attack because of their unsettled status within the larger professions of medicine and statistics. Forensic doctors interested in the biological sources of the self-destructive individual were certainly in a precarious position by the end of the 1920s, given the growing campaign against eugenics, the study of the criminal personality, and neolombrosianism.[17] Moreover, little new had been published on the basis of the forensic-medical questionnaires since 1926–27, perhaps a sign that the goal of producing a regular, nationwide accounting of self-destruction had been superseded by other interests or even by the work of the Department of Moral Statistics.[18] Whatever hope existed for the anketa program ended with the removal of its chief patron, Iakov Leibovich, from his position as chief medical examiner in 1930–31 amid a general crackdown on the discipline.[19] Leibovich left Moscow and

15. Susan Gross Solomon discusses the thorny issues of responsibility within Soviet social science in "David and Goliath in Soviet Public Health: The Rivalry of Social Hygienists and Psychiatrists over the *Bytovoi* Alcoholic," *Soviet Studies* 41, no. 2 (April 1989): 254–75; and "The Expert and the State in Russian Public Health: Continuities and Changes Across the Revolutionary Divide," in *The History of Public Health Under the Modern State,* ed. Dorothy Porter (Amsterdam, 1994), 195–210.

16. Martin A. Miller and Ylana N. Miller, "Suicide and Suicidology in the Soviet Union," *Suicide and Life-Threatening Behavior* 18, no. 4 (Winter 1988): 303–21.

17. L. O. Ivanov and L. V. Il'ina, *Puti i sud'by otechestvennoi kriminologii* (Moscow, 1991), 196–97.

18. Also suggestive in this regard is the 1928–29 claim of the Central Statistical Administration that no other governmental department was doing suicide statistics. RGAE, f. 1562, op. 1, d. 490, l. 9ob.

19. For example, the flagship journal *Forensic-Medical Expertise* was closed in 1931. This was preceded by the closure in Leningrad of several scientific organizations and faculties devoted to forensic medicine.

went on to develop forensic-medical departments at institutions of higher education in Tomsk and Vinitsa; however, his eventual fate remains a mystery.[20] Much more is known about Mikhail Gernet. With the closure of the Department of Moral Statistics in 1931 and the transfer of its activities to other departments within the Central Statistical Administration's Social Statistics Sector, Gernet personally came under attack for his adherence to an insufficiently Marxist approach to criminology. Still, despite his deteriorating eyesight, he continued his academic pursuits and published a major history of the tsarist prison system. The prerevolutionary social order, which had once held back his ambitions, now became a safe haven for his scholarship.[21]

The demise of the forensic-medical and moral statistical studies, however, did not mean that the Soviet state lost interest in suicide. Suicide during the 1930s remained an object of concern from a demographic, criminal, and political-moral standpoint, and its study assumed a mostly secretive character because of the sensitive nature of the topic. Statisticians in the Central Statistical Administration, for example, included suicides in their internal accounts of mortality across the USSR, a practice that became increasingly dangerous given the regime's desire to present a robust population despite the many deaths from industrial accidents, famine, forced labor, and the Great Purges.[22] Meanwhile, both local and secret police officials continued to carry out investigations of suspicious deaths in order to establish the presence of a crime, be it a personal or overtly political act, and the data from such inquiries were then shared with both the Communist Party leadership and legal officials, including the country's chief prosecutor, Andrei Vyshinskii.[23] Consistent with their responsibilities as part of the Soviet legal system, forensic-medical doctors also participated in the study of suspected suicides. Reports of suicides in the Red Army and Komsomol during the 1930s mention their involvement on several occasions. Generally, the forensic autopsy established the

---

20. According to a recent biographical sketch, Leibovich disappeared during the Nazi occupation of Ukraine. See Iu. A. Nekliudov, "Iakov L'vovich Leibovich—vidnyi deiatel' otechestvennoi sudebnoi meditsiny," *Sudebno-meditsinskaia ekspertiza*, no. 5 (2003): 48–49.

21. In a short autobiographical piece, Gernet claims that he resigned his position because his vision was deteriorating. "Avtobiografiia," Otdel Rukopisei RGB, f. 603, k. 1, d. ll. 5–7.

22. Most notorious in this regard is the tragic fate that befell statisticians who directed the 1937 census, which showed a greater-than-anticipated loss of population. Many of these officials were arrested and later executed.

23. Gábor T. Rittersporn, "Le message des données introuvables: L'État et les statistiques du suicide en Russie et en URSS," *Cahiers du Monde russe* 38, no. 4 (October–December 1997): 515–19.

fact of suicide, the precise cause of death, and the general physical condition of the individual at the time of the incident. However, there are no references in these records to degeneration or the physiological signs of the self-destructive personality.

As a consequence of these developments, suicide ceased to be a visible or widespread problem troubling the Soviet population. Like other social pathologies, it could have no place within the socialist order that was eventually proclaimed with the adoption of the Stalin Constitution of 1936. Suicide's disappearance from the public realm represented the realization of the Bolsheviks' dream—a society where their ideology held sway and where bourgeois or liberal individualism no longer existed. The actions of any person who still ran counter to such tendencies could only be a "social anomaly" (*sotsial'naia anomaliia*), an idea that was in circulation during the 1920s but assumed greater prominence in the decade that followed. Linguistically and conceptually, this way of thinking about asocial behavior separated the deviant part from the healthy whole. It found concrete expression in Soviet psychology of the 1930s. Environmental theories of human behavior, which dominated in the 1920s, were increasingly displaced by explanations that focused on personal responsibility. Psychologists and others could therefore treat the deviant individual as an outlier and someone unreflective of the dominant social order.[24] As late as 1963, in fact, the author of an article on suicide in the *Great Soviet Encyclopedia* claimed that suicide was no longer a social problem in the USSR. The few acts that did occur were simply "residual" phenomena from the capitalist past.[25]

To defend society against these human residues, the Soviet state called more insistently upon the institutions and practices that had been developed during the first full decade of the revolution. Carrying out surveillance, utilizing the powers of the police and criminal-legal system, organizing collective opinion, conducting educational work, and studying the individual were all intensified in an effort to identify, isolate, and liquidate the revolution's increasingly desperate enemies. Most active in the realm of investigating suicides were the state and political organs concerned with maintaining order and ideological health. The civilian world was actively monitored by the People's Commissariat of Internal Affairs (NKVD), while the military population fell under the watchful gaze

---

24. See Raymond Bauer, *The New Man in Soviet Psychology* (Cambridge, MA, 1952).

25. Miller and Miller, "Suicide and Suicidology," 305–7. Soviet ethnographers working in the early 1930s also adopted the idea of prerevolutionary "survivals" (*perezhitki*) to explain nonracially the failure of certain peoples to follow the script of revolutionary change. See Francine Hirsch, *Empire of Nations: Ethnographic Knowledge and the Making of the Soviet Union* (Ithaca, 2005), 217–21.

of the Political Administration, the Special Section of the State Political Directorate (OOGPU), and the Military Procurator's office. Of course, the Communist Party and its youth wing devoted special attention to self-destructive acts among the country's current and future political elite. The net effect was to reinforce the political-moral dimensions of both attempted and completed suicide.

A survey of these institutions' activities during the 1930s suggests some strong patterns of continuity from the previous decade. Acts of self-destruction, above all, remained an illegitimate response to life's difficulties, especially now that the country was poised for the final triumph of socialist construction and besieged on all fronts by its capitalist adversaries. They continued to be seen as isolated incidents largely committed by the weakest and least stable members of society.[26] Furthermore, by counting them along with the other "extraordinary events" (which included the misappropriation of weapons, fires, desertions, murders, and self-inflicted injuries), the Red Army reinforced the idea that suicides were outside the norm and harmful to the readiness of the armed forces.[27] Military units and party cells also maintained the association between suicide and betrayal of the socialist cause. One resolution passed amid the outbreak of war in late September 1939 condemned an unsuccessful suicide as an act that discredited the honor of the unit. Echoing earlier associations of suicide with desertion, the resolution deemed the attempt "a disgraceful flight from responsibility and from his military duty" at a time when the entire country was mobilized for its self-defense.[28] More generally, the themes of alienation and isolation from the collective remained prominent in official narratives. Various suicides, as a consequence of both their weak will and the failures of political officials, were thought to have fallen away from the party's salubrious influence. Well into the late 1930s, for example, an interest in Esenin's poetry was interpreted as a sign of despondency and the individual's moral and political disintegration outside the collective's purview.[29]

26. On the linkage of suicide, weakness, and instability see, for example, "O faktakh samoubiistva komsomol'tsev i pionerov v Zapsibkrae," RGASPI, f. M-1, op. 23, d. 1072, ll. 39–40; and "Vneocherednoe politdonesenie," RGVA, f. 9, op. 36, d. 500, l. 14–14ob.

27. See the various reports in RGVA, f. 9, op. 36, d. 1786; and "Karto-donesenie o chrez-vychainom proisshestvom," RGVA, f. 9, op. 36, 3372, ll. 125–125ob.

28. "Rezoliutsiia. Priniataia na obshchem sobranii komandnogo, politicheskogo i nachal'stvuiushchego sostava v/chasti 8588 21-ogo sentiabria 1939 goda," RGVA, f. 9, op. 36, d. 3714, l. 107.

29. "O faktakh samoubiistva komsomol'tsev i pionerov," l. 47; and report of August 31, 1939, on the attempted suicide of the Red Army man S. G. Voitko, RGVA, f. 9, op. 36, d. 3372, l. 127. Suicides among proletarian school children were explicitly linked to their isolation

Suicides also continued to be a form of revelation in the hands of Soviet investigators. In particular, they were thought to reflect the inner self, the state of affairs inside the respective military unit or party organization, and the level of activity on the part of local officials and political leaders. Investigators considered the 1939 suicide of Viacheslav Trofimovich Dalenko, for example, to be a "serious signal that speaks to the fact that the party leaders of unit 6593 carry out their responsibilities to strengthen work on people very poorly."[30] This evaluative approach carried over to the rest of the unit or party cell, whose mood following the suicide was described as part of the general diagnosis of collective health. Red Army reports from the 1930s usually provided a sampling of responses to the act. Ranging from improper expressions of sympathy to sharp condemnations, these reactions suggested that the significance of Soviet suicide continued to be negotiated, as multiple meanings persisted amid the desire for interpretive uniformity among the citizenry. Investigators noted with disapproval the organization of funeral rites for the deceased, the purposeful hiding of suicides from upper-level political organs, and the failure to appreciate the political significance of the act. One report noted with particular alarm that the local political leaders were more concerned about what music to play at the funeral than with investigating the causes and meaning of the suicide.[31] By contrast, healthy reactions were those where the members of the collective condemned and even denigrated the suicide. An exemplary set referred to the suicide as a fool and a stain on the unit and included the suggestion that he be shot for acting in a way that played into the hands of the country's class enemies.[32] The recording and shaping of such responses were all part of the process of forming collective opinion, which according to one report remained among the Red Army's most powerful disciplinary "levers" (*richagi*) and a vital component of its "political work." Still, even this tool required regulation. Accusations of improper behavior had to be leveled with care, since in some instances

---

from the kollektiv, a state of being that compounded their mental instability. Gur-Gurevich, "Samoubiistva," 102.

30. "O samoubiistve starshego pisaria sverkhsrochnoi sluzhby v/ch 6593 Dalenko Viacheslava Trofimovicha," RGVA, f. 9, op. 36, d. 3372, ll. 101–2.

31. On problematic responses to suicides see "O faktakh samoubiistva komsomol'tsev i pionerov," ll. 46, 50, 52; and "Politdonesenie o sostoianii informatsionnoi raboty v v/s 5284 i priniatykh merakh," RGVA, f. 9, op. 36, d. 3713, ll. 162–63. The latter source noted that the regiment's political leaders incorrectly regarded some "extraordinary occurrences" as "common everyday phenomena" and thus failed to report them to the Political Administration of the Red Army and the military district.

32. "Politdonesenie. O pokushenii na samoubiistvo kr-tsa 42-go OKSV t. Orekhova," RGVA, f. 9, op. 36, d. 1278, l. 9.

collective opinion could incite suicides among weak individuals unable to bear the ensuing shame and social pressure.[33] As during the 1920s, full transparency and intimate knowledge of the individual were deemed essential to the proper functioning of the Soviet regime's diagnostic and disciplinary apparatus.

While this book has demonstrated that interest in the individual personality was already strong in the 1920s, there was an important shift in Soviet discourse throughout the following decade. Most notably, the matter of personal responsibility assumed greater prominence in the evaluation of the causal factors and the meaning ascribed to suicide. To be sure, concerns with responsibility certainly did not spring up overnight and are an almost universal feature of responses to suicide. Investigators of the 1920s, for example, assigned blame to a variety of "culprits" (*vinovniki*): faulty heredity, physiological degeneration, others' callousness, environmental conditions, and even the embryonic state of mutual surveillance. Oftentimes the matter was raised only implicitly and was not pursued with a great deal of vigor, perhaps as a result of the incompleteness of the Soviet experiment. Under Stalin, however, there was a qualitatively different set of expectations and attitudes amid the heightened struggle against enemies and after socialism had been declared achieved. Quite simply, the regime was no longer willing to accept the presence of hostile forces within its borders, as it did with some reluctance during the transition period of the New Economic Policy. In his study of Communist autobiographies, for example, Igal Halfin sees a move away from medicalization and toward the criminalization of suicides among party members during the Great Purges. Those who took their own lives were no longer seen as sick but as possessing an innately "wicked will" that derived from their irredeemable class psychology. Suicide, in other words, was tantamount to a confession of one's guilt or hostility to the regime.[34] While we should be careful not to apply this interpretation too broadly and too categorically, especially before the Great Purges and declaration of socialism's achievement in 1936, there is ample evidence to suggest that a search for culprits did animate many of the investigations into suicide during the 1930s.[35]

---

33. On the significance and potential danger of collective opinion see "Obzor o samoubiistvakh v chastiakh RKKA," RGVA, f. 9, op. 36, d. 834, l. 64. According to a summary report from western Siberia, two young pioneers killed themselves in part because they feared the "growing collective opinion" about their membership in an anti-Soviet organization. "O faktakh samoubiistva komsomol'tsev i pionerov," l. 51.

34. Halfin, *Terror in My Soul*, 276–78.

35. In a noteworthy shift, the authors of a 1930 Red Army report sharply criticized the failure of local political workers to identify and go after the "concrete culprits" of suicides.

This search, of course, began with the suicide. In the 1934 case of the Komsomol teacher Liapunov, for example, party representatives concluded that he had revealed his true self by taking his own life. Liapunov's outward social and political activism, they argued, had been "only a mask that hid his decay, despondency, and complete moral and ideological disintegration."[36] Another Red Army investigation observed that the study of suicides committed by exposed class enemies "sometimes reveals and shows the suppressed hatred toward the Soviet system among these representatives of the liquidated classes, the totality of their rottenness, and their impotent fury."[37] The regime's concern with counterrevolutionary political outlooks was also expressed in several cases of multiple suicides that led to the discovery of anti-Soviet youth groups. The NKVD investigation into the triple suicide in the city of Ordzhonikidze found that all three participants had belonged to an organization consisting of twenty to thirty young people, many of whom came from suspicious class backgrounds. They regularly gathered to read the poetry of Esenin, sing counterrevolutionary songs, drink and engage in sexual activity, and generally act out against their sense of boredom and dissatisfaction with life.[38] That same year (1934) investigators in western Siberia linked the suicides of two fifteen-year-old schoolgirls, who shot themselves with the same bullet, to the revelation of their participation in a band of hooligans.[39]

Still, the assessment of responsibility was directed most aggressively toward the living, not the dead. Here there were two main villains: class enemies who had acted with hostile intent toward the suicide and flawed party leaders who had failed to carry out their duties with sufficient zeal. Party investigators in Siberia, for example, uncovered a number of cases where young Communists had been hounded to their death in a sort of reverse purge. Fearing exposure by these vigilant youth, class enemies running several local schools sought to eliminate the threat from their midst by using the force of collective opinion to their advantage. In the village of Lagushino, the Komsomol members Kliueva and Krasniakova fell prey to the machinations of an assortment of unsavory characters. The latter spread the false rumor that both young women were prostitutes and purposefully sowed discord between Krasniakova and her parents. Using

"Statisticheskii ezhegodnik za 1928/29 god. Politiko-moral'noe sostoianie RKKA," RGVA, f. 54, op. 4, d. 64, ll 45–45ob.

36. "O faktakh samoubiistva komsomol'tsev i pionerov," l. 44.

37. "Obzor o samoubiistvakh v chastiakh RKKA," l. 66.

38. Report of March 8, 1935, from Assistant Procurator Niurin to Nikolai Ezhov, head of the Party Control Commission, RGASPI, f. M-1, op. 23, d. 1107, ll. 55–57.

39. "O faktakh samoubiistva komsomol'tsev i pionerov," l. 51.

a similar method, Shemetova, the head of the Petropavlovka village school who had hidden her socially alien background, drove the Komsomol secretary E. L. Senchilo to kill himself. The summary report explained, "Knowing Senchilo to be an active, firm, and politically literate Komsomolist who could unmask her, Shemetova set her task to remove Senchilo not just from the school but from the village." To achieve this goal, Shemetova sought to "badger" (*zatravit'*) Senchilo and ruin his reputation among his fellow Communists and Komsomol comrades through false accusations of theft and malfeasance.[40] Such stories, when considered within the framework of the Bolsheviks' vision of an ongoing struggle between good and evil, appear a rewriting of older religious and supernatural explanations of suicide. Where the devil or sinister spirits were once to blame, now the tormentors of Soviet life were class enemies who drove weakened, and sometimes devout, individuals to lose faith and take their own lives.

Poor political leaders were also blamed for their less direct, but no less significant, role in causing suicides. In almost every case surveyed, the investigators faulted the local political organizations for their failure to follow through with policies that would have forestalled acts of self-destruction. They had failed to carry out a vigilant search for class enemies, which allowed such dangerous individuals as Shemetova to hold positions of authority and create an unhealthy atmosphere. Or they had failed to carry out the party's edicts to study individuals and to conduct serious educational work with each of them. Thus, the disintegration of the teacher Liapunov went unseen despite the fact that he had talked openly of suicide and showed a fascination with Esenin in his poetry and notebooks.[41] Red Army investigators looking into suicides due to "the unmasking of a socially alien origin" linked them to the failure of commanders and party organizations to study the "class physiognomy" of the individuals under their guidance. How else to explain their presence in the first place?[42] The search for culpability even extended to cases of suicide that were deemed to have resulted from a physical or mental illness. Doctors and other medical personnel were criticized for their failure to monitor the condition of the troops and for their callous approach to soldiers who came to them for assistance.[43]

---

40. Ibid., ll. 40–43. The tale of young women being hounded to their deaths by class enemies was a common trope in Soviet educational literature of the late 1920s and early 1930s. See the discussion in E. Thomas Ewing, "Personal Acts with Public Meanings: Suicides by Women Teachers in the Early Stalin Era," *Gender & History* 14, no. 1 (April 2002): 117–37.

41. "O faktakh samoubiistva komsomol'tsev i pionerov," l. 44.

42. "Obzor o samoubiistvakh v chastiakh RKKA," ll. 65–67.

43. Ibid., ll. 67–68.

Whether such failures were the result of intentional malice, bureaucratic mentalities, or simple inexperience, they harmed the cause of socialism and demanded the punishment of those deemed responsible. Compared with many of the reports written during the 1920s, the investigatory summaries from the 1930s are noteworthy for including some mention of the measures adopted against the culprits. These ranged from simple reprimands to expulsions and even criminal prosecutions. In the case of the young Communists hounded to their death in Siberia, for example, action was taken against both the "concrete culprits" (who were turned over to the courts) and the party leaders who had failed to take any measures before and after the suicides.[44] Criminal action was similarly taken in 1936 against two individuals in connection with the "collective suicide" of four schoolchildren in Ukraine. Found to have "systematically" tormented the youths, they were turned over for prosecution under article 54-14 of the Ukrainian Criminal Code.[45] Even in cases where suicides asked in their farewell letters that nobody be blamed for their action, Soviet officials meted out punishments. This was the case with the Red Army man and Komsomolist Vasilii Mikhailovich Cherkas, who killed himself in 1939 because of the humiliation of his chronic incontinence. Cherkas took full responsibility for ending his own life. Nevertheless, his doctors, as well as his commander and political instructor, were reprimanded for their formal and uncaring attitude toward him.[46]

These prosecutions reflected heightened expectations of transparency and control organized around an individualized approach to every citizen. Reports from the period are replete with discussions about the treatment of the individual in the affected group or institution. They frequently attributed the suicide—whatever the immediate cause—to the disregard of commanding officers and political leaders for the study and tutoring of the men and women entrusted to their care. The 1934 summary of suicides in western Siberia contended that many investigators had failed to draw the proper "political conclusions" about self-destruction. Citing despondency, infection by Eseninism, and unrequited love as causes missed the point, since in truth the majority of cases were conditioned by "the weakening of vigilance by local Komsomol and party organizations, feeble work with

44. "O faktakh samoubiistva komsomol'tsev i pionerov," ll. 41–43.

45. Report of May 15, 1936, by F. Starovoitov, procurator of the Kiev oblast, to A. Ia. Vyshinskii, procurator of the USSR, GARF, f. 8131, op. 37, d. 72, ll. 26–30. Article 54 was the Ukrainian equivalent of the infamous article 58 of the RSFSR's Criminal Code. Both dealt with counterrevolutionary crimes that were intended to damage or overthrow Soviet power.

46. "Politdonesenie nachal'nika politicheskogo otdela voiskovoi chasti 6565. 23 ianvaria 1939 g.," RGVA, f. 9, op. 36, d. 3372, ll. 2–3.

every Komsomolist, and not knowing how Komsomol members live." As a consequence, claimed the report's authors, "individual Komsomolists who are unstable and politically unformed fall under the influence of class-enemy elements. Not receiving the timely support of the Komsomol organizations, they reach the point of decomposition and faintheartedness, and see suicide as their only way out."[47] To reinforce their criticism of the local organization's performance, several reports cited the 1933 directive of the Political Administration's director, Ian Gamarnik, who as we know ended up taking his own life in 1937. Gamarnik observed that most attempted suicides could be prevented through a "comradely" rather than "bureaucratic" approach to the individual, and he called more broadly for improving internal party work.[48]

The failure to study the individual undermined the practice of mutual surveillance and prevented the commander or political organization from recognizing the signs of suicide that were often before them. Political workers and officers, in particular, were reminded that personal life was not to be treated as sacrosanct. They had to open up the subjects completely in order to know their circumstances, uncover their thoughts and aspirations, and even visit their parents or family in order to fully understand them as individuals. Otherwise, they would be blind to their needs and unable to gauge the effect of events or disciplinary measures upon them. This is how investigators interpreted the suicide of the Red Army man Efim Kuz'menko, who hanged himself in November 1936. Kuz'menko showed himself to be a disciplined and earnest soldier, but he had difficulty with his studies and complained frequently about headaches and a poor memory. Consequently, he fared badly on his exams and was passed over during the selection of junior commanders, a rejection that ultimately led to his suicide. However, according to the report sent to Gamarnik, the breakdown of surveillance was also to blame. It stated, "The command and lead staff, the Party-Komsomol organization of the platoon, while knowing about Kuz'menko's mood and isolation [*zamknutnost'*], did not get close to him, did not study him, and did not help him."[49] In particular, the Political Administration's investigators criticized Gorenko, the platoon's political instructor. He and the political organizations certainly knew about Kuz'menko's "unhappiness." But they "worked with him generally, and not concretely, did not know Kuz'menko, and did not

47. "O faktakh samoubiistva komsomol'tsev i pionerov," l. 53.

48. "Obzor o samoubiistvakh v chastiakh RKKA," l. 69; and "Politdonesenie Nachal'nika Politotdela Aviatsionnoi Brigady VVA. O dopolnitel'nykh dannykh prichin samoubiistva mladshego aviatekhnika Pavlovicha i o meropriatiiakh, priniatykh komandovaniem i partpolit-aparatom Aviabrigady," RGVA, f. 9, op. 36, d. 626, l. 2ob.

49. Report of November 14, 1936, to Gamarnik, RGVA, f. 9, op. 36, d. 2161, ll. 35–36.

prevent his misconduct [*prostupok*]." Had Gorenko really taken an interest, he would have found that Kuz'menko had a prior history of mental
illness, that his family was in tight material circumstances, and that he had
pinned many hopes on a promotion. Since he did not know Kuz'menko's
personality, however, the political instructor's observational and restor-
ative powers were diminished. As one summary of the suicide concluded,
"In conversation with Kuz'menko, comrade Gorenko was unable to detect
his dark mood and arrive at the appropriate conclusions."[50]

We see similar expectations of knowledge and openness expressed in
the work of investigators looking into the suicides of children in the Ukrainian Republic. One particularly distressing case involved a schoolboy who
accidentally broke a bust of Lenin in his classroom. The school authorities
insisted that he pay for the bust and that his parents be informed of his
act, not knowing, however, that the father regularly beat his son. Fearing what awaited him at home, the boy shot himself.[51] Komsomol officials
regarded this and other school-aged suicides as proof that local officials
were not fulfilling their obligation to "work with every Komsomolist and
Young Pioneer individually [*v otdel'nosti*]" and to acquaint themselves fully
with their "everyday living conditions and personal life." This lapse only
opened the door for the country's enemies. Wrote the investigators, "The
policy of noninterference in the personal life of Komosomolists, and the
dulling of class vigilance on the part of individual Komsomol organizations, creates the grounds for the penetration of class-enemy influences
into individual Komsomolists and Pioneers, and pulls the weakest among
them onto the path unworthy of a Komsomolist and the youth of our
country—suicide."[52]

The intense need to assign personal responsibility reflected and esca-
lated the increasingly vicious, paranoid, and conflict-ridden world of the
late 1930s. Given the fact that each action or inaction could be construed
as the product of one's attitude toward the regime, everyone involved in
the drama of self-destruction was potentially at fault. Suicide was therefore
fraught with peril for the living as well as the dead. Instructive in this regard

50. "Donesenie o sluchae samoubiistva dnevnal'nogo po koniushne," RGVA, f. 9, op. 36,
d. 2161, ll. 31–33; "Politdonesenie Politicheskogo otdela 99 strelkovoi divizii," RGVA, f. 9, op.
36, d. 2161, l. 41; and "Donesenie No. 1. 'O sluchae samoubiistva dneval'nogo po koniushne
khoz. vzvoda 297 str. polka, Kr-tsa Kuz'menko, E. P. 13/XI 1936 g.,'" RGVA, f. 9, op. 36, d.
2161, ll. 27–29.
51. "Ob otdel'nykh faktakh samoubiistva," l. 117.
52. Ibid., ll. 118–19. The failure to explore personal life was also cited in the case of
the suicide Iurii Babkin, who was said to have lived "under the influence of the philistine
[*obyvatel'skii*] environment of his family." "Politdonesenie o chrezvychainom proisshestvii,"
RGVA, f. op. 36, d. 3713, l. 283.

is the case of the sailor Mikhail Bagrov, who in April 1937 shot himself and his girlfriend while on leave. Bagrov's actions led to an investigation by the NKVD and military political authorities, who ended up uncovering a series of unsavory facts about life in the deceased man's village soviet. They included an existing pattern of suicides (thirteen total since the previous year) and preparations for a group suicide by members of the local Komsomol organization. In fact, the youth of the village soviet were deemed "utterly infected with Eseninist despondency" due to the lack of sufficient political work among them. Most ominously, the investigators concluded that behind the instigator of the group suicide (the Komsomol secretary Il'ina) lurked a "bigger counterrevolutionary figure" whose identity had yet to be discovered.[53]

There is some evidence to suggest that individuals who killed themselves were aware of the high stakes involved. Some wrote to absolve others of blame, perhaps because they knew what could happen to friends, relatives, and colleagues after they were gone.[54] Others, however, chose to name the culprits in their notes. The suicide of the physician Mikhailichenko, whose suicide was flagged for special attention in a 1934 summary report, is a case in point. In his final letter, Mikhailichenko claimed that he was ending his life primarily because of improper treatment by his regimental commander, Povestkin, whom he called a "parasite" and "piece of White Guard trash."[55] In a similar fashion, a fifteen-year-old girl accused the teacher Solov'eva of causing her suicide. Solov'eva, claimed the young suicide, had prevented her from going on to higher education by incorrectly grading her work.[56] While such notes and accusations might

53. See the report of the battalion commissar Adamson to the regimental commissar Teslenko, RGASPI, f. M-1, op. 23, d. 1245, ll. 228–29.

54. In so doing, they continued a long-standing pattern in Russian suicide. Given the fact that even before the revolution the law had punished individuals who instigated a suicide, suicide notes in Russia often contained a plea that no one be blamed for the death. The prerevolutionary physician Grigorii Gordon even argued that such requests were a "purely Russian peculiarity." G. I. Gordon, "Samoubiitsy i ikh pis'ma," *Novyi zhurnal dlia vsekh*, no. 28 (February 1911): 107. On the issue of responsibility prior to 1917, see Susan K. Morrissey, "Patriarchy on Trial: Suicide, Discipline, and Governance in Imperial Russia," *Journal of Modern History* 75 (March 2003): 23–58.

55. The report, however, does not mention the fate of Povestkin. "Obzor o samoubiistvakh v chastiakh RKKA," l. 63. Five years later, the suicide Viacheslav Dalenko also found fault with the way he had been treated by others. In his view, they had failed to help him and took no interest in his problems. "O samoubiistve starshego pisaria sverkhsrochnoi sluzhby v/ch 6593 Dalenko Viacheslava Trofimovicha," l. 101.

56. The report states only that an investigation was ongoing. "Ob otdel'nyhk faktakh samoubiistva," ll. 117–18. Authorities in Moscow also reported somewhat similar "scandalous facts" in 1937. A young girl reportedly attempted suicide because she was harassed by her teacher, who accused her of sexual promiscuity, while a male student hanged himself

have been a simple expression of bitterness and injured pride, within the tumultuous conditions of early Stalinism they took on the form of a denunciation. They remind us of the important fact that the practices surrounding suicide and other so-called illnesses during the 1920s helped to establish the parameters, and thus the possibilities, for how individuals could think of themselves and their place in the new socialist world. Consistent with Bolshevik notions of the organic society, the Soviet citizen of the 1930s was expected at all times—perhaps even as a final act before dying—to display loyalty through particular forms of public participation, including the identification and reporting of individuals who threatened the social order.[57]

Most significantly, the accounts of the 1930s promoted individual agency, an inclination that went against the general trend in modern explanations of self-destructive behavior. As we have seen, sociological as well as medical theories tended to view the suicide as the victim of impersonal forces, whether these were the alienating world of the city, the vicissitudes of industrial capitalism, or the destabilizing effects of one's diseased psyche and faulty heredity.[58] In Soviet discourse, by contrast, individual action as well as inaction drove the narrative forward. Whether discussion centered on the suicides or on those who lived and toiled around them, there were no abstractions at work, only concrete enemies and culprits. To a large degree, the overt politicization and criminalization of deviant behavior had much to do with this shift toward individual agency. Killing oneself was seen as an intentional act, be it to escape from one's tormentors, to protest living conditions and the actions of others, or to strike a blow at the cause of socialism. Even in cases where the suicide was cast in the role of victim, human agency found a face in the form of class enemies, callous physicians, and uninterested political officers.

The ascription of all events, good and evil, to human actions had important consequences for thinking about the Soviet social world. First

---

because of displeasure with the grade he had received on a drawing. "Dokladnaia zapiska," RGASPI, f. M-1, op. 23, d. 1265, l. 34.

57. For more on the important relationship between conceptions of society and expectations of public activism see Michael David-Fox, "From Illusory 'Society' to Intellectual 'Public' Works: VOKS, International Travel and Party-Intelligentsia Relations in the Interwar Period," *Contemporary European History* 2, no. 1 (2002): 7–32; and David-Fox, Review of *Obshchestvennye organizatsii Rossii v 1920-e gody*, by Irina Nikolaevna Il'ina, *Kritika* 3, no. 1 (Winter 2002): 173–81.

58. Agency becomes doubly problematic when the conversation turns to female suicides, who were represented as reactive creatures ruled by emotion rather than intellect. For an attempt to discern agency in several female suicides of the Soviet period see Ewing, "Personal Acts with Public Meanings."

and foremost, it absolved the socialist environment from any liability for suicides and other deviant actions. Soviet investigators certainly believed that the milieu played a key role in developing the personality and shaping human psychology. However, the existence of any unhealthy pockets within the body politic could only be the product of class enemies or residual social elements that resisted the progressive developments of socialism. The sources of childhood suicides, for instance, were thought to reside in the traditional family and not in the restructured Soviet school.[59] At the same time, the emphasis on individual responsibility preserved the sanctity of the proletariat and its guardians in the Communist Party. Suicides among these two privileged groups, who seemed to have the greatest reason to live under socialism, suggested either irredeemable personal flaws that were now coming into the open or the machinations and mistakes of others. Writing about the few suicides among proletarian schoolchildren, V. M. Gur-Gurevich explained, "The blame for these suicides falls in the majority of cases on the collective surrounding the suicide, on his comrades. Frequently, instead of straightening out their comrade and pulling him from the incorrect path in a timely manner, his friends and comrades abandon him, leaving him to the mercy of fate."[60]

Here, in this reference to suicide and fate, we see the complementarity of individual agency and collectivism within Soviet socialism. The modern social sciences emerged in Europe as a consequence of the broader epistemological shift toward seeing society as a human artifact; rather than being fixed and preordained, the social world could be refashioned toward the goal of promoting individual emancipation, fulfillment, and potential. The historical and self-reflexive quality of such thinking rationalized the emergence of governmental technologies that promised increased control over fate by providing the tools to manage and shape populations. It also gave rise to transformational ideologies like Marxism and its Bolshevist variant, which envisaged new forms of organization to counter the alienating effects and uncertainty of urban industrial life. Viewed in this context, Soviet socialism was a distinct response to the impersonal character and unsettling vagaries of the modern world. It theoretically blended the cool objectivity of scientific rationality with the warmth of tightly knit human relations to produce a stable, predictable, and nurturing environment for the emergence of complete human beings. With the final construction of socialism in Russia, an achievement consecrated in the 1936 Stalin Constitution, the external impediments to individual self-realization had been

59. Markovin, "Samoubiistvo sredi detei," 375.
60. Gur-Gurevich, "Samoubiistva," 102.

officially removed. Human agency as a force of history again reigned supreme, although it was now channeled through the collective rather than the egoistic and avaricious pursuits that left individuals under capitalism isolated from their fellow citizens and exposed before the outside world.

The sharpened individuation of suicide was thus part and parcel of the broader shift from the masses to the individual in Soviet culture and politics of the 1930s. As scholars have demonstrated, Bolshevik visions of socialism promoted a set of practices designed to promote individual self-reflection that encouraged citizens to develop their political selves and to inscribe themselves into the narrative of the revolution.[61] Images of the heroic struggle to build socialism emphasized volition and the ability of conscious persons to make their own history and conquer all obstacles. Standing in their way was a set of villains—wreckers, spies, and class enemies—whose existence and repression were equally individualized.[62] In the case of self-destruction, it is tempting to see suicides as writing themselves out of the revolution's story or at least seeking to construct a version at odds with the dominant narrative. Perhaps they already felt outside the great endeavor and found oblivion preferable to the painful awareness of their separation. Or perhaps they saw suicide as a final sacrifice on behalf of the group. Both possibilities are suggested in the words of Nikolai Petrovich Zelenskii, who attempted suicide in September 1939. He wrote, "I no longer wish to be a corpse before my wife and the party.... I am rotten, and the rot must be cut out in order to save the living."[63] Still, within the framework of Soviet socialism, becoming a corpse did not end one's relationship to the collective, since its discovery set in motion the entire machinery of the social science state. The suicide was counted, the body was opened up, and the life was interrogated for what it revealed about the deceased and the rest of society. With each pull of the trigger, each constriction of the noose, and each gram of poison ingested, the suicide reaffirmed an undeniable truth about Soviet life: the collective's greatest resource and greatest threat was the individual.

61. Jochen Hellbeck, *Revolution on My Mind: Writing a Diary under Stalin* (Cambridge, MA, 2006); Frederick C. Corney, *Telling October: Memory and the Making of the Bolshevik Revolution* (Ithaca, 2004); Oleg Kharkhordin, *The Collective and the Individual in Russia: A Study of Practices* (Berkeley, 1999); and Halfin, *Terror in My Soul.*

62. Hellbeck, *Revolution on My Mind*, 32–35.

63. Copy of suicide note belonging to Nikolai Petrovich Zelenskii, RGVA, f. 9, op. 36, d. 3714, l. 108. According to the official report on Zelenskii's case, material was being gathered to "call him to account." RGVA, f. 9, op. 36, d. 3714, l. 106.

Bibliography

ARCHIVES CONSULTED

The Central Archive of the City of Moscow (TsAGM)
Fond 1609: Moscow State University (Number 1).

The Central Historical Archive of Moscow (TsIAM)
Fond 459: Office of the Administrator of the Moscow School District.

The Central State Archive of the Highest Organs of Government and Administration of Ukraine (TsDAVO), Kiev
Fond 582: State Statistical Committee UkrSSR.

The Central State Archive of Historico-Political Records of St. Petersburg (TsGAIPD (SPb))
Fond 601: Leningrad Provincial Committee VLKSM.

The Central State Archive of St. Petersburg (TsGA SPb)
Fond 164: Statistical Department of the Executive Committee of the Leningrad Provincial Soviet (1918–27).

Manuscript Division of the Russian State Library (Otdel Rukopisei RGB), Moscow
Fond 603: Personal fond of Mikhail Nikolaevich Gernet.

Russian State Archive for Literature and the Arts (RGALI), Moscow
Fond 199: Personal fond of Dmitrii Nikolaevich Zhbankov.

Russian State Archive of the Economy (RGAE), Moscow
Fond 1562: Central Statistical Administration.

Russian State Historical Archive (RGIA), St. Petersburg
Fond 733: Ministry of Public Education.

Russian State Military Archive (RGVA), Moscow
Fond 9: Political Administration of the Red Army (PUR).
Fond 34: Main Military-Sanitary Administration (GVSU).
Fond 54: Main Administration RKKA (GURKKA).

Russian State Archive for Social-Political History (RGASPI), Moscow
Fond M-1: Central Committee VLKSM.
Fond 17: Central Committee VKP(b).
Fond 82: Personal fond of Viacheslav Mikhailovich Molotov.

State Archive of Iaroslavl' Oblast (GAIaO), Iaroslavl'
Fond 844: Bureau of Forensic-Medical Expertise. Iaroslavl' Province.

State Archive of the Russian Federation (GARF), Moscow
Fond 374: Central Control Commission VKP(b).
Fond 482: People's Commissariat of Public Health RSFSR.
Fond 4042: Main Prison Administration.
Fond 8131: Procurator SSSR.

State Archive of Tula Oblast (GATO), Tula
Fond 451: Medical-Sanitary Department of the Executive Committee of the Tula Oblast.

Primary Sources

Anosov, I. I. "Tashkentskie samoubiistva (1927–1929 g.g.) (po materialam rassledovanii militsii)." *Meditsinskaia mysl' Uzbekistana i Turkmenistana* 4, nos. 9–10 (June–July 1930): 101–10.

Bekhterev, V. M. *O prichinakh samoubiistva i o vozmozhnoi bor'be s nim.* St. Petersburg: T-vo Khudozhestvnnoi Pechati, 1912.

Belen'kii, G. S., and E. V. Eremeeva. "O sotsial'no-bytovykh motivakh samoubiistva zhenshchin." *Leningradskii meditsinskii zhurnal,* no. 4 (April 1928): 3–15.

Bobryshev, I. *Melkoburzhuaznye vliianiia sredi molodezhi.* Moscow-Leningrad: Molodaia gvardiia, 1928.

Bogatina, Sofiia. "Samoubiistva sredi zhenshchin." *Zhenskii vestnik,* no. 11 (November 1910): 219–22.

Brukhanskii, N. P. "O samoubiistvakh i samoubiitsakh." *Klinicheskaia meditsina* 4, no. 3 (March 1926): 110–15.

———. *Samoubiitsy.* Moscow-Leningrad: Priboi, 1927.

Bychkov, I. Ia., and S. Ia. Rachkovskii. "Samoubiistva v RSFSR posredstvom otravleniia za 1920–1924 gg." In *Trudy II Vserossiiskogo s"ezda sudebno-meditsinskikh ekspertov. Moskva, 25 fevralia-3 marta 1926 g,* edited by Ia. Leibovich, 228–38. Ulyanovsk, 1926.

Chuprov, A. A. "Nravstvennaia statistika." In *Entsiklopedicheskii slovar' F. A. Brokgauz i I. A. Efron.* Vol. 21, 403–8. St. Petersburg, 1897.

Diurkgeim, E. *Samoubiistvo: Sotsiologicheskii etiud.* Translated by A. N. Il'inskii. Edited by V. A. Bazarov. St. Petersburg: N. N. Karbasnikov, 1912.

Doklady pravleniia i komissii XII-mu Pirogovskomu s"ezdu vrachei (S.-Peterburg, 29 maia-6 iiunia 1913 g.). Moscow: N. N. Levenson, 1913.

Dubrovskii, M., and A. Lipkin. "O samoubiistvakh." *Revoliutsiia i kul'tura,* March 15, 1929, 33–36.

Durkheim, Émile. *Suicide: A Study in Sociology.* Translated by John A. Spaulding and George Simpson. New York: Free Press, 1951.

Erdman, Nikolai. "Samoubiitsa." In *P'esy, intermedii, pis'm, dokumenty, vospominaniia sovremennikov,* 80–164. Moscow: Iskusstvo, 1990.

Ermilov, V. I. *Protiv meshchanstva i upadochnichestva.* Moscow-Leningrad, 1927.

Esaulov, N. N. "K organizatsii sudebno-meditsinskoi ekspertizy v RSFSR." *Rabochekrest'ianskaia militsiia,* no. 1 (November 1922): 42–44.

Gaikovich, R. I. "Samoubiistvo v voiskakh russkoi armii za 15 let." *Russkii vrach,* March 10, 1907, 344–45.

Galant, I. B. "O dushevnoi bolezni S. Esenina." *Klinicheskii arkhiv genial'nosti i odarennosti (evropatologii)* 2, no. 2 (1926): 115–32.

Gavrilovskii, V. P. "K voprosu ob anatomicheskikh izmeneniiakh na trupakh samoubiits." *Sudebno-meditsinskaia ekspertiza,* no. 11 (1929): 59–60.

Gernet, M. N. *Izbrannye proizvedeniia.* Moscow: Iuridicheskaia literatura, 1974.

———. *Moral'naia statistika (ugolovnaia statistika i statistika samoubiistv).* Moscow: Izdanie Tsentral'nogo Statisticheskogo Upravleniia, 1922.

———. "Noveishie dannye statistiki samoubiistv za granitsei." *Administrativnyi vestnik,* no. 2 (1927): 6–12.

———. *Prestupnost' i samoubiistva vo vremia voiny i posle nee.* Moscow: Izdanie TsSU SSR, 1927.

———. *Prestupnost' za granitsei i v SSSR.* Moscow: Sovetskoe zakonodatel'stvo, 1931.

———. "Samoubiistva v starcheskom vozraste." *Statisticheskoe obozrenie,* no. 7 (July 1929): 105–14.

———. "Statistika samoubiistv v SSSR." *Administrativnyi vestnik,* no. 3 (1927): 17–22.

———. *Ukazatel' russkoi i inostrannoi literatury po statistike prestuplenii, nakazanii i samoubiistv.* Moscow, 1924.

———. "Vozrast samoubiits v SSSR." *Statisticheskoe obozrenie,* no. 6 (June 1927): 92–95.

Gernet, M. N., and D. P. Rodin. "Statistika osuzhdennykh v 1922 g. i statistika samoubiistv v 1922–23 gg." *Biulleten' Tsentral'nogo statisticheskogo upravleniia,* no. 84 (1924): 113–25.

Giliarovskii, V. A. "K psikhopatologii detskikh samoubiistv." In *Psikhopatologiia i psikhoprofilaktika detskogo vozrasta. Sbornik rabot sotrudnikov Detskogo otdeleniia Donskoi nervno-psikhiatricheskoi lechebnitsy—psikhiatricheskoi kliniki 2 MGU,* edited by V. A. Giliarovskii, 66–82. Moscow: Izdatel'stvo Moszdravotdela, 1929.

Gordon, G. I. "Samoubiistva detei." In *Trudy XI Pirogovskogo S"ezda,* edited by P. N. Bulatev, 2:56–57. St. Petersburg, 1911.

———. "Samoubiistva molodezhi i ee nervna-psikhicheskaia neustoichivosti." *Novyi zhurnal dlia vsekh,* no. 9 (September 1912): 105–10.

———. "Samoubiistva uchashcheisia molodezhi." *Novoe slovo,* no. 9 (September 1911): 29–35.

———. "Samoubiistva v Rossii." *Bodroe slovo,* no. 15 (August 1909): 69–78.

———. "Samoubiitsy i ikh pis'ma." *Novyi zhurnal dlia vsekh,* no. 28 (February 1911): 107–14.

———. "Sovremennye samoubiistva." *Russkaia mysl',* no. 5 (1912): 74–93.

Gor'kii, Maksim. "O solitere." *Nashi dostizheniia,* no. 6 (June 1930): 3–6.

Gur-Gurevich, V. M. "Samoubiistva sredi detskogo i iunoshevskogo vozrasta do i posle revoliutsii." *Pedologiia,* no. 1 (1930): 98–106.

Iakovenko, V. "Zdorovye i boleznennye proiavleniia v psikhike sovremennogo russkogo obshchestva." *Zhurnal Obshchestva Russkikh vrachei v pamiat' N. I. Pirogova* 13, no. 4 (May 1907): 269–87.

Iaroslavskii, E. "Filosofiia upadochnichestva." *Bol'shevik,* December 31, 1927, 135–44.

———. "Nuzhno surovo osudit' samoubiistva." *Pravda,* October 9, 1924, 4.

Ignat'ev, V. "Militsiia kak organ doznaniia." *Raboche-krest'ianskaia militsiia,* no. 1 (November 1922): 40–41.

Ingulov, S. "Protiv khuliganstva v pechati." *Zhurnalist,* no. 10 (October, 1926): 3.

Ionov, P. "Bez cheremukhi." *Pravda,* December 4, 1926, 5.

Khalfin, V. "Samoubiistvo (Po materialam TsAU NKVD)." *Raboche-krest'ianskaia militsiia,* no. 1 (1924): 17–20.

Khlopin, G. V. *Samoubiistva, pokusheniia na samoubiistva i neschastnye sluchai sredi uchashchikhsia russkikh uchebnykh zavedenii. Sanitarno-statisticheskoe issledovanie.* St. Petersburg: 1906.

Koni, A. F. *Samoubiistvo v zakone i zhizni.* Moscow: Pravo i zhizn', 1923.

Korchazhinskaia, Ol'ga Ivanovna. *Samoubiistva v Kazani v 1921 godu.* Kazan: Izdanie Statisticheskogo Upravleniia T.S.S.R., 1922.

Kosorotov, P. *Uchebnik sudebnoi-meditsiny.* 2nd ed. Edited by Ia. L. Leibovich. Moscow-Leningrad: Gosudarstvennoe izdatel'stvo, 1926.

———. *Uchebnik sudebnoi-meditsiny.* 3rd ed. Edited by Ia. L. Leibovich. Moscow-Leningrad: Gosudarstvennoe izdatel'stvo, 1928.

Kovalenko, I. Z. "Opyt izucheniia pokushenii i zakochennykh samoubiistv sredi gorodskogo naseleniia." *Profilakticheskaia meditsina,* no. 10 (1926): 45–58.

———. "Opyt izucheniia pokushenii i zakochennykh samoubiistv sredi gorodskogo naseleniia (okonchanie)." *Profilakticheskaia meditsina,* no. 11 (1926): 47–60.

Kriukov, A. I. "K voprosu o prichinakh samoubiistva." *Nevrologiia i psikhiatriia. Trudy gosudarstvennogo meditsinskogo instituta v Moskve* 1, no. 1 (1923): 286–97.

———. "O degeneratsii cherepa." *Arkhiv kriminologii i sudebnoi meditsiny* 1, nos. 2–3 (1927): 705–14.

———. "O degeneratsii cherepa u samoubiits." *Sudebno-meditsinskaia ekspertiza*, no. 1 (1925): 18–24.

Krylov, A. "Boleznennye iavleniia v partorganizatsii krasnoi armii i flota." *Politrabotnik*, nos. 4–5 (April–May 1924): 47–51.

Leibovich, Ia. "K kharakteristike sovremennykh samoubiistv v Sovetskoi Rossii." *Ezhenedel'nik sovetskoi iustitsii*, no. 14 (April 12, 1923): 315–17.

———. "Piat' let sudebnoi meditsiny." *Ezhenedel'nik sovetskoi iustitsii*, August 30, 1923, 775–77.

———. *Prakticheskoe rukovodstvo po sudebnoi meditsiny*. Moscow, 1922.

———. "Sovremennye samoubiistva v Sovetskoi Rossii." In P. Kosorotov, *Uchebnik sudebnoi-meditsiny*. 2nd ed. Edited by Ia. L. Leibovich, 295–307. Moscow-Leningrad: Gosudarstvennoe izdatel'stvo, 1926.

———. "Sudebno-meditsinskaia ekspertiza pri NEP'e." *Ezhenedel'nik sovetskoi iustitsii*, January 23, 1923, 36–38.

———. *1000 sovremmenykh samoubiistv (Sotsiologicheskii ocherk)*. Moscow: VKhUTEMAS, 1923.

———. "Tri goda sudebnoi meditsiny." *Izvestiia narodnogo komissariata zdravookhraneniia*, nos. 1–2 (1922): 12–13.

———. "Zhenskie samoubiistva." *Rabochii sud*, no. 8 (April 1926): 551–59.

———. "Zhenskie samoubiistva (Okonchanie)." *Rabochii sud*, no. 9 (May 1926): 623–32.

Leplinskii, I. M. "K voprosu o samoubiistvakh v Azerbaidzhane." *Zhurnal teorii i praktiki meditsiny* 2, nos. 1–3 (1926): 277–86.

Liadov, Martyn Nikolaevich. *Voprosy byta (Doklad na sobranii iacheiki sverdlovskogo kommun. Un-ta)*. Moscow: Izdanie kommunisticheskogo universiteta im. Ia. M. Sverdlova, 1925.

Maliutin. "Mysli vslukh (Ob upadochnicheskikh nastroeniiakh i bo'rbe s nimi)." *Voennyi vestnik*, June 11, 1927, 61–62.

Markovin, I. V. "Samoubiistvo sredi detei shkol'nikov." *Trudy sredneaziatskogo meditsinskogo instituta* 1, no. 1 (1935): 371–75.

Maskin, P. A. "Samoubiistva v Leningrade s 1922 g. po 1925 god (Avtoreferat)." *Sudebno-meditsinskaia ekspertiza*, no. 6 (1927): 71–75.

Matveev, S. N. "Ubiistvo ili samoubiistvo?" *Arkhiv kriminologii i sudebnoi meditsiny* 1, nos. 2–3 (1927): 781–88.

Mirel'zon, L. A. "K voprosu o samoubiistve u golodaiushchikh." *Sovremennaia meditsina*, nos. 4–6 (May–July 1924): 61–70.

Moseichuk. "O nekotorykh momentakh prakticheskoi raboty v sviazi s chistkoi partii." *Voennyi vestnik*, May 21, 1929, 34–36.

Murakhovskaia, I. N. "K genezu detskikh samoubiistv." In *Problemy psikhiatrii i Psikhopatologii*, edited by S. N. Davidenkov, 567–75. Moscow: Biomedgiz, 1935.

"O samoubiistve. Nasha anketa." *Vecherniaia moskva*, January 7, 9, and 11, 1926, 2 (of each issue).

Novosel'skii, S. *Demografiia i statistika (Izbrannye proizvedeniia)*. Edited by L. E. Poliakov. Moscow: Statistika, 1979.

———. "Estestvennoe dvizhenie naseleniia v Petrograde v 1920 godu." In *Materialy po statistike Petrograda i petrogradskoi gubernii*, 5: 43–44. Petrograd, 1921.

———. "Samoubiistva, ubiistva i smertel'nye neschastnye sluchai v Leningrade."
Biulleten' Leningradskogo gubstatotdela, no. 14 (July–September 1925): 117–25.

———. "Samoubiistva v Leningrade." *Statisticheskii biulleten'*, no. 24 (1930): 67–71.

Parabuchev, A. V. "*Status thymicus* u samoubiits kak morfologicheskii pokazatel'
rasstroistva inkretornoi sistemy (avtoreferat)." In *Vtoroi s"ezd khirurgov Severo-
kavkazskogo kraia. 12–15 ianvaria 1927 g.*, 263–67. Rostov-on-Don: 1927.

Partiinaia etika. Dokumenty i materialy diskussii 20-kh godov. Moscow: Izdatel'stvo
politicheskoi literatury, 1989.

Partiino-politicheskaia rabota v Krasnoi Armii: Dokumenty 1921–1929 gg. Moscow:
Voennoe izdatel'stvo Ministerstva Oborony SSSR, 1981.

"Pervyi Vserossiiskii s"ezd sudebno-meditsinskikh ekspertov 20–25 sentiabria
1920 g." *Izvestiia Narodnogo Komissariata Zdravookhraneniia*, nos. 1–4 (1921):
13–14.

Petukhov, I. *Partiinaia organizatsiia i partiinaia rabota v RKKA*. Moscow-Leningrad:
Gosizdat, 1928.

Podsotskii, K. "Vnimanie k zhizni partiitsa." *Voennyi vestnik*, April 9, 1927, 40–41.

Pokrovskii, G. *Esenin—Eseninshchina—religiia*. Moscow: Ateist, 1929.

Popov, N. V., and O. V. Krasovskaia. "Sluchai samoubiistva v degenerativnoi sem'e."
Russkii evgenicheskii zhurnal 3, no. 1 (1925): 67–71.

"Po povodu odnogo samoubiistva." *Voennyi vestnik*, March 8, 1924, 25.

Prozorov, L. A. "Profilaktika i terapiia samoubiistva." In *Nevrologiia, nevropatologiia,
psikhologiia, psikhiatriia. Sbornik posviashchennyi 40-letiiu nauchnoi vrachebnoi
i pedagogicheskoi deiatel'nosti Prof. G. I. Rossolimo 1884–1924*, 47–59. Moscow:
Narkomzdrav-Glavnauka, 1925.

———. *Samoubiistva voennykh*. Moscow, 1914.

Radek, Karl. "Pamiati tov. Iuriia Lutovinova." *Pravda*, May 10, 1925, 5.

Rodin, D. "O moral'noi statistiki." *Vestnik statistiki*, nos. 9–12 (September–December
1922): 105–15.

———. "O postanovke statistiki samoubiistv v Rossii." *Vestnik statistiki*, nos. 5–8 (May–
August 1921): 84–97.

Romanov, Panteleimon. "Pravo na zhizn', ili Problema bespartiinosti." In *Izbrannye
proizvedeniia*, 252–91. Moscow: Khudozhestvennaia literatura, 1988.

Rozhanovskii, V. A. "Sudebno-meditsinskaia ekspertiza v dorevoliutsionnoi Rossii i
v SSSR." *Sudebno-meditsinskaia ekspertiza*, no. 6 (1927): 1–105 (supplement).

S. A. "Samoubiistva na Ukraine." *Statisticheskoe obozrenie*, no. 9 (September 1928):
97–100.

S. N. "Samoubiistva v Petrograde." *Biulleten' Petrogradskogo gubstatotdela*, no. 3 (June
1923): 62–64.

Samoubiistva v SSSR 1922–1925. Moscow: Tsentral'noe statisticheskoe upravlenie
SSSR, 1927.

Samoubiistva v SSSR 1925 i 1926 g.g. Moscow: Tsentral'noe statisticheskoe upravlenie SSSR, 1929.

Semashko, N. "Ugrozhaet li nam epidemiia samoubiistv?" *Izvestiia TsIK Sovetov*,
January 22, 1926, 5.

Serebrianikov, P. V. "Neskol'ko zamechanii k stat'e prof. Kriukova 'O degeneratsii
cherepa u samoubiits.'" *Sudebno-meditsinskaia ekspertiza*, no. 7 (1928), 81–84.

Serge, Victor. *Memoirs of a Revolutionary, 1901–1941.* Edited and translated by Peter Sedgwick. London: Oxford University Press, 1963.

Sharbe, T. A. "Sudebnyi medik i Status Thymico-Lymphaticus." *Sudebno-meditsinskaia ekspertiza,* no. 7 (1928): 68–72.

Shaverdov, A. S. "K voprosu of samoubiistvakh v Tiflise." *Meditsinskii sbornik zhelezno-dorozhnykh vrachei Zakavkaz'ia,* no. 2 (April–June 1923): 153–74.

Shepilov, *Samoubiistva v Iakutii (etiud).* Yakutsk: Tipografiia iakutgosizdata, 1928.

Skliar. "K voprosu o chisle samobuiistv v nostoiashchee vremia." *Vlast' sovetov,* nos. 8–9 (August–September 1923): 95–99.

Stal'nov, Ia. I. "Puti bio-khimicheskogo analiza lichnosti samoubiitsy." *Sudebno-meditsinskaia ekspertiza,* no. 5 (1927): 7–11.

Tarnovskii, E. N. "Svedeniia o samoubiistvakh v Zapadnoi Evrope i v RSFSR za poslednee desiatiletie." *Problemy prestupnosti,* no. 1 (1926): 192–214.

Teodorovich, M. F. *Samoubiistvo: Ukazatel' literatury na russkom iazike.* Moscow: 1928.

Trudy II Vserossiskogo s"ezda sudebno-meditsinskikh ekspertov. Moskva, 25 fevralia–3 marta 1926 g. Edited by Ia. Leibovich. Ulyanovsk, 1926.

Tsel'min, P. "O samoubiistvakh." *Sputnik politrabotnika,* March 31, 1926: 20–22.

Uchevatov, A. "Samoubiistva i organy doznaniia." *Raboche-krest'ianskaia militsiia,* nos. 7–8 (July–August 1924): 21–23.

Upadochnoe nastroenie sredi molodezhi: Eseninshchina. Moscow-Leningrad: Izd-vo Kommunisticheskoi akademii, 1927.

Vasilevskaia, L. A., and L. M. Vasilevskii. *Golodanie. Populiarnyi i mediko-sanitarnyi ocherk.* Ufa, 1922.

Velichkin, V. "Pravo na smert'." *Sovetskii vrach,* nos. 17–18 (1930): 765–66.

Visherskii, N. N. "Kolichestvo samoubiistv v Iaroslavskoi gub. (10 uezdov), za pervoe polugodie 1923 goda." *Iaroslavskii statisticheskii vestnik,* no. 2 (September 1923): 15–16.

——. "Samoubiistva v Iaroslavskoi gubernii." *Sotsial'naia gigiena,* no. 1 (1929): 90–96.

——. "Statistika samoubiistv v Iaroslavskoi gubernii za 1922 godu (5 uezdov)." *Iaroslavskii statisticheskii vestnik,* no. 1 (August 1923): 24–25.

Vongrodskii, V. A. "Samoubiistvo v Tomske po anketnym dannym." In *Trudy pervogo s"ezda vrachei Sibiri,* 291. Tomsk: 1927.

Zalkind, A. B. *Revoliutsiia i molodezh'.* Moscow: Izdanie Kommunisticheskogo universiteta im. Sverdlova, 1925.

Zhbankov, D. N. "O samoubiistvakh v poslednee vremia." *Prakticheskii vrach* 5, nos. 26–29 (1906): 437–39, 455–57, 470–72, 489–91.

——. "Travmaticheskaia epidemiia v Rossii (aprel'–mai 1905 g.)." *Prakticheskii vrach* 4, nos. 32–35 (1905): 633–37, 656–61, 681–86, 703–6.

——. "Travmaticheskaia epidemiia v Rossii (fevral' 1905 g.–iiun' 1907 g.)." *Prakticheskii vrach* 6, nos. 34–38 (1907): 609–15, 624–25, 644–45, 661–64, 680–83.

——. "Travmaticheskaia krovovaia epidemiia v Rossii." *Prakticheskii vrach* 5, nos. 32–35 (1906): 533–36, 552–55, 569–71, 584–88.

Ziskind, D. I. "Degeneratsiia cherepa kak faktor, pomogaiushchii stavit' differentsial'nyi diagnoz mezhdu ubiistvom i samoubiistvom." *Sudebno-meditsinskaia ekspertiza,* no. 14 (1930): 48–50.

SECONDARY SOURCES

Adams, Mark B. "Eugenics as Social Medicine in Revolutionary Russia: Prophets, Patrons, and the Dialectics of Discipline-Building." In *Health and Society in Revolutionary Russia,* edited by Susan Gross Solomon and John F. Hutchinson, 200–223. Bloomington: Indiana University Press, 1990.

———. "Eugenics in Russia 1900–1940." In *The Wellborn Science: Eugenics in Germany, France, Brazil, and Russia,* edited by Mark B. Adams, 153–216. Oxford: Oxford University Press, 1990.

Avdeev, Alexandre, Alain Blum, and Irina Troitskaya. "The History of Abortion Statistics in Russia and the USSR from 1900 to 1991." *Population: An English Selection* 7 (1995): 39–66.

Balzer, Harley. "The Problem of Professions in Imperial Russia." In *Between Tsar and People: Educated Society and the Quest for Public Identity in Late Imperial Russia,* edited by Edith W. Clowes, Samuel D. Kassow, and James L. West, 183–98. Princeton: Princeton University Press, 1991.

Bauer, Raymond. *The New Man in Soviet Psychology.* Cambridge, MA: Harvard University Press, 1952.

Becker, Elisa M. "Judicial Reform and the Role of Medical Expertise in Late Imperial Russian Courts." *Law and History Review* 17, no. 1 (Spring 1999): 1–26.

Beer, Daniel. "The Medicalization of Religious Deviance in the Russian Orthodox Church (1880–1905)." *Kritika: Explorations in Russian and Eurasian History* 5, no. 3 (Summer 2004): 451–82.

———. "'Microbes of the Mind': Moral Contagion in Late Imperial Russia." *Journal of Modern History* 79 (September 2007): 531–71.

———. *Renovating Russia: The Human Sciences and the Fate of Liberal Modernity, 1880–1930.* Ithaca: Cornell University Press, 2008.

Beirne, Piers. *Inventing Criminology: Essays on the Rise of Homo Criminalis.* Albany: State University of New York Press, 1993.

Bernstein, Frances Lee. *The Dictatorship of Sex: Lifestyle Advice for the Soviet Masses.* DeKalb: Northern Illinois University Press, 2007.

Blum, Alain. "Society, Politics and Demography: The Example of Soviet History." *Czech Sociological Review* 4, no. 1 (1996): 81–95.

Blum, Alain, and Martine Mespoulet. *L'anarchie bureaucratique: Pouvoir et statistique sous Staline.* Paris: Éditions la Découverte, 2003.

Brown, Julie V. "Revolution and Psychosis: The Mixing of Science and Politics in Russian Psychiatric Medicine." *Russian Review* 46 (1987): 282–302.

Brubaker, Rogers, and Frederick Cooper. "Beyond 'Identity.'" *Theory and Society* 29, no. 1 (February 2000): 1–47.

Bruner, Jerome. *Acts of Meaning.* Cambridge, MA: Harvard University Press, 1990.

Bulmer, Martin, Kevin Bales, and Kathryn Kish Sklar, eds. *The Social Survey in Historical Perspective.* Cambridge: Cambridge University Press, 1991.

Burney, Ian A. *Bodies of Evidence: Medicine and the Politics of the English Inquest, 1830–1926.* Baltimore: Johns Hopkins University Press, 2000.

Caplan, Jane, and John Torpey, eds. *Documenting Individual Identity: The Development of State Practices in the Modern World.* Princeton: Princeton University Press, 2001.

Carleton, Gregory. *Sexual Revolution in Bolshevik Russia.* Pittsburgh: University of Pittsburgh Press, 2005.

Chkhartishvili, Grigorii. *Samoubiistvo i pisatel'.* Moscow: Novoe literaturnoe obozrenie, 1999.

Clark, Katerina. *The Soviet Novel: History as Ritual.* 3rd ed. Bloomington: Indiana University Press, 2000.

Cole, Joshua. *The Power of Large Numbers: Population, Politics, and Gender in Nineteenth-Century France.* Ithaca: Cornell University Press, 2000.

Corney, Frederick. *Telling October: Memory and the Making of the Bolshevik Revolution.* Ithaca: Cornell University Press, 2004.

Curtis, Bruce. "Foucault on Governmentality and Population: The Impossible Discovery." *Canadian Journal of Sociology* 27, no. 4 (Autumn 2002): 505–33.

——. "Surveying the Social: Techniques, Practices, Power." *Histoire sociale/Social History* 35 (2002): 83–108.

Dally, Ann. "Status Lymphaticus: Sudden Death in Children from 'Visitation of God' to Cot Death." *Medical History* 41 (January 1997): 70–85.

David-Fox, Michael. "From Illusory 'Society' to Intellectual 'Public' Works: VOKS, International Travel and Party-Intelligentsia Relations in the Interwar Period." *Contemporary European History* 2, no. 1 (2002): 7–32.

——. *Revolution of the Mind: Higher Learning among the Bolsheviks, 1918–1929.* Ithaca: Cornell University Press, 1997.

Desrosières, Alain. *The Politics of Large Numbers: A History of Statistical Reasoning.* Translated by Camille Naish. Cambridge, MA: Harvard University Press, 1998.

Engelstein, Laura. *The Keys to Happiness: Sex and the Search for Modernity in Fin-de-Siècle Russia.* Ithaca: Cornell University Press, 1992.

Ewing, E. Thomas. "Personal Acts with Public Meanings: Suicides by Women Teachers in the Early Stalin Era." *Gender & History* 14, no. 1 (April 2002): 117–37.

Fitzpatrick, Sheila. "Ascribing Class: The Construction of Social Identity in Soviet Russia." *Journal of Modern History* 65, no. 4 (December 1993): 745–70.

——. "The Bolsheviks' Dilemma: The Class Issue in Party Politics and Culture." In *The Cultural Front: Power and Culture in Revolutionary Russia,* 16–36. Ithaca: Cornell University Press, 1992.

Frieden, Nancy Mandelker. *Russian Physicians in an Era of Reform and Revolution, 1856–1905.* Princeton: Princeton University Press, 1981.

Giddens, Anthony. *The Consequences of Modernity.* Stanford: Stanford University Press, 1990.

Gorsuch, Anne E. *Youth in Revolutionary Russia: Enthusiasts, Bohemians, Delinquents.* Bloomington: Indiana University Press, 2000.

Hacking, Ian. "Biopower and the Avalanche of Printed Numbers." *Humanities in Society* 5, no. 3/4 (Summer/Fall 1982): 279–95.

——. "How Numerical Sociology Began by Counting Suicides: From Medical Pathology to Social Pathology." In *The Natural Sciences and the Social Sciences: Some Critical and Historical Perspectives,* edited by I. Bernard Cohen, 101–33. Dordrecht: Kluwer, 1994.

——. "Making Up People." In *Reconstructing Individualism: Autonomy, Individuality, and the Self in Western Thought,* edited by Morton Sosna, Thomas C. Heller, and David E. Wellbery, 222–36. Stanford: Stanford University Press, 1986.

———. *The Taming of Chance*. Cambridge: Cambridge University Press, 1990.

Hagenloh, Paul M. "'Socially Harmful Elements' and the Great Terror." In *Stalinism: New Directions (Rewriting History)*, edited by Sheila Fitzpatrick, 286–308. New York: Routledge, 2000.

Halberstam, Michael. "Totalitarianism as a Problem for the Modern Conception of Politics." *Political Theory* 26, no. 4 (August 1998): 459–88.

Halfin, Igal. *From Darkness to Light: Class, Consciousness, and Salvation in Revolutionary Russia*. Pittsburgh: University of Pittsburgh Press, 2000.

———. *Terror in My Soul: Communist Autobiographies on Trial*. Cambridge, MA: Harvard University Press, 2003.

Healey, Dan. "Early Soviet Forensic Psychiatric Approaches to Sex Crime, 1917–1934." In *Madness and the Mad in Russian Culture*, edited by Angela Brintlinger and Ilya Vinitsky, 150–68. Toronto: University of Toronto Press, 2007.

———. *Homosexual Desire in Revolutionary Russia: The Regulation of Sexual and Gender Dissent*. Chicago: University of Chicago Press, 2001.

Healy, Róisín. "Suicide in Early Modern and Modern Europe." *Historical Review* 49, no. 3 (2006): 903–19.

Hellbeck, Jochen. *Revolution on My Mind: Writing a Diary under Stalin*. Cambridge, MA: Harvard University Press, 2005.

———. "Self-Realization in the Stalinist System: Two Soviet Diaries of the 1930s." In *Russian Modernity: Politics, Knowledge, Practices*, edited by David L. Hoffmann and Yanni Kotsonis, 221–42. London: Macmillan, 2000.

Hershkovitz, Israel, Bruce Latimer, Olivier Dutour, Lyman M. Jellema, Susanne Wish-Baratz, Christine Rothschild, and Bruce M. Rothschild. "Why Do We Fail in Aging the Skull from the Sagittal Suture?" *American Journal of Physical Anthropology* 103, no. 3 (July 1997): 393–99.

Higonnet, Margaret. "Suicide: Representations of the Feminine in the Nineteenth Century." *Poetics Today* 6, nos. 1–2 (1985): 103–18.

Hirsch, Francine. *Empire of Nations: Ethnographic Knowledge and the Making of the Soviet Union*. Ithaca: Cornell University Press, 2005.

Hoffmann, David L. "European Modernity and Soviet Socialism." In *Russian Modernity: Politics, Knowledge, Practices*, edited by David L. Hoffmann and Yanni Kotsonis, 245–60. London: Macmillan, 2000.

———. *Stalinist Values: The Cultural Norms of Soviet Modernity, 1917–1941*. Ithaca: Cornell University Press, 2002.

Hoffmann, David L., and Yanni Kotsonis, eds. *Russian Modernity: Politics, Knowledge, Practices*. London: Macmillan, 2000.

Holquist, Peter. "Anti-Soviet *Svodki* from the Civil War: Surveillance as a Shared Feature of Russian Political Culture." *Russian Review* 56, no. 3 (July 1997): 445–50.

———. "'Information Is the Alpha and Omega of Our Work': Bolshevik Surveillance in Its Pan-European Context." *Journal of Modern History* 69, no. 3 (September 1997): 415–50.

———. *Making War, Forging Revolution: Russia's Continuum of Crisis, 1914–1921*. Cambridge, MA: Harvard University Press, 2002.

———. "What's So Revolutionary about the Russian Revolution? State Practices and the New-Style Politics, 1914–21." In *Russian Modernity: Politics, Knowledge,*

Practices, edited by David L. Hoffmann and Yanni Kotsonis, 87–111. London: Macmillan, 2000.

Horn, David G. "The Norm Which Is Not One: Reading the Female Body in Lombroso's Anthropology." In *Deviant Bodies,* edited by Jennifer Terry and Jacqueline Urla, 109–28. Bloomington: Indiana University Press, 1995.

———. *Social Bodies: Science, Reproduction, and Italian Modernity.* Princeton: Princeton University Press, 1994.

Hutchinson, John F. *Politics and Health in Revolutionary Russia, 1890–1918.* Baltimore: Johns Hopkins University Press, 1990.

Ingerflom, Claudio Sergio, and Tamara Kondratieva. "Pourquoi la Russie s'agite-t-elle autour du corps de Lénine?" In *La Mort du Roi. Autour de François Mitterand. Essai d'ethnographic politique comparée,* edited by Jacques Julliard, 261–92. Paris: Éditions Gallimard, 1999.

Ivanov, L. O., and L. V. Il'ina. *Puti i sud'by otechestvennoi kriminologii.* Moscow: Nauka, 1991.

Izmozik, Vladlen Semenovich. *Glaza i ushi rezhima: Gosudarstvennyi politicheskii kontrol' za naseleniem Sovetskoi Rossii v 1918–1928 godakh.* St. Petersburg: Izdatel'stvo Sankt-Peterburgskogo universiteta ekonomiki i finansov, 1995.

Janoušek, Jaromír, and Irina Sirotkina. "Psychology in Russia and Central and Eastern Europe." In *The Cambridge History of Science.* Vol. 7, *The Modern Social Sciences,* edited by Theodore M. Porter and Dorothy Ross, 431–49. Cambridge: Cambridge University Press, 2003.

Joravsky, David. *Russian Psychology: A Critical History.* Oxford: Basil Blackwell, 1989.

Kharkhordin, Oleg. *The Collective and the Individual in Russia: A Study of Practices.* Berkeley: University of California Press, 1999.

Klevniuk, O. V. *1937-i: Stalin, NKVD i sovetskoe obshchestvo.* Moscow: Izdatel'stvo "Respublika," 1992.

Kotkin, Stephen. *Magnetic Mountain: Stalinism as a Civilization.* Berkeley: University of California Press, 1995.

Kotsonis, Yanni. "'Face-to-Face': The State, the Individual, and the Citizen in Russian Taxation, 1863–1917." *Slavic Review* 63, no. 2 (Summer 2004): 221–46.

———. *Making Peasants Backward: Agricultural Cooperatives and the Agrarian Question in Russia, 1861–1914.* London: Macmillan, 1999.

———. "'No Place to Go': Taxation and State Transformation in Late Imperial and Early Soviet Russia." *Journal of Modern History* 76 (September 2004): 531–77.

Kowalsky, Sharon A. "Who's Responsible for Female Crime? Gender, Deviance, and the Development of Social Norms in Revolutionary Russia." *Russian Review* 62 (July 2003): 366–86.

Krylova, Anna. "Beyond the Spontaneity-Consciousness Paradigm: 'Class Instinct' as a Promising Category of Historical Analysis." *Slavic Review* 62, no. 1 (Spring 2003): 1–23.

Kushner, Howard I. *American Suicide: A Psychocultural Exploration.* New Brunswick: Rutgers University Press, 1991.

———. "Suicide, Gender, and the Fear of Modernity in Nineteenth-Century Medical and Social Thought." *Journal of Social History* 26, no. 3 (Spring 1993): 461–90.

———. "Women and Suicide in Historical Perspective." *Signs* 10, no. 3 (Spring 1985): 537–52.

Kuznetsov, Vladimir Evgen'evich. "Etapy razvitiia otechestvennoi dorevoliutsion-noi suitsidologii: Psikhiatricheskii i mezhditsiplinarnyi aspekty." Candidate diss., Moscow Scientific-Investigative Institute of Psychiatry, 1987.

Lebina, Natalia Borisovna. *Povsednevnaia zhizn' sovetskogo goroda: Normy i anomalii: 1920–1930 gody.* St. Petersburg: Letnii sad, 1999.

Lieberman, Lisa. *Leaving You: The Cultural Meaning of Suicide.* Chicago: Ivan R. Dee, 2003.

MacDonald, Michael. "The Secularization of Suicide in England 1660–1800." *Past and Present,* no. 111 (May 1986): 50–100.

MacDonald, Michael, and Terence R. Murphy. *Sleepless Souls: Suicide in Early Modern England.* Oxford: Oxford University Press, 1990.

Maslov, A. V. *Petlia i pulia. Issledovanie obstoiatel'stv gibeli Sergeia Esenina i Vladimira Maiakovskogo.* St. Petersburg: Inapress, 2004.

Merridale, Catherine. *Nights of Stone: Death and Memory in Twentieth-Century Russia.* New York: Viking, 2000.

Meyer, John W. "Myths of Socialization and of Personality." In *Reconstructing Individualism: Autonomy, Individuality, and the Self in Western Thought,* edited by Thomas C. Heller, Morton Sosna, and David E. Wellbery, 208–21. Stanford: Stanford University Press, 1986.

Mikhailov, Aleksandr. *Zhizn' Maiakovskogo. Ia svoe zemnoe ne dozhil.* Moscow: Tsentropoligraf, 2001.

Miller, Martin A., and Ylana N. Miller. "Suicide and Suicidology in the Soviet Union." *Suicide and Life-Threatening Behavior* 18, no. 4 (Winter 1988): 303–21.

Morrissey, Susan K. "Drinking to Death: Suicide, Vodka and Religious Burial in Russia." *Past and Present,* no. 186 (February 2005): 117–46.

——. "Patriarchy on Trial: Suicide, Discipline, and Governance in Imperial Russia." *Journal of Modern History* 75 (March 2003): 23–58.

——. "Suicide and Civilization in Late Imperial Russia." *Jahrbücher für Geschichte Osteuropas* 43, no. 2 (1995): 201–17.

——. *Suicide and the Body Politic in Imperial Russia.* Cambridge: Cambridge University Press, 2007.

Naiman, Eric. *Sex in Public: The Incarnation of Early Soviet Ideology.* Princeton: Princeton University Press, 1997.

Nekliudov, Iu. A. "Iakov L'vovich Leibovich—vidnyi deiatel' otechestvennoi sudebnoi meditsiny." *Sudebno-meditsinskaia ekspertiza,* no. 5 (2003): 48–49.

Nesbet, Anne. "Suicide as Literary Fact in the 1920s." *Slavic Review* 50, no. 4 (Winter 1991): 827–35.

Offord, Derek. "*Lichnost'*: Notions of Individual Identity." In *Constructing Russian Culture in the Age of Revolution: 1881–1940,* edited by Catriona Kelly and David Shepherd, 113–23. Oxford: Oxford University Press, 1998.

Paperno, Irina. *Suicide as a Cultural Institution in Dostoevsky's Russia.* Ithaca: Cornell University Press, 1997.

Patriarca, Silvana. *Numbers and Nationhood: Writing Statistics in Nineteenth-Century Italy.* New York: Cambridge University Press, 1996.

Pick, Daniel. *Faces of Degeneration: A European Disorder, c. 1848–c. 1918.* Cambridge: Cambridge University Press, 1989.

Porter, Theodore M. *The Rise of Statistical Thinking 1820–1900.* Princeton: Princeton University Press, 1986.

Rittersporn, Gábor T. "Le message des données introuvables: L'État et les statistiques du suicide en Russie et en URSS." *Cahiers du Monde russe* 38, no. 4 (October–December 1997): 511–24.

Sanborn, Joshua A. *Drafting the Russian Nation: Military Conscription, Total War, and Mass Politics, 1905–1925.* DeKalb: Northern Illinois University Press, 2003.

Shelly, Louise. "Soviet Criminology: Its Birth and Demise, 1917–1936." *Slavic Review* 38, no. 4 (December 1979): 614–28.

Sirotkina, Irina. *Diagnosing Literary Genius: A Cultural History of Psychiatry in Russia, 1880–1930.* Baltimore: Johns Hopkins University Press, 2002.

Solokhin, Anatolii A., and Iurii A. Solokhin. *Sudebno-meditsinskaia nauka v Rossii i SSSR v XIX i XX stoletiiakh.* Moscow, 1998.

Solomon, Jr., Peter H. "Soviet Criminology: Its Demise and Rebirth, 1928–1963." *Soviet Union/Union Sovietique* 1, no. 2 (1974): 122–40.

Solomon, Susan. "David and Goliath in Soviet Public Health: The Rivalry of Social Hygienists and Psychiatrists for Authority over the *Bytovoi* Alcoholic." *Soviet Studies* 41, no. 2 (April 1989): 254–75.

——. "The Expert and the State in Russian Public Health: Continuities and Changes across the Revolutionary Divide." In *The History of Public Health and the Modern State,* edited by Dorothy Porter, 183–223. Amsterdam: Editions Rodopi B. V., 1994.

Solomon, Susan Gross, and John F. Hutchinson, eds. *Health and Society in Revolutionary Russia.* Bloomington: Indiana University Press, 1990.

Spivak, Monika. *Posmertnaia diagnostika genial'nosti. Eduard Bagritskii, Andrei Belyi, Vladimir Maiakovskii v kollektsii Instituta mozga (materialy iz arkhiva G. I. Poliakova).* Moscow: Agraf, 2001.

Terry, Jennifer. "Anxious Slippages between 'Us' and 'Them': A Brief History of the Scientific Search for Homosexual Bodies." In *Deviant Bodies: Critical Perspectives on Difference in Science and Popular Culture,* edited by Jennifer Terry and Jacqueline Urla, 129–69. Bloomington: Indiana University Press, 1995.

Tiazhel'nikova, Viktoriia S. "Samoubiistva kommunistov v 1920-e gody." *Otechestvennaia istoriia,* no. 6 (1998): 158–73.

Unnithan, N. Prabha, Lin Huff-Corzine, Jay Corzine, and Hugh P. Whitt. *The Currents of Lethal Violence: An Integrated Model of Suicide and Homicide.* Albany: State University of New York Press, 1994.

van Ree, Eric. "Stalin's Organic Theory of the Party." *Russian Review* 52, no. 1 (January 1993): 43–57.

von Hagen, Mark. *Soldiers in the Proletarian Dictatorship: The Red Army and the Socialist State, 1917–1930.* Ithaca: Cornell University Press, 1990.

Weinberg, Elizabeth A. *Sociology in the Soviet Union and Beyond: Social Enquiry and Social Change.* Hants, UK: Ashgate, 2004.

Weiner, Amir. "Nature, Nurture, and Memory in the Socialist Utopia: Delineating the Soviet Socio-Ethnic Body in the Age of Socialism." *American Historical Review* 104, no. 4 (October 1999): 1114–55.

Weitz, Eric D. "Racial Politics without the Concept of Race: Reevaluating Soviet Ethnic and National Purges." *Slavic Review* 61, no. 1 (Spring 2002): 1–29.

Index